Physician Travelers

Travels in the
Interior Districts of Africa

Mungo Park

Arno Press & The New York Times
New York * 1971

PHYSICIAN TRAVELERS

Editor
ROBERT M. GOLDWYN, M.D.

This book is reprinted from a copy in the
Francis A. Countway Library of Medicine

Library of Congress Catalog Card No. 74-115623
ISBN 0-405-01718-9
ISBN for complete set 0-405-01710-3

Manufactured in the United States of America, 1971

About the Author

ONE OF THE EARLIEST PIONEERS to penetrate the interior of Africa was Mungo Park, who was born in Selkirk, Scotland, in 1771. The seventh child in a family of thirteen, he was educated at home and, at age fifteen, was apprenticed to a local surgeon. In 1789, he entered Edinburgh University, where he studied medicine and botany. He obtained his surgical diploma and proceeded to London in 1791. Through his brother-in-law he met Sir Joseph Banks, then president of the Royal Society. Through Banks' influence, Park was appointed assistant medical officer on a voyage to Sumatra in the service of the East India Company. Upon his return, he presented new species of fish and plants to the Linnaean Society; some members were so impressed that they arranged for Park to replace Major Daniel Houghton, who had died during an unsuccessful search for the source of the Niger River, known to Europeans only by hearsay.

Parks' account of his own efforts, *Travels in the Interior Districts of Africa,* is literary evidence of man's penchant for finding obstacles to overcome. He stated his credo: "I had a passionate desire to examine into the production of a country so little known; and to become experimentally acquainted with the modes of life and character of the natives . . . if I should perish in my journey, I was willing that my hopes and expectations should perish with me . . ."

The objectives of his expedition were "to pass on to the river Niger either by way of Bambouk or by such other routes as should be found most convenient, to ascertain the course, and if possible the rise and termination of that River."

In July, 1795, Park arrived as Pisania, two hundred miles up the Gambia River. He remained at that place for five months learning the Madingo language and recovering from his first severe attack of malaria. After a series of incredible misfortunes, Park reached Segou on the Niger River and thus became the first European to view its waters. A slave ship bound for America eventually took him to England in 1799. Following a hero's reception, he began medical practice in Peebles, Scotland, where he married the daughter of his former teacher of medicine.

The "call of the wild" was dormant but not extinct. Africa reclaimed him after six years in this quiet community. Now an accredited explorer, he left Britain in 1805 with his brother-in-law—a surgeon—and a well-staffed and a well-supplied expedition to find the termination of the Niger River. Dysentery, however, took a heavy toll: after a few months, twenty-nine of forty Europeans, including his brother-in-law, were dead. Despondent yet determined, Park constructed a flat-bottomed boat out of two canoes and descended the uncharted Niger. He perished after an attack by natives but not before he had navigated a thousand miles of its then legendary waters. He had failed to reach the sea, four hundred miles beyond; a quarter of a century had to pass before this feat could be accomplished.

Park was survived by three sons, a daughter, and his wife. His second son, a midshipman, hoped to discover something further about his father's fate but in his search the younger Park also died in Africa.

R. M. G.

REFERENCE:
Goldwyn, R. M.: "Medical Explorers in Africa," *Journal of the American Medical Association,* 208: 135-138, 1969.

TRAVELS

IN THE

INTERIOR DISTRICTS OF AFRICA.

Mr. M. Park.

Publish'd April 5.1799, by G. Nicol, Pall Mall.

TRAVELS

IN THE

INTERIOR DISTRICTS OF AFRICA:

PERFORMED UNDER THE

DIRECTION AND PATRONAGE

OF THE,

AFRICAN ASSOCIATION,

IN THE

YEARS 1795, 1796, AND 1797.

BY MUNGO PARK, SURGEON.

WITH

AN APPENDIX,

CONTAINING

GEOGRAPHICAL ILLUSTRATIONS OF AFRICA.

BY MAJOR RENNELL.

——— egens Libyæ deserta peragro. VIRG.

LONDON:

PRINTED BY W. BULMER AND CO. FOR THE AUTHOR;

AND SOLD BY G. AND W. NICOL, BOOKSELLERS TO HIS MAJESTY,
PALL-MALL. 1799.

TO THE

NOBLEMEN AND GENTLEMEN,

ASSOCIATED FOR THE PURPOSE OF EXPLORING

THE

INTERIOR REGIONS OF AFRICA,

THIS

JOURNAL OF TRAVELS

ON THAT CONTINENT,

PERFORMED UNDER THEIR PATRONAGE,

IS,

WITH ALL HUMILITY,

INSCRIBED,

BY THEIR FAITHFUL

AND OBLIGED HUMBLE SERVANT,

April 10*th,* 1799.   MUNGO PARK.

a

PREFACE.

THE following Journal, drawn up from original minutes and notices made at the proper moment and preserved with great difficulty, is now offered to the Public by the direction of my noble and honourable employers, the Members of the African Association. I regret that it is so little commensurate to the patronage I have received. As a composition, it has nothing to recommend it, but *truth*. It is a plain, unvarnished tale; without pretensions of any kind, except that it claims to enlarge, in some degree, the circle of African geography. For this purpose, my services were offered, and accepted by the Association; and, I trust, I have not laboured altogether in vain. The work, however, must speak for itself; and I should not have thought any preliminary observations necessary, if I did not consider myself called upon, both by justice and gratitude, to offer those which follow.

Immediately after my return from Africa, the acting Committee of the Association,* taking notice of the time it would

* This Committee consists of the following Noblemen and Gentlemen; Earl of Moira, Lord Bishop of Landaff, Right Hon. Sir Joseph Banks, President of the

a 2

require to prepare an account in detail, as it now appears; and being desirous of gratifying, as speedily as possible, the curiosity which many of the Members were pleased to express concerning my discoveries, determined that an epitome, or abridgment of my travels, should be forthwith prepared from such materials and oral communications as I could furnish, and printed for the use of the Association; and also, that an engraved Map of my route should accompany it. A memoir, thus supplied and improved, was accordingly drawn up in two parts, by Members of the Association, and distributed among the Society: the first part consisting of a narrative, in abstract, of my travels, by Bryan Edwards, Esq.; the second, of Geographical Illustrations of my progress, by Major James Rennell, F. R. S. Major Rennell was pleased also to add, not only a Map of my route, constructed in conformity to my own observations and sketches (when freed from those errors, which the Major's superior knowledge, and distinguished accuracy in geographical researches, enabled him to discover and correct), but also a General Map, shewing the progress of discovery, and improvement in the Geography of North Africa; together with a Chart of the

Royal Society; Andrew Stewart, Esq. F. R. S. and Bryan Edwards, Esq. F. R. S. Concerning the original institution of the Society itself, and the progress of discovery, previous to my expedition, the fullest information has already been given in the various publications which the Society have caused to be made.

lines of magnetic variation, in the seas around that immense continent.

Availing myself therefore, on the present occasion, of assistance like this, it is impossible that I can present myself before the Public, without expressing how deeply and gratefully sensible I am of the honour and advantage which I derive from the labours of those Gentlemen; for Mr. Edwards has kindly permitted me to incorporate, as occasion offered, the whole of his narrative into different parts of my work; and Major Rennell, with equal good will, allows me not only to embellish and elucidate my Travels, with the Maps beforementioned, but also to subjoin his Geographical Illustrations *entire*.

Thus aided and encouraged, I should deliver this volume to the world, with that confidence of a favourable reception, which no merits of my own could authorize me to claim; were I not apprehensive that expectations have been formed, by some of my subscribers, of discoveries to be unfolded, which I have not made, and of wonders to be related, of which I am utterly ignorant. There is danger that those who feel a disappointment of this nature, finding less to astonish and amuse in my book, than they had promised to themselves beforehand, will not even allow me the little merit which I really possess. Painful as this circumstance may prove to my feelings, I shall console myself under it, if the distinguished persons, under whose auspices I entered on my mission, shall allow that I have executed the duties of it to their satisfaction; and that they consider the Journal which I have now the honour to present to them, to be, what I have endeavoured to make it, an honest and faithful report of my proceedings and observations in their service, from the outset of my journey to its termination.

M. P.

CONTENTS.

CHAPTER VIII.

CHAPTER IX.

CHAPTER X.

CHAPTER XI.

b

CHAPTER XVI.

CHAPTER XVII.

CHAPTER XVIII.

CHAPTER XIX.

CHAPTER XX.

CHAPTER XXI.

CHAPTER XXII.

CHAPTER XXIII.

CHAPTER XXIV.

CHAPTER XXV.

CHAPTER XXVI.

APPENDIX.

The following AFRICAN WORDS, *recurring very frequently in the course of the Narrative, it is thought necessary to prefix an Explanation of them for the Reader's convenience.*

———————

Mansa. A king or chief governor.

Alkaid. The head magistrate of a town or province, whose office is commonly hereditary.

Dooty. Another name for the chief magistrate of a town or province : this word is used only in the interior countries.

Palaver. A court of justice ; a public meeting of any kind.

Bushreen. A mussulman.

Kafir. A Pagan native; an unbeliever.

Sonakee. Another term for an unconverted native; it signifies one who drinks strong liquors, and is used by way of reproach.

Slatees. Free black merchants, who trade chiefly in slaves.

Coffle or *Caffila.* A caravan of slaves, or a company of people travelling with any kind of merchandize.

Bar. Nominal money; a single bar is equal in value to two shillings sterling, or thereabouts.

Minkalli. A quantity of gold, nearly equal in value to ten shillings sterling.

Kowries. Small shells, which pass for money in the Interior.

Korree. A watering-place, where shepherds keep their cattle.

Bentang. A sort of stage, erected in every town, answering the purpose of a town hall.

Baloon.   A room in which strangers are commonly lodged.

Soofroo.   A skin for containing water.

Saphie.   An amulet or charm.

Kouskous.   A dish prepared from boiled corn.

Shea-toulou.   Vegetable butter.

Calabash.   A species of gourd, of which the Negroes make bowls and dishes.

Paddle.   A sort of hoe used in husbandry.

ERRATA.

Page 13, line 9, after the word *of*, insert *the*.

—— 18, the third line from the bottom, for *Mandigoes*, read *Mandingoes*. This error occurs in some other places.

—— 20, line 6, after the word *as*, insert *counsel*.

—— 30, line 8, dele *and*.

—— 47, line 14, after *expression*, insert *even*.

—— 60, line 14, after *Prophet* dele the period.

—— 91, third line from the bottom, after *difficulty*, insert *and*.

—— 136, line 4, dele *there*.

—— 261, third line from the bottom, for *is*, read *was*.

☞ The *Mandingo* language being merely oral, it sometimes unavoidably happened to the Author, in reducing African terms to writing, to express the same word differently, in different parts of his journal. Thus, on revising his papers, he found *Jillifree* and *Jillifrey* used indiscriminately for the name of the same town; and in like manner *Kinyeto* and *Kenneyetoo*; *Cancaba* and *Kancaba*; *Tambacunda* and *Tombaconda*; and some others. As this was not observed until many of the sheets were printed, some of these instances of inattention will be found in the ensuing work, which it is hoped the good-natured reader will excuse. In cases of doubt, the Map of the Author's route is generally to be considered as the best authority; and to that also he refers for the course and distance of each day's progress.

SUBSCRIBERS' NAMES.

HIS MAJESTY'S LIBRARY.

ABERCORN, the most Noble the
Marquis of
Ailesbury, the Rt. Hon. the Earl of
Aylesford, the Rt. Hon. the Coun-
tess of
Archer, the Rt. Hon. Lady
Annesley, the Hon. Richard
Anderson, Mr. James
Archer, Edward, Esq.
Ashton, Nicholas, Esq.
Atkinson, Thomas, Esq.
Arts, &c. the Society for the en-
couragement of

B.

Buccleuch, his Grace the Duke of
Buccleuch, her Grace the Dut-
chess of
Banks, the Rt. Hon. Sir Joseph,
Bart. K.B.
Burges, Lady

Bruhl, Count de
Baillie, Dr.
Baker, John, Esq.
Baker, William, Esq,
Balan, Mr.
Bale, the Rev. Mr.
Balfour, General James
Baring, Sir Francis, Bart. M. P.
Baring, J. Esq. M. P.
Barker, Samuel, Esq.
Barratt, Mr.
Barrow, Mr. John
Bathurst, the Rev. Charles
Bedford, Charles, Esq.
Bensley, William, Esq.
Bickerdike, G. Esq.
Biddulph, Charles, Esq.
Bill, Charles, Esq.
Birmingham, the Library at
Blackburne, John, Esq.
Blackeston, Mr.

c

Blith, James, Esq.

Boddington, S. Esq.

Bonar, Mr. James

Boosey, Mr.

Boys, Mr. John

Braithwaite, Daniel, Esq.

Bramston, John, Esq.

Brand, Mr.

Bristol, the Library Society at

Brodie, Alexander, Esq.

Brompton, the Book Society of

Brown, Mr. Thomas

Bull, Mr.

Burgh, William, Esq.

Bush, F. Mr.

C.

Chesterfield, the Rt. Hon. the
    Earl of

Chichester, the Bishop of

Carnegie, Sir David, Bart.

Cotton, Sir Charles, Bart.

Cavendish, the Hon. Henry

Carter, the Rev. John, M. A.
    and F. S. A.

Chalmers, George, Esq.

Clarke, Dr. James

Claxton, ——, Esq.

Cleeve, the Rev. Mr.

Cockfield, Mr. Joseph

Collins, David, Esq.

Comings, Thomas Gray, Esq.

Cooper, R. B. Esq.

Cornwall, the County Library of

Corser, the Rev. William

Costeker, John, Esq.

Coussmaker, Mr. W. K.

Coxe, the Rev. Mr.

Cracherode, the Rev. Mr.

Creser, Mr. Thomas

Crowe, James, Esq.

Curtis, the Rev. Mr.

Cure, Capel, Esq.

D.

Dalkeith, the Rt. Hon. the Earl of

Durham, the Bishop of

Douglas, the Rt. Hon. Lord

Dundas, the Rt. Hon. Lord

Dalrymple, Sir John, Bart.

Drummond, William, Esq. M.P.

Dalrymple, Alexander, Esq.

Dalton, Mrs. Jane

Dawson, John, Esq.

Deacon, James, Esq.

Deal, the Book Society at

Denman, Dr.

Dick, Mungo, Esq.

Dickson, Mr. James
Dickinson, Caleb, Esq.
Dickenson, Rev. Samuel, LL.B.
Disney, the Rev. Dr.
Douce, Francis, Esq.
Douglas, Andrew, Esq.
Douglas, Miss
Dulwich College, the Library of

E.

Egremont, the Rt. Hon. the Earl of
Edwards, Bryan, Esq. M. P.
    F. R. S. and A. S.
Edwards, Z. B. Esq.
Ellis, George, Esq. M. P.
Ellis, Charles, Esq. M. P.
East, Mr.
Eden, Robert, Esq.
Edmondsbury, Saint, the new Pub-
    lic Library of
Edwards, Mr.
Egerton, the Hon. and Rev. Francis
Escher, Mr.
Eyre, Francis, Esq.
Exeter, the Book Society of

F.

Falconar, the Rev. Mr.
Fearnside, Mr.

Ferriday, William, Esq.
Fitzhugh, Thomas, Esq.
Forbes, James, Esq.
Fox, James, Esq.
Fraser, Mr.
Fry, Nicholas, L. Esq.

G.

Grafton, his Grace the Duke of
Glasgow, the Rt. Hon. the Earl of
Grantham, the Rt. Hon. Lady
Garthshore, Dr. 4 copies
Garrow, William, Esq.
Gebhardt, Mr.
Gillett, Mr.
Gisborne, the Rev. Thomas
Gordon, Thomas, Esq.
Gore, Colonel
Greene, Thomas, Esq.
Green, Mrs.
Gregory, Robert, Esq.
Gregory, the Rev. Edward
Greville, Robert, Esq.

H.

Howe, the Rt. Hon. Earl
Howe, the Rt. Hon. Sir William
Howe, the Hon. Caroline.
Howard, the Rt. Hon. Lady Julia

Hawkins, Sir Christopher, Bart.

Hort, Sir John, Bart.

Hudson, Sir Charles Grave, Bart.

Hale, Curteis, Esq.

Haliburton, David, Esq.

Halifax, the Library of

Hall, J. G. Esq.

Hammond, G. Esq.

Hanbury, Sampson, Esq.

Hardcastle, Joseph, Esq.

Harris, Mr. Nathaniel

Harvey, Mr.

Hedgland, Mr. P.

Heinemman, Mr. J. H.

Hill, Mr. William

Hislop, Mr.

Hislop, Mrs.

Hoare, Charles, Esq.

Hoare, Henry Hugh, Esq.

Hobhouse, Benjamin, Esq. M.P.

Hogarth, Mr. John

Hoffman, Mr.

Home, Miss

Hooper, the Rev. W. B. D. and F. A. S.

Horne, Edward, Esq.

Howarth, Mr.

Hussey, Phineas, Esq.

I.

James, Houghton, Esq.

Jarrett, Herbert, Esq.

Jennings, David, Esq.

Jenyns, the Rev. George

Imeson, Mr. William

Ingram, Francis, Esq.

Innis, John, Esq.

Johnes, Thomas, Esq.

Jones, Mrs.

Jones, Miss

Judge, Mr. John

Ivatts, Mr. Thomas

K.

Kerry, the Rt. Hon. the Earl of

King, the Rt. Hon. Lord

Kemble, John Philip, Esq.

Kendal, the Library at

Knowles, Mr.

L.

Landaff, the Bishop of

Lucas, the Rt. Hon. Lady

Leyser, Le Baron de

Lee, Thomas, Esq.

Leeds, the Library of

Leeds, the new Subscription Library at

Lindsey, the Rev. Theoph. A. M.
Long, William, Esq.
Long, Edward, Esq.

M.

Montrose, his Grace the Duke of
Moira, the Rt. Hon. the Earl of
Middleton, the Rt. Hon. Lord
   Viscount
Middleton, Sir Charles, Bart.
Macclesfield, Subscription Li-
   brary at
Maitland, Ebenezer, Esq.
Maitland, John, Esq.
Mappleton, Dr.
Martin, the Rev. Mr.
Mason, Major
Mavor, John, Esq.
Melville, General
Michell, Charles, Esq.
Miles, William, Esq.
Millman, Dr.
Miller, Charles, Esq.
Mills, Dr.
Monro, Captain George
Mordaunt, General
Morgan, William, Esq.
Morland, Mr. Thomas

Morris, Lieut. Col.
Morris, Charles, Esq.

N.

Northumberland, his Grace the
   Duke of
Neave, Sir Richard, Bart. 2 copies
Newbery, Francis, Esq.
Newcastle upon Tyne, the Lite-
   rary Society of
Newcomen, William, Esq.
Nicholls, John, Esq. M. P.
Norris, H. H. Esq.
North, Percival, Esq.

O.

Oglander, Sir William, Bart.
Ogle, Rev. Dr.
Ogle, Nathaniel, Esq.
Onslow, Arthur, Esq.
Ormerod, the Rev. R.

P.

Palmerston, the Rt. Hon. Lord
   Viscount.
Peachey, the Hon. John
Pelham, the Hon. Mr.
Penryhn, the Rt. Hon. Lord

Price, the Rt. Hon. Lady Maria
Pulteney, Sir William, Bart.
Parker, Samuel, Esq.
Parker, Mrs.
Palmer, Thomas, Esq.
Paulett, Norton, Esq.
Pearson, George, M. D.
Pearson, the Rev. Mr.
Peart, Dr.
Peltier, Mons.
Philips, the Rev. John
Pickering, the Rev. Joseph
Pryme, Mr.

R.

Roxburghe, his Grace the Duke of
Riddell, Sir John Buchanan,
    Bart.
Rainsford, General
Repton, Book Society of
Reyner, Joseph, Esq.
Rennell, Major
Rennie, John, Esq.
Reynolds, Richard, Esq.
Rippon, Cuthbert, Esq.
Roberts, the Rev. Thomas
Robley, Joseph, Esq.
Robley, John, Esq.

Rochester, the Book Society of
Rudge, Samuel, Esq.
Russell, Claud, Esq,

S.

Stopford, the Rt. Hon. Lord Vis-
    count
Suffield, the Rt. Hon. Lord
Sheffield, the Rt. Hon. Lord
Stepney, Sir John, Bart.
Staunton, Sir George, Bart.
Stephens, Sir Philip, Bart. M. P.
    F. R. S. and S. A.
Samuda, Mr. David, Jun.
Sharp, William, Esq.
Sharpe, the Rev. Mr.
Shepherd, Tuffen, Esq.
Simmons, Samuel Froart, M. D.
    F. R. S.
Sittingbourn, the Library of
Skipp, John, Esq.
Skirrow, Mr.
Sloane, Hans, Esq.
Smith, Mr. James
Smith, the Rev. John
Smith, Thomas, Esq.
Smith, William, Esq. M. P.
Soane, John, Esq.

Spann, John, Esq.

Spooner, Isaac, Esq.

Stainsforth, George, Esq.

Stamford, the Library at

Stanhope, Mr. Spencer

Stanley, Colonel

Stead, Mr. John

Stephens, Francis, Esq.

Stonard, the Rev. John

Stonhewer, Richard, Esq.

Stratford, the Rev. Wm. A.M.

Stuart, And. Esq. M.P. 3 copies

Sulivan, R. J. Esq.

Symmons, John, Esq. 3 copies

Symes, the Rev. James

T.

Tate, the Rev. B. B. D.

Taylor, the Rev. Dr.

Thomas, Mr. L.

Thompson, Mr.

Thornton, Henry, Esq. M. P.

Toulmin, T. Esq.

Travers, Benjamin, Esq.

Travers, Joseph, Esq.

Trevelyan, Sir John, Bart.

Trist, the Rev. Mr.

Trowbridge and Warminster Book Society

Tunnard, Mr.

Turner, Charles, Esq.

Turney, Mr. John

V.

Upper Ossory, the Rt. Hon. the Earl of

Vaughan, William, Esq.

W.

Winchester, the Bishop of

Walley, Josiah, Esq.

Walker, J. Esq. F.R.S. and S.A.

Walls, the Rev. Edward

Warburton, John, Esq.

Warmintser, the Book Society at

Warwick, the Library of

Watson, William, Esq.

West, the Rev. Mr.

Weston, the Rev. Stephen

Whitaker, Mrs.

White, James, Esq,

Whitehead, Miss

Whitfeld, the Rev. Henry, D.D.

Wilberforce, William, Esq. M.P.

DIRECTIONS FOR PLACING THE PLATES.

APPENDIX.

POSTSCRIPT.

THE incident of the Negro Song, related in the 15th Chapter of this work (p. 198), having been communicated to a Lady, who is not more distinguished for her rank, than for her beauty and accomplishments; she was pleased to think so highly of this simple and unpremeditated effusion, as to make a version of it with her own pen; and cause it to be set to music by an eminent Composer. With this elegant production, in both parts of which the plaintive simplicity of the original is preserved and improved, the Author thinks himself highly honoured in being permitted to adorn his book; and he laments only that he had not an opportunity of inserting it in its proper place in the body of the work.

SONG.

A NEGRO SONG,

FROM MR. PARK'S TRAVELS.

I.

THE loud wind roar'd, the rain fell fast;
The White Man yielded to the blast:
He sat him down, beneath our tree;
For weary, sad, and faint was he;
And ah, no wife, or mother's care,
For him, the milk or corn prepare:

CHORUS.

The White Man, shall our pity share;
Alas, no wife or mother's care,
For him, the milk or corn prepare.

II.

The storm is o'er; the tempest past;
And Mercy's voice has hush'd the blast.
The wind is heard in whispers low;
The White Man, far away must go;—
But ever in his heart will bear
Remembrance of the Negro's care.

CHORUS.

Go, White Man, go;—but with thee bear
The Negro's wish, the Negro's prayer;
Remembrance of the Negro's care.

S O N G
from M.r Park's Travels

The Words by the Dutchess of Devonshire.

The Music by G. G. Ferrari.

The loud wind roar'd, the rain fell fast, the white man yeilded to the blast: he sat him down beneath our tree, for weary, sad and faint was he, and ah! no

wife or mother's care, for him the milk or corn prepare; for him the

rinf

Chorus

milk or corn prepare. The white man shall our pity

sf *p*

share; alas! no wife or mother's care, the milk or corn for him pre_

_pare; the milk or corn for him prepare.

rinf *p*

TRAVELS

IN THE

INTERIOR OF AFRICA.

CHAPTER I.

The Author's Motives for undertaking the Voyage—his Instruc-
tions and Departure—arrives at Jillifree, on the Gambia River
—proceeds to Vintain.—Some Account of the Feloops.—Proceeds
up the River for Jonkakonda—arrives at Dr. Laidley's.—Some
Account of Pisania, and the British Factory established at that
Place.—The Author's Employment during his Stay at Pisania—
his Sickness and Recovery—the Country described—prepares to
set out for the Interior.

Soon after my return from the East Indies in 1793, having
learnt that the Noblemen and Gentlemen, associated for the
purpose of prosecuting Discoveries in the Interior of Africa,
were desirous of engaging a person to explore that continent,
by the way of the Gambia river, I took occasion, through means
of the President of the Royal Society, to whom I had the
honour to be known, of offering myself for that service. I had
been informed, that a gentleman of the name of Houghton, a

B

Captain in the army, and formerly Fort-Major at Goree, had already sailed to the Gambia, under the direction of the Association, and that there was reason to apprehend he had fallen a sacrifice to the climate, or perished in some contest with the natives; but this intelligence, instead of deterring me from my purpose, animated me to persist in the offer of my services with the greater solicitude. I had a passionate desire to examine into the productions of a country so little known; and to become experimentally acquainted with the modes of life, and character of the natives. I knew that I was able to bear fatigue; and I relied on my youth, and the strength of my constitution, to preserve me from the effects of the climate. The salary which the Committee allowed was sufficiently large, and I made no stipulation for future reward. If I should perish in my journey, I was willing that my hopes and expectations should perish with me; and if I should succeed in rendering the geography of Africa more familiar to my countrymen, and in opening to their ambition and industry new sources of wealth, and new channels of commerce, I knew that I was in the hands of men of honour, who would not fail to bestow that remuneration which my successful services should appear to them to merit. The Committee of the Association, having made such inquiries as they thought necessary, declared themselves satisfied with the qualifications that I possessed, and accepted me for the service; and with that liberality which on all occasions distinguishes their conduct, gave me every encouragement which it was in their power to grant, or which I could with propriety ask.

It was at first proposed that I should accompany Mr. James Willis, who was then recently appointed Consul at Senegambia, and whose countenance in that capacity it was thought might have served and protected me; but Government afterwards rescinded his appointment, and I lost that advantage. The kindness of the Committee, however, supplied all that was necessary. Being favoured by the Secretary of the Association, the late Henry Beaufoy, Esq. with a recommendation to Dr. John Laidley (a gentleman who had resided many years at an English factory on the banks of the Gambia), and furnished with a letter of credit on him for £200, I took my passage in the brig Endeavour, a small vessel trading to the Gambia for bees-wax and ivory, commanded by Captain Richard Wyatt, and I became impatient for my departure.

My instructions were very plain and concise. I was directed, on my arrival in Africa, " to pass on to the river Niger, either by the way of Bambouk, or by such other route as should be found most convenient. That I should ascertain the course, and, if possible, the rise and termination of that river. That I should use my utmost exertions to visit the principal towns or cities in its neighbourhood, particularly Tombuctoo and Houssa; and that I should be afterwards at liberty to return to Europe, either by the way of the Gambia, or by such other route, as, under all the then existing circumstances of my situation and prospects, should appear to me to be most advisable."

We sailed from Portsmouth on the 22d day of May, 1795. On the 4th of June, we saw the mountains over Mogadore, on the coast of Africa; and on the 21st of the same month, after a pleasant voyage of thirty days, we anchored at Jillifree, a town on the northern bank of the river Gambia, opposite to James's Island, where the English had formerly a small fort.

The kingdom of Barra, in which the town of Jillifree is situated, produces great plenty of the necessaries of life ; but the chief trade of the inhabitants is in salt ; which commodity they carry up the river in canoes as high as Barraconda, and bring down in return Indian corn, cotton cloths, elephants' teeth, small quantities of gold dust, &c. The number of canoes and people constantly employed in this trade, make the King of Barra more formidable to Europeans than any other chieftain on the river ; and this circumstance probably encouraged him to establish those exorbitant duties, which traders of all nations are obliged to pay at entry, amounting to nearly £20. on every vessel, great and small. These duties, or customs, are generally collected in person by the Alkaid, or Governor of Jillifree, and he is attended on these occasions by a numerous train of dependants, among whom are found many who, by their frequent intercourse with the English, have acquired a smattering of our language ; but they are commonly very noisy, and very troublesome ; begging for every thing they fancy with such earnestness and importunity, that traders, in order to get quit of them, are frequently obliged to grant their requests.

On the 23d we departed from Jillifree, and proceeded to Vintain, a town situated about two miles up a creek on the southern side of the river. This place is much resorted to by Europeans, on account of the great quantities of bees-wax which are brought hither for sale : the wax is collected in the woods by the Feloops, a wild and unsociable race of people ; their country, which is of considerable extent, abounds in rice ; and the natives supply the traders, both on the Gambia, and Cassamansa rivers, with that article, and also with goats and poultry, on very reasonable terms. The honey which they collect is chiefly used by themselves in making a strong intoxicating liquor, much the same as the mead which is produced from honey in Great Britain.

In their traffic with Europeans, the Feloops generally employ a factor, or agent, of the Mandingo nation, who speaks a little English, and is acquainted with the trade of the river. This broker makes the bargain ; and, with the connivance of the European, receives a certain part only of the payment ; which he gives to his employer as the whole ; the remainder (which is very truly called the *cheating money*) he receives when the Feloop is gone, and appropriates to himself, as a reward for his trouble.

The language of the Feloops is appropriate and peculiar ; and as their trade is chiefly conducted, as hath been observed, by Mandingoes, the Europeans have no inducement to learn it. The numerals are as follow :

One	——	*Enory.*
Two	——	*Sickaba, or Cookaba.*
Three	——	*Sisajee.*
Four	——	*Sibakeer.*
Five	——	*Footuck.*
Six	——	*Footuck-Enory.*
Seven	——	*Footuck Cookaba.*

Eight ——— *Footuck-Sisajee.*
Nine ——— *Footuck-Sibakeer.*
Ten ——— *Sibankonyen.*

On the 26th we left Vintain, and continued our course up the river, anchoring whenever the tide failed us, and frequently towing the vessel with the boat. The river is deep and muddy; the banks are covered with impenetrable thickets of mangrove; and the whole of the adjacent country appears to be flat and swampy.

The Gambia abounds with fish, some species of which are excellent food; but none of them that I recollect are known in Europe. At the entrance from the sea, sharks are found in great abundance; and, higher up, alligators, and the hippopotamus (or river horse) are very numerous. The latter might with more propriety be called the river-elephant, being of an enormous and unwieldy bulk. and his teeth furnish good ivory. This animal is amphibious, with short and thick legs, and cloven hoofs; it feeds on grass, and such shrubs as the banks of the river afford, boughs of trees, &c. seldom venturing far from the water, in which it seeks refuge on hearing the approach of man. I have seen many, and always found them of a timid and inoffensive disposition.

In six days after leaving Vintain, we reached Jonkakonda, a place of considerable trade, where our vessel was to take in part of her lading. The next morning, the several European traders came from their different factories to receive their letters, and learn the nature and amount of the cargo; and the Captain dispatched a messenger to Dr. Laidley to inform him of my arrival. He came to Jonkakonda the morning following, when I delivered him Mr Beaufoy's letter, and he gave me a kind invitation to spend my time at his house until an opportunity should offer of prosecuting my journey. This invitation was too acceptable to be refused, and being furnished by the Doctor with a horse and guide, I set out from Jonkakonda at daybreak on the 5th of July, and at eleven o'clock arrived at Pisania, where I was accommodated with a room, and other conveniences in the Doctor's house.

Pisania is a small village in the King of Yany's dominions, established by British subjects as a factory for trade, and inhabited solely by them and their black servants. It is situated on the banks of the Gambia, sixteen miles above Jonkakonda. The white residents, at the time of my arrival there, consisted only of Dr. Laidley, and two gentlemen who were brothers, of the name of Ainsley ; but their domestics were numerous. They enjoyed perfect security under the king's protection, and being highly esteemed and respected by the natives at large, wanted no accommodation or comfort which the country could supply ; and the greatest part of the trade in slaves, ivory, and gold, was in their hands.

Being now settled for some time at my ease, my first object was to learn the Mandingo tongue, being the language in almost general use throughout this part of Africa ; and without which I was fully convinced that I never could acquire an extensive knowledge of the country or its inhabitants. In this pursuit I was greatly assisted by Dr. Laidley, who, by a long residence in the country, and constant intercourse with the natives, had made himself completely master of it. Next to the language, my great object was to collect information concerning the countries I intended to visit. On this occasion I was referred to certain traders called Slatees. These are free black merchants, of great consideration in this part of Africa, who come down from the interior countries, chiefly with enslaved Negroes for sale ; but I soon discovered that very little dependance could be placed on the accounts which they gave ; for they contradicted each other in the most important particulars, and all of them seemed extremely unwilling that I should prosecute my journey. These circumstances increased my anxiety to ascertain the truth from my own personal observations.

In researches of this kind, and in observing the manners and customs of the natives, in a country so little known to the nations of Europe, and furnished with so many striking and uncommon objects of nature, my time passed not unpleasantly ; and I began to flatter myself that I had escaped the fever, or seasoning, to which Europeans, on their first arrival in hot climates, are generally subject. But, on the 31st of July, I imprudently exposed myself to the night dew, in observing an eclipse of the moon, with a view to determine the longitude of the place : the next day I found myself attacked with a smart fever and delirium ; and such an illness followed, as confined me to the house during the greatest part of August. My recovery was very slow : but I embraced every short interval of convalescence to walk out, and make myself acquainted with the productions of the country. In one of those excursions, having rambled farther than usual, in a hot day, I brought on a return of my fever, and on the 10th of September I was again confined to my bed. The fever, however, was not so violent as before; and in the course of three weeks I was able, when the weather would permit, to renew my botanical excursions; and when it rained, I amused myself with drawing plants, &c. in my chamber. The care and attention of Dr. Laidley contributed greatly to alleviate my sufferings; his company and conversation beguiled the tedious hours during that gloomy season, when the rain falls in torrents; when suffocating heats oppress by day, and when the night is spent by the terrified traveller in listening to the croaking of frogs, (of which the numbers are beyond imagination,) the shrill cry of the jackall, and the deep howling of the hyæna; a dismal concert, interrupted only by the roar of such tremendous thunder as no person can form a conception of but those who have heard it.

The country itself being an immense level, and very generally covered with woods, presents a tiresome and gloomy uniformity to the eye; but although nature has denied to the inhabitants the beauties of romantic landscapes, she has bestowed on them, with a liberal hand, the more important blessings of fertility and abundance. A little attention to cultivation procures a sufficiency of corn; the fields afford a rich pasturage for cattle; and the natives are plentifully supplied with excellent fish, both from the Gambia river and the Walli creek.

The grains which are chiefly cultivated are Indian corn, (*zea mays*); two kinds of *holcus spicatus*, called by the natives *soono* and *sanio*; *holcus niger*, and *holcus bicolor*; the former of which

C

they have named *bassi woolima,* and the latter *bassiqui.* These, together with rice, are raised in considerable quantities; besides which, the inhabitants, in the vicinity of the towns and villages, have gardens which produce onions, calavances, yams, cassavi, ground-nuts, pompions, gourds, water melons, and some other esculent plants.

I observed likewise, near the towns, small patches of cotton and indigo. The former of these articles supplies them with clothing, and with the latter they dye their cloth of an excellent blue colour, in a manner that will hereafter be described.

In preparing their corn for food, the natives use a large wooden mortar called a *paloon*, in which they bruise the seed until it parts with the outer covering, or husk, which is then separated from the clean corn, by exposing it to the wind; nearly in the same manner as wheat is cleared from the chaff in England. The corn thus freed from the husk, is returned to the mortar, and beaten into meal; which is dressed variously in different countries; but the most common preparation of it among the nations of the Gambia, is a sort of pudding, which they call *kouskous.* It is made by first moistening the flour with water, and then stirring and shaking it about in a large calabash, or gourd, till it adheres together in small granules, resembling sago. It is then put into an earthen pot, whose bottom is perforated with a number of small holes; and this pot being placed upon another, the two vessels are luted together, either with a paste of meal and water, or with cows' dung, and placed upon the fire. In the lower vessel is commonly some animal food and water, the steam or vapour of which ascends through the perforations in the bottom of the upper vessel, and softens and prepares the *kouskous*, which is very much esteemed throughout all the countries that I visited. I am informed, that the same manner of preparing flour, is very generally used on the Barbary coast, and that the dish so prepared, is there called by the same name. It is therefore probable, that the Negroes borrowed the practice from the Moors.

For gratifying a taste for variety, another sort of pudding, called *nealing*, is sometimes prepared from the meal of corn; and they have also adopted two or three different modes of dressing their rice. Of vegetable food, therefore, the natives have no want; and although the common class of people are but sparingly supplied with animal food, yet this article is not wholly withheld from them.

Their domestic animals are nearly the same as in Europe. Swine are found in the woods, but their flesh is not esteemed: probably the marked abhorrence in which this animal is held by the votaries of Mahomet, has spread itself among the Pagans. Poultry of all kinds (the turkey excepted) is every where to be had. The Guinea fowl and red partridge, abound in the fields; and the woods furnish a small species of antelope, of which the venison is highly and deservedly prized.

Of the other wild animals in the Mandingo countries, the most common are the hyæna, the panther, and the elephant. Considering the use that is made of the latter in the East Indies, it may be thought extraordinary, that the natives of Africa have not, in any part of this immense continent, acquired the skill of taming this powerful and docile creature, and applying his strength

and faculties to the service of man. When I told some of the
natives that this was actually done in the countries of the East,
my auditors laughed me to scorn, and exclaimed, *Tobaubo fonnio!*
(a white man's lie.) The Negroes frequently find means to
destroy the elephant by fire arms; they hunt it principally for
the sake of the teeth, which they transfer in barter to those
who sell them again to the Europeans. The flesh they eat, and
consider it as a great delicacy.

The usual beast of burthen in all the Negro territories, is the
ass. The application of animal labour to the purposes of agriculture, is no where adopted; the plough, therefore, is wholly
unknown. The chief implement used in husbandry is the hoe,
which varies in form in different districts; and the labour is
universally performed by slaves.

On the 6th of October the waters of the Gambia were at the
greatest height, being fifteen feet above the high-water mark
of the tide; after which they began to subside; at first slowly,
but afterwards very rapidly; sometimes sinking more than
a foot in twenty-four hours: by the beginning of November
the river had sunk to its former level, and the tide ebbed and
flowed as usual. When the river had subsided, and the atmosphere grew dry, I recovered apace, and began to think of my
departure; for this is reckoned the most proper season for travelling: the natives had completed their harvest, and provisions were every where cheap and plentiful.

Dr. Laidley was at this time employed in a trading voyage
at Jonkakonda. I wrote to him to desire that he would use his
interest with the slatees, or slave merchants, to procure me the

company and protection of the first *coffle* (or caravan,) that might leave Gambia for the interior country ; and in the mean time I requested him to purchase for me a horse, and two asses. A few days afterwards the Doctor returned to Pisania, and informed me that a coffle would certainly go for the interior, in the course of the dry season ; but that as many of the merchants belonging to it had not yet completed their assortment of goods, he could not say at what time they would set out.

As the characters and dispositions of slatees, and people that composed the caravan, were entirely unknown to me, and as they seemed rather averse to my purpose, and unwilling to enter into any positive engagements on my account ; and the time of their departure being withal very uncertain, I resolved, on further deliberation, to avail myself of the dry season, and proceed without them.

Dr. Laidley approved my determination, and promised me every assistance in his power, to enable me to prosecute my journey with comfort and safety.

This resolution having been formed, I made preparations accordingly. And now, being about to take leave of my hospitable friend, (whose kindness and solicitude continued to the moment of my departure,*) and to quit, for many months, the countries bordering on the Gambia, it seems proper, before I proceed with my narrative, that I should, in this place, give some account of the several Negro nations which inhabit the banks

* Dr. Laidley, to my infinite regret, has since paid the debt of nature. He left Africa in the latter end of 1797, intending to return to Great Britain by way of the West Indies ; and died soon after his arrival at Barbadoes.

of this celebrated river; and the commercial intercourse that
subsists between them, and such of the nations of Europe as
find their advantage in trading to this part of Africa. The observations which have occurred to me on both these subjects,
will be found in the following Chapter.

CHAPTER II.

*Description of the Feloops, the Jaloffs, the Foulahs, and Man-
dingoes.—Some Account of the Trade between the Nations of
Europe and the Natives of Africa by the way of the Gambia,
and between the native Inhabitants of the Coast and the Nations of the interior Countries—their Mode of selling and
buying, &c.*

THE natives of the countries bordering on the Gambia, though
distributed into a great many distinct governments, may, I
think, be divided into four great classes ; the Feloops, the Jaloffs,
the Foulahs, and the Mandingoes. Among all these nations, the
religion of Mahomet has made, and continues to make, considerable progress ; but, in most of them, the body of the people,
both free and enslaved, persevere in maintaining the blind but
harmless superstitions of their ancestors, and are called by the
Mahomedans *kafirs*, or infidels.

Of the Feloops, I have little to add to what has been observed
concerning them in the former Chapter. They are of a gloomy
disposition, and are supposed never to forgive an injury. They
are even said to transmit their quarrels as deadly feuds to their
posterity ; insomuch that a son considers it as incumbent on
him, from a just sense of filial obligation, to become the avenger
of his deceased father's wrongs. If a man loses his life in one
of those sudden quarrels, which perpetually occur at their feasts,

when the whole party is intoxicated with mead, his son, or the eldest of his sons (if he has more than one), endeavours to procure his father's sandals, which he wears *once a year*, on the anniversary of his father's death, until a fit opportunity offers of revenging his fate, when the object of his resentment seldom escapes his pursuit.   This fierce and unrelenting disposition is, however, counterbalanced by many good qualities : they display the utmost gratitude and affection towards their benefactors ; and the fidelity with which they preserve whatever is intrusted to them is remarkable.   During the present war they have, more than once, taken up arms to defend our merchant vessels from French privateers ; and English property, of considerable value, has frequently been left at Vintain, for a long time, entirely under the care of the Feloops ; who have uniformly manifested on such occasions the strictest honesty and punctuality.   How greatly is it to be wished, that the minds of a people so determined and faithful, could be softened and civilized, by the mild and benevolent spirit of Christianity !

The Jaloffs (or Yaloffs) are an active, powerful, and warlike race, inhabiting great part of that tract which lies between the river Senegal, and the Mandingo States on the Gambia ; yet they differ from the Mandingoes, not only in language, but likewise in complexion and features. The noses of the Jaloffs are not so much depressed, nor the lips so protuberant, as among the generality of Africans ; and although their skin is of the deepest black, they are considered by the white traders, as the most sightly Negroes in this part of the Continent.

They are divided into several independent states or kingdoms ;

which are frequently at war either with their neighbours, or with each other. In their manners, superstitions, and government, however, they have a greater resemblance to the Mandingoes (of whom I shall presently speak) than to any other nation; but excel them in the manufacture of cotton cloth; spinning the wool to a finer thread, weaving it in a broader loom, and dying it of a better colour.

Their language is said to be copious and significant; and is often learnt by Europeans trading to Senegal. I cannot say much of it from my own knowledge; but have preserved their numerals, which are these:

One	——	*Wean.*
Two	——	*Yar.*
Three	——	*Yat.*
Four	——	*Yanet.*
Five	——	*Judom.*
Six	——	*Judom wean.*
Seven	——	*Judom Yar.*
Eight	——	*Judom Yat.*
Nine	——	*Judom Yanet.*
Ten	——	*Fook.*
Eleven	——	*Fook aug wean,* &c.

The Foulahs (or Pholeys), such of them at least as reside near the Gambia, are chiefly of a tawny complexion, with soft silky hair, and pleasing features. They are much attached to a pastoral life, and have introduced themselves into all the kingdoms on the windward coast, as herdsmen and husbandmen, paying a

D

tribute to the sovereign of the country for the lands which they hold. Not having many opportunities however, during my residence at Pisania, of improving my acquaintance with these people, I defer entering at large into their character, until a fitter occasion occurs, which will present itself when I come to Bondou.

The Mandingoes, of whom it remains to speak, constitute in truth, the bulk of the inhabitants in all those districts of Africa which I visited ; and their language, with a few exceptions, is universally understood, and very generally spoken, in that part of the continent. Their numerals are these : *

One	——	*Killin.*
Two	——	*Foola.*
Three	——	*Sabba.*
Four	——	*Nani.*
Five	——	*Loolo.*
Six	——	*Woro.*
Seven	——	*Oronglo.*
Eight	——	*Sie.*
Nine	——	*Conunta.*
Ten	——	*Tang.*
Eleven	——	*Tan ning killin,* &c.

They are called Mandigoes, I conceive, as having originally migrated from the interior state of Manding, of which some account will hereafter be given ; but, contrary to the present

---

* In the Travels of Francis Moore the reader will find a pretty copious vocabulary of the Mandingo language, which in general is correct.

constitution of their parent country, which is republican, it appeared to me that the government in all the Mandingo states, near the Gambia, is monarchical. The power of the sovereign is, however, by no means unlimited. In all affairs of importance, the king calls an assembly of the principal men, or elders, by whose councils he is directed, and without whose advice he can neither declare war, nor conclude peace.

In every considerable town there is a chief magistrate, called the *Alkaid*, whose office is hereditary, and whose business it is to preserve order, to levy duties on travellers, and to preside at all conferences in the exercise of local jurisdiction and the administration of justice. These courts are composed of the elders of the town (of free condition), and are termed *palavers;* and their proceedings are conducted in the open air with sufficient solemnity. Both sides of a question are freely canvassed, witnesses are publicly examined, and the decisions which follow generally meet with the approbation of the surrounding audience.

As the Negroes have no written language of their own, the general rule of decision is an appeal to *ancient custom;* but since the system of Mahomet has made so great progress among them, the converts to that faith have gradually introduced, with the religious tenets, many of the civil institutions of the Prophet; and where the Koran is not found sufficiently explicit, recourse is had to a commentary called *Al Sharra*, containing, as I was told, a complete exposition or digest of the Mahomedan laws, both civil and criminal, properly arranged and illustrated.

D 2

This frequency of appeal to written laws, with which the Pagan natives are necessarily unacquainted, has given rise in their palavers to (what I little expected to find in Africa) professional advocates, or expounders of the law, who are allowed to appear and to plead for plaintiff or defendant, much in the same manner as in the law courts of Great Britain. They are Mahomedan Negroes who have made, or affect to have made, the laws of the Prophet their peculiar study; and if I may judge from their harangues, which I frequently attended, I believe that in the forensic qualifications of procrastination and cavil, and the arts of confounding and perplexing a cause, they are not always surpassed by the ablest pleaders in Europe. While I was at Pisania a cause was heard which furnished the Mahomedan lawyers with an admirable opportunity of displaying their professional dexterity. The case was this: an ass belonging to a Serawoolli Negro (a native of an interior country near the river Senegal) had broke into a field of corn belonging to one of the Mandingo inhabitants, and destroyed great part of it. The Mandingo having caught the animal in his field, immediately drew his knife and cut its throat. The Serawoolli thereupon called a *palaver* (or in European terms, *brought an action*) to recover damages for the loss of his beast, on which he set a high value. The defendant confessed he had killed the ass, but pleaded a *set off*, insisting that the loss he had sustained by the ravage in his corn, was equal to the sum demanded for the animal. To ascertain this fact was the point at issue, and the learned advocates contrived to puzzle the cause in such a manner, that after a hearing of three days, the court broke up without coming to any determination upon it; and a second palaver was, I suppose, thought necessary.

The Mandingoes, generally speaking, are of a mild, sociable, and obliging disposition. The men are commonly above the middle size, well shaped, strong, and capable of enduring great labour; the women are good-natured, sprightly and agreeable. The dress of both sexes is composed of cotton cloth, of their own manufacture; that of the men is a loose frock, not unlike a surplice, with drawers which reach half way down the leg; and they wear sandals on their feet, and white cotton caps on their heads. The women's dress consists of two pieces of cloth, each of which is about six feet long, and three broad; one of these they wrap round the waist, which hanging down to the ancles answers the purpose of a petticoat: the other is thrown negligently over the bosom and shoulders.

This account of their clothing is indeed nearly applicable to the natives of all the different countries in this part of Africa; a peculiar national mode is observable only in the head dresses of the women.

Thus, in the countries of the Gambia, the females wear a sort of bandage, which they call *Jalla*. It is a narrow stripe of cotton cloth, wrapped many times round, immediately over the forehead. In Bondou the head is encircled with strings of white beads, and a small plate of gold is worn in the middle of the forehead. In Kasson, the ladies decorate their heads in a very tasteful and elegant manner, with white sea-shells. In Kaarta and Ludamar, the women raise their hair to a great height by the addition of a pad (as the ladies did formerly in Great

Britain) which they decorate with a species of coral, brought from the Red sea by pilgrims returning from Mecca, and sold at a great price.

In the construction of their dwelling houses the Mandigoes also conform to the general practice of the African nations on this part of the continent, contenting themselves with small and incommodious hovels. A circular mud wall about four feet high, upon which is placed a conical roof, composed of the bamboo cane, and thatched with grass, forms alike the palace of the king, and the hovel of the slave. Their household furniture is equally simple. A hurdle of canes placed upon upright stakes, about two feet from the ground, upon which is spread a mat or bullock's hide, answers the purpose of a bed : a water jar, some earthen pots for dressing their food, a few wooden bowls and calabashes, and one or two low stools, compose the rest.

As every man of free condition has a plurality of wives, it is found necessary (to prevent, I suppose, matrimonial disputes) that each of the ladies should be accommodated with a hut to herself ; and all the huts belonging to the same family are sur-rounded by a fence, constructed of bamboo canes, split and formed into a sort of wicker-work. The whole inclosure is called a *sirk*, or *surk*. A number of these inclosures, with narrow passages between them, form what is called a town ; but the huts are ge-nerally placed without any regularity, according to the caprice of the owner. The only rule that seems to be attended to, is placing the door towards the south-west, in order to admit the sea breeze.

In each town is a large stage called the *bentang*, which answers the purpose of a public hall or town-house; it is composed of interwoven canes, and is generally sheltered from the sun by being erected in the shade of some large tree. It is here that all public affairs are transacted and trials conducted ; and here the lazy and indolent meet to smoke their pipes and hear the news of the day. In most of the towns the Mahomedans have also a *missura,* or mosque, in which they assemble and offer up their daily prayers, according to the rules of the Koran.

In the account which I have thus given of the natives, the reader must bear in mind, that my observations apply chiefly to persons of *free condition,* who constitute, I suppose, not more than one-fourth part of the inhabitants at large ; the other three-fourths are in a state of hopeless and hereditary slavery ; and are employed in cultivating the land, in the care of cattle, and in servile offices of all kinds, much in the same manner as the slaves in the West Indies. I was told, however, that the Mandingo master can neither deprive his slave of life, nor sell him to a stranger. without first calling a palaver on his conduct ; or, in other words, bringing him to a public trial : but this degree of protection is extended only to the native or domestic slave. Captives taken in war, and those unfortunate victims who are condemned to slavery for crimes or insolvency, and, in short, all those unhappy people who are brought down from the interior countries for sale, have no security whatever, but may be treated and disposed of in all respects as the owner thinks proper. It sometimes happens, indeed, when no ships are on the Coast, that a humane and considerate master, incorporates his purchased slaves among his domestics; and their offspring at least, if not the parents, become entitled to all the privileges of the native class.

The preceding remarks, concerning the several nations that inhabit the banks of the Gambia, are all that I recollect as necessary to be made in this place, at the outset of my journey. With regard to the Mandingoes, however, many particulars are yet to be related; some of which are necessarily interwoven into the narrative of my progress, and others will be given in a summary, at the end of my work; together with all such observations as I have collected on the country and climate, which I could not with propriety insert in the regular detail of occurrences. What remains of the present Chapter will therefore relate solely to the trade which the nations of Christendom have found means to establish with the natives of Africa, by the channel of the Gambia; and the inland traffic which has arisen, in consequence of it, between the inhabitants of the Coast, and the nations of the interior countries.

The earliest European establishment on this celebrated river was a factory of the Portugueze; and to this must be ascribed the introduction of the numerous words of that language which are still in use among the Negroes. The Dutch, French, and English, afterwards successively possessed themselves of settlements on the Coast; but the trade of the Gambia became, and continued for many years, a sort of monopoly in the hands of the English. In the travels of Francis Moore, is preserved an account of the Royal African Company's establishments in this river, in the year 1730; at which time James's factory alone consisted of a governor, deputy governor, and two other principal

officers ; eight factors, thirteen writers, twenty inferior attendants and tradesmen ; a company of soldiers, and thirty-two
Negro servants, besides sloops, shallops, and boats, with their
crews ; and there were no less than eight subordinate factories
in other parts of the river.

The trade with Europe, by being afterwards laid open, was
almost annihilated ; the share which the subjects of England at
this time hold in it, supports not more than two or three annual
ships ; and I am informed that the gross value of British exports
is under £20,000. The French and Danes still maintain a
small share, and the Americans have lately sent a few vessels
to the Gambia by way of experiment.

The commodities exported to the Gambia from Europe consist chiefly of fire-arms and ammunition, iron ware, spiritu-
ous liquors, tobacco, cotton caps, a small quantity of broad
cloth, and a few articles of the manufacture of Manchester ; a
small assortment of India goods, with some glass beads, amber,
and other trifles : for which are taken in exchange slaves, gold-
dust, ivory, bees-wax, and hides. Slaves are the chief article,
but the whole number which at this time are annually exported from the Gambia by all nations, is supposed to be under
one thousand.

Most of these unfortunate victims are brought to the Coast in
periodical caravans ; many of them from very remote inland
countries ; for the language which they speak is not understood
by the inhabitants of the maritime districts. In a subsequent
part of my work I shall give the best information I have been
able to collect concerning the manner in which they are ob-

E

tained. On their arrival at the Coast, if no immediate opportunity offers of selling them to advantage, they are distributed among the neighbouring villages, until a slave ship arrives, or until they can be sold to black traders, who sometimes purchase on speculation. In the meanwhile, the poor wretches are kept constantly fettered, two and two of them being chained together, and employed in the labours of the field : and I am sorry to add, are very scantily fed, as well as harshly treated. The price of a slave varies according to the number of purchasers from Europe, and the arrival of caravans from the interior ; but in general I reckon, that a young and healthy male, from 16 to 25 years of age, may be estimated on the spot from £18. to £20. sterling.

The Negro slave merchants, as I have observed in the former Chapter ; are called *Slatees ;* who, besides slaves, and the merchandize which they bring for sale to the whites, supply the inhabitants of the maritime districts with native iron, sweet smelling gums and frankincense, and a commodity called *Shea-toulou,* which, literally translated, signifies *tree-butter.* This commodity is extracted, by means of boiling water, from the kernel of a nut, as will be more particularly described hereafter : it has the consistence and appearance of butter; and is in truth an admirable substitute for it. It forms an important article in the food of the natives, and serves also for every domestic purpose in which oil would otherwise be used. The demand for it is therefore very great.

In payment of these articles, the maritime states supply the interior countries with salt, a scarce and valuable commodity, as I frequently and painfully experienced in the course of my journey. Considerable quantities of this article, however, are also supplied to the inland natives by the Moors; who obtain it from the salt-pits in the Great Desart, and receive in return corn, cotton cloth, and slaves.

In thus bartering one commodity for another, many inconveniences must necessarily have arisen at first from the want of coined money, or some other visible and determinate medium, to settle the balance, or difference of value, between different articles; to remedy which, the natives of the interior make use of small shells called *kowries*, as will be shewn hereafter. On the Coast, the inhabitants have adopted a practice which I believe is peculiar to themselves.

In their early intercourse with Europeans, the article that attracted most notice was iron. Its utility, in forming the instruments of war and husbandry, made it preferable to all others; and iron soon became the measure by which the value of all other commodities was ascertained. Thus a certain quantity of goods of whatever denomination, appearing to be equal in value to a bar of iron, constituted, in the trader's phraseology, a bar of that particular merchandize. Twenty leaves of tobacco, for instance, were considered as *a bar* of tobacco; and a gallon of spirits (or rather half spirits and half water), as *a bar* of rum; a bar of one commodity being reckoned equal in value to a bar of another commodity.

As, however, it must unavoidably happen, that according to the plenty or scarcity of goods at market in proportion to the demand, the relative value would be subject to continual fluc-

E 2

tuation, greater precision has been found necessary ; and at this
time, the current value of a single bar of any kind is fixed by
the whites at two shillings sterling. Thus a slave, whose price
is £15. is said to be worth 150 bars.

In transactions of this nature, it is obvious that the white
trader has infinitely the advantage over the African, whom,
therefore, it is difficult to satisfy ; for, conscious of his own ignorance, he naturally becomes exceedingly suspicious and wa-
vering ; and indeed so very unsettled and jealous are the Negroes
in their dealings with the whites, that a bargain is never considered by the European as concluded, until the purchase money
is paid, and the party has taken leave.

Having now brought together such general observations on
the country, and its inhabitants, as occurred to me during my
residence in the vicinage of the Gambia, I shall detain the
reader no longer with introductory matter, but proceed, in the
next Chapter, to a regular detail of the incidents which happened, and the reflections which arose in my mind, in the
course of my painful and perilous journey, from its commencement, until my return to the Gambia.

CHAPTER III.

The Author sets out from Pisania—his Attendants—reaches Jindey.
—Story related by a Mandingo Negro.—Proceeds to Medina,
the capital of Woolli.—Interview with the King.—Saphies or
Charms.—Proceeds to Kolor.—Description of Mumbo Jumbo—
arrives at Koojar—wrestling Match.—Crosses the Wilderness,
and arrives at Tallika, in the Kingdom of Bondou.

ON the 2d of December, 1795, I took my departure from the
hospitable mansion of Dr. Laidley. I was fortunately provided
with a Negro servant, who spoke both the English and Mandingo tongues. His name was *Johnson*. He was a native of
this part of Africa; and having in his youth been conveyed to
Jamaica as a slave, he had been made free, and taken to England by his master, where he had resided many years; and at
length found his way back to his native country. As he was
known to Dr. Laidley, the Doctor recommended him to me,
and I hired him as my interpreter, at the rate of ten bars
monthly, to be paid to himself, and five bars a month to be
paid to his wife, during his absence. Dr. Laidley furthermore
provided me with a Negro boy of his own, named *Demba*; a
sprightly youth, who, besides Mandingo, spoke the language
of the Serawoollies, an inland people (of whom mention will

hereafter be made), residing on the banks of the Senegal ; and to induce him to behave well, the Doctor promised him his freedom on his return, in case I should report favourably of his fidelity and services. I was furnished with a horse for myself, (a small, but very hardy and spirited beast, which cost me to the value of £7. 10 s.) and two asses for my interpreter and servant. My baggage was light, consisting chiefly of provisions for two days ; and a small assortment of beads, amber, and tobacco, for the purchase of a fresh supply, as I proceeded : a few changes of linen, and other necessary apparel, an umbrella, a pocket sextant, a magnetic compass, and a thermometer ; together with two fowling pieces, two pair of pistols, and some other small articles.

A free man (a Bushreen or Mahomedan), named Madiboo, who was travelling to the kingdom of Bambara, and two Slatees, or slave merchants of the Serawoolli nation, and of the same sect, who were going to Bondou, offered their services as far as they intended respectively to proceed ; as did likewise a Negro named Tami, (also a Mahomedan,) a native of Kasson, who had been employed some years by Dr. Laidley as a blacksmith, and was returning to his native country with the savings of his labours. All these men travelled on foot, driving their asses before them.

Thus I had no less than six attendants, all of whom had been taught to regard me with great respect ; and to consider that their safe return hereafter, to the countries on the Gambia, would depend on my preservation.

Dr. Laidley himself, and Messrs. Ainsley, with a number of

their domestics, kindly determined to accompany me the two first days ; and, I believe, they secretly thought they should never see me afterwards.

We reached Jindey the same day, having crossed the Walli creek, a branch of the Gambia, and rested at the house of a black woman, who had formerly been the *chere amie* of a white trader named Hewett ; and who, in consequence thereof, was called, by way of distinction, *Seniora*. In the evening we walked out to see an adjoining village, belonging to a Slatee named Jemaffoo Mamadoo, the richest of all the Gambia traders. We found him at home ; and he thought so highly of the honour done him by this visit, that he presented us with a fine bullock, which was immediately killed, and part of it dressed for our evening's repast.

The Negroes do not go to supper till late ; and in order to amuse ourselves while our beef was preparing, a Mandingo was desired to relate some diverting stories ; in listening to which, and smoking tobacco, we spent three hours. These stories bear some resemblance to those in the Arabian Nights Entertainments ; but, in general, are of a more ludicrous cast. I shall here abridge one of them for the reader's amusement.

" Many years ago (said the relator), the people of Doomasansa (a town on the Gambia), were much annoyed by a lion, that came every night, and took away some of their cattle. By continuing his depredations, the people were at length so much enraged, that a party of them resolved to go and hunt the monster. They accordingly proceeded in search of the common enemy, who they found concealed in a thicket ; and immediately firing at him, were lucky enough to wound him in such a manner, that, in springing from the thicket towards the people, he fell down among the grass, and was unable to rise. The animal, however, manifested such appearance of vigour, that nobody cared to approach him singly; and a consultation was held, concerning the properest means of taking him alive; a circumstance, it was said, which, while it furnished undeniable proof of their prowess, would turn out to great advantage, it being resolved to convey him to the Coast, and sell him to the Europeans. While some persons proposed one plan, and some another, an old man offered a scheme. This was, to strip the roof of a house of its thatch, and to carry the bamboo frame (the pieces of which are well secured together by thongs), and throw it over the lion. If, in approaching him, he should attempt to spring upon them, they had nothing to do but to let down the roof upon themselves, and fire at the lion through the rafters.

" This proposition was approved and adopted. The thatch was taken from the roof of a hut, and the lion-hunters, supporting the fabric, marched courageously to the field of battle; each person carrying a gun in one hand, and bearing his share of the roof on the opposite shoulder. In this manner they approached the enemy: but the beast had by this time recovered his strength; and such was the fierceness of his countenance, that the hunters, instead of proceeding any further, thought it prudent to provide for their own safety, by covering themselves with the roof. Unfortunately, the lion was too nimble for them; for, making a spring while the roof was setting down, both the beast and his pursuers were caught in the same cage, and the lion devoured them at his leisure, to the great astonishment and mortification of the people of Doomasansa; at which place it is dangerous even at this day to tell the story; for it is become the subject of laughter and derision in the neighbouring countries, and nothing will enrage an inhabitant of that town so much as desiring him to catch a lion alive."

About one o'clock in the afternoon of the 3d of December, I took my leave of Dr. Laidley and Messrs. Ainsley, and rode slowly into the woods. I had now before me a boundless forest, and a country, the inhabitants of which were strangers to civilized life, and to most of whom a white man was the object of curiosity or plunder. I reflected that I had parted from the last European I might probably behold, and perhaps quitted for ever the comforts of Christian society. Thoughts like these would necessarily cast a gloom over the mind, and I rode musing along for about three miles, when I was awakened from my reverie by a body of people, who came running up and stopped the asses, giving me to understand that I must go with them to Peckaba, to present myself to the King of Walli, or pay customs to them. I endeavoured to make them comprehend that the object of my journey not being traffic, I ought not to be subjected to a tax like the Slatees, and other merchants, who travel for gain; but I reasoned to no purpose. They said it was usual for travellers of all descriptions to make a present to the King of Walli, and without doing so I could not be permitted to proceed. As they were more numerous than my attendants, and withal very noisy, I thought it prudent to comply

F

with their demand, and having presented them with four bars of tobacco, for the king's use, I was permitted to continue my journey, and at sunset reached a village near Kootacunda, where we rested for the night.

In the morning of December 4th, I passed Kootacunda, the last town of Walli, and stopped about an hour at a small adjoining village to pay customs to an officer of the King of Woolli ; we rested the ensuing night at a village called Tabajang ; and at noon the next day (December 5th) we reached Medina, the capital of the King of Woolli's dominions.

The kingdom of Woolli is bounded by Walli on the west, by the Gambia on the south, by the small river Walli on the north-west ; by Bondou on the north-east ; and on the east, by the Simbani wilderness.

The country every where rises into gentle acclivities, which are generally covered with extensive woods, and the towns are situated in the intermediate valleys. Each town is surrounded by a tract of cultivated land, the produce of which, I presume, is found sufficient to supply the wants of the inhabitants ; for the soil appeared to me to be every where fertile, except near the tops of the ridges, where the red iron stone and stunted shrubs sufficiently marked the boundaries between fertility and barrenness. The chief productions are cotton, tobacco, and esculent vegetables ; all which are raised in the valleys, the rising grounds being appropriated to different sorts of corn.

The inhabitants are Mandigoes ; and, like most of the Mandingo nations, are divided into two great sects, the Mahomedans, who are called *Bushreens*, and the Pagans who are called indiscriminately *Kafirs* (unbelievers) and *Sonakies* (*i. e.* men who drink strong liquors.) The Pagan natives are by far the most numerous, and the government of the country is in their hands; for though the most respectable among the Bushreens are frequently consulted in affairs of importance, yet they are never permitted to take any share in the executive government, which rests solely in the hands of the *Mansa*, or sovereign, and great officers of the state. Of these, the first in point of rank is the presumptive heir of the crown, who is called the *Farbanna;* next to him are the *Alkaids*, or provincial governors, who are more frequently called *Keamos*. Then follow the two grand divisions of freemen and slaves*; of the former, the Slatees, so frequently mentioned in the preceding pages, are considered as the principal: but in all classes, great respect is paid to the authority of aged men.

On the death of the reigning monarch, his eldest son (if he has attained the age of manhood) succeeds to the regal authority. If there is no son, or if the son is under the age of discretion, a meeting of the great men is held, and the late monarch's nearest relation (commonly his brother), is called to the government, not as regent, or guardian to the infant son, but in full right, and to the exclusion of the minor. The charges of the government are defrayed by occasional tributes from the people, and by duties on goods transported across the country. Travellers, on going from the Gambia towards the interior, pay customs in European merchandize. On returning, they pay in iron and *shea-toulou:* these taxes are paid at every town.

* The term which signifies a man of free condition is *Horea*, that of a slave, *Jong*.

Medina * the capital of the kingdom, at which I was now
arrived, is a place of considerable extent; and may contain
from eight hundred to one thousand houses. It is fortified in
the common African manner, by a surrounding high wall built
of clay, and an outward fence of pointed stakes and prickly
bushes; but the walls are neglected, and the outward fence
has suffered considerably from the active hands of busy house-
wives, who pluck up the stakes for firewood. I obtained a
lodging at one of the king's near relations, who apprized me,
that at my introduction to the king, I must not presume *to
shake hands with him*. It was not usual, he said, to allow this
liberty to strangers. Thus instructed, I went in the afternoon
to pay my respects to the sovereign; and ask permission to
pass through his territories to Bondou. The king's name was
Jatta. He was the same venerable old man of whom so favourable an account was transmitted by Major Houghton. I
found him seated upon a mat before the door of his hut: a
number of men and women were arranged on each side, who
were singing and clapping their hands. I saluted him respect-
fully, and informed him of the purport of my visit. The king
graciously replied, that he not only gave me leave to pass
through his country, but would offer up his prayers for my
safety. On this, one of my attendants, seemingly in return for
the king's condescension, began to sing, or rather to roar, an
Arabic song; at every pause of which, the king himself, and
all the people present, struck their hands against their fore-

* Medina in the Arabic signifies a city; the name is not uncommon among
the Negroes, and has probably been borrowed from the Mahomedans.

heads, and exclaimed, with devout and affecting solemnity, *Amen, amen!* * The king told me furthermore, that I should have a guide the day following, who would conduct me safely to the frontier of his kingdom. I then took my leave, and in the evening sent the king an order upon Dr. Laidley for three gallons of rum, and received in return great store of provisions.

Dec. 6th, early in the morning, I went to the king a second time, to learn if the guide was ready. I found his majesty sitting upon a bullock's hide, warming himself before a large fire ; for the Africans are sensible of the smallest variation in the temperature of the air, and frequently complain of cold when a European is oppressed with heat. He received me with a benevolent countenance, and tenderly entreated me to desist from my purpose of travelling into the interior ; telling me, that Major Houghton had been killed in his route, and that if I followed his footsteps, I should probably meet with his fate. He said that I must not judge of the people of the eastern country by those of Woolli : that the latter were acquainted with white men, and respected them, whereas the people of the east had never seen a white man, and would certainly destroy me. I thanked the king for his affectionate solicitude, but told him that I had considered the matter, and was determined, notwithstanding all dangers, to proceed. The king shook his

* It may seem from hence that the king was a Mahomedan ; but I was assured to the contrary. He joined in prayer on this occasion probably from the mere dictates of his benevolent mind ; considering perhaps that prayers to the Almighty, offered up with true devotion and sincerity, were equally acceptable, whether from Bushreen or Pagan.

head, but desisted from further persuasion; and told me the
guide should be ready in the afternoon.

About two o'clock, the guide appearing, I went and took my
last farewell of the good old king, and in three hours reached
Konjour, a small village, where we determined to rest for the
night. Here I purchased a fine sheep for some beads, and my
Serawoolli attendants killed it with all the ceremonies prescribed by their religion : part of it was dressed for supper;
after which a dispute arose between one of the Serawoolli
Negroes and Johnson, my interpreter, about the sheep's horns.
The former claimed the horns as his perquisite, for having acted
the part of our butcher, and Johnson contested the claim. I
settled the matter by giving a horn to each of them. This
trifling incident is mentioned as introductory to what follows :
for it appeared on inquiry that these horns were highly
valued, as being easily convertible into portable sheaths, or
cases, for containing and keeping secure certain charms or
amulets called *saphies*, which the Negroes constantly wear about
them. These saphies are prayers, or rather sentences, from the
Koran, which the Mahomedan priests write on scraps of paper, and
sell to the simple natives, who consider them to possess very extraordinary virtues. Some of the Negroes wear them to guard
themselves against the bite of snakes or alligators; and on this occasion the saphie is commonly inclosed in a snake's or alligator's
skin, and tied round the ancle. Others have recourse to them in
time of war, to protect their persons against hostile weapons; but
the common use to which these amulets are applied, is to prevent or cure bodily diseases; to preserve from hunger and thirst,

and generally to conciliate the favour of superior powers under all the cirumstances and occurrences of life.*

In this case, it is impossible not to admire the wonderful contagion of superstition ; for, notwithstanding that the majority of the Negroes are Pagans, and absolutely reject the doctrines of Mahomet, I did not meet with a man, whether a Bushreen or Kafir, who was not fully persuaded of the powerful efficacy of these amulets. The truth is, that all the natives of this part of Africa consider the art of writing as bordering on magic : and it is not in the doctrines of the Prophet, but in the arts of the magician, that their confidence is placed It will hereafter be seen that I was myself lucky enough, in circumstances of distress, to turn the popular credulity in this respect to good account.

On the 7th I departed from Konjour, and slept at a village called Malla (or Mallaing) ; and on the 8th about noon I arrived at Kolor, a considerable town ; near the entrance into which I observed, hanging upon a tree, a sort of masquerade habit, made of the bark of trees. which I was told on inquiry belonged to MUMBO JUMBO. This is a strange bugbear, common to all the Mandingo towns, and much employed by the Pagan natives in keeping their women in subjection ; for as the Kafirs are not restricted in the number of their wives, every one marries as many as he can conveniently maintain ; and as it frequently happens that the ladies disagree among themselves, family

* I believe that similar charms or amulets, under the names of *domini*, *grigri*, *fetich*, &c. &c. are common in all parts of Africa.

quarrels sometime rise to such a height, that the authority of the husband can no longer preserve peace in his household. In such cases, the interposition of Mumbo Jumbo is called in, and is always decisive.

This strange minister of justice (who is supposed to be either the husband himself, or some person instructed by him), disguised in the dress that has been mentioned and armed with the rod of public authority, announces his coming (whenever his services are required) by loud and dismal screams in the woods near the town. He begins the pantomime at the approach of night; and as soon as it is dark, he enters the town, and proceeds to the Bentang at which all the inhabitants immediately assemble.

It may easily be supposed that this exhibition is not much relished by the women; for as the person in disguise is entirely unknown to them, every married female suspects that the visit may possibly be intended for herself; but they dare not refuse to appear when they are summoned; and the ceremony commences with songs and dances. which continue till midnight, about which time Mumbo fixes on the offender. This unfortunate victim being thereupon immediately seized, is stripped naked, tied to a post, and severely scourged with Mumbo's rod, amidst the shouts and derision of the whole assembly; and it is remarkable, that the rest of the women are the loudest in their exclamations on this occasion against their unhappy sister. Daylight puts an end to this indecent and unmanly revel.

December 9th. As there was no water to be procured on the road, we travelled with great expedition until we reached

Tambacunda, and departing from thence early the next morning, the 10th ; we reached in the evening Kooniakary, a town of nearly the same magnitude as Kolor. About noon on the 11th we arrived at Koojar, the frontier town of Woolli, towards Bondou, from which it is separated by an intervening Wilderness of two days' journey.

The guide appointed by the King of Woolli being now to return, I presented him with some amber for his trouble : and having been informed that it was not possible at all times to procure water in the Wilderness, I made inquiry for men who would serve both as guides and water-bearers during my journey across it. Three Negroes, elephant hunters, offered their services for these purposes, which I accepted, and paid them 3 bars each in advance, and the day being far spent, I determined to pass the night in my present quarters.

The inhabitants of Koojar, though not wholly unaccustomed to the sight of Europeans (most of them having occasionally visited the countries on the Gambia) beheld me with a mixture of curiosity and reverence, and in the evening invited me to see a *neobering*, or wrestling match, at the Bentang. This is an exhibition very common in all the Mandingo countries. The spectators arranged themselves in a circle, leaving the intermediate space for the wrestlers, who were strong active young men, full of emulation, and accustomed I suppose from their infancy to this sort of exertion. Being stripped of their clothing, except a short pair of drawers, and having their skin anointed with oil, or *shea* butter, the combatants approached each other on all fours, parrying with, and occasionally extending a hand

G

for some time, till at length one of them sprang forward, and caught his rival by the knee. Great dexterity and judgment were now displayed; but the contest was decided by superior strength; and I think that few Europeans would have been able to cope with the conqueror. It must not be unobserved, that the combatants were animated by the music of a drum, by which their actions were in some measure regulated.

The wrestling was succeeded by a dance, in which many performers assisted, all of whom were provided with little bells, which were fastened to their legs and arms; and here too the drum regulated their motions. It was beaten with a crooked stick, which the drummer held in his right hand, occasionally using his left to deaden the sound, and thus vary the music. The drum is likewise applied on these occasions to keep order among the spectators, by imitating the sound of certain Mandingo sentences: for example, when the wrestling match is about to begin, the drummer strikes what is understood to signify *ali bœ si*,—sit all down; upon which the spectators immediately seat themselves; and when the combatants are to begin, he strikes *amuta amuta*,—take hold, take hold.

In the course of the evening I was presented, by way of refreshment, with a liquor which tasted so much like the strong-beer of my native country (and very good beer too), as to induce me to inquire into its composition; and I learnt, with some degree of surprise, that it was actually made from corn which had been previously malted, much in the same manner as barley is malted in Great Britain: a root yielding a grateful bitter, was used in lieu of hops, the name of which I have forgot; but the corn which yields the wort, is the *holcus spicatus* of botanists.

Early in the morning (the 12th) I found that one of the elephant hunters had absconded with the money he had received from me in part of wages; and in order to prevent the other two from following his example, I made them instantly fill their calabashes (or gourds) with water, and as the sun rose I entered the Wilderness that separates the kingdoms of Woolli and Bondou.

We had not travelled more than a mile before my attendants insisted on stopping, that they might prepare a saphie, or charm, to insure us a safe journey. This was done by muttering a few sentences, and spitting upon a stone, which was thrown before us on the road. The same ceremony was repeated three times, after which the Negroes proceeded with the greatest confidence; every one being firmly persuaded that the stone (like the scape goat) had carried with it every thing that could induce superior powers to visit us with misfortune.

We continued our journey without stopping any more until noon, when we came to a large tree, called by the natives *Neema Taba*. It had a very singular appearance, being decorated with innumerable rags or scraps of cloth, which persons travelling across the Wilderness had, at different times, tied to the branches; probably, at first, to inform the traveller that water was to be found near it; but the custom has been so greatly sanctioned by time, that nobody now presumes to pass without hanging up something. I followed the example, and suspended a handsome piece of cloth on one of the boughs, and

being told that either a well, or pool of water, was at no
great distance, I ordered the Negroes to unload the asses, that
we might give them corn, and regale ourselves with the provisions we had brought. In the mean time, I sent one of the
elephant hunters to look for the well, intending, if water was to
be obtained, to rest here for the night. A pool was found, but
the water was thick and muddy, and the Negro discovered near
it the remains of a fire recently extinguished, and the fragments
of provisions, which afforded a proof that it had been lately visited, either by travellers or banditti. The fears of my attendants supposed the latter; and believing that robbers lurked
near us, I was persuaded to change my resolution of resting
here all night, and proceed to another watering place, which I
was assured we might reach early in the evening.

We departed accordingly, but it was eight o'clock at night
before we came to the watering place; and being now sufficiently fatigued with so long a day's journey, we kindled a large
fire, and lay down, surrounded by our cattle, on the bare ground,
more than a gun-shot from any bush; the Negroes agreeing to
keep watch by turns to prevent surprise.

I knew not indeed that any danger was justly to be dreaded,
but the Negroes were unaccountably apprehensive of banditti,
during the whole of the journey. As soon therefore as daylight
appeared, we filled our *soofros* (skins) and calabashes at the
pool, and set out for Tallika, the first town in Bondou, which we
reached about eleven o'clock in the forenoon (the 13th of
December). I cannot, however, take leave of Woolli, without
observing that I was every where well received by the natives;

and that the fatigues of the day were generally alleviated by a hearty welcome at night ; and although the African mode of living was at first unpleasant to me, yet I found, at length, that custom surmounted trifling inconveniences, and made every thing palatable and easy.

CHAPTER IV.

Some Account of the Inhabitants of Tallika.—The Author proceeds for Fatteconda—Incidents on the Road.—Crosses the Neriko, arrives at Koorkarany—reaches the River Falemé—Fishery on that River—proceeds along its Bank to Naye or Nayemow—crosses the Falemé and arrives at Fatteconda.—Has an Interview with Almami, the Sovereign of Bondou.—Description of the King's Dwelling—has a second Interview with the King, who begs the Author's Coat.—Author visits the King's Wives—is permitted to depart on friendly Terms.—Journey by Night—arrives at Joag.—Some Account of Bondou and its Inhabitants the Foulahs.

Tallika, the frontier town of Bondou towards Woolli, is inhabited chiefly by Foulahs of the Mahomedan religion, who live in considerable affluence, partly by furnishing provisions to the *coffles*, or caravans, that pass through the town, and partly by the sale of ivory, obtained by hunting elephants; in which employment the young men are generally very successful. Here, an officer belonging to the King of Bondou constantly resides, whose business it is to give timely information of the arrival of the caravans; which are taxed according to the number of loaded asses that arrive at Tallika.

I took up my residence at this officer's house, and agreed with him to accompany me to Fatteconda, the residence of the king ; for which he was to receive five bars ; and before my departure I wrote a few lines to Dr. Laidley, and gave my letter to the master of a caravan bound for the Gambia. This caravan consisted of five asses loaded with ivory. The large teeth are conveyed in nets, two on each side of the ass ; the small ones are wrapped up in skins, and secured with ropes.

December 14th. We left Tallika, and rode on very peaceably for about two miles, when a violent quarrel arose between two of my fellow-travellers, one of whom was the blacksmith, in the course of which they bestowed some opprobrious terms upon each other ; and it is worthy of remark, that an African will sooner forgive a blow, than a term of reproach applied to his ancestors : " Strike me, but do not curse my mother," is a common expression among the slaves. This sort of abuse, therefore, so enraged one of the disputants that he drew his cutlass upon the blacksmith, and would certainly have ended the dispute in a very serious manner, if the others had not laid hold of him, and wrested the cutlass from him. I was obliged to interfere, and put an end to this disagreeable business, by desiring the blacksmith to be silent, and telling the other, who I thought was in the wrong, that if he attempted in future to draw his cutlass, or molest any of my attendants, I should look upon him as a robber, and shoot him without further ceremony. This threat had the desired effect, and we marched sullenly along till the afternoon, when we arrived at a number of small villages scattered over an open and fertile plain; at one of these called Ganado we took up our residence for the night : here an exchange of presents and a good supper terminated all animosities among my attendants; and the night was far advanced before any of us thought of going to sleep. We were amused by an itinerant *singing man*,* who told a number of diverting stories, and played some sweet airs, by blowing his breath upon a bow-string, and striking it at the same time with a stick.

December 15th. At daybreak my fellow-travellers, the Sera-woollies, took leave of me, with many prayers for my safety. About a mile from Ganado, we crossed a considerable branch of the Gambia, called Neriko. The banks were steep, and cover-ed with *mimosas;* and I observed in the mud a number of large muscles, but the natives do not eat them. About noon, the sun being exceedingly hot, we rested two hours in the shade of a tree, and purchased some milk and pounded corn from some Foulah herdsmen, and at sunset reached a town called Koor-karany, where the blacksmith had some relations; and here we rested two days.

Koorkarany is a Mahomedan town, surrounded by a high wall, and is provided with a mosque. Here I was shewn a number of Arabic manuscripts, particularly a copy of the book before mentioned called *Al Shara*. The *Maraboo*, or priest, in whose possession it was, read and explained to me in Man-dingo, many of the most remarkable passages; and in return I shewed him Richardson's Arabic grammar, which he very much admired.

On the evening of the second day (Dec. 17th) we departed

* These are a sort of travelling bards and musicians, who sing extempore songs in praise of those who employ them. A fuller account of them will be given hereafter.

from Koorkarany. We were joined by a young man who was travelling to Fatteconda for salt; and as night set in we reached Dooggi, a small village about three miles from Koorkarany.

Provisions were here so cheap that I purchased a bullock for six small stones of amber; for I found my company increase or diminish according to the good fare they met with.

Dec. 18th. Early in the morning we departed from Dooggi, and being joined by a number of Foulahs and other people, made a formidable appearance; and were under no apprehension of being plundered in the woods. About eleven o'clock one of the asses proving very refractory, the Negroes took a curious method to make him tractable. They cut a forked stick, and putting the forked part into the ass's mouth, like the bit of a bridle, tied the two smaller parts together above his head, leaving the lower part of the stick of sufficient length to strike against the ground, if the ass should attempt to put his head down. After this, the ass walked along quietly, and gravely enough, taking care, after some practice, to hold his head sufficiently high to prevent the stones or roots of trees from striking against the end of the stick, which experience had taught him would give a severe shock to his teeth. This contrivance produced a ludicrous appearance, but my fellow-travellers told me it was constantly adopted by the Slatees, and always proved effectual.

In the evening we arrived at a few scattered villages, surrounded with extensive cultivation; at one of which, called Buggil, we passed the night in a miserable hut, having no other

H

bed than a bundle of corn stalks, and no provisions but what we brought with us. The wells here are dug with great ingenuity, and are very deep. I measured one of the bucket ropes, and found the depth of the well to be 28 fathoms.

Dec. 19th. We departed from Buggil, and travelled along a dry, stony height, covered with *mimosas*, till mid-day; when the land sloped towards the east, and we descended into a deep valley, in which I observed abundance of whin-stone, and white quartz. Pursuing our course to the eastward, along this valley, in the bed of an exhausted river course, we came to a large village, where we intended to lodge. We found many of the natives, dressed in a thin French gauze, which they called *Byqui;* this being a light airy dress, and well calculated to display the shape of their persons, is much esteemed by the ladies. The manners of these females, however, did not correspond with their dress; for they were rude and troublesome in the highest degree; they surrounded me in numbers, begging for amber, beads, &c.; and were so vehement in their solicitations, that I found it impossible to resist them. They tore my cloak, cut the buttons from my boy's clothes, and were proceeding to other outrages, when I mounted my horse and rode off, followed for half a mile by a body of these harpies.

In the evening we reached Soobrudooka, and as my company was numerous, (being fourteen) I purchased a sheep, and abundance of corn for supper; after which we lay down by the bundles, and passed an uncomfortable night in a heavy dew.

Dec. 20th. We departed from Soobrudooka, and at two o'clock reached a large village situated on the banks of the Falemé river, which is here rapid and rocky. The natives were employed in fishing in various ways. The large fish were taken in long baskets made of split cane, and placed in a strong current, which was created by walls of stone built across the stream, certain open places being left, through which the water rushed with great force. Some of these baskets were more than 20 feet long, and when once the fish had entered one of them, the force of the stream prevented it from returning. The small fish were taken in great numbers in hand-nets, which the natives weave of cotton, and use with great dexterity. The fish last mentioned are about the size of sprats, and are prepared for sale in different ways; the most common is by pounding them entire as they come from the stream, in a wooden mortar, and exposing them to dry in the sun, in large lumps, like sugar loaves. It may be supposed that the smell is not very agreeable; but in the Moorish countries to the north of the Senegal, where fish is scarcely known, this preparation is esteemed as a luxury, and sold to considerable advantage. The manner of using it by the natives is, by dissolving a piece of this black loaf in boiling water, and mixing it with their *kouskous*.

I thought it very singular, at this season of the year, to find the banks of the Faleme every where covered with large and beautiful fields of corn; but on examination I found it was not the same species of grain as is commonly cultivated on the Gambia; it is called by the natives *Manio*; and grows in the dry season, is very prolific, and is reaped in the month of January. It is the same which, from the depending position of the ear, is called by botanical writers *holcus cernuus*.

H 2

On returning to the village, after an excursion to the river side, to inspect the fishery, an old Moorish shereeff came to bestow his blessing upon me, and beg some paper to write saphies upon. This man had seen Major Houghton in the kingdom of Kaarta, and told me that he died in the country of the Moors. I gave him a few sheets of paper, and he levied a similar tribute from the blacksmith; for it is customary for young Mussulmen to make presents to the old ones, in order to obtain their blessing, which is pronounced in Arabic, and received with great humility.

About three in the afternoon we continued our course along the bank of the river, to the northward, till eight o'clock, when we reached Nayemow; here the hospitable master of the town received us kindly, and presented us with a bullock. In return, I gave him some amber and beads.

Dec. 21st. In the morning, having agreed for a canoe to carry over my bundles, I crossed the river, which came up to my knees, as I sat on my horse; but the water is so clear, that from the high bank, the bottom is visible all the way over.

About noon we entered Fatteconda, the capital of Bondou; and in a little time received an invitation to the house of a respectable Slatee : for as there are no public houses in Africa, it is customary for strangers to stand at the Bentang, or some other place of public resort, till they are invited to a lodging by some of the inhabitants. We accepted the offer; and in an hour afterwards, a person came and told me that he was sent on purpose to conduct me to the king, who was very desirous of seeing me immediately, if I was not too much fatigued.

I took my interpreter with me, and followed the messenger till we got quite out of the town, and crossed some corn fields; when suspecting some trick I stopped, and asked the guide whither he was going. Upon which he pointed to a man sitting under a tree at some little distance; and told me that the king frequently gave audience in that retired manner in order to avoid a crowd of people; and that nobody but myself and my interpreter must approach him. When I advanced, the king desired me to come and sit by him upon the mat; and after hearing my story, on which he made no observation, he asked if I wished to purchase any slaves, or gold. being answered in the negative, he seemed rather surprised; but desired me to come to him in the evening, and he would give me some provisions.

This monarch was called Almami; a Moorish name, though I was told that he was not a Mahomedan, but a Kafir, or Pagan. I had heard that he had acted towards Major Houghton with great unkindness, and caused him to be plundered. His behaviour, therefore, towards myself at this interview, though much more civil than I expected, was far from freeing me from uneasiness. I still apprehended some double dealing; and as I was now entirely in his power, I thought it best to smooth the way by a present; accordingly I took with me in the evening, one cannister of gunpowder, some amber, tobacco, and my umbrella; and as I considered that my bundles would inevitably be searched, I concealed some few articles in the roof of the hut where I lodged, and I put on my new blue coat, in order to preserve it.

All the houses belonging to the king and his family are surrounded by a lofty mud wall, which converts the whole into a kind
of citadel. The interior is subdivided into different courts. At
the first place of entrance I observed a man standing with a musket on his shoulder; and I found the way to the presence very
intricate, leading through many passages, with centinels placed
at the different doors. When we came to the entrance of the
court in which the king resides, both my guide and interpreter,
according to custom, took off their sandals; and the former pronounced the king's name aloud, repeating it till he was answered
from within. We found the monarch sitting upon a mat, and
two attendants with him. I repeated what I had before told
him concerning the object of my journey, and my reasons for
passing through his country. He seemed, however, but half satisfied. The notion of travelling for curiosity, was quite new to
him. He thought it impossible, he said, that any man in his
senses would undertake so dangerous a journey, merely to look
at the country, and its inhabitants: however, when I offered to
shew him the contents of my portmanteau, and every thing belonging to me, he was convinced; and it was evident that his
suspicion had arisen from a belief, that every white man must
of necessity be a trader. When I had delivered my presents, he
seemed well pleased, and was particularly delighted with the
umbrella, which he repeatedly furled and unfurled, to the great
admiration of himself and his two attendants; who could not
for some time comprehend the use of this wonderful machine.
After this I was about to take my leave, when the king, desiring me to stop a while, began a long preamble in favour of the

whites ; extolling their immense wealth, and good dispositions. He next proceeded to an eulogium on my blue coat, of which the yellow buttons seemed particularly to catch his fancy ; and he concluded by entreating me to present him with it ; assuring me, for my consolation under the loss of it, that he would wear it on all public occasions, and inform every one who saw it, of my great liberality towards him. The request of an African prince, in his own dominions, particularly when made to a stranger, comes little short of a command. It is only a way of obtaining by gentle means, what he can, if he pleases, take by force ; and as it was against my interest to offend him by a refusal, I very quietly took off my coat, the only good one in my possession, and laid it at his feet.

In return for my compliance, he presented me with great plenty of provisions, and desired to see me again in the morning. I accordingly attended, and found him sitting upon his bed. He told me he was sick, and wished to have a little blood taken from him ; but I had no sooner tied up his arm, and displayed the lancet, than his courage failed ; and he begged me to postpone the operation till the afternoon, as he felt himself, he said, much better than he had been, and thanked me kindly for my readiness to serve him. He then observed, that his women were very desirous to see me, and requested that I would favour them with a visit. An attendant was ordered to conduct me ; and I had no sooner entered the court appropriated to the ladies, than the whole seraglio surrounded me ; some begging for physic, some for amber ; and all of them desirous of trying that great African specific, *blood-letting*. They were 10 or 12 in number, most of them young and handsome, and wearing on their heads ornaments of gold, and beads of amber.

They rallied me with a good deal of gaiety on different subjects; particularly upon the whiteness of my skin, and the prominency of my nose. They insisted that both were artificial. The first, they said, was produced when I was an infant, by dipping me in milk; and they insisted that my nose had been pinched every day, till it had acquired its present unsightly and unnatural conformation. On my part, without disputing my own deformity, I paid them many compliments on African beauty. I praised the glossy jet of their skins, and the lovely depression of their noses; but they said that flattery, or (as they emphatically termed it) *honey-mouth*, was not esteemed in Bondou. In return, however, for my company or my compliments (to which, by the way, they seemed not so insensible as they affected to be), they presented me with a jar of honey and some fish, which were sent to my lodging; and I was desired to come again to the king a little before sunset.

I carried with me some beads and writing paper, it being usual to present some small offering on taking leave: in return for which, the king gave me five drachms of gold; observing, that it was but a trifle, and given out of pure friendship; but would be of use to me in travelling, for the purchase of provisions. He seconded this act of kindness by one still greater; politely telling me, that though it was customary to examine the baggage of every traveller passing through his country, yet, in the present instance, he would dispense with that ceremony; adding, I was at liberty to depart when I pleased.

Accordingly, on the morning of the 23d, we left Fatteconda, and about eleven o'clock came to a small village, where we determined to stop for the rest of the day.

In the afternoon my fellow-travellers informed me, that as this was the boundary between Bondou and Kajaaga, and dangerous for travellers, it would be necessary to continue our journey by night, until we should reach a more hospitable part of the country. I agreed to the proposal, and hired two people for guides through the woods; and as soon as the people of the village were gone to sleep (the moon shining bright) we set out. The stillness of the air, the howling of the wild beasts, and the deep solitude of the forest, made the scene solemn and impressive. Not a word was uttered by any of us, but in a whisper; all were attentive, and every one anxious to shew his sagacity, by pointing out to me the wolves and hyænas as they glided, like shadows, from one thicket to another. Towards morning, we arrived at a village called Kimmoo, where our guides awakened one of their acquaintances, and we stopped to give the asses some corn, and roast a few ground-nuts for ourselves. At daylight we resumed our journey, and in the afternoon arrived at Joag in the kingdom of Kajaaga.

Being now in a country, and among a people, differing in many respects from those that have as yet fallen under our observation, I shall, before I proceed further, give some account of Bondou (the territory we have left), and its inhabitants, the Foulahs, the description of whom I purposely reserved for this part of my work.

Bondou is bounded on the east by Bambouk; on the south-

I

east, and south, by Tenda, and the Simbani Wilderness ; on the south-west by Woolli ; on the west, by Foota Torra ; and on the north, by Kajaaga.

The country, like that of Woolli, is very generally covered with woods, but the land is more elevated, and towards the Falemé river, rises into considerable hills. In native fertility the soil is not surpassed, I believe, by any part of Africa.

From the central situation of Bondou, between the Gambia and Senegal rivers, it is become a place of great resort, both for the Slatees, who generally pass through it, in going from the coast to the interior countries ; and for occasional traders, who frequently come hither from the inland countries, to purchase salt.

These different branches of commerce are conducted principally by Mandingoes and Serawoollies, who have settled in the country. These merchants likewise carry on a considerable trade with Gedumah, and other Moorish countries, bartering corn and blue cotton clothes for salt ; which they again barter in Dentila and other districts for iron, shea-butter, and small quantities of gold-dust. They likewise sell a variety of sweet smelling gums packed up in small bags, containing each about a pound. These gums, being thrown on hot embers, produce a very pleasant odour, and are used by the Mandingoes for perfuming their huts and clothes.

The customs, or duties on travellers, are very heavy ; in almost every town an ass load pays a bar of European merchandize, and at Fatteconda, the residence of the king, one Indian baft, or a musket, and six bottles of gunpowder, are exacted as the common tribute. By means of these duties, the King of Bondou is well supplied with arms and ammunition; a circumstance which makes him formidable to the neighbouring states.

The inhabitants differ in their complexions and national manners from the Mandingoes and Serawoollies, with whom they are frequently at war. Some years ago the King of Bondou crossed the Falemé river with a numerous army, and after a short and bloody campaign totally defeated the forces of Samboo King of Bambouk, who was obliged to sue for peace, and surrender to him all the towns along the eastern bank of the Falemé.

The Foulahs in general (as has been observed in a former Chapter) are of a tawny complexion, with small features, and soft silky hair; next to the Mandingoes they are undoubtedly the most considerable of all the nations in this part of Africa. Their original country is said to be Fooladoo (which signifies the country of the Foulahs); but they possess at present many other kingdoms at a great distance from each other: their complexion, however, is not exactly the same in the different districts; in Bondou, and the other kingdoms which are situated in the vicinity of the Moorish territories, they are of a more yellow complexion than in the southern states.

The Foulahs of Bondou are naturally of a mild and gentle disposition, but the uncharitable maxims of the Koran has made them less hospitable to strangers, and more reserved in their behaviour than the Mandingoes. They evidently consider all the Negro natives as their inferiors; and when talking of different nations, always rank themselves among the white people.

I 2

Their government differs from that of the Mandingoes chiefly in this, that they are more immediately under the influence of the Mahomedan laws ; for all the chief men (the king excepted) and a large majority of the inhabitants of Bondou, are Mussulmen, and the authority and laws of the Prophet, are every where looked upon as sacred and decisive. In the exercise of their faith, however, they are not very intolerant towards such of their countrymen as still retain their ancient superstitions. Religious persecution is not known among them, nor is it necessary ; for the system of Mahomet is made to extend itself by means abundantly more efficacious. By establishing small schools in the different towns, where many of the Pagan as well as Mahomedan children are taught to read the Koran, and instructed in the tenets of the Prophet. The Mahomedan priests fix a bias on the minds, and form the character of their young disciples, which no accidents of life can ever afterwards remove or alter. Many of these little schools I visited in my progress through the country, and observed with pleasure the great docility and submissive deportment of the children, and heartily wished they had had better instructors, and a purer religion.

With the Mahomedan faith is also introduced the Arabic language, with which most of the Foulahs have a slight acquaintance. Their native tongue abounds very much in liquids, but there is something unpleasant in the manner of pronouncing it. A stranger on hearing the common conversation of two Foulahs, would imagine that they were scolding each other. Their numerals are these :—

One	——	*Go.*
Two	——	*Deeddee.*
Three	——	*Tettee.*
Four	——	*Nee.*
Five	——	*Jouee.*
Six	——	*Jego.*
Seven	——	*Jedeeddee.*
Eight	——	*Je Tettee.*
Nine	——	*Je Nee.*
Ten	——	*Sappo.*

The industry of the Foulahs, in the occupations of pasturage and agriculture, is every where remarkable. Even on the banks of the Gambia, the greater part of the corn is raised by them; and their herds and flocks are more numerous and in better condition than those of the Mandingoes; but in Bondou they are opulent in a high degree, and enjoy all the necessaries of life in the greatest profusion. They display great skill in the management of their cattle, making them extremely gentle by kindness and familiarity. On the approach of night, they are collected from the woods, and secured in folds, called korrees, which are constructed in the neighbourhood of the different villages. In the middle of each korree is erected a small hut, wherein one or two of the herdsmen keep watch during the night, to prevent the cattle from being stolen, and to keep up the fires which are kindled round the korree to frighten away the wild beasts.

The cattle are milked in the mornings and evenings: the milk is excellent; but the quantity obtained from any one cow is by no means so great as in Europe. The Foulahs use the milk chiefly as an article of diet, and that, not until it is quite sour. The cream which it affords is very thick, and is converted into butter by stirring it violently in a large calabash. This butter, when melted over a gentle fire, and freed from impurities, is preserved in small earthen pots, and forms a part in most of their dishes; it serves likewise to anoint their heads, and is bestowed very liberally on their faces and arms.

But although milk is plentiful, it is somewhat remarkable that the Foulahs, and indeed all the inhabitants of this part of Africa, are totally unacquainted with the art of making cheese. A firm attachment to the customs of their ancestors, makes them view with an eye of prejudice every thing that looks like innovation. The heat of the climate, and the great scarcity of salt, are held forth as unanswerable objections; and the whole process appears to them too long and troublesome, to be attended with any solid advantage.

Besides the cattle, which constitute the chief wealth of the Foulahs, they possess some excellent horses, the breed of which seems to be a mixture of the Arabian with the original African.

CHAPTER V.

*Account of Kajaaga.—Serawoollies—their Manners and Language.
—Account of Joag.—The Author is ill treated, and robbed of
half of his Effects, by Order of Batcheri, the King.—Charity of
a female Slave.—The Author is visited by Demba Sego, Nephew
of the King of Kasson, who offers to conduct him in safety to that
Kingdom.—Offer accepted.—The Author and his Protector, with
a numerous Retinue, set out and reach Samee, on the Banks of
the Senegal.—Proceed to Kayee, and crossing the Senegal, arrive in the Kingdom of Kasson.*

THE kingdom of Kajaaga, in which I was now arrived, is called
by the French, Gallam; but the name that I have adopted is
universally used by the natives. This country is bounded on
the south-east and south by Bambouk; on the west by Bondou
and Foota Torra; and on the north by the river Senegal.

The air and climate are, I believe, more pure and salubrious
than at any of the settlements towards the Coast; the face of
the country is every where interspersed with a pleasing variety
of hills and vallies; and the windings of the Senegal river,
which descends from the rocky hills of the interior, make the
scenery on its banks very picturesque and beautiful.

The inhabitants are called Serawoollies, or (as the French
write it) *Seracolets*. Their complexion is a jet black: they are
not to be distinguished in this respect from the Jaloffs.

The government is monarchical; and the regal authority, from what I experienced of it, seems to be sufficiently formidable. The people themselves, however, complain of no oppression; and seemed all very anxious to support the king, in a contest he was going to enter into with the sovereign of Kasson. The Serawoollies are habitually a trading people; they formerly carried on a great commerce with the French, in gold and slaves, and still maintain some traffic in slaves with the British factories on the Gambia. They are reckoned tolerably fair and just in their dealings, but are indefatigable in their exertions to acquire wealth, and they derive considerable profits by the sale of salt, and cotton cloth, in distant countries. When a Serawoolli merchant returns home from a trading expedition, the neighbours immediately assemble to congratulate him upon his arrival. On these occasions the traveller displays his wealth and liberality, by making a few presents to his friends; but if he has been unsuccessful, his levee is soon over; and every one looks upon him as a man of no understanding, who could perform a long journey, and (as they express it) *bring back nothing but the hair upon his head.*

Their language abounds much in gutturals, and is not so harmonious as that spoken by the Foulahs: it is, however, well worth acquiring by those who travel through this part of the African continent; it being very generally understood in the kingdoms of Kasson, Kaarta, Ludamar, and the northern parts of Bambara. In all these countries the Serawoollies are the chief traders. Their numerals are,

One	——	*Bani.*
Two	——	*Fillo.*
Three	——	*Sicco.*
Four	——	*Narrato,*
Five	——	*Karrago.*
Six	——	*Toomo.*
Seven	——	*Nero.*
Eight	——	*Sego.*
Nine	——	*Kabbo.*
Ten	——	*Tamo.*
Twenty	——	*Tamo di fillo.*

We arrived at Joag, the frontier town of this kingdom on the 24th of December; and took up our residence at the house of the chief man, who is here no longer known by the title of *Alkaid,* but is called the *Dooty.* He was a rigid Mahomedan, but distinguished for his hospitality. This town may be supposed, on a gross computation, to contain two thousand inhabitants. It is surrounded by a high wall, in which are a number of port holes, for musquetry to fire through, in case of an attack. Every man's possession is likewise surrounded by a wall; the whole forming so many distinct citadels; and amongst a people unacquainted with the use of artillery, these walls answer all the purposes of stronger fortifications. To the westward of the town is a small river, on the banks of which the natives raise great plenty of tobacco and onions.

The same evening Madiboo the Bushreen, who had accompanied me from Pisania, went to pay a visit to his father and

K

mother, who dwelt at a neighbouring town called Dramanet. He was joined by my other attendant the blacksmith; and as soon as it was dark, I was invited to see the sports of the inhabitants, it being their custom on the arrival of strangers, to welcome them by diversions of different kinds. I found a great crowd surrounding a party who were dancing, by the light of some large fires, to the music of four drums, which were beat with great exactness and uniformity. The dances, however, consisted more in wanton gestures, than in muscular exertion or graceful attitudes. The ladies vied with each other in displaying the most voluptuous movements imaginable.

December 25th. About two o'clock in the morning a number of horsemen came into the town, and having awakened my landlord, talked to him for some time in the Serawoolli tongue; after which they dismounted, and came to the Bentang on which I had made my bed. One of them thinking that I was asleep, attempted to steal the musket that lay by me on the mat; but finding that he could not effect his purpose undiscovered, he desisted; and the strangers sat down by me till daylight.

I could now easily perceive, by the countenance of my interpreter, Johnson, that something very unpleasant was in agitation. I was likewise surprised to see Madiboo and the blacksmith so soon returned. On inquiring the reason, Madiboo informed me that as they were dancing at Dramanet, ten horsemen belonging to Batcheri, king of the country, with his second son at their head, had arrived there, inquiring if the white man had passed; and on being told that I was at Joag, they rode off without stopping. Madiboo added, that on hearing this, he and the blacksmith hastened back to give me notice of their coming. Whilst I was listening to this narrative, the ten horsemen mentioned by Madiboo arrived; and coming to the Bentang, dismounted and seated themselves with those who had come before, the whole being about twenty in number, forming a circle round me, and each man holding his musket in his hand. I took this opportunity to observe to my landlord, that as I did not understand the Serawoolli tongue, I hoped, whatever the men had to say, they would speak in Mandingo. To this they agreed, and a short man, loaded with a remarkable number of saphies, opened the business in a very long harangue, informing me that I had entered the king's town without having first paid the duties, or giving any present to the king, and that, according to the laws of the country, my people, cattle, and baggage were forfeited. He added, that they had received orders from the king to conduct me to Maana,* the place of his residence; and if I refused to come with them, their orders were to bring me by force; upon his saying which, all of them rose up and asked me if I was ready. It would have been equally vain and imprudent in me to have resisted or irritated such a body of men; I therefore affected to comply with their commands, and begged them only to stop a little until I had given my horse a feed of corn, and settled matters with my landlord. The poor blacksmith, who was a native of Kasson, mistook

* Maana is within a short distance of the ruins of Fort St. Joseph, on the Senegal river, formerly a French factory.

K 2

this feigned compliance for a real intention, and taking me away from the company, told me, that he had always behaved towards me as if I had been his father and master; and he hoped I would not entirely ruin him, by going to Maana; adding, that as there was every reason to believe a war would soon take place between Kasson and Kajaaga, he should not only lose his little property, the savings of four years' industry, but should certainly be detained and sold as a slave, unless his friends had an opportunity of paying two slaves for his redemption. I saw this reasoning in its full force, and determined to do my utmost to preserve the blacksmith from so dreadful a fate. I therefore told the king's son that I was ready to go with him, upon condition that the blacksmith, who was an inhabitant of a distant kingdom, and entirely unconnected with me, should be allowed to stay at Joag, till my return; to this they all objected, and insisted that as we had all acted contrary to the laws, we were all equally answerable for our conduct.

I now took my landlord aside, and giving him a small present of gunpowder, asked his advice in so critical a situation: he was decidedly of opinion that I ought not to go to the king: he was fully convinced, he said, that if the king should discover any thing valuable in my possession, he would not be over scrupulous about the means of obtaining it. This made me the more solicitous to conciliate matters with the king's people; and I began by observing, that what I had done did not proceed from any want of respect towards the king, nor from any wish to violate his laws, but wholly from my own inexperience and ignorance, being a stranger, totally unacquainted with the laws and customs of their country; I had indeed entered the king's frontier, without knowing that I was to pay the duties beforehand, but I was ready to pay them now: which I thought was all they could reasonably demand. I then tendered them, as a present to the king, the five drams of gold which the King of Bondou had given me; this they accepted, but insisted on examining my baggage, which I opposed in vain. The bundles were opened; but the men were much disappointed in not finding in them so much gold and amber as they expected: they made up the deficiency, however, by taking whatever things they fancied; and after wrangling and debating with me till sunset, they departed; having first robbed me of half my goods. These proceedings dispirited my people, and our fortitude was not strengthened by a very indifferent supper, after a long fast. Madiboo begged me to turn back; Johnson laughed at the thoughts of proceeding without money, and the blacksmith was afraid to be seen, or even to speak, lest any one should discover him to be a native of Kasson. In this disposition, we passed the night by the side of a dim fire, and our situation the next day was very perplexing: it was impossible to procure provisions without money, and I knew that if I produced any beads or amber, the king would immediately hear of it, and I should probably lose the few effects I had concealed. We therefore resolved to combat hunger for the day; and wait some favourable opportunity of purchasing or begging provisions.

Towards evening, as I was sitting upon the Bentang, chewing straws, an old female slave, passing by with a basket upon her head, asked me *if I had got my dinner*. As I thought she only laughed at me, I gave her no answer ; but my boy, who was sitting close by, answered for me ; and told her, that the King's people had robbed me of all my money. On hearing this, the good old woman, with a look of unaffected benevolence, immediately took the basket from her head, and shewing me that it contained ground-nuts, asked me if I could eat them ; being answered in the affirmative, she presented me with a few handfuls, and walked away, before I had time to thank her for this seasonable supply. This trifling circumstance gave me peculiar satisfaction. I reflected with pleasure on the conduct of this poor untutored slave, who, without examining into my character or circumstances, listened implicitly to the dictates of her own heart. Experience had taught her that hunger was painful, and her own distresses made her commiserate those of others.

The old woman had scarcely left me, when I received information that a nephew of Demba Sego Jalla, the Mandingo King of Kasson, was coming to pay me a visit. He had been sent on an embassy to Batcheri, King of Kajaaga, to endeavour to settle the disputes which had arisen between his uncle and the latter ; but after debating the matter four days without success, he was now on his return ; and hearing that a white man was at Joag, in his way to Kasson, curiosity brought him to see me. I represented to him my situation and distresses ; when he frankly offered me his protection, and said he would be my guide to Kasson (provided I would set out the next morning), and be answerable for my safety. I readily and gratefully accepted his offer ; and was ready, with my attendants, by day-light on the morning of the 27th of December.

My protector, whose name was Demba Sego, probably after his uncle, had a numerous retinue. Our company at leaving Joag, consisted of thirty persons and six loaded asses ; and we rode on cheerfully enough for some hours, without any remark-able occurrence, until we came to a species of tree, for which my interpreter, Johnson, had made frequent inquiry. On find-ing it, he desired us to stop ; and producing a white chicken, which he had purchased at Joag for the purpose, he tied it by the leg to one of the branches, and then told us we might now safely proceed, for that our journey would be prosperous. This circumstance is mentioned merely to illustrate the disposition of the Negroes, and to shew the power of superstition over their minds ; for although this man had resided seven years in England, it was evident that he still retained the prejudices and notions he had imbibed in his youth. He meant this cere-mony, he told me, as an offering, or sacrifice, to the spirits of the woods ; who were, he said, a powerful race of beings of a white colour, with long flowing hair. I laughed at his folly, but could not condemn the piety of his motives.

At noon we had reached Gungadi, a large town, where we stopped about an hour, until some of the asses that had fallen behind came up. Here I observed a number of date trees, and a mosque built of clay, with six turrets, on the pinnacles of which were placed six ostrich eggs. A little before sunset we arrived at the town of Samee, on the banks of the Senegal, which is here a beautiful, but shallow river, moving slowly over a bed of sand and gravel. The banks are high, and covered with verdure; the country is open and cultivated; and the rocky hills of Felow and Bambouk, add much to the beauty of the landscape.

December 28. We departed from Samee, and arrived in the afternoon at Kayee, a large village, part of which is situated on the north, and part on the south side of the river. A little above this place is a considerable cataract, where the river flows over a ledge of whin-stone rock, with great force: below this, the river is remarkably black and deep; and here it was proposed to make our cattle swim over. After hollooing, and firing some muskets, the people on the Kasson side observed us, and brought over a canoe to carry our baggage. I did not, however, think it possible to get the cattle down the bank, which is here more than forty feet above the water; but the Negroes seized the horses, and launched them one at a time, down a sort of trench or gully, that was almost perpendicular, and seemed to have been worn smooth by this sort of use. After the terrified cattle had been plunged in this manner to the water's edge, every man got down as well as he could. The ferryman then taking hold of the most steady of the horses by a rope, led him into the water, and paddled the canoe a little from the brink; upon which a general attack commenced upon the other horses, who finding themselves pelted and kicked on all sides, unanimously plunged into the river, and followed their companion. A few boys swam in after them; and by laving water upon them when they attempted to return, urged them onwards; and we had the satisfaction, in about fifteen minutes, to see them all safe on the other side. It was a matter of greater difficulty to manage the asses: their natural stubborn-ness of disposition made them endure a great deal of pelting and shoving before they would venture into the water; and when they had reached the middle of the stream, four of them turned back, in spite of every exertion to get them forwards. Two hours were spent in getting the whole of them over; an hour more was employed in transporting the baggage; and it was near sunset before the canoe returned, when Demba Sego and myself embarked in this dangerous passage-boat, which the least motion was like to overset. The king's ne-phew thought this a proper time to have a peep into a tin box of mine, that stood in the fore part of the canoe; and in stretching out his hand for it, he unfortunately destroyed the equilibrium, and overset the canoe. Luckily we were not far advanced, and got back to the shore without much difficulty; from whence, after wringing the water from our clothes, we took a fresh departure, and were soon afterwards safely landed in Kasson.

L

CHAPTER VI.

Arrival at Teesee.—Interview with Tiggity Sego, the King's Bro-
ther—the Author's Detention at Teesee—some Account of that
Place and its Inhabitants—Incidents which occurred there.—
Rapacious Conduct of Tiggity Sego toward the Author on his
Departure.—Sets out for Kooniakary, the Capital of the King-
dom.—Incidents on the Road, and Arrival at Kooniakary.

WE no sooner found ourselves safe in Kasson, than Demba
Sego told me that we were now in his uncle's dominions, and he
hoped I would consider, being now out of danger, the obligation
I owed to him, and make him a suitable return for the trouble he
had taken on my account by a handsome present. This, as he
knew how much had been pilfered from me at Joag, was rather
an unexpected proposition ; and I began to fear that I had not
much improved my condition by crossing the water, but as it
would have been folly to complain, I made no observation upon
his conduct, and gave him seven bars of amber, and some tobacco ; with which he seemed to be content.

After a long day's journey, in the course of which I observed
a number of large loose nodules of white granite, we arrived at
Teesee on the evening of Dec. 29th, and were accommodated in
Demba Sego's hut. The next morning he introduced me to his
father Tiggity Sego, brother to the King of Kasson, chief of

Teesee. The old man viewed me with great earnestness, having never, he said, beheld but one white man before, whom by his description I immediately knew to be Major Houghton. I related to him, in answer to his inquiries, the motives that induced me to explore the country. But he seemed to doubt the truth of what I asserted ; thinking, I believe, that I secretly meditated some project which I was afraid to avow. He told me, it would be necessary I should go to Kooniakary, the residence of the king, to pay my respects to that prince ; but desired me to come to him again before I left Teesee.

In the afternoon one of his slaves eloped; and a general alarm being given, every person that had a horse rode into the woods, in the hopes of apprehending him ; and Demba Sego begged the use of my horse for the same purpose. I readily consented ; and in about an hour they all returned with the slave, who was severely flogged, and afterwards put in irons. On the day following (Dec. 31.) Demba Sego was ordered to go with twenty horsemen to a town in Gedumah, to adjust some dispute with the Moors, a party of whom were supposed to have stolen three horses from Teesee. Demba begged, a second time, the use of my horse; adding, that the sight of my bridle and saddle would give him consequence among the Moors. This request also I readily granted, and he promised to return at the end of three days. During his absence I amused myself with walking about the town, and conversing with the natives, who attended me every where with great kindness and curiosity, and supplied me with milk, eggs, and what other provisions I wanted, on very easy terms.

Teesee is a large unwalled town, having no security against the attack of an enemy, except a sort of citadel, in which Tiggity and his family constantly reside. This town, according to the report of the natives, was formerly inhabited only by a few Foulah shepherds, who lived in considerable affluence by means of the excellent meadows in the neighbourhood, in which they reared great herds of cattle. But their prosperity attracting the envy of some Mandingoes, the latter drove out the shepherds, and took possession of their lands.

The present inhabitants, though they possess both cattle and corn in abundance, are not over nice in articles of diet; rats, moles, squirrels, snakes, locusts, &c. are eaten without scruple by the highest and lowest. My people were one evening invited to a feast given by some of the townsmen, where, after making a hearty meal of what they thought fish and kouskous, one of them found a piece of hard skin in the dish, and brought it along with him, to shew me what sort of fish they had been eating. On examining the skin, I found they had been feasting on a large snake. Another custom still more extraordinary, is that no woman is allowed *to eat an egg*. This prohibition, whether arising from ancient superstition, or from the craftiness of some old Bushreen who loved eggs himself, is rigidly adhered to, and nothing will more affront a woman of Teesee than to offer her an egg. The custom is the more singular, as the men eat eggs without scruple in the presence of their wives, and I never observed the same prohibition in any other of the Mandingo countries.

The third day after his son's departure, Tiggity Sego held a palaver on a very extraordinary occasion, which I attended ; and the debates on both sides of the question displayed much ingenuity. The case was this. A young man, a Kafir, of considerable affluence, who had recently married a young and handsome wife, applied to a very devout Bushreen, or Mussulman priest, of his acquaintance, to procure him saphies for his protection during the approaching war. The Bushreen complied with the request ; and in order, as he pretended, to render the saphies more efficacious, enjoined the young man to avoid any nuptial intercourse with his bride for the space of six weeks. Severe as the injunction was, the Kafir strictly obeyed ; and without telling his wife the real cause, absented himself from her company. In the mean time it began to be whispered at Teesee, that the Bushreen, who always performed his evening devotions at the door of the Kafir's hut, was more intimate with the young wife than he ought to be. At first, the good husband was unwilling to suspect the honour of his sanctified friend, and one whole month elapsed before any jealousy rose in his mind ; but hearing the charge repeated, he at last interrogated his wife on the subject, who frankly confessed that the Bushreen had seduced her. Hereupon the Kafir put her into confinement and called a palaver upon the Bushreen's conduct. The fact was clearly proved against him ; and he was sentenced to be sold into slavery, or to find two slaves for his redemption, according to the pleasure of the complainant. The injured husband, however, was unwilling to proceed against his friend to such extremity, and desired rather to have him publicly flogged before Tiggity Sego's gate. This was agreed to, and the sentence was immediately executed. The culprit was tied by the hands to a strong stake; and a long black rod being brought forth, the executioner, after flourishing it round his head for some time, applied it with such force and dexterity to the Bushreen's back, as to make him roar until the woods resounded with his screams. The surrounding multitude, by their hooting and laughing, manifested how much they enjoyed the punishment of this old gallant; and it is worthy of remark, that the number of stripes was precisely the same as are enjoined by the Mosaic law, *forty, save one.*

As there appeared great probability that Teesee, from its being a frontier town, would be much exposed during the war to the predatory excursions of the Moors of Gadumah, Tiggity Sego had, before my arrival, sent round to the neighbouring villages, to beg or to purchase as much provisions as would afford subsistence to the inhabitants for one whole year, independently of the crop on the ground, which the Moors might destroy. This project was well received by the country people, and they fixed a day on which to bring all the provisions they could spare to Teesee, and as my horse was not yet returned, I went, in the afternoon of January 4th, 1796, to meet the escort with the provisions.

It was composed of about 400 men, marching in good order, with corn and ground nuts in large calabashes upon their heads. They were preceded by a strong guard of bowmen, and followed by eight musicians or singing men. As soon as they approached the town, the latter began a song, every verse of which was answered by the company, and succeeded by a few strokes on the large drums. In this manner they proceeded, amidst the acclamations of the populace, till they reached the house of Tiggity Sego, where the loads were deposited; and in the evening they all assembled under the Bentang tree, and spent the night in dancing and merriment. Many of these strangers remained at Teesee for three days, during which time I was constantly attended by as many of them as could conveniently see me; one party giving way to another, as soon as curiosity was gratified.

On the 5th of January an embassy of ten people belonging to Almami Abdulkader, King of Foota Torra, a country to the west of Bondou, arrived at Teesee; and desiring Tiggity Sego to call an assembly of the inhabitants, announced publicly their king's determination, to this effect: " That unless all the people of Kasson would embrace the Mahomedan religion, and evince their conversion by saying eleven public prayers, he (the King of Foota Torra) could not possibly stand neuter in the present contest, but would certainly join his arms to those of Kajaaga." A message of this nature, from so powerful a prince, could not fail to create great alarm; and the inhabitants of Teesee, after a long consultation, agreed to conform to his good pleasure, humiliating as it was to them. Accordingly, one and all publicly offered up eleven prayers, which were considered a sufficient testimony of their having renounced Paganism, and embraced the doctrines of the Prophet.

It was the 8th of January before Demba Sego returned with my horse; and being quite wearied out with the delay, I went immediately to inform his father, that I should set out for Kooniakary early the next day. The old man made many frivolous objections; and at length gave me to understand, that I must not think of departing, without first paying him the same duties he was entitled to receive from all travellers; besides which, he expected, he said, some acknowledgment for his kindness towards me. Accordingly, on the morning of the 9th, my friend Demba, with a number of people, came to me, and said that they were sent by Tiggity Sego for my present, and wished to see what goods I had appropriated for that purpose. I knew that resistance was hopeless, and complaint unavailing; and being in some measure prepared, by the intimation I had received the night before, I quietly offered him seven bars of amber, and five of tobacco. After surveying these articles for some time very coolly, Demba laid them down, and told me, this was not a present for a man of Tiggity Sego's consequence, who had it in his power to take whatever he pleased from me. He added, that if I did not consent to make him a larger offering, he would carry all my baggage to his father, and let him choose for himself. I had no time for reply; for Demba and his attendants immediately began to open my bundles, and spread the different articles upon the floor, where they underwent a more strict examination than they had done at Joag. Every thing that pleased them, they took without scruple, and amongst other things, Demba seized the tin box, which had so much attracted his attention in crossing the river. Upon collecting the scattered remains of my little fortune after these people had left me, I found that, as at Joag, I had been plundered of half, so here, without even the shadow of accusation, I was deprived of half the remainder. The blacksmith himself, though a native of Kasson, had also been compelled to open his bundles, and take an oath that the different articles they contained were his own exclusive property. There was, however, no remedy; and having been under some obligation to Demba Sego for his attention towards me in the journey from Joag, I did not reproach him for his rapacity, but determined to quit Teesee at all events the next morning. In the meanwhile, in order to raise the drooping spirits of my attendants, I purchased a fat sheep, and had it dressed for our dinner.

Early in the morning of January 10th, therefore, I left Teesee, and about mid-day ascended a ridge, from whence we had a distant view of the hills round Kooniakary. In the evening we reached a small village where we slept, and departing from thence the next morning, crossed in a few hours a narrow but deep stream called Krieko, a branch of the Senegal. About two miles farther to the eastward, we passed a large town called Madina; and at two o'clock came in sight of Jumbo, the blacksmith's native town, from whence he had been absent more than four years. Soon after this his brother, who had by some means been apprized of his coming, came out to meet him, accompanied by a singing man: he brought a horse for the blacksmith, that he might enter his native town in a dignified manner; and he desired each of us to put a good charge of powder into our guns. The singing man now led the way, followed by the two brothers; and we were presently joined by

M

a number of people from the town, all of whom demonstrated
great joy at seeing their old acquaintance the blacksmith, by
the most extravagant jumping and singing.   On entering the
town, the singing man began an extempore song in praise of
the blacksmith, extolling his courage in having overcome so
many difficulties ; and concluding with a strict injunction to his
friends to dress him plenty of victuals.

When we arrived at the blacksmith's place of residence, we
dismounted and fired our muskets.   The meeting between
him and his relations was very tender ; for these rude children
of nature, free from restraint, display their emotions in the
strongest and most expressive manner.   Amidst these trans-
ports, the blacksmith's aged mother was led forth, leaning upon
a staff.   Every one made way for her ; and she stretched out
her hand to bid her son welcome.   Being totally blind, she
stroked his hands, arms, and face, with great care, and seemed
highly delighted that her latter days were blessed by his return,
and that her ears once more heard the music of his voice.   From
this interview I was fully convinced, that whatever difference
there is between the Negro and European in the conformation
of the nose and the colour of the skin, there is none in the
genuine sympathies and characteristic feelings of our common
nature.

During the tumult of these congratulations, I had seated myself apart, by the side of one of the huts, being unwilling to
interrupt the flow of filial and parental tenderness ; and the
attention of the company was so entirely taken up with the
blacksmith, that I believe none of his friends had observed me.

When all the people present had seated themselves, the black-smith was desired by his father to give them some account of his adventures; and silence being commanded, he began; and after repeatedly thanking God for the success that had attended him, related every material occurrence that had happened to him from his leaving Kasson to his arrival at the Gambia; his employment and success in those parts; and the dangers he had escaped in returning to his native country. In the latter part of his narration, he had frequently occasion to mention me; and after many strong expressions concerning my kind-ness to him, he pointed to the place where I sat, and exclaim-ed, *affille ibi siring*, " see him sitting there." In a moment all eyes were turned upon me; I appeared like a being dropped from the clouds; every one was surprised that they had not observed me before; and a few women and children expressed great uneasiness at being so near a man of such an uncommon appearance. By degrees, however, their apprehensions sub-sided; and when the blacksmith assured them that I was per-fectly inoffensive, and would hurt nobody, some of them ven-tured so far as to examine the texture of my clothes; but many of them were still very suspicious; and when by accident I happened to move myself, or look at the young children, their mothers would scamper off with them with the greatest pre-cipitation. In a few hours, however, they all became reconciled to me.

With these worthy people I spent the remainder of that, and the whole of the ensuing day, in feasting and merriment; and the blacksmith declared he would not quit me during my stay

M 2

at Kooniakary, for which place we set out early on the morning of the 14th of January, and arrived about the middle of the day at Soolo, a small village three miles to the south of it.

As this place was somewhat out of the direct road, it is necessary to observe, that I went thither to visit a Slatee, or Gambia trader, of great note and reputation, named Salim Daucari. He was well known to Dr. Laidley, who had trusted him with effects to the value of five slaves, and had given me an order for the whole of the debt. We luckily found him at home, and he received me with great kindness and attention.

It is remarkable, however, that the King of Kasson was, by some means, immediately apprized of my motions; for I had been at Soolo but a few hours, before Sambo Sego, his second son, came thither with a party of horse, to inquire what had prevented me from proceeding to Kooniakary, and waiting immediately upon the king, who, he said, was impatient to see me. Salim Daucari made my apology, and promised to accompany me to Kooniakary the same evening: we accordingly departed from Soolo at sunset, and in about an hour entered Kooniakary. But as the king had gone to sleep, we deferred the interview till next morning, and slept at the hut of Sambo Sego.

My interview with the king, and the incidents which occurred to me in the kingdoms of Kasson and Kaarta, will be the subject of the ensuing Chapter.

CHAPTER VII.

*The Author admitted to an Audience of the King of Kasson, whom
he finds well disposed towards him.—Incidents during the
Author's stay at Kooniakary.—Departs thence for Kemmoo,
the Capital of Kaarta.—Is received with great kindness by the
King of Kaarta, who dissuades him from prosecuting his Journey, on Account of approaching Hostilities with the King of
Bambarra.—The Author determines, notwithstanding, to proceed; and the usual Routes being obstructed, takes the Path to
Ludamar, a Moorish Kingdom.—Is accommodated by the King
with a Guide to Jarra, the frontier Town of the Moorish Territories; and sets out for that Place, accompanied by Three of
the King's Sons, and 200 Horsemen.*

ABOUT eight o'clock in the morning of January 15, 1796, we
went to an audience of the king (Demba Sego Jalla); but the
crowd of people to see me was so great, that I could scarcely
get admittance. A passage being at length obtained, I made
my bow to the monarch, whom we found sitting upon a mat, in
a large hut: he appeared to be a man of about sixty years of
age: his success in war, and the mildness of his behaviour in
time of peace, had much endeared him to all his subjects. He
surveyed me with great attention; and when Salim Daucari
explained to him the object of my journey, and my reasons for

passing through his country, the good old king appeared not only perfectly satisfied, but promised me every assistance in his power. He informed me that he had seen Major Houghton, and presented him with a white horse; but that after crossing the kingdom of Kaarta, he had lost his life among the Moors; in what manner he could not inform me. When this audience was ended we returned to our lodging, and I made up a small present for the king, out of the few effects that were left me; for I had not yet received any thing from Salim Daucari. This present, though inconsiderable in itself, was well received by the king, who sent me in return a large white bullock. The sight of this animal quite delighted my attendants; not so much on account of its bulk, as from its being of a white colour; which is considered as a particular mark of favour. But although the king himself was well disposed towards me, and readily granted me permission to pass through his territories, I soon discovered that very great and unexpected obstacles were likely to impede my progress. Besides the war which was on the point of breaking out between Kasson and Kajaaga, I was told that the next kingdom of Kaarta, through which my route lay, was involved in the issue; and was furthermore threatened with hostilities on the part of Bambarra. The king himself informed me of these circumstances; and advised me to stay in the neighbourhood of Kooniakary, till such time as he could procure proper information respecting Bambarra, which he expected to do in the course of four or five days, as he had already, he said, sent four messengers into Kaarta for that purpose. I readily submitted to this proposal, and went to Soolo, to stay there till the return of one of those messengers. This afforded me a favourable opportunity of receiving what money Salim Daucari could spare me on Dr. Laidley's account. I succeeded in receiving the value of three slaves, chiefly in gold dust ; and being anxious to proceed as quickly as possible, I begged Daucari to use his interest with the king to allow me a guide by the way of Fooladoo, as I was informed that the war had already commenced between the Kings of Bambarra and Kaarta. Daucari accordingly set out for Kooniakary on the morning of the 20th, and the same evening returned with the king's answer, which was to this purpose ; that the king had, many years ago, made an agreement with Daisey, King of Kaarta, to send all merchants and travellers through his dominions ; but that if I wished to take the route through Fooladoo, I had his permission so to do ; though he could not, consistently with his agreement, lend me a guide. Having felt the want of regal protection in a former part of my journey, I was unwilling to hazard a repetition of the hardships I had then experienced, especially as the money I had received was probably the last supply that I should obtain ; I therefore determined to wait for the return of the messengers from Kaarta.

In the interim, it began to be whispered abroad that I had received plenty of gold from Salim Daucari ; and on the morning of the 23d, Sambo Sego paid me a visit with a party of horsemen. He insisted upon knowing the exact amount of the money I had obtained ; declaring, that whatever the sum was, one half of it must go to the king ; besides which, he intimated that he expected a handsome present for himself, as being the

king's son ; and for his attendants, as being the king's relations. The reader will easily perceive, that if all these demands
had been satisfied, I should not have been overburthened with
money ; but though it was very mortifying to me to comply
with the demands of injustice, and so arbitrary an exaction,
yet, thinking it was highly dangerous to make a foolish resistance, and irritate the lion when within the reach of his paw, I
prepared to submit ; and if Salim Daucari had not interposed,
all my endeavours to mitigate this oppressive claim would have
been of no avail. Salim at last prevailed upon Sambo to accept sixteen bars of European merchandize, and some powder
and ball, as a complete payment of every demand that could be
made upon me in the kingdom of Kasson.

January 26th, in the forenoon, I went to the top of a high
hill to the southward of Soolo, where I had a most enchanting
prospect of the country. The number of towns and villages,
and the extensive cultivation around them, surpassed every
thing I had yet seen in Africa. A gross calculation may be
formed of the number of inhabitants in this delightful plain, by
considering, that the King of Kasson can raise four thousand
fighting men by the sound of his war drum. In traversing the
rocky eminences of this hill, which are almost destitute of vegetation, I observed a number of large holes in the crevices and
fissures of the rocks, where the wolves and hyenas take refuge
during the day. Some of these animals paid us a visit on the
evening of the 27th ; their approach was discovered by the dogs
of the village ; and on this occasion it is remarkable, that the
dogs did not bark, but howl in the most dismal manner. The

inhabitants of the village no sooner heard them than, knowing the cause, they armed themselves; and providing bunches of dry grass, went in a body to the inclosure in the middle of the village where the cattle were kept. Here they lighted the bunches of grass, and, waving them to and fro, ran hooping and hallooing towards the hills. This manœuvre had the desired effect of frightening the wolves away from the village; but on examination, we found that they had killed five of the cattle, and torn and wounded many others.

February 1st. The messengers arrived from Kaarta, and brought intelligence that the war had not yet commenced between Bambarra and Kaarta, and that I might probably pass through Kaarta before the Bambarra army invaded that country.

Feb. 3d. Early in the morning, two guides on horseback came from Kooniakary to conduct me to the frontiers of Kaarta. I accordingly took leave of Salim Daucari, and parted for the last time from my fellow-traveller the blacksmith, whose kind solicitude for my welfare had been so conspicuous; and about ten o'clock departed from Soolo. We travelled this day through a rocky and hilly country, along the banks of the river Krieko, and at sunset came to the village of Soomoo, where we slept.

Feb. 4th. We departed from Soomoo, and continued our route along the banks of the Krieko, which are every where well cultivated, and swarm with inhabitants. At this time they were increased by the number of people that had flown thither from Kaarta, on account of the Bambarra war. In the afternoon we reached Kimo, a large village, the residence of

N

Madi Konko, governor of the hilly country of Kasson, which is called Sorroma. From hence the guides appointed by the King of Kasson returned, to join in the expedition against Kajaaga; and I waited until the 6th, before I could prevail on Madi Konko to appoint me a guide to Kaarta.

Feb. 7th. Departing from Kimo, with Madi Konko's son as a guide, we continued our course along the banks of the Krieko until the afternoon, when we arrived at Kangee, a considerable town. The Krieko is here but a small rivulet; this beautiful stream takes its rise a little to the eastward of this town, and descends with a rapid and noisy current until it reaches the bottom of the high hill called Tappa, where it becomes more placid, and winds gently through the lovely plains of Kooniakary; after which, having received an additional branch from the north, it is lost in the Senegal, somewhere near the Falls of Felow.

Feb. 8th. This day we travelled over a rough stony country, and having passed Seimpo and a number of other villages, arrived in the afternoon at Lackarago, a small village, which stands upon the ridge of hills that separates the kingdoms of Kasson and Kaarta. In the course of the day we passed many hundreds of people flying from Kaarta, with their families and effects.

Feb. 9th. Early in the morning, we departed from Lackarago, and a little to the eastward came to the brow of a hill, from whence we had an extensive view of the country. Towards the south-east were perceived some very distant hills, which our guide told us were the mountains of Fooladoo. We

travelled with great difficulty down a stony and abrupt precipice, and continued our way in the bed of a dry river course;
where the trees, meeting over head, made the place dark and
cool. In a little time we reached the bottom of this romantic
glen, and about ten o'clock emerged from between two rocky hills,
and found ourselves on the level and sandy plains of Kaarta. At
noon we arrived at a Korree, or watering-place, where, for a few
strings of beads, I purchased as much milk and corn-meal as we
could eat; indeed provisions are here so cheap, and the shepherds live in such affluence, that they seldom ask any return for
what refreshments a traveller receives from them. From this
Korree, we reached Feesurah at sunset, where we took up our
lodging for the night.

Feb. 10th. We continued at Feesurah all this day, to have
a few clothes washed, and learn more exactly the situation of
affairs before we ventured towards the capital.

Feb. 11th. Our landlord, taking advantage of the unsettled
state of the country, demanded so extravagant a sum for
our lodging, that suspecting he wished for an opportunity to
quarrel with us, I refused to submit to his exorbitant demand;
but my attendants were so much frightened at the reports of
approaching war, that they refused to proceed any farther, unless
I could settle matters with him, and induce him to accompany
us to Kemmoo, for our protection on the road. This I accomplished with some difficulty by a present of a blanket, which I
had brought with me to sleep in, and for which our landlord
had conceived a very great liking, matters were at length

amicably adjusted, and he mounted his horse and led the way. He was one of those Negroes who, together with the ceremonial part of the Mahomedan religion, retain all their ancient superstitions, and even drink strong liquors. They are called Johars, or Jowers, and in this kingdom form a very numerous and powerful tribe. We had no sooner got into a dark and lonely part of the first wood, than he made a sign for us to stop, and taking hold of a hollow piece of bamboo, that hung as an amulet round his neck, whistled very loud, three times. I confess I was somewhat startled, thinking it was a signal for some of his companions to come and attack us; but he assured me that it was done merely with a view to ascertain what success we were likely to meet with on our present journey. He then dismounted, laid his spear across the road, and having said a number of short prayers, concluded with three loud whistles; after which he listened for some time, as if in expectation of an answer, and receiving none, told us we might proceed without fear, for there was no danger. About noon we passed a number of large villages quite deserted, the inhabitants having fled into Kasson to avoid the horrors of war. We reached Karankalla at sunset; this formerly was a large town, but having been plundered by the Bambarrans about four years ago, nearly one half of it is still in ruins.

Feb. 12th. At daylight, we departed from Karankalla, and as it was but a short day's journey to Kemmoo, we travelled slower than usual, and amused ourselves by collecting such eatable fruits as grew near the road side. In this pursuit

I had wandered a little from my people, and being uncertain whether they were before or behind me, I hastened to a rising ground to look about me. As I was proceeding towards this eminence, two Negro horsemen, armed with muskets, came galloping from among the bushes: on seeing them I made a full stop; the horsemen did the same, and all three of us seemed equally surprised and confounded at this interview. As I approached them their fears increased, and one of them, after casting upon me a look of horror, rode off at full speed; the other, in a panic of fear, put his hand over his eyes, and continued muttering prayers until his horse, seemingly without the rider's knowledge, conveyed him slowly after his companion. About a mile to the westward, they fell in with my attendants, to whom they related a frightful story: it seems their fears had dressed me in the flowing robes of a tremendous spirit, and one of them affirmed, that when I made my appearance, a cold blast of wind came pouring down upon him from the sky like so much cold water. About noon we saw at a distance the capital of Kaarta, situated in the middle of an open plain, the country for two miles round being cleared of wood, by the great consumption of that article for building and fuel, and we entered the town about two o'clock in the afternoon.

We proceeded, without stopping, to the court before the King's residence; but I was so completely surrounded by the gazing multitude, that I did not attempt to dismount, but sent in the landlord and Madi Konko's son, to acquaint the king of my arrival. In a little time they returned, accompanied by a messenger from the king, signifying that he would see me in the evening; and in the mean time, the messenger had orders to procure me a lodging, and see that the crowd did not molest me. He conducted me into a court, at the door of which he stationed a man, with a stick in his hand, to keep off the mob, and then shewed me a large hut, in which I was to lodge. I had scarcely seated myself in this spacious apartment, when the mob entered ; it was found impossible to keep them out, and I was surrounded by as many as the hut could contain. When the first party, however, had seen me, and asked a few questions, they retired, to make room for another company ; and in this manner the hut was filled and emptied thirteen different times.

A little before sunset, the king sent to inform me that he was at leisure, and wished to see me. I followed the messenger through a number of courts surrounded with high walls, where I observed plenty of dry grass bundled up like hay, to fodder the horses, in case the town should be invested. On entering the court in which the king was sitting, I was astonished at the number of his attendants, and at the good order that seemed to prevail among them : they were all seated ; the fighting men on the king's right hand, and the women and children on the left, leaving a space between them for my passage. The king, whose name was Daisy Koorabarri, was not to be distinguished from his subjects by any superiority in point of dress ; a bank of earth, about two feet high, upon which was spread a leopard's skin, constituted the only mark of royal dignity. When I had seated myself upon the ground before him, and related the various circumstances that had induced me to pass through his country, and my reasons for soliciting his protection, he appeared perfectly satisfied; but said it was not in his power at present to afford me much assistance; for that all sort of communication between Kaarta and Bambarra had been interrupted for some time past ; and as Mansong, the King of Bambarra, with his army, had entered Fooladoo in his way to Kaarta, there was but little hope of my reaching Bambarra by any of the usual routes, inasmuch as, coming from an enemy's country, I should certainly be plundered, or taken for a spy. If his country had been at peace, he said, I might have remained with him until a more favourable opportunity offered ; but, as matters stood at present, he did not wish me to continue in Kaarta, for fear some accident should befal me, in which case my countrymen might say that he had murdered a white man. He would therefore advise me to return into Kasson, and remain there until the war should terminate, which would probably happen in the course of three or four months ; after which, if he was alive, he said, he would be glad to see me, and if he was dead, his sons would take care of me.

This advice was certainly well meant on the part of the king; and perhaps I was to blame in not following it ; but I reflected that the hot months were approaching, and I dreaded the thoughts of spending the rainy season in the interior of Africa. These considerations, and the aversion I felt at the idea of returning without having made a greater progress in discovery, made me determine to go forwards; and though the king could not give me a guide to Bambarra, I begged that he would allow a man to accompany me as near the frontiers of his kingdom as was consistent with safety. Finding that I was determined to proceed, the king told me that one route still remained, but that, he said, was by no means free from danger; which was to go from Kaarta into the Moorish kingdom of Ludamar, from whence I might pass, by a circuitous route, into Bambarra. If I wished to follow this route, he would appoint people to conduct me to Jarra, the frontier town of Ludamar. He then inquired very particularly how I had been treated since I had left the Gambia, and asked in a jocular way how many slaves I expected to carry home with me on my return. He was about to proceed, when a man mounted on a fine Moorish horse, which was covered with sweat and foam, entered the court, and signifying that he had something of importance to communicate, the king immediately took up his sandals, which is the signal to strangers to retire. I accordingly took leave, but desired my boy to stay about the place, in order to learn something of the intelligence that this messenger had brought. In about an hour the boy returned, and informed me that the Bambarra army had left Fooladoo, and was on its march towards Kaarta; that the man I had seen, who had brought this intelligence, was one of the scouts or watchmen employed by the king, each of whom has his particular station (commonly on some rising ground) from whence he has the best view of the country, and watches the motions of the enemy.

In the evening the king sent me a fine sheep; which was very acceptable, as none of us had tasted victuals during the day. Whilst we were employed in dressing supper, evening prayers were announced; not by the call of the priest, as usual,

but by beating on drums, and blowing through large elephants'
teeth, hollowed out in such a manner as to resemble bugle
horns; the sound is melodious, and, in my opinion, comes
nearer to the human voice than any other artificial sound. As
the main body of Daisy's army was, at this juncture, at Kemmoo, the mosques were very much crowded; and I observed
that the disciples of Mahomet composed nearly one half of the
army of Kaarta.

Feb. 13th. At daylight I sent my horse-pistols and holsters
as a present to the king, and being very desirous to get away
from a place which was likely soon to become the seat of war,
I begged the messenger to inform the king that I wished to
depart from Kemmoo as soon as he should find it convenient
to appoint me a guide. In about an hour the king sent his
messenger to thank me for the present, and eight horsemen
to conduct me to Jarra. They told me that the king wished
me to proceed to Jarra with all possible expedition, that they
might return before any thing decisive should happen between
the armies of Bambarra and Kaarta; we accordingly departed
forthwith from Kemmoo, accompanied by three of Daisy's sons,
and about two hundred horsemen, who kindly undertook to see
me a little way on my journey.

O

CHAPTER VIII.

*Journey from Kemmoo to Funingkedy.—Some Account of the
Lotus.—A Youth murdered by the Moors—interesting Scene at
his Death.—Author passes through Simbing.—Some Particu-
culars concerning Major Houghton.—Author reaches Jarra—
Situation of the surrounding States at the Period of his Arrival
there, and a brief Account of the War between Kaarta and
Bambarra.*

On the evening of the day of our departure from Kemmoo,
(the king's eldest son and great part of the horsemen having returned) we reached a village called Marina, where we slept.
During the night some thieves broke into the hut where I
had deposited my baggage, and having cut open one of my
bundles, stole a quantity of beads, part of my clothes, and
some amber and gold, which happened to be in one of the
pockets. I complained to my protectors, but without effect.
The next day (Feb. 14,) was far advanced before we departed
from Marina, and we travelled slowly, on account of the excessive heat, until four o'clock in the afternoon, when two Negroes
were observed sitting among some thorny bushes at a little
distance from the road. The king's people, taking it for granted
that they were runaway slaves, cocked their muskets, and rode
at full speed in different directions through the bushes, in order

to surround them, and prevent their escaping. The Negroes, however, waited with great composure until we came within bowshot of them, when each of them took from his quiver a handful of arrows, and putting two between his teeth and one in his bow, waved to us with his hand to keep at a distance; upon which one of the king's people called out to the strangers to give some account of themselves. They said that " they were natives of Toorda, a neighbouring village, and had come to that place to gather *tomberongs*." These are small farinaceous berries, of a yellow colour and delicious taste, which I knew to be the fruit of the *rhamnus lotus* of Linnæus. The Negroes shewed us two large baskets full, which they had collected in the course of the day. These berries are much esteemed by the natives, who convert them into a sort of bread, by exposing them for some days to the sun, and afterwards pounding them gently in a wooden mortar, until the farinaceous part of the berry is separated from the stone. This meal is then mixed with a little water, and formed into cakes; which, when dried in the sun, resemble in colour and flavour the sweetest gingerbread. The stones are afterwards put into a vessel of water, and shaken about so as to separate the meal which may still adhere to them : this communicates a sweet and agreeable taste to the water, and with the addition of a little pounded millet, forms a pleasant gruel called *fondi,* which is the common breakfast in many parts of Ludamar, during the months of February and March. The fruit is collected by spreading a cloth upon the ground, and beating the branches with a stick.

The lotus is very common in all the kingdoms which I visited;

but is found in the greatest plenty on the sandy soil of Kaarta, Ludamar, and the northern parts of Bambarra, where it is one of the most common shrubs of the country. I had observed the same species at Gambia, and had an opportunity to make a drawing of a branch in flower, of which an engraving is given. The leaves of the desert shrub are, however, much smaller; and more resembling, in that particular, those represented in the engraving given by Desfontaines, in the Mémoires de l'Académie Royale des Sciences, 1788, p. 443.

As this shrub is found in Tunis, and also in the Negro kingdoms, and as it furnishes the natives of the latter with a food resembling bread, and also with a sweet liquor, which is much relished by them, there can be little doubt of its being the lotus mentioned by Pliny, as the food of the Lybian Lotophagi. An army may very well have been fed with the bread I have tasted, made of the meal of the fruit, as is said by Pliny to have been done in Lybia; and as the taste of the bread is sweet and agreeable, it is not likely that the soldiers would complain of it.

We arrived in the evening at the village of Toorda; when all the rest of the king's people turned back except two, who remained with me as guides to Jarra.

Feb. 15th. I departed from Toorda, and about two o'clock came to a considerable town called Funingkedy. As we approached the town the inhabitants were much alarmed; for, as one of my guides wore a turban, they mistook us for some Moorish banditti. This misapprehension was soon cleared up, and we were well received by a Gambia Slatee, who resides at this town, and at whose house we lodged.

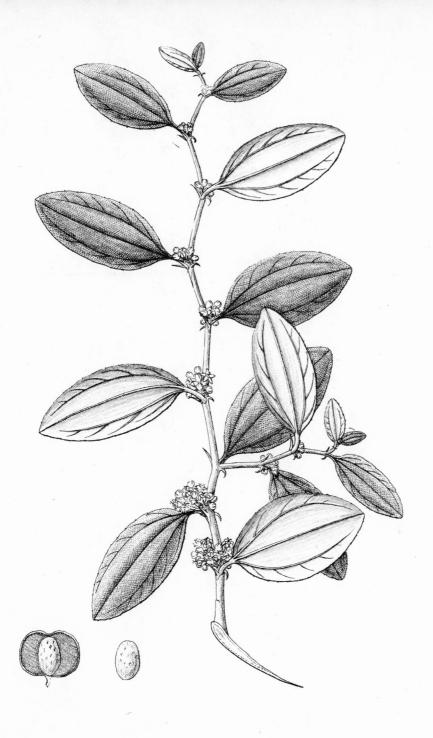

Rhamnus Lotus.

Published as the Act directs, by George Nicol, Pall Mall, January 1.1799.

McKenzie sculp.^t

Feb. 16th. We were informed that a number of people would go from this town to Jarra on the day following ; and as the road was much infested by the Moors, we resolved to stay and accompany the travellers. In the meantime we were told, that a few days before our arrival, most of the Bushreens and people of property in Funingkedy had gone to Jarra, to consult about removing their families and effects to that town, for fear of the approaching war ; and that the Moors, in their absence, had stolen some of their cattle.

About two o'clock, as I was lying asleep upon a bullock's hide behind the door of the hut, I was awakened by the screams of women, and a general clamour and confusion among the inhabitants. At first I suspected that the Bambarrans had actually entered the town ; but observing my boy upon the top of one of the huts, I called to him to know what was the matter. He informed me that the Moors were come a second time to steal the cattle, and that they were now close to the town. I mounted the roof of the hut, and observed a large herd of bullocks coming towards the town, followed by five Moors on horseback, who drove the cattle forward with their muskets. When they had reached the wells, which are close to the town, the Moors selected from the herd sixteen of the finest beasts, and drove them off at full gallop. During this transaction, the townspeople, to the number of five hundred, stood collected close to the walls of the town ; and when the Moors drove the cattle away, though they passed within pistol-shot of them, the inhabitants scarcely made a shew of resistance. I only saw four muskets fired, which, being loaded with gunpowder of the

Negroes' own manufacture, did no execution. Shortly after this I observed a number of people supporting a young man upon horseback, and conducting him slowly towards the town. This was one of the herdsmen, who, attempting to throw his spear, had been wounded by a shot from one of the Moors. His mother walked on before, quite frantic with grief, clapping her hands, and enumerating the good qualities of her son. *Ee maffo fonio*, (he never told a lie) said the disconsolate mother, as her wounded son was carried in at the gate—*Ee maffo fonio abada* (he never told a lie; no, never.) When they had conveyed him to his hut, and laid him upon a mat, all the spectators joined in lamenting his fate, by screaming and howling in the most piteous manner.

After their grief had subsided a little, I was desired to examine the wound. I found that the ball had passed quite through his leg, having fractured both bones a little below the knee: the poor boy was faint from the loss of blood, and his situation withal so very precarious, that I could not console his relations with any great hopes of his recovery. However, to give him a possible chance, I observed to them that it was necessary to cut off his leg above the knee; this proposal made every one start with horror: they had never heard of such a method of cure, and would by no means give their consent to it; indeed they evidently considered me as a sort of cannibal for proposing so cruel and unheard of an operation, which in their opinion would be attended with more pain and danger than the wound itself. The patient was therefore committed to the care of some old Bushreens, who endeavoured to secure him a passage into Paradise, by whispering in his ear some Arabic sentences, and desiring him to repeat them. After many unsuccessful attempts, the poor Heathen at last pronounced, *la illah el allah, Mahamet rasowl allahi*,* and the disciples of the Prophet assured his mother that her son had given sufficient evidence of his faith, and would be happy in a future state. He died the same evening.

Feb. 17th. My guides informed me, that in order to avoid the Moorish banditti, it was necessary to travel in the night; we accordingly departed from Funingkedy in the afternoon, accompanied by about thirty people, carrying their effects with them into Ludamar, for fear of the war. We travelled with great silence and expedition until midnight, when we stopped in a sort of inclosure, near a small village; but the thermometer being so low as 68°, none of the Negroes could sleep on account of the cold.

At daybreak on the 18th, we resumed our journey, and at eight o'clock passed *Simbing*, the frontier village of Ludamar, situated in a narrow pass between two rocky hills, and surrounded with a high wall. From this village Major Houghton (being deserted by his Negro servants, who refused to follow him into the Moorish country) wrote his last letter with a pencil to Dr. Laidley. This brave but unfortunate man, having surmounted many difficulties, had taken a northerly direction, and endeavoured to pass through the kingdom of Ludamar, where I afterwards learned the following particulars concerning his me-

---

* There is but one god, and Mahomet is his Prophet.

lancholy fate. On his arrival at Jarra, he got acquainted with certain Moorish merchants who were travelling to Tisheet (a place near the salt pits in the great Desert, ten days' journey to the northward) to purchase salt ; and the Major, at the expence of a musket and some tobacco, engaged them to convey him thither. It is impossible to form any other opinion on this determination, than that the Moors intentionally deceived him, either with regard to the route that he wished to pursue, or the state of the intermediate country between Jarra and Tombuctoo. Their intention probably was to rob and leave him in the Desert. At the end of two days he suspected their treachery, and insisted on returning to Jarra. Finding him persist in this determination, the Moors robbed him of every thing he possessed, and went off with their camels ; the poor Major being thus deserted, returned on foot to a watering place in possession of the Moors, called Tarra. He had been some days without food, and the unfeeling Moors refusing to give him any, he sunk at last under his distresses. Whether he actually perished of hunger, or was murdered outright by the savage Mahomedans, is not certainly known ; his body was dragged into the woods, and I was shewn at a distance, the spot where his remains were left to perish.

About four miles to the north of Simbing, we came to a small stream of water, where we observed a number of wild horses : they were all of one colour, and galloped away from us at an easy rate, frequently stopping and looking back. The Negroes hunt them for food, and their flesh is much esteemed.

About noon we arrived at Jarra, a large town situated at the bottom of some rocky hills. But before I proceed to describe the place itself, and relate the various occurrences which befel me there, it will not be improper to give my readers a brief recital of the origin of the war which induced me to take this route ; an unfortunate determination, the immediate cause of all the misfortunes and calamities which afterward befel me. The recital which I propose to give in this place, will prevent interruptions hereafter.

This war, which desolated Kaarta soon after I had left that kingdom, and spread terror into many of the neighbouring states, arose in the following manner. A few bullocks belonging to a frontier village of Bambarra having been stolen by a party of Moors, were sold to the Dooty, or chief man, of a town in Kaarta. The villagers claimed their cattle, and being refused satisfaction, complained of the Dooty to their sovereign, Mansong, King of Bambarra, who probably beheld with an eye of jealousy the growing prosperity of Kaarta, and availed himself of this incident to declare hostilities against that kingdom.

With this view he sent a messenger and a party of horsemen to Daisy King of Kaarta, to inform him that the King of Bambarra, with nine thousand men, would visit Kemmoo in the course of the dry season ; and to desire that he (Daisy) would direct his slaves to sweep the houses, and have every thing ready for their accommodation. The messenger concluded this insulting notification by presenting the king with a pair of *iron sandals;* at the same time adding, that " until such time as Daisy had worn out these sandals in his flight, he should never be secure from the arrows of Bambarra."

P

Daisy, having consulted with his chief men about the best means of repelling so formidable an enemy, returned an answer of defiance, and made a Bushreen write in Arabic, upon a piece of thin board, a sort of proclamation, which was suspended to a tree in the public square; and a number of aged men were sent to different places to explain it to the common people. This proclamation called upon all the friends of Daisy to join him immediately; but to such as had no arms, or were afraid to enter into the war, permission was given to retire into any of the neighbouring kingdoms; and it was added, that provided they observed a strict neutrality, they should always be welcome to return to their former habitations; if, however, they took any active part against Kaarta, they had then " broken the key of their huts, and could never afterwards enter the door." Such was the expression.

This proclamation was very generally applauded: but many of the Kaartans, and amongst others the powerful tribes of Jower and Kakaroo, availing themselves of the indulgent clause, retired from Daisy's dominions, and took refuge in Ludamar and Kasson. By means of these desertions, Daisy's army was not so numerous as might have been expected; and when I was at Kemmoo, the whole number of effective men, according to report, did not exceed four thousand; but they were men of spirit and enterprize, and could be depended on.

On the 22d of February (four days after my arrival at Jarra), Mansong, with his army, advanced towards Kemmoo; and Daisy, without hazarding a battle, retired to Joko, a town to the north-west of Kemmoo, where he remained three days, and then took

refuge in a strong town called Gedingooma, situated in the hilly
country, and surrounded with high walls of stone. When Daisy
departed from Joko, his sons refused to follow him, alledging
that " the singing-men would publish their disgrace, as soon as
it should be known that Daisy and his family had fled from Joko
without firing a gun." They were therefore left behind with
a number of horsemen to defend Joko; but, after many skir-
mishes, they were totally defeated, and one of Daisy's sons taken
prisoner; the remainder fled to Gedingooma, which Daisy had
stored with provisions, and where he determined to make his
final stand.

Mansong, finding that Daisy was determined to avoid a
pitched battle, placed a strong force at Joko to watch his motions, and separating the remainder of his army into small
detachments, ordered them to over-run the country, and seize
upon the inhabitants, before they had time to escape. These
orders were executed with such promptitude, that in a few
days the whole kingdom of Kaarta became a scene of desolation. Most of the poor inhabitants of the different towns and
villages, being surprised in the night, fell an easy prey; and
their corn, and every thing which could be useful to Daisy, was
burnt and destroyed. During these transactions, Daisy was
employed in fortifying Gedingooma: this town is built in a
narrow pass between two high hills, having only two gates, one
towards Kaarta, and the other towards Jaffnoo; the gate
towards Kaarta, was defended by Daisy in person; and that towards Jaffnoo was committed to the charge of his sons. When
the army of Bambarra approached the town, they made some

attempts to storm it; but were always driven back with great loss; and Mansong, finding Daisy more formidable than he expected, resolved to cut off his supplies, and starve him into submission. He accordingly sent all the prisoners he had taken, into Bambarra; and having collected a considerable quantity of provisions, remained with his army two whole months in the vicinity of Gedingooma, without doing any thing decisive. During this time he was much harassed by sallies from the besieged; and his stock of provisions being nearly exhausted, he sent to Ali, the Moorish King of Ludamar, for two hundred horsemen, to enable him to make an attack upon the north gate of the town, and give the Bambarrans an opportunity of storming the place. Ali, though he had made an agreement with Mansong at the commencement of the war, to afford him assistance, now refused to fulfil his engagement; which so enraged Mansong, that he marched part of his army to Funingkedy, with a view to surprise the camp of Benowm; but the Moors having received intelligence of his design, fled to the northward; and Mansong, without attempting any thing farther, returned to Sego. This happened while I was myself in captivity in Ali's camp, as will hereafter be seen.

As the King of Kaarta had now got quit of his most formidable antagonist, it might have been hoped that peace would have been restored to his dominions; but an extraordinary incident involved him, immediately afterward, in hostilities with Kasson; the king of which country dying about that time, the succession was disputed by his two sons. The younger (Sambo Sego, my old acquaintance) prevailed; and drove his brother from the country. He fled to Gedingooma; and being pursued thither, Daisy, who had lived in constant friendship with both the brothers, refused to deliver him up; at the same time declaring that he would not support his claim, nor any way interfere in the quarrel. Sambo Sego, elated with success, and proud of the homage that was paid him as sovereign of Kasson, was much displeased with Daisy's conduct, and joined with some disaffected fugitive Kaartans in a plundering expedition against him. Daisy, who little expected such a visit, had sent a number of people to Joko, to plant corn, and collect together such cattle as they might find straying in the woods, in order to supply his army. All these people fell into the hands of Sambo Sego, who carried them to Kooniakary, and afterwards sent them in caravans, to be sold to the French at Fort Louis, on the river Senegal.

This attack was soon retaliated; for Daisy, who was now in distress for want of provisions, thought he was justified in supplying himself from the plunder of Kasson. He accordingly took with him eight hundred of his best men, and marching secretly through the woods, surprised, in the night, three large villages near Kooniakary, in which many of his traitorous subjects, who were in Sambo's expedition, had taken up their residence; all these, and indeed all the able men that fell into Daisy's hands, were immediately put to death.

After this expedition, Daisy began to indulge the hopes of peace; many of his discontented subjects had returned to their allegiance, and were repairing the towns which had been desolated by the war; the rainy season was approaching; and every thing wore a favourable appearance, when he was suddenly attacked from a different quarter.

The Jowers, Kakaroos, and some other Kaartans, who had deserted from him at the commencement of the war, and had shewn a decided preference to Mansong and his army during the whole campaign, were now afraid or ashamed to ask forgiveness of Daisy, and being very powerful in themselves, joined together to make war upon him. They solicited the Moors to assist them in their rebellion (as will appear hereafter) and having collected a considerable army, they plundered a large village belonging to Daisy, and carried off a number of prisoners.

Daisy immediately prepared to revenge this insult; but the Jowers, and indeed almost all the Negro inhabitants of Ludamar, deserted their towns and fled to the eastward; and the rainy season put an end to the war of Kaarta, which had enriched a few individuals, but destroyed the happiness of thousands.

Such was the state of affairs among the nations in the neighbourhood of Jarra, soon after the period of my arrival there. I shall now proceed, after giving some description of that place, with the detail of events as they occurred.

CHAPTER IX.

Some Account of Jarra, and the Moorish Inhabitants.—The Author applies for, and obtains Permission from Ali, the Moorish Chief or Sovereign, of Ludamar, to pass through his Territories. —Departs from Jarra, and arrives at Deena—ill treated by the Moors.—Proceeds to Sampaka—finds a Negro who makes Gunpowder.—Continues his Journey to Samee, where he is seized by some Moors who are sent for that Purpose by Ali—is conveyed a Prisoner to the Moorish Camp at Benowm, on the Borders of the Great Desert.

THE town of Jarra is of considerable extent: the houses are built of clay and stone intermixed; the clay answering the purpose of mortar. It is situated in the Moorish kingdom of Ludamar; but the major part of the inhabitants are Negroes, from the borders of the southern states, who prefer a precarious protection under the Moors, which they purchase by a tribute, rather than continue exposed to their predatory hostilities. The tribute they pay is considerable; and they manifest towards their Moorish superiors the most unlimited obedience and submission, and are treated by them with the utmost indignity and contempt. The Moors of this, and the other states adjoining the country of the Negroes, resemble in their persons the Mulattoes of the West Indies to so great a degree, as not easily to

be distinguished from them ; and in truth, the present generation seem to be a mixed race between the Moors (properly
so called) of the North, and the Negroes of the South ; possessing many of the worst qualities of both nations.

Of the origin of these Moorish tribes, as distinguished from
the inhabitants of Barbary, from whom they are divided by the
Great Desert, nothing farther seems to be known than what
is related by John Leo, the African ; whose account may be
abridged as follows :

Before the Arabian Conquest, about the middle of the seventh
century, all the inhabitants of Africa, whether they were descended from Numidians, Phœnicians, Carthaginians, Romans,
Vandals, or Goths, were comprehended under the general name
of *Mauri*, or Moors. All these nations were converted to the
religion of Mahomet, during the Arabian empire under the
Kaliphs. About this time many of the Numidian tribes, who
led a wandering life in the Desert, and supported themselves
upon the produce of their cattle, retired southward across the
Great Desert, to avoid the fury of the Arabians ; and by one of
those tribes, says Leo, (that of Zanhaga) were discovered and
conquered the Negro nations on the Niger. By the Niger, is
here undoubtedly meant the river of Senegal, which in the
Mandingo language is called *Bafing*, or the Black River.

To what extent these people are now spread over the African
continent, it is difficult to ascertain. There is reason to believe,
that their dominion stretches from West to East, in a narrow
line or belt, from the mouth of the Senegal (on the northern side
of that river) to the confines of Abyssinia. They are a subtle

and treacherous race of people; and take every opportunity of cheating and plundering the credulous and unsuspecting Negroes. But their manners and general habits of life will be best explained, as incidents occur in the course of my narrative.

On my arrival at Jarra, I obtained a lodging at the house of Daman Jumma, a Gambia Slatee. This man had formerly borrowed goods from Dr. Laidley, who had given me an order for the money, to the amount of six slaves; and though the debt was of five years standing, he readily acknowledged it, and promised me what money he could raise. He was afraid, he said, in his present situation, he could not pay more than two slaves' value. He gave me his assistance however in exchanging my beads and amber for gold, which was a more portable article, and more easily concealed from the Moors.

The difficulties we had already encountered, the unsettled state of the country, and, above all, the savage and overbearing deportment of the Moors, had so completely frightened my attendants, that they declared they would rather relinquish every claim to reward, than proceed one step farther to the eastward. Indeed the danger they incurred of being seized by the Moors, and sold into slavery, became every day more apparent; and I could not condemn their apprehensions. In this situation, deserted by my attendants, and reflecting that my retreat was cut off by the war behind me, and that a Moorish country of ten days' journey lay before me, I applied to Daman to obtain permission from Ali, the chief or sovereign of Ludamar, that I might pass through his country unmolested, into Bambarra; and I hired one of Daman's slaves to accompany me thither, as

Q

soon as such permission should be obtained. A messenger was
dispatched to Ali, who at this time was encamped near Benowm;
and as a present was necessary, in order to insure success, I sent
him five garments of cotton cloth, which I purchased of Daman,
for one of my fowling-pieces. Fourteen days elapsed in settling
this affair; but, on the evening of the 26th of February, one of
Ali's slaves arrived with directions, as he pretended, to conduct
me in safety, as far as Goomba; and told me I was to pay him
one garment of blue cotton cloth for his attendance. My faithful boy observing that I was about to proceed ·without him,
resolved to accompany me; and told me, that though he wished
me to turn back, he never had entertained any serious thoughts
of deserting me, but had been advised to it by Johnson, with
a view to induce me to return immediately for Gambia.

Feb. 27th. I delivered most of my papers to Johnson, to
convey them to Gambia as soon as possible, reserving a dupli-
cate for myself, in case of accidents. I likewise left in Daman's
possession a bundle of clothes, and other things that were not
absolutely necessary; for I wished to diminish my baggage as
much as possible, that the Moors might have fewer induce-
ments to plunder us.

Things being thus adjusted, we departed from Jarra in the
forenoon, and slept at Troomgoomba, a small walled village,
inhabited by a mixture of Negroes and Moors. On the day
following (Feb. 28th) we reached Quira; and on the 29th,
after a toilsome journey over a sandy country, we came to
Compe, a watering place belonging to the Moors; from whence
on the morning following, we proceeded to Deena, a large town,

and, like Jarra, built of stone and clay. The Moors are here in greater proportion to the Negroes than at Jarra. They assembled round the hut of the Negro where I lodged, and treated me with the greatest insolence: they hissed, shouted, and abused me; they even spit in my face, with a view to irritate me, and afford them a pretext for seizing my baggage. But, finding such insults had not the desired effect, they had recourse to the final and decisive argument, that I was a Christian, and of course that my property was lawful plunder to the followers of Mahomet. They accordingly opened my bundles, and robbed me of every thing they fancied. My attendants finding that every body could rob me with impunity, insisted on returning to Jarra.

The day following (March 2d) I endeavoured, by all the means in my power, to prevail upon my people to go on; but they still continued obstinate; and having reason to fear some further insult from the fanatic Moors, I resolved to proceed alone. Accordingly the next morning, about two o'clock I departed from Deena. It was moonlight; but the roaring of the wild beasts made it necessary to proceed with caution.

When I had reached a piece of rising ground about half a mile from the town, I heard somebody halloo, and looking back, saw my faithful boy running after me. He informed me, that Ali's man had gone back to Benowm, and that Daman's Negro was about to depart for Jarra; but he said he had no doubt, if I would stop a little, that he could persuade the latter to accompany us. I waited accordingly, and in about an hour the boy returned with the Negro; and we continued travelling over

Q 2

a sandy country, covered with *asclepias gigantica,* until mid-day, when we came to a number of deserted huts ; and seeing some appearances of water at a little distance, I sent the boy to fill a soofroo ; but as he was examining the place for water, the roaring of a lion, that was probably on the same pursuit, induced the frightened boy to return in haste, and we submitted patiently to the disappointment. In the afternoon we reached a town inhabited chiefly by Foulahs, called Samamingkoos.

Next morning (March 4th) we set out for Sampaka ; which place we reached about two o'clock. On the road we observed immense quantities of locusts: the trees were quite black with them. These insects devour every vegetable that comes in their way, and in a short time completely strip a tree of its leaves. The noise of their excrement falling upon the leaves and withered grass, very much resembles a shower of rain. When a tree is shaken or struck, it is astonishing to see what a cloud of them will fly off. In their flight they yield to the current of the wind, which at this season of the year is always from the N. E. Should the wind shift, it is difficult to conceive where they could collect food, as the whole of their course was marked with desolation.

Sampaka is a large town, and when the Moors and Bambarrans were at war, was thrice attacked by the former ; but they were driven off with great loss, though the King of Bambarra was afterwards obliged to give up this, and all the other towns as far as Goomba, in order to obtain a peace. Here I lodged at the house of a Negro who practised the art of making gunpowder. He shewed me a bag of nitre, very white, but the crystals were much smaller than common. They procure it in considerable quantities from the ponds which are filled in the rainy season, and to which the cattle resort for coolness during the heat of the day. When the water is evaporated, a white efflorescence is observed on the mud, which the natives collect and purify in such a manner as to answer their purpose. The Moors supply them with sulphur from the Mediterranean; and the process is completed by pounding the different articles together in a wooden mortar. The grains are very unequal, and the sound of its explosion is by no means so sharp as that produced by European gunpowder.

March 5th. We departed from Sampaka at daylight. About noon we stopped a little at a village called Dangali; and in the evening arrived at Dalli. We saw upon the road two large herds of camels feeding. When the Moors turn their camels to feed, they tie up one of their fore legs, to prevent their straying. This happened to be a feast day at Dalli, and the people were dancing before the Dooti's house. But when they were informed that a white man was come into the town, they left off dancing, and came to the place where I lodged, walking in regular order, two and two, with the music before them. They play upon a sort of flute; but instead of blowing into a hole in the side, they blow obliquely over the end, which is half shut by a thin piece of wood: they govern the holes on the side with their fingers, and play some simple and very plaintive airs. They continued to dance and sing until midnight: during which time I was surrounded by so great a crowd, as made it necessary for me to satisfy their curiosity, by sitting still.

March 6th. We stopt here this morning, because some of the townspeople, who were going for Goomba on the day following, wished to accompany us; but in order to avoid the crowd of people which usually assembled in the evening, we went to a Negro village to the east of Dalli, called Samee, where we were kindly received by the hospitable Dooti, who on this occasion killed two fine sheep, and invited his friends to come and feast with him.

March 7th. Our landlord was so proud of the honour of entertaining a white man, that he insisted on my staying with him and his friends until the cool of the evening, when he said he would conduct me to the next village. As I was now within two days' journey of Goomba, I had no apprehensions from the Moors, and readily accepted the invitation. I spent the forenoon very pleasantly with these poor Negroes: their company was the more acceptable, as the gentleness of their manners presented a striking contrast to the rudeness and barbarity of the Moors. They enlivened their conversation by drinking a fermented liquor made from corn; the same sort of beer that I have described in a former chapter; and better I never tasted in Great Britain.

In the midst of this harmless festivity, I flattered myself that all danger from the Moors was over. Fancy had already placed me on the banks of the Niger, and presented to my imagination a thousand delightful scenes in my future progress, when a party of Moors unexpectedly entered the hut, and dispelled the golden dream. They came, they said, by Ali's orders, to convey me to his camp at Benowm. If I went peaceably, they told me, I had nothing to fear; but if I refused, they had orders to bring me by force. I was struck dumb by surprise and terror, which the Moors observing, endeavoured to calm my apprehensions, by repeating the assurance that I had nothing to fear. Their visit, they added, was occasioned by the curiosity of Ali's wife, *Fatima*, who had heard so much about Christians, that she was very anxious to see one: as soon as her curiosity should be satisfied, they had no doubt, they said, that Ali would give me a handsome present, and send a person to conduct me to Bambarra. Finding entreaty and resistance equally fruitless, I prepared to follow the messengers, and took leave of my landlord and his company with great reluctance. Accompanied by my faithful boy (for Daman's slave made his escape on seeing the Moors), we reached Dalli in the evening; where we were strictly watched by the Moors during the night.

March 8th. We were conducted by a circuitous path through the woods to Dangali, where we slept.

March 9th. We continued our journey, and in the afternoon arrived at Sampaka. On the road we saw a party of Moors, well armed, who told us that they were hunting for a runaway slave; but the townspeople informed us, that a party of Moors had attempted to steal some cattle from the town in the morning, but were repulsed; and, on their describing the persons, we were satisfied that they were the same banditti that we had seen in the woods.

Next morning (March 10th) we set out for Samaning Koos. On the road we overtook a woman and two boys, with an ass: she informed us that she was going for Bambarra, but had been stopped on the road by a party of Moors, who had taken most of her clothes, and some gold from her ; and that she would be under the necessity of returning to Deena till the fast moon was over. The same evening the new moon was seen, which ushered in the month Rhamadan. Large fires were made in different parts of the town, and a greater quantity of victuals than usual dressed upon the occasion.

March 11th. By daylight the Moors were in readiness ; but as I had suffered much from thirst on the road, I made my boy fill a soofroo of water for my own use ; for the Moors assured me that they should not taste either meat or drink until sunset. However, I found that the excessive heat of the sun, and the dust we raised in travelling, overcame their scruples, and made my soofroo a very useful part of our baggage. On our arrival at Deena, I went to pay my respects to one of Ali's sons. I found him sitting in a low hut, with five or six more of his companions, washing their hands and feet, and frequently taking water into their mouths, gargling, and spitting it out again. I was no sooner seated, than he handed me a double-barreled gun, and told me to dye the stock of a blue colour, and repair one of the locks. I found great difficulty in persuading him that I knew nothing about the matter. However, says he, if you cannot repair the gun, you shall give me some knives and scissars immediately ; and when my boy, who acted as interpreter, assured him that I had no such articles, he hastily snatched up a musket that stood by him, cocked it, and putting the muzzle close to the boy's ear, would certainly have shot him dead upon the spot, had not the Moors wrested the musket from him, and made signs for us to retreat. The boy, being terrified at this treatment, attempted to make his escape in the night, but was prevented by the vigilance of the Moors, who guarded us with strict attention; and at night always went to sleep by the door of the hut, in such a situation that it was almost impossible to pass, without stepping upon them.

March 12. We departed from Deena towards Benowm, and about nine o'clock came to a Korree, whence the Moors were preparing to depart to the southward, on account of the scarcity of water; here we filled our soofroo, and continued our journey over a hot sandy country, covered with small stunted shrubs, until about one o'clock, when the heat of the sun obliged us to stop. But our water being expended, we could not prudently remain longer than a few minutes to collect a little gum, which is an excellent succedaneum for water; as it keeps the mouth moist, and allays, for a time, the pain in the throat.

About five o'clock we came in sight of Benowm, the residence of Ali. It presented to the eye a great number of dirty looking tents, scattered, without order, over a large space of ground; and among the tents appeared large herds of camels, cattle, and goats. We reached the skirts of this camp, a little before sunset, and, with much entreaty, procured a little water. My arrival was no sooner observed, than the people who drew water at the wells threw down their buckets; those in the tents mounted their horses; and men, women, and children, came running or galloping towards me. I soon found myself surrounded by such a crowd, that I could scarcely move; one pulled

R

my clothes, another took off my hat, a third stopped me to examine my waistcoat buttons, and a fourth called out, *la illa
el allah Mahamet rasowl allahi,** and signified, in a threatening manner, that I must repeat those words. We reached
at length the king's tent, where we found a great number of
people, men and women, assembled. Ali was sitting upon a black
leather cushion, clipping a few hairs from his upper lip; a female
attendant holding up a looking glass before him. He appeared to
be an old man, of the Arab cast, with a long white beard; and
he had a sullen and indignant aspect. He surveyed me with attention, and inquired of the Moors if I could speak Arabic: being
answered in the negative, he appeared much surprised, and
continued silent. The surrounding attendants, and especially
the ladies, were abundantly more inquisitive: they asked a
thousand questions; inspected every part of my apparel, searched my pockets, and obliged me to unbutton my waistcoat, and
display the whiteness of my skin: they even counted my toes
and fingers, as if they doubted whether I was in truth a human
being. In a little time the priest announced evening prayers;
but before the people departed, the Moor who had acted as
interpreter, informed me that Ali was about to present me
with something to eat; and looking round, I observed some
boys bringing a wild hog, which they tied to one of the tent
strings, and Ali made signs to me to kill and dress it for supper.
Though I was very hungry, I did not think it prudent to eat
any part of an animal so much detested by the Moors, and
therefore told him that I never eat such food. They then

* See page 103.

J. C. Barrow delt. from a Sketch by M. Park.

A VIEW of ALI'S TENT at the CAMP of BENOWM.

J. Mills sculpt.

untied the hog, in hopes that it would run immediately at me; for they believe that a great enmity subsists between hogs and Christians; but in this they were disappointed; for the animal no sooner regained his liberty, than he began to attack indiscriminately every person that came in his way, and at last took shelter under the couch upon which the King was sitting. The assembly being thus dissolved, I was conducted to the tent of Ali's chief slave, but was not permitted to enter, nor allowed to touch any thing belonging to it. I requested something to eat, and a little boiled corn, with salt and water, was at length sent me in a wooden bowl; and a mat was spread upon the sand before the tent, on which I passed the night, surrounded by the curious multitude.

At sunrise, Ali, with a few attendants, came on horseback to visit me, and signified that he had provided a hut for me, where I would be sheltered from the sun. I was accordingly conducted thither, and found the hut comparatively cool and pleasant. It was constructed of corn stalks set up on end, in the form of a square, with a flat roof of the same materials, supported by forked sticks; to one of which was tied the wild hog before mentioned. This animal had certainly been placed there by Ali's order, out of derision to a Christian; and I found it a very disagreeable inmate, as it drew together a number of boys, who amused themselves by beating it with sticks, until they had so irritated the hog that it ran and bit at every person within its reach.

I was no sooner seated in this my new habitation, than the Moors assembled in crowds to behold me; but I found it rather a troublesome levee, for I was obliged to take off one of my stockings, and show them my foot, and even to take off my jacket and waistcoat, to show them how my clothes were put on and off; they were much delighted with the curious contrivance of buttons. All this was to be repeated to every succeeding visitor; for such as had already seen these wonders, insisted on their friends seeing the same; and in this manner I was employed, dressing and undressing, buttoning and unbuttoning, from noon to night. About eight o'clock, Ali sent me for supper, some kouskous and salt and water, which was very acceptable, being the only victuals I had tasted since morning.

I observed that, in the night, the Moors kept regular watch, and frequently looked into the hut, to see if I was asleep, and if it was quite dark, they would light a wisp of grass. About two o'clock in the morning, a Moor entered the hut, probably with a view to steal something, or perhaps to murder me; and groping about, he laid his hand upon my shoulder. As night visitors were at best but suspicious characters, I sprang up the moment he laid his hand upon me; and the Moor, in his haste to get off, stumbled over my boy, and fell with his face upon the wild hog, which returned the attack by biting the Moor's arm. The screams of this man alarmed the people in the King's tent, who immediately conjectured that I had made my escape, and a number of them mounted their horses, and prepared to pursue me. I observed upon this occasion that Ali did not sleep in his own tent, but came galloping upon a white horse from a small tent at a considerable distance; indeed, the tyrannical and cruel behaviour of this man made him so jealous of every person around him, that even his own slaves and domestics knew not where he slept. When the Moors had explained to him the cause of this outcry, they all went away, and I was permitted to sleep quietly until morning.

March 13th. With the returning day commenced the same round of insult and irritation: the boys assembled to beat the hog, and the men and women to plague the Christian. It is impossible for me to describe the behaviour of a people who study mischief as a science, and exult in the miseries and misfortunes of their fellow-creatures. It is sufficient to observe, that the rudeness, ferocity, and fanaticism, which distinguish the Moors from the rest of mankind, found here a proper subject whereon to exercise their propensities. I was a *stranger*, I was *unprotected*, and I was a *Christian;* each of these circumstances is sufficient to drive every spark of humanity from the heart of a Moor; but when all of them, as in my case, were combined in the same person, and a suspicion prevailed withal, that I had come as a *spy* into the country, the reader will easily imagine that, in such a situation, I had every thing to fear. Anxious, however, to conciliate favour, and, if possible, to afford the Moors no pretence for ill treating me, I readily complied with every command, and patiently bore every insult; but never did any period of my life pass away so heavily: from sunrise to sunset, was I obliged to suffer, with an unruffled countenance, the insults of the rudest savages on earth.

CHAPTER X.

*Various Occurrences during the Author's Confinement at Benowm
—is visited by some Moorish Ladies.—A Funeral and Wedding.—The Author receives an extraordinary Present from the
Bride.—Other Circumstances illustrative of the Moorish Character and Manners.*

T<small>HE</small> Moors, though very indolent themselves, are rigid task-
masters, and keep every person under them in full employment.
My boy Demba was sent to the woods to collect withered grass
for Ali's horses; and after a variety of projects concerning myself, they at last found out an employment for me: this was
no other than the respectable office of *barber.* I was to make
my first exhibition in this capacity in the royal presence, and
to be honoured with the task of shaving the head of the young
prince of Ludamar. I accordingly seated myself upon the sand,
and the boy, with some hesitation, sat down beside me. A small
razor, about three inches long, was put into my hand, and I
was ordered to proceed; but whether from my own want of
skill, or the improper shape of the instrument, I unfortunately
made a slight incision in the boy's head, at the very commencement of the operation; and the King observing the awkward
manner in which I held the razor, concluded that his son's

head was in very improper hands, and ordered me to resign the razor, and walk out of the tent. This I considered as a very fortunate circumstance; for I had laid it down as a rule, to make myself as useless and insignificant as possible, as the only means of recovering my liberty.

March 18. Four Moors arrived from Jarra with Johnson my interpreter, having seized him before he had received any intimation of my confinement; and bringing with them a bundle of clothes that I had left at Daman Jumma's house, for my use in case I should return by the way of Jarra. Johnson was led into Ali's tent and examined; the bundle was opened, and I was sent for, to explain the use of the different articles. I was happy, however, to find that Johnson had committed my papers to the charge of one of Daman's wives. When I had satisfied Ali's curiosity respecting the different articles of apparel, the bundle was again tied up, and put into a large cow-skin bag, that stood in a corner of the tent. The same evening Ali sent three of his people to inform me, that there were many thieves in the neighbourhood, and that to prevent the rest of my things from being stolen, it was necessary to convey them all into his tent. My clothes, instruments, and every thing that belonged to me, were accordingly carried away; and though the heat and dust made clean linen very necessary and refreshing, I could not procure a single shirt out of the small stock I had brought along with me. Ali was however disappointed, by not finding among my effects the quantity of gold and amber that he expected; but to make sure of every thing, he sent the same people, on the morning following, to examine whether I had any thing concealed about my

person.   They, with their usual rudeness, searched every part of
my apparel, and stripped me of all my gold, amber, my watch,
and one of my pocket compasses; I had fortunately, in the night,
buried the other compass in the sand; and this, with the clothes
I had on, was all that the tyranny of Ali had now left me.

The gold and amber were highly gratifying to Moorish
avarice, but the pocket compass soon became an object of superstitious curiosity.   Ali was very desirous to be informed, why
that small piece of iron, the needle, always pointed to the Great
Desert; and I found myself somewhat puzzled to answer the
question.   To have pleaded my ignorance, would have created a
suspicion that I wished to conceal the real truth from him; I
therefore told him, that my mother resided far beyond the sands
of Zaharra, and that whilst she was alive the piece of iron would
always point that way, and serve as a guide to conduct me to
her, and that if she was dead it would point to her grave.   Ali
now looked at the compass with redoubled amazement; turned
it round and round repeatedly; but observing that it always
pointed the same way, he took it up with great caution and
returned it to me, manifesting that he thought there was
something of magic in it, and that he was afraid of keeping
so dangerous an instrument in his possession.

March 20th.   This morning a council of chief men was held
in Ali's tent respecting me: their decisions, though they were
all unfavourable to me, were differently related by different
persons.   Some said that they intended to put me to death;
others that I was only to lose my right hand; but the most
probable account was that which I received from Ali's own son,

a boy about nine years of age, who came to me in the evening, and, with much concern, informed me that his uncle had persuaded his father to put out my eyes, which they said resembled those of a cat, and that all the Bushreens had approved of this measure. His father however, he said, would not put the sentence into execution until Fatima the queen, who was at present in the north, had seen me.

March 21st. Anxious to know my destiny, I went to the king early in the morning; and as a number of Bushreens were assembled, I thought this a favourable opportunity of discovering their intentions. I therefore began by begging his permission to return to Jarra; which was flatly refused: his wife, he said, had not yet seen me, and I must stay until she came to Benowm, after which I should be at liberty to depart; and that my horse, which had been taken away from me the day after I arrived, should be again restored to me. Unsatisfactory as this answer was, I was forced to appear pleased; and as there was little hopes of making my escape, at this season of the year, on account of the excessive heat, and the total want of water in the woods, I resolved to wait patiently until the rains had set in, or until some more favourable opportunity should present itself;— but *hope deferred maketh the heart sick.* This tedious procrastination from day to day, and the thoughts of travelling through the Negro kingdoms in the rainy season, which was now fast approaching, made me very melancholy; and having passed a restless night, I found myself attacked, in the morning, by a smart fever. I had wrapped myself close up in my cloak, with a view to induce perspiration, and was asleep when a party of Moors en-

S

tered the hut, and with their usual rudeness pulled the cloak from me. I made signs to them that I was sick, and wished much to sleep; but I solicited in vain: my distress was matter of sport to them, and they endeavoured to heighten it, by every means in their power. This studied and degrading insolence, to which I was constantly exposed, was one of the bitterest ingredients in the cup of captivity; and often made life itself a burthen to me. In those distressing moments I have frequently envied the situation of the slave; who, amidst all his calamities, could still possess the enjoyment of his own thoughts; a happiness to which I had, for some time, been a stranger. Wearied out with such continual insults, and perhaps a little peevish from the fever, I trembled lest my passion might unawares overleap the bounds of prudence, and spur me to some sudden act of resentment, when death must be the inevitable consequence. In this perplexity, I left my hut, and walked to some shady trees at a little distance from the camp, where I lay down. But even here, persecution followed me; and solitude was thought too great an indulgence for a distressed Christian. Ali's son, with a number of horsemen, came galloping to the place, and ordered me to rise and follow them. I begged they would allow me to remain where I was, if it was only for a few hours; but they paid little attention to what I said; and after a few threatening words, one of them pulled out a pistol from a leather bag, that was fastened to the pummel of his saddle, and presenting it towards me, snapped it twice. He did this with so much indifference, that I really doubted whether the pistol was loaded; he cocked it a third time, and was striking the flint with a piece of steel, when I begged them to desist, and returned with them to the camp. When we entered Ali's tent, we found him much out of humour. He called for the Moor's pistol, and amused himself for some time with opening and shutting the pan; at length, taking up his powder horn, he fresh primed it; and turning round to me with a menacing look, said something in Arabic, which I did not understand. I desired my boy, who was sitting before the tent, to inquire what offence I had committed; when I was informed that having gone out of the camp without Ali's permission, they suspected that I had some design of making my escape; and that, in future, if I was seen without the skirts of the camp, orders had been given that I should be shot by the first person that observed me.

In the afternoon the horizon, to the eastward, was thick and hazy, and the Moors prognosticated a sand wind; which accordingly commenced on the morning following, and lasted, with slight intermissions, for two days. The force of the wind was not in itself very great: it was what a seaman would have denominated a *stiff breeze;* but the quantity of sand and dust carried before it, was such as to darken the whole atmosphere. It swept along from east to west, in a thick and constant stream, and the air was at times so dark and full of sand, that it was difficult to discern the neighbouring tents. As the Moors always dress their victuals in the open air, this sand fell in great plenty amongst the kouskous: it readily adhered to the skin, when moistened by perspiration, and formed a cheap and universal hair powder. The Moors wrap a cloth round their face, to prevent them from inhaling the sand, and always turn their

backs to the wind when they look up, to prevent the sand falling into their eyes.

About this time, all the women of the camp had their feet,
and the ends of their fingers, stained of a dark saffron colour.
I could never ascertain whether this was done from motives of
religion, or by way of ornament. The curiosity of the Moorish
ladies had been very troublesome to me ever since my arrival
at Benowm; and on the evening of the 25th (whether from
the instigation of others, or impelled by their own ungovernable curiosity, or merely out of frolic, I cannot affirm) a party
of them came into my hut, and gave me plainly to understand
that the object of their visit was to ascertain, by actual inspection, whether the rite of circumcision extended to the Nazarenes,
(Christians,) as well as to the followers of Mahomet. The
reader will easily judge of my surprise at this unexpected declaration; and in order to avoid the proposed scrutiny, I thought
it best to treat the business jocularly. I observed to them, that
it was not customary in my country to give ocular demonstration in such cases, before so many beautiful women; but that if
all of them would retire, except the young lady to whom I pointed, (selecting the youngest and handsomest), I would satisfy her
curiosity. The ladies enjoyed the jest; and went away laughing
heartily; and the young damsel herself to whom I had given
the preference, (though she did not avail herself of the privi-
lege of inspection), seemed no way displeased at the compli-
ment; for she soon afterwards sent me some meal and milk for
my supper.

March 28th. This morning a large herd of cattle arrived

from the eastward; and one of the drivers, to whom Ali had lent my horse, came into my hut with the leg of an antelope as a present, and told me that my horse was standing before Ali's tent. In a little time Ali sent one of his slaves to inform me, that, in the afternoon, I must be in readiness to ride out with him, as he intended to shew me to some of his women.

About four o'clock, Ali, with six of his courtiers, came riding to my hut, and told me to follow them. I readily complied. But here a new difficulty occurred: the Moors, accustomed to a loose and easy dress, could not reconcile themselves to the appearance of my *nankeen breeches*, which they said were not only inelegant, but, on account of their tightness, very indecent; and as this was a visit to ladies, Ali ordered my boy to bring out the loose cloak which I had always worn since my arrival at Benowm, and told me to wrap it close round me. We visited the tents of four different ladies, at every one of which I was presented with a bowl of milk and water. All these ladies were remarkably corpulent, which is considered here as the highest mark of beauty. They were very inquisitive, and examined my hair and skin with great attention; but affected to consider me as a sort of inferior being to themselves, and would knit their brows, and seem to shudder, when they looked at the whiteness of my skin. In the course of this evening's excursion, my dress and appearance afforded infinite mirth to the company, who galloped round me as if they were baiting a wild animal; twirling their muskets round their heads, and exhibiting various feats of activity and horsemanship, seemingly to display their superior prowess over a miserable captive.

The Moors are certainly very good horsemen. They ride without fear; their saddles, being high before and behind, afford them a very secure seat; and if they chance to fall, the whole country is so soft and sandy, that they are very seldom hurt. Their greatest pride, and one of their principal amusements, is to put the horse to his full speed, and then stop him with a sudden jerk, so as frequently to bring him down upon his haunches. Ali always rode upon a milk-white horse, with its tail dyed red. He never walked, unless when he went to say his prayers; and even in the night, two or three horses were always kept ready saddled, at a little distance from his own tent. The Moors set a very high value upon their horses; for it is by their superior fleetness that they are enabled to make so many predatory excursions into the Negro countries. They feed them three or four times a day, and generally give them a large quantity of sweet milk in the evening, which the horses appear to relish very much.

April 3d. This forenoon a child, which had been some time sickly, died in the next tent; and the mother and relations immediately began the death howl. They were joined by a number of female visitors, who came on purpose to assist at this melancholy concert. I had no opportunity of seeing the burial, which is generally performed secretly, in the dusk of the evening, and frequently at only a few yards distance from the tent. Over the grave, they plant one particular shrub; and no stranger is allowed to pluck a leaf, or even to touch it; so great a veneration have they for the dead.

April 7th. About four o'clock in the afternoon, a whirlwind passed through the camp, with such violence that it overturned three tents, and blew down one side of my hut. These whirl-winds come from the Great Desert, and, at this season of the year, are so common, that I have seen five or six of them at one time. They carry up quantities of sand to an amazing height, which resemble, at a distance, so many moving pillars of smoke.

The scorching heat of the sun, upon a dry and sandy country, makes the air insufferably hot. Ali having robbed me of my thermometer, I had no means of forming a comparative judg-ment; but in the middle of the day, when the beams of the vertical sun are seconded by the scorching wind from the Desert, the ground is frequently heated to such a degree, as not to be borne by the naked foot; even the Negro slaves, will not run from one tent to another, without their sandals. At this time of the day, the Moors lie stretched at length in their tents, either asleep, or unwilling to move; and I have often felt the wind so hot, that I could not hold my hand in the current of air which came through the crevices of my hut, without feeling sensible pain.

April 8th. This day the wind blew from the south-west, and in the night there was a heavy shower of rain, accompanied with thunder and lightning.

April 10th. In the evening the Tabala, or large drum, was

beat, to announce a wedding, which was held at one of the neighbouring tents. A great number of people of both sexes assembled, but without that mirth and hilarity which take place at a Negro wedding: here there was neither singing, nor dancing; nor any other amusement that I could perceive. A woman was beating the drum, and the other women joining at times, like a chorus, by setting up a shrill scream; and at the same time, moving their tongues from one side of the mouth to the other, with great celerity. I was soon tired, and had returned into my hut, where I was sitting almost asleep, when an old woman entered, with a wooden bowl in her hand, and signified that she had brought me a present from the bride. Before I could recover from the surprise which this message created, the woman discharged the contents of the bowl full in my face. Finding that it was the same sort of holy water, with which, among the Hottentots, a priest is said to sprinkle a new married couple, I began to suspect that the old lady was actuated by mischief, or malice; but she gave me seriously to understand, that it was a nuptial benediction from the bride's own person; and which, on such occasions, is always received by the young unmarried Moors as a mark of distinguished favour. This being the case, I wiped my face, and sent my acknowledgments to the lady. The wedding drum continued to beat, and the women to sing, or rather whistle, all night. About nine in the morning, the bride was brought in state from her mother's tent, attended by a number of women, who carried her tent, (a present from the husband) some bearing up the poles, others holding by the strings; and in this manner they marched, whistling as formerly, until they came to the place appointed for her residence, where they pitched the tent. The husband followed, with a number of men leading four bullocks, which they tied to the tent strings; and having killed another, and distributed the beef among the people, the ceremony was concluded.

T

CHAPTER XI.

Occurrences at the Camp continued.—Information collected by the
Author, concerning Houssa and Tombuctoo; and the Situation
of the latter.—The Route described from Morocco to Benowm.
—The Author's Distress from Hunger.—Ali removes his Camp
to the Northward.—The Author is carried Prisoner to the
new Encampment, and is presented to Queen Fatima.—Great
Distress from the Want of Water.

ONE whole month had now elapsed since I was led into captivity; during which time, each returning day brought me
fresh distresses. I watched the lingering course of the sun with
anxiety, and blessed his evening beams as they shed a yellow
lustre along the sandy floor of my hut; for it was then that my
oppressors left me, and allowed me to pass the sultry night in
solitude and reflection.

About midnight, a bowl of kouskous with some salt and water
was brought for me and my two attendants; this was our common fare, and it was all that was allowed us, to allay the cravings
of hunger, and support nature for the whole of the following
day: for it is to be observed, that this was the Mahomedan Lent;
and as the Moors keep the fast with a religious strictness, they
thought it proper to compel me, though a Christain, to a similar
observance. Time, however, somewhat reconciled me to my

situation : I found that I could bear hunger and thirst better than I expected ; and at length, I endeavoured to beguile the tedious hours, by learning to write Arabic. The people who came to see me, soon made me acquainted with the characters; and I discovered, that by engaging their attention in this way, they were not so troublesome as otherwise they would have been : indeed, when I observed any person whose countenance I thought bore malice towards me, I made it a rule to ask him, either to write in the sand himself, or to decipher what I had already written ; and the pride of shewing his superior attainments, generally induced him to comply with my request.

April 14th. As Queen Fatima had not yet arrived, Ali proposed to go to the north, and bring her back with him ; but as the place was two days' journey from Benowm, it was necessary to have some refreshment on the road ; and Ali, suspicious of those about him, was so afraid of being poisoned, that he never eat any thing but what was dressed under his own immediate inspection. A fine bullock was therefore killed, and the flesh being cut up into thin slices, was dried in the sun ; and this, with two bags of dry kouskous, formed his travelling provisions.

Previous to his departure, the black people of the town of Benowm came, according to their annual custom, to shew their arms, and bring their stipulated tribute of corn and cloth. They were but badly armed ; twenty-two with muskets, forty or fifty with bows and arrows ; and nearly the same number of men and boys, with spears only : they arranged themselves before the tent, where they waited until their arms were examined, and some little disputes settled.

T 2

About midnight on the 16th, Ali departed quietly from Benowm, accompanied by a few attendants. He was expected
to return in the course of nine or ten days.

April 18th. Two days after the departure of Ali, a Shereef
arrived with salt, and some other articles, from Walet, the
capital of the kingdom of Biroo. As there was no tent appropriated for him, he took up his abode in the same hut with me.
He seemed to be a well informed man, and his acquaintance
both with the Arabic and Bambarra tongues, enabled him to
travel, with ease and safety, through a number of kingdoms; for
though his place of residence was Walet, he had visited Houssa,
and had lived some years at Tombuctoo. Upon my inquiring
so particularly about the distance, from Walet to Tombuctoo,
he asked me if I intended to travel that way; and being answered
in the affirmative, he shook his head, and said, *it would not do*;
for that Christians were looked upon there as the devil's
children, and enemies to the Prophet. From him I learned the
following particulars; that Houssa was the largest town he had
ever seen: that Walet was larger than Tombuctoo; but being
remote from the Niger, and its trade consisting chiefly of salt,
it was not so much resorted to by strangers: that between Benowm and Walet was ten days' journey; but the road did not
lead through any remarkable towns, and travellers supported
themselves by purchasing milk from the Arabs, who keep their
herds by the watering-places: two of the days' journies, was
over a sandy country, without water. From Walet to Tombuctoo, was eleven days more; but water was more plentiful, and the journey was usually performed upon bullocks. He

said there were many Jews at Tombuctoo, but they all spoke Arabic, and used the same prayers as the Moors. He frequently pointed his hand to the south-east quarter, or rather the east by south; observing, that Tombuctoo was situated in that direction; and though I made him repeat this information, again and again, I never found him to vary more than half a point, which was to the southward.

April 24th. This morning Shereef Sidi Mahomed Moora Abdalla, a native of Morocco, arrived with five bullocks loaded with salt. He had formerly resided some months at Gibraltar, where he had picked up as much English, as enabled him to make himself understood. He informed me, that he had been five months in coming from Santa Cruz; but that great part of the time had been spent in trading. When I requested him to enumerate the days employed in travelling from Morocco to Benowm, he gave them as follows :—to Swera, three days; to Agadier, three; to Jiniken, ten; to Wadenoon, four; to Lakeneig, five; to Zeeriwin-zeriman, five; to Tisheet, ten; to Benowm, ten; in all fifty days: but travellers usually rest a long while at Jiniken and Tisheet; at the latter of which places they dig the rock salt, which is so great an article of commerce with the Negroes.

In conversing with these Shereefs, and the different strangers that resorted to the camp, I passed my time with rather less uneasiness than formerly. On the other hand, as the dressing of my victuals was now left entirely to the care of Ali's slaves, over whom I had not the smallest control, I found myself but ill supplied, worse even than in the fast month: for two successive nights, they neglected to send us our accustomed meal, and though my boy went to a small Negro town near the camp, and begged with great diligence from hut to hut, he could only procure a few handfuls of ground nuts, which he readily shared with me. Hunger, at first, is certainly a very painful sensation ; but when it has continued for some time, this pain is succeeded by languor and debility; in which case, a draught of water, by keeping the stomach distended, will greatly exhilarate the spirits, and remove for a short time every sort of uneasiness. Johnson and Demba were very much dejected. They lay stretched upon the sand, in a sort of torpid slumber ; and even when the kouskous arrived, I found some difficulty in awakening them. I felt no inclination to sleep, but was affected with a deep convulsive respiration, like constant sighing ; and, what alarmed me still more, a dimness of sight, and a tendency to faint when I attempted to sit up. These symptoms did not go off until some time after I had received nourishment.

We had been for some days in daily expectation of Ali's return from Saheel (or the north country) with his wife Fatima. In the meanwhile Mansong, King of Bambarra, as I have related in Chapter VIII, had sent to Ali for a party of horse to assist in storming Gedingooma. With this demand Ali had not only refused to comply, but had treated the messengers with great haughtiness and contempt ; upon which Mansong gave up all thoughts of taking the town, and prepared to chastize Ali for his contumacy.

Things were in this situation when, on the 29th of April, a messenger arrived at Benowm with the disagreeable intelligence that the Bambarra army was approaching the frontiers of Lu-damar. This threw the whole country into confusion; and in the afternoon Ali's son with about twenty horsemen arrived at Benowm. He ordered all the cattle to be driven away imme-diately, all the tents to be struck, and the people to hold them-selves in readiness to depart at daylight the next morning.

April 30th. At daybreak the whole camp was in motion. The baggage was carried upon bullocks, the two tent poles being placed one on each side, and the different wooden articles of the tent distributed in like manner; the tent cloth was thrown over all, and upon this was commonly placed one or two women; for the Moorish women are very bad walkers. The king's fa-vourite concubines rode upon camels, with a saddle of a parti-cular construction, and a canopy to shelter them from the sun. We proceeded to the northward until noon, when the king's son ordered the whole company, except two tents, to enter a thick low wood, which was upon our right. I was sent along with the two tents, and arrived in the evening at a Negro town called Farani: here we pitched the tents in an open place, at no great distance from the town.

The hurry and confusion which attended this decampment, prevented the slaves from dressing the usual quantity of victuals; and lest their dry provisions should be exhausted before they reached their place of destination, (for as yet none but Ali and the chief men knew whither we were going,) they thought proper to make me observe this day as a day of fasting.

May 1st. As I had some reason to suspect that this day was also to be considered as a fast, I went in the morning to the

Negro town of Farani, and begged some provisions from the
Dooti, who readily supplied my wants, and desired me to come to
his house every day during my stay in the neighbourhood. These
hospitable people are looked upon by the Moors as an abject
race of slaves, and are treated accordingly. Two of Ali's household slaves, a man and a woman, who had come along with the
two tents, went this morning to water the cattle from the town
wells, at which there began to be a great scarcity. When the
Negro women observed the cattle approaching, they took up
their pitchers and ran with all possible haste towards the town,
but before they could enter the gate, they were stopped by the
slaves, who compelled them to bring back the water they had
drawn for their own families, and empty it into the troughs for
the cattle. When this was exhausted, they were ordered to
draw water until such time as the cattle had all drank ; and the
woman slave actually broke two wooden bowls over the heads
of the black girls, because they were somewhat dilatory in
obeying her commands.

May 3d. We departed from the vicinity of Farani, and after
a circuitous route through the woods, arrived at Ali's camp in
the afternoon. This encampment was larger than that of Benowm, and was situated in the middle of a thick wood about two
miles distant from a Negro town, called Bubaker. I immediately waited upon Ali, in order to pay my respects to Queen
Fatima, who had come with him from Saheel. He seemed much
pleased with my coming ; shook hands with me, and informed
his wife that I was the Christian. She was a woman of the Arab
cast, with long black hair, and remarkably corpulent. She

appeared at first rather shocked at the thought of having a Christian so near her : but when I had (by means of a Negro boy, who spoke the Mandingo and Arabic tongues) answered a great many questions, which her curiosity suggested, respecting the country of the Christians, she seemed more at ease, and presented me with a bowl of milk ; which I considered as a very favourable omen.

The heat was now almost insufferable ; all nature seemed sinking under it. The distant country presented to the eye a dreary expanse of sand, with a few stunted trees and prickly bushes, in the shade of which the hungry cattle licked up the withered grass, while the camels and goats picked off the scanty foliage. The scarcity of water was greater here than at Benowm. Day and night the wells were crowded with cattle, lowing and fighting with each other to come at the trough : excessive thirst made many of them furious ; others, being too weak to contend for the water, endeavoured to quench their thirst by devouring the black mud from the gutters near the wells ; which they did with great avidity, though it was commonly fatal to them.

This great scarcity of water was felt severely by all the people of the camp, and by none more than myself ; for though Ali allowed me a skin for containing water, and Fatima, once or twice, gave me a small supply, when I was in distress, yet such was the barbarous disposition of the Moors at the wells, that, when my boy attempted to fill the skin, he commonly received a sound drubbing for his presumption. Every one was astonished that the slave of a Christian should attempt to draw

U

water from wells which had been dug by the followers of the Prophet. This treatment, at length, so frightened the boy, that I believe he would sooner have perished with thirst, than attempted again to fill the skin ; he therefore contented himself with begging water from the Negro slaves that attended the camp ; and I followed his example ; but with very indifferent success ; for though I let no opportunity slip, and was very urgent in my solicitations, both to the Moors and Negroes, I was but ill supplied, and frequently passed the night in the situation of *Tantalus*. No sooner had I shut my eyes, than fancy would convey me to the streams and rivers of my native land : there, as I wandered along the verdant brink, I surveyed the clear stream with transport, and hastened to swallow the delightful draught ;—but alas! disappointment awakened me ; and I found myself a lonely captive, perishing of thirst amidst the wilds of Africa!

One night, having solicited in vain for water at the camp, and being quite feverish, I resolved to try my fortune at the wells, which were about half a mile distant from the camp. Accordingly, I set out about midnight, and, being guided by the lowing of the cattle, soon arrived at the place ; where I found the Moors very busy drawing water. I requested permission to drink, but was driven away, with outrageous abuse. Passing, however, from one well to another, I came at last to one where there was only an old man and two boys. I made the same request to this man, and he immediately drew me up a bucket of water ; but, as I was about to take hold of it, he recollected that I was a Christian, and fearing that his bucket might be polluted by my lips, he dashed the water into the trough, and told me to drink from thence. Though this trough was none of the largest, and three cows were already drinking in it, I resolved to come in for my share; and kneeling down, thrust my head between two of the cows, and drank with great pleasure, until the water was nearly exhausted; and the cows began to contend with each other for the last mouthful.

In adventures of this nature, I passed the sultry month of May, during which no material change took place in my situation. Ali still considered me as a lawful prisoner; and Fatima, though she allowed me a larger quantity of victuals than I had been accustomed to receive at Benowm, had as yet said nothing on the subject of my release. In the meantime, the frequent changes of the wind, the gathering clouds, and distant lightning, with other appearances of approaching rain, indicated that the wet season was at hand; when the Moors annually evacuate the country of the Negroes, and return to the skirts of the Great Desert. This made me consider that my fate was drawing towards a crisis, and I resolved to wait for the event without any seeming uneasiness: but circumstances occurred which produced a change in my favour, more suddenly than I had foreseen, or had reason to expect. The case was this: the fugitive Kaartans, who had taken refuge in Ludamar, as I have related in Chapter VIII. finding that the Moors were about to leave them, and dreading the resentment of their own sovereign, whom they had so basely deserted, offered to treat with Ali, for two hundred Moorish horsemen, to co-operate with them in an effort to expel Daisy from Gedingooma; for until Daisy should be vanquished, or humbled, they considered that they could neither return to their native towns, nor live in security in any of the neighbouring kingdoms. With a view to extort money from these people, by means of this treaty, Ali dispatched his son to Jarra, and prepared to follow him in the course of a few days. This was an opportunity of too great consequence to me, to be neglected. I immediately applied to Fatima (who, I found, had the chief direction in all affairs of state), and begged her interest with Ali, to give me permission to accompany him to Jarra. This request, after some hesitation, was favourably received. Fatima looked kindly on me, and, I believe, was at length moved with compassion towards me. My bundles were brought from the large cow-skin bag that stood in the corner of Ali's tent, and I was ordered to explain the use of the different articles, and shew the method of putting on the boots, stockings, &c.; with all which I cheerfully complied, and was told that, in the course of a few days, I should be at liberty to depart.

Believing, therefore, that I should certainly find the means of escaping from Jarra, if I should once get thither; I now freely indulged the pleasing hope that my captivity would soon terminate; and happily not having been disappointed in this idea, I shall pause, in this place, to collect and bring into one point of view, such observations on the Moorish character, and country, as I had no fair opportunity of introducing into the preceding narrative.

CHAPTER XII.

Containing some further miscellaneous Reflections on the Moorish Character, and Manners.—Observations concerning the Great Desert, its Animals, wild and domestic, &c. &c.

THE Moors of this part of Africa, are divided into many separate tribes; of which the most formidable, according to what was reported to me, are those of Trasart and Il Braken, which inhabit the northern bank of the Senegal river. The tribes of Gedumah, Jafnoo, and Ludamar, though not so numerous as the former, are nevertheless very powerful and warlike; and are each governed by a chief, or king, who exercises absolute jurisdiction over his own horde, without acknowledging allegiance to a common sovereign. In time of peace, the employment of the people is pasturage. The Moors, indeed, subsist chiefly on the flesh of their cattle; and are always in the extreme of either gluttony or abstinence. In consequence of the frequent and severe fasts which their religion enjoins, and the toilsome journies, which they sometimes undertake across the Desert, they are enabled to bear both hunger and thirst, with surprising fortitude; but whenever opportunities occur of satisfying their appetite, they generally devour more at one meal, than would serve an European for three. They pay but little attention to agriculture; purchasing their corn, cotton-cloth, and other necessaries, from the Negroes, in exchange for salt, which they dig from the pits in the Great Desert.

The natural barrenness of the country is such, that it furnishes but few materials for manufacture. The Moors, however, contrive to weave a strong cloth, with which they cover their tents: the thread is spun by their women, from the hair of goats; and they prepare the hides of their cattle, so as to furnish saddles, bridles, pouches, and other articles of leather. They are likewise sufficiently skilful, to convert the native iron, which they procure from the Negroes, into spears and knives, and also into pots for boiling their food; but their sabres and other weapons, as well as their fire-arms and ammunition, they purchase from the Europeans, in exchange for the Negro slaves which they obtain in their predatory excursions. Their chief commerce of this kind is with the French traders, on the Senegal river.

The Moors are rigid Mahomedans, and possess, with the bigotry and superstition, all the intolerance, of their sect. They have no mosques at Benowm, but perform their devotions in a sort of open shed, or inclosure made of mats. The priest is, at the same time, schoolmaster to the juniors. His pupils assemble every evening before his tent; where, by the light of a large fire, made of brush-wood and cows' dung, they are taught a few sentences from the Koran, and are initiated into the principles of their creed. Their alphabet differs but little from that in Richardson's Arabic Grammar. They always write with the vowel points. Their priests even affect to know something of foreign literature. The priest of Benowm assured me, that he could read the writings of the Christians: he shewed me a number of barbarous characters, which he asserted were the Roman alphabet; and he produced another specimen, equally unintelligible, which he declared to be the *Kallam il Indi*, or Persian. His library consisted of nine volumes in quarto; most of them, I believe, were books of religion; for the name of Mahomet appeared, in red letters, in almost every page of each. His scholars wrote their lessons upon thin boards; paper being too expensive for general use. The boys were diligent enough, and appeared to possess a considerable share of emulation; carrying their boards slung over their shoulders, when about their common employments. When a boy has committed to memory a few of their prayers, and can read and write certain parts of the Koran, he is reckoned sufficiently instructed; and, with this slender stock of learning, commences his career of life. Proud of his acquirements, he surveys with contempt the unlettered Negro; and embraces every opportunity of displaying his superiority over such of his countrymen, as are not distinguished by the same accomplishments.

The education of the girls is neglected altogether: mental accomplishments are but little attended to by the women; nor is the want of them considered by the men, as a defect in the female character. They are regarded, I believe, as an inferior species of animals; and seem to be brought up for no other purpose, than that of administering to the sensual pleasures of their imperious masters. Voluptuousness is, therefore, considered as their chief accomplishment, and slavish submission as their indispensable duty.

The Moors have singular ideas of feminine perfection. The gracefulness of figure and motion, and a countenance enlivened by expression, are by no means essential points in their standard: with them, corpulence and beauty appear to be terms nearly synonymous. A woman, of even moderate pretensions, must be one who cannot walk without a slave under each arm, to support her; and a perfect beauty is a load for a camel. In consequence of this prevalent taste for unwieldiness of bulk, the Moorish ladies take great pains to acquire it early in life; and for this purpose, many of the young girls are compelled, by their mothers, to devour a great quantity of kouskous, and drink a large bowl of camels' milk every morning. It is of no importance, whether the girl has an appetite or not; the kouskous and milk must be swallowed; and obedience is frequently enforced by blows. I have seen a poor girl sit crying, with the bowl at her lips, for more than an hour; and her mother, with a stick in her hand, watching her all the while, and using the stick without mercy, whenever she observed that her daughter was not swallowing. This singular practice, instead of producing indigestion and disease, soon covers the young lady with that degree of plumpness, which, in the eye of a Moor, is perfection itself.

As the Moors purchase all their clothing from the Negroes, the women are forced to be very economical in the article of dress. In general, they content themselves with a broad piece of cotton cloth, which is wrapped round the middle, and hangs down like a petticoat, almost to the ground: to the upper part of this, are sewed two square pieces, one before, and the other behind, which are fastened together over the shoulders. The head-dress, is commonly a bandage of cotton cloth, with some parts of it broader than others, which serve to conceal the face when they walk in the sun; frequently, however, when they go abroad, they veil themselves from head to foot.

The employment of the women varies, according to their degrees of opulence. Queen Fatima, and a few others of high rank, like the great ladies in some parts of Europe, pass their time chiefly in conversing with their visitors, performing their devotions; or admiring their charms in a looking-glass. The women of inferior class, employ themselves in different domestic duties. They are very vain, and talkative; and when any thing puts them out of humour, they commonly vent their anger upon their female slaves, over whom they rule with severe and despotic authority; which leads me to observe, that the condition of these poor captives is deplorably wretched. At daybreak, they are compelled to fetch water from the wells, in large skins, called *girbas;* and as soon as they have brought water enough to serve the family for the day, as well as the horses (for the Moors seldom give their horses the trouble of going to the wells), they are then employed in pounding the corn, and dressing the victuals. This being always done in the open air, the slaves are exposed to the combined heat of the sun, the sand, and the fire. In the intervals, it is their business to sweep the tent, churn the milk, and perform other domestic offices. With all this they are badly fed, and oftentimes cruelly punished.

The men's dress, among the Moors of Ludamar, differs but

X

little from that of the Negroes (which has been already described,) except that they have all adopted that characteristic of
the Mahomedan sect, the *turban;* which is here universally
made of white cotton cloth.   Such of the Moors as have long
beards, display them with a mixture of pride and satisfaction,
as denoting an Arab ancestry.   Of this number was Ali himself; but among the generality of the people, the hair is short
and bushy, and universally black.   And here I may be permitted to observe, that if any one circumstance excited among them
favourable thoughts towards my own person, it was my beard;
which was now grown to an enormous length, and was always
beheld with approbation or envy.   I believe in my conscience,
they thought it too good a beard for a Christian.

The only diseases which I observed to prevail among the
Moors, were the intermittent fever, and dysentery: for the
cure of which, nostrums are sometimes administered by their
old women; but, in general, nature is left to her own operations.
Mention was made to me of the small-pox, as being sometimes
very destructive; but it had not, to my knowledge, made its
appearance in Ludamar, while I was in captivity.   That it prevails, however, among some tribes of the Moors, and that it is
frequently conveyed by them to the Negroes in the southern
states, I was assured, on the authority of Dr. Laidley; who also
informed me, that the Negroes on the Gambia practise inocu-
lation.

The administration of criminal justice, as far as I had opportunities of observing, was prompt and decisive.   For, although
civil rights were but little regarded in Ludamar, it was neces-

sary, when crimes were committed, that examples should sometimes be made. On such occasions, the offender was brought
before Ali, who pronounced, of his sole authority, what judgment he thought proper. But I understood that capital punishment was seldom or never inflicted, except on the Negroes.

Although the wealth of the Moors consists chiefly in their
numerous herds of cattle; yet, as the pastoral life does not afford
full employment, the majority of the people are perfectly idle,
and spend the day in trifling conversation about their horses,
or in laying schemes of depredation on the Negro villages.

The usual place of rendezvous for the indolent, is the King's
tent; where great liberty of speech seems to be exercised by the
company towards each other; while in speaking of their chief,
they express but one opinion. In praise of their sovereign, they
are unanimous. Songs are composed in his honour, which the
company frequently sing in concert; but they are so loaded with
gross adulation, that no man but a Moorish despot, could hear
them without blushing. The king is distinguished by the fineness of his dress; which is composed of blue cotton cloth,
brought from Tombuctoo, or white linen or muslin from Morocco. He has likewise a larger tent than any other person,
with a white cloth over it: but, in his usual intercourse with
his subjects, all distinctions of rank are frequently forgotten. He
sometimes eats out of the same bowl with his camel driver, and
reposes himself, during the heat of the day, upon the same bed.
The expences of his government and household are defrayed by
a tax upon his Negro subjects, which is paid by every house-
holder, either in corn, cloth, or gold dust; a tax upon the dif-

X 2

ferent Moorish Korrees, or watering-places, which is commonly levied in cattle ; and a tax upon all merchandize which passes through the kingdom, and is generally collected in kind. But a considerable part of the king's revenue arises from the plunder of individuals. The Negro inhabitants of Ludamar, and the travelling merchants, are afraid of appearing rich ; for Ali, who has spies stationed in the different towns, to give him information concerning the wealth of his subjects, frequently invents some frivolous plea for seizing their property, and reducing the opulent to a level with their fellow citizens.

Of the number of Ali's Moorish subjects, I had no means of forming a correct estimate. The military strength of Ludamar consists in cavalry. They are well mounted, and appear to be very expert in skirmishing and attacking by surprise. Every soldier furnishes his own horse, and finds his accoutrements, consisting of a large sabre, a double barrelled gun, a small red leather bag for holding his balls, and a powder horn slung over the shoulder. He has no pay, nor any remuneration but what arises from plunder. This body is not very numerous ; for when Ali made war upon Bambarra, I was informed that his whole force did not exceed two thousand cavalry. They constitute, however, by what I could learn, but a very small proportion of his Moorish subjects. The horses are very beautiful, and so highly esteemed, that the Negro princes will sometimes give from twelve to fourteen slaves for one horse.

Ludamar has for its northern boundary, the Great Desert of Sahara. From the best inquiries I could make, this vast ocean of sand, which occupies so large a space in Northern Africa, may be pronounced almost destitute of inhabitants; except where the scanty vegetation which appears in certain spots, affords pasturage for the flocks of a few miserable Arabs, who wander from one well to another. In other places, where the supply of water and pasturage is more abundant, small parties of the Moors have taken up their residence. Here they live, in independent poverty, secure from the tyrannical government of Barbary. But the greater part of the Desert, being totally destitute of water, is seldom visited by any human being; unless where the trading caravans trace out their toilsome and dangerous route across it. In some parts of this extensive waste, the ground is covered with low stunted shrubs, which serve as landmarks for the caravans, and furnish the camels with a scanty forage. In other parts, the disconsolate wanderer, wherever he turns, sees nothing around him but a vast interminable expanse of sand and sky; a gloomy and barren void, where the eye finds no particular object to rest upon, and the mind is filled with painful apprehensions of perishing with thirst. " Surrounded by this dreary solitude, the traveller sees the dead bodies of birds, that the violence of the wind has brought from happier regions; and, as he ruminates on the fearful length of his remaining passage, listens with horror to the voice of the driving blast; the only sound that interrupts the awful repose of the Desert."*

The few wild animals which inhabit these melancholy regions, are the antelope and the ostrich; their swiftness of foot

* Proceedings of the African Association, Part I.

enabling them to reach the distant watering-places. On the
skirts of the Desert, where water is more plentiful, are found
lions, panthers, elephants, and wild boars.

Of domestic animals, the only one that can endure the
fatigue of crossing the Desert, is the camel. By the particular
conformation of the stomach, he is enabled to carry a supply of
water sufficient for ten or twelve days; his broad and yielding
foot, is well adapted for a sandy country; and by a singular
motion of his upper lip, he picks the smallest leaves from the
thorny shrubs of the Desert as he passes along. The camel is,
therefore, the only beast of burden employed by the trading
caravans, which traverse the Desert in different directions,
from Barbary to Nigritia. As this useful and docile creature
has been sufficiently described by systematical writers, it is
unnecessary for me to enlarge upon his properties. I shall
only add, that his flesh, though to my own taste dry and un-
savoury, is preferred by the Moors to any other; and that the
milk of the female is in universal esteem, and is indeed sweet,
pleasant, and nutritive.

I have observed that the Moors, in their complexion, resemble
the Mulattoes of the West Indies; but they have something
unpleasant in their aspect, which the Mulattoes have not. I
fancied that I discovered in the features of most of them, a
disposition towards cruelty, and low cunning; and I could never
contemplate their physiognomy, without feeling sensible uneasiness. From the staring wildness of their eyes, a stranger
would immediately set them down as a nation of lunatics. The
treachery and malevolence of their character, are manifested

in their plundering excursions against the Negro villages. Oftentimes, without the smallest provocation, and sometimes, under the fairest professions of friendship, they will suddenly seize upon the Negroes' cattle, and even on the inhabitants themselves. The Negroes very seldom retaliate. The enterprizing boldness of the Moors, their knowledge of the country, and, above all, the superior fleetness of their horses, make them such formidable enemies, that the petty Negro states which border upon the Desert, are in continual terror while the Moorish tribes are in the vicinity, and are too much awed to think of resistance.

Like the roving Arabs, the Moors frequently remove from one place to another; according to the season of the year, or the convenience of pasturage. In the month of February, when the heat of the sun scorches up every sort of vegetation in the Desert, they strike their tents, and approach the Negro country to the south; where they reside until the rains commence, in the month of July. At this time, having purchased corn, and other necessaries from the Negroes, in exchange for salt, they again depart to the northward, and continue in the Desert until the rains are over, and that part of the country becomes burnt up and barren.

This wandering and restless way of life, while it inures them to hardships, strengthens, at the same time, the bonds of their little society, and creates in them an aversion towards strangers, which is almost insurmountable. Cut off from all intercourse with civilized nations, and boasting an advantage over the Negroes, by possessing, though in a very limited degree, the knowledge of letters, they are at once the vainest and proudest, and, perhaps, the most bigotted, ferocious, and intolerant of all the nations on the earth: combining in their character, the blind superstition of the Negro, with the savage cruelty and treachery of the Arab.

It is probable that many of them had never beheld a white man, before my arrival at Benowm : but they had all been taught to regard the Christian name with inconceivable abhorrence, and to consider it nearly as lawful to murder a European, as it would be to kill a dog. The melancholy fate of Major Houghton, and the treatment I experienced during my confinement among them, will, I trust, serve as a warning to future travellers to avoid this inhospitable district.

The reader may probably have expected from me a more detailed and copious account of the manners, customs, superstitions, and prejudices, of this secluded and singular people ; but it must not be forgotten, that the wretchedness of my situation among them, afforded me but few opportunities of collecting information. Some particulars, however, might be added in this place ; but being equally applicable to the Negroes to the southward, they will appear in a subsequent page.

CHAPTER XIII.

*Ali departs for Jarra, and the Author allowed to follow him thi-
ther.—The Author's faithful Servant, Demba, seized by Ali's
Order, and sent back into Slavery.—Ali returns to his Camp, and
permits the Author to remain at Jarra, who, thenceforward,
meditates his Escape.—Daisy, King of Kaarta, approaching with
his Army towards Jarra, the Inhabitants quit the Town, and the
Author accompanies them in their Flight.—A Party of Moors over-
take him at Queira.—He gets away from them at Daybreak:—
is again pursued by another Party, and robbed; but finally effects
his Escape.*

HAVING, as hath been related, obtained permission to accompany Ali to Jarra, I took leave of Queen Fatima, who with much
grace and civility, returned me part of my apparel; and the
evening before my departure, my horse, with the saddle and
bridle, were sent me by Ali's order.

Early on the morning of the 26th of May, I departed from the
camp of Bubaker, accompanied by my two attendants, Johnson
and Demba, and a number of Moors on horseback; Ali, with
about fifty horsemen, having gone privately from the camp
during the night. We stopped about noon at Farani, and were

Y

there joined by twelve Moors riding upon camels, and with them
we proceeded to a watering-place in the woods, where we overtook Ali and his fifty horsemen. They were lodged in some low
shepherds' tents near the wells. As the company was numerous,
the tents could scarcely accommodate us all ; and I was ordered
to sleep in the open space, in the centre of the tents, where
every one might observe my motions. During the night, there
was much lightning from the north-east ; and about daybreak
a very heavy sand-wind commenced, which continued with
great violence until four in the afternoon. The quantity of sand
which passed to the westward in the course of this day, must
have been prodigiously great. At times it was impossible to look
up; and the cattle were so tormented by the particles lodging
in their ears and eyes, that they ran about like mad creatures,
and I was in continual danger of being trampled to death by
them.

May 28th. Early in the morning the Moors saddled their
horses, and Ali's chief slave ordered me to get in readiness.
In a little time the same messenger returned, and taking my boy
by the shoulder, told him in the Mandingo language, that " Ali
was to be his master in future ;" and then turning to me, " the
business is settled at last (said he); " the boy, and every thing
but your horse, goes back to Bubaker ; but you may take the
old fool (meaning Johnson the interpreter) with you to Jarra."
I made him no answer ; but being shocked beyond description
at the idea of losing the poor boy, I hastened to Ali, who was
at breakfast before his tent, surrounded by many of his courtiers. I told him (perhaps in rather too passionate a strain,) that

whatever imprudence I had been guilty of, in coming into his country, I thought I had already been sufficiently punished for it, by being so long detained; and then plundered of all my little property; which, however, gave me no uneasiness, when compared with what he had just now done to me. I observed, that the boy which he had now seized upon, was not a slave, and had been accused of no offence: he was indeed one of my attendants; and his faithful services in that station, had procured him his freedom: his fidelity and attachment had made him follow me into my present situation; and as he looked up to me for protection, I could not see him deprived of his liberty, without remonstrating against such an act, as the height of cruelty and injustice. Ali made no reply, but with a haughty air and malignant smile, told his interpreter, that if I did not mount my horse immediately, he would send me back likewise. There is something in the frown of a tyrant which rouzes the most secret emotions of the heart: I could not suppress my feelings; and for once entertained an indignant wish to rid the world of such a monster.

Poor Demba was not less affected than myself; he had formed a strong attachment towards me, and had a cheerfulness of disposition, which often beguiled the tedious hours of captivity: he was likewise a proficient in the Bambarra tongue, and promised on that account to be of great utility to me in future. But it was in vain to expect any thing favourable to humanity, from people who are strangers to its dictates. So having shaken hands with this unfortunate boy, and blended my tears with his, assuring him, however, that I would do my utmost to redeem him, I saw him led off by three of Ali's slaves, towards the camp at Bubaker.

When the Moors had mounted their horses, I was ordered to follow them; and after a toilsome journey through the woods, in a very sultry day, we arrived in the afternoon at a walled village, called Doombani; where we remained two days, waiting for the arrival of some horsemen from the northward.

On the 1st of June, we departed from Doombani towards Jarra. Our company now amounted to two hundred men, all on horseback; for the Moors never use infantry in their wars. They appeared capable of enduring great fatigue; but from their total want of discipline, our journey to Jarra was more like a fox-chase, than the march of an army.

At Jarra, I took up my lodging at the house of my old acquaintance, Daman Jumma; and informed him of every thing that had befallen me. I particularly requested him to use his interest with Ali, to redeem my boy, and promised him a bill upon Dr. Laidley, for the value of two slaves, the moment he brought him to Jarra. Daman very readily undertook to negotiate the business; but found that Ali considered the boy as my principal interpreter, and was unwilling to part with him, lest he should fall a second time into my hands; and be instrumental in conducting me to Bambarra. Ali therefore put off the matter from day to day; but withal told Daman, that if he wished to purchase the boy for himself, he should have him thereafter, at the common price of a slave; which Daman agreed to pay for him, whenever Ali should send him to Jarra.

The chief object of Ali, in this journey to Jarra, as I have already related, was to procure money from such of the Kaartans, as had taken refuge in his country. Some of these had solicited his protection, to avoid the horrors of war; but by far the greatest number of them were dissatisfied men, who wished the ruin of their own sovereign. These people no sooner heard that the Bambarran army had returned to Sego without subduing Daisy, as was generally expected, than they resolved to make a sudden attack themselves upon him, before he could recruit his forces, which were now known to be much diminished by a bloody campaign, and in great want of provisions. With this view, they solicited the Moors to join them, and offered to hire of Ali two hundred horsemen; which Ali, with the warmest professions of friendship, agreed to furnish, upon condition that they should previously supply him with four hundred head of cattle, two hundred garments of blue cloth, and a considerable quantity of beads and ornaments. The raising this impost, somewhat perplexed them; and in order to procure the cattle, they persuaded the king to demand one-half the stipulated number from the people of Jarra; promising to replace them in a short time. Ali agreed to this proposal, and the same evening (June 2d) the drum was sent through the town; and the crier announced, that if any person suffered his cattle to go into the woods, the next morning, before the king had chosen his quota of them, his house should be plundered, and his slaves taken from him. The people dared not disobey the proclamation; and next morning about two hundred of their best cattle were selected, and delivered to the Moors: the full complement was made up afterwards, by means equally unjust and arbitrary.

June 8th. In the afternoon, Ali sent his chief slave to inform me, that he was about to return to Bubaker; but as he would only stay there a few days, to keep the approaching festival (*Banna Salee*), and then return to Jarra, I had permission to remain with Daman until his return. This was joyful news to me; but I had experienced so many disappointments, that I was unwilling to indulge the hope of its being true, until Johnson came and told me that Ali, with part of the horsemen, were actually gone from the town, and that the rest were to follow him in the morning.

June 9th. Early in the morning, the remainder of the Moors departed from the town. They had, during their stay, committed many acts of robbery; and this morning, with the most unparalleled audacity, they seized upon three girls, who were bringing water from the wells, and carried them away into slavery.

The anniversary of *Banna Salee*, at Jarra, very well deserved to be called a festival. The slaves were all finely clad on this occasion, and the householders vied with each other in providing large quantities of victuals, which they distributed to all their neighbours, with the greatest profusion: hunger was literally banished from the town; man, woman, and child, bond and free, all had as much as they could eat.

June 12th. Two people, dreadfully wounded, were discovered at a watering-place, in the woods; one of them had just breathed his last, but the other was brought alive to Jarra,

On recovering a little, he informed the people, that he had fled through the woods from Kasson; that Daisy had made war upon Sambo, the king of that country; had surprised three of his towns, and put all the inhabitants to the sword. He enumerated by name, many of the friends of the Jarra people, who had been murdered in Kasson. This intelligence made the death-howl universal in Jarra, for the space of two days.

This piece of bad news, was followed by another, not less distressing. A number of runaway slaves, arrived from Kaarta on the 14th, and reported that Daisy, having received information concerning the intended attack upon him, was about to visit Jarra. This made the Negroes call upon Ali for the two hundred horsemen, which he was to furnish them, according to engagement. But Ali paid very little attention to their remonstrances; and at last plainly told them, that his cavalry were otherwise employed. The Negroes, thus deserted by the Moors, and fully apprized that the king of Kaarta would shew them as little clemency, as he had shewn the inhabitants of Kasson, resolved to collect all their forces, and hazard a battle before the king, who was now in great distress for want of provisions, should become too powerful for them. They therefore assembled about eight hundred effective men in the whole; and with these they entered Kaarta, on the evening of the 18th of June.

June 19th. This morning the wind shifted to the south-west; and about two o'clock in the afternoon, we had a heavy tornado, or thunder squall, accompanied with rain, which greatly revived the face of nature, and gave a pleasant coolness to the air. This was the first rain that had fallen for many months.

As every attempt to redeem my boy had hitherto been unsuccessful, and in all probability would continue to prove so, whilst I remained in the country; I found that it was necessary for me to come to some determination concerning my own safety, before the rains should be fully set in; for my landlord, seeing no likelihood of being paid for his trouble, began to wish me away; and Johnson, my interpreter, refusing to proceed, my situation became very perplexing. If I continued where I was, I foresaw that I must soon fall a victim to the barbarity of the Moors; and yet if I went forward singly, it was evident that I must sustain great difficulties, both from the want of means to purchase the necessaries of life, and of an interpreter to make myself understood. On the other hand, to return to England without accomplishing the object of my mission, was worse than either. I therefore determined to avail myself of the first opportunity of escaping, and to proceed directly for Bambarra, as soon as the rains had set in for a few days, so as to afford me the certainty of finding water in the woods.

Such was my situation, when, on the evening of the 24th of June, I was startled by the report of some muskets close to the town, and inquiring the reason, was informed that the Jarra army had returned from fighting Daisy, and that this firing was by way of rejoicing. However, when the chief men of the town had assembled, and heard a full detail of the expedition, they were by no means relieved from their uneasiness on Daisy's account. The deceitful Moors having drawn back from the confederacy, after being hired by the Negroes, greatly dispirited the insurgents ; who, instead of finding Daisy with a few friends concealed in the strong fortress of Gedingooma, had found him at a town near Joka, in the open country, surrounded by so numerous an army, that every attempt to attack him was at once given up ; and the confederates only thought of enriching themselves, by the plunder of the small towns in the neighbourhood. They accordingly fell upon two of Daisy's towns, and carried off the whole of the inhabitants; but lest intelligence of this might reach Daisy, and induce him to cut off their retreat, they returned through the woods by night, bringing with them the slaves and cattle which they had captured.

June 26th. This afternoon, a spy from Kaarta, brought the alarming intelligence, that Daisy had taken Simbing in the morning, and would be in Jarra some time in the course of the ensuing day. A number of people were immediately stationed on the tops of the rocks, and in the different passages leading into the town, to give early intelligence of Daisy's motions ; and the women set about making the necessary preparations for quitting the town as soon as possible. They continued beating corn, and packing up different articles, during the night ; and early in the morning, nearly one half of the townspeople took the road for Bambarra, by the way of Deena.

Their departure was very affecting : the women and children crying; the men sullen and dejected; and all of them looking back with regret on their native town ; and on the wells and rocks, beyond which their ambition had never tempted them to

Z

stray, and where they had laid all their plans of future happiness; all of which they were now forced to abandon, and to seek shelter among strangers.

June 27th. About eleven o'clock in the forenoon, we were alarmed by the centinels, who brought information that Daisy was on his march towards Jarra, and that the confederate army had fled before him without firing a gun. The terror of the townspeople on this occasion is not easily to be described.— Indeed, the screams of the women and children, and the great hurry and confusion that every where prevailed, made me suspect that the Kaartans had already entered the town; and although I had every reason to be pleased with Daisy's behaviour to me, when I was at Kemmoo, I had no wish to expose myself to the mercy of his army, who might, in the general confusion, mistake me for a Moor. I therefore mounted my horse, and taking a large bag of corn before me, rode slowly along with the townspeople, until we reached the foot of a rocky hill, where I dismounted, and drove my horse up before me. When I had reached the summit, I sat down, and having a full view of the town, and the neighbouring country, could not help lamenting the situation of the poor inhabitants, who were thronging after me, driving their sheep, cows, goats, &c. and carrying a scanty portion of provisions, and a few clothes. There was a great noise and crying every where upon the road; for many aged people and children were unable to walk, and these, with the sick, were obliged to be carried, otherwise they must have been left to certain destruction.

About five o'clock we arrived at a small farm, belonging to the

Jarra people, called Kadeeja; and here I found Daman and Johnson employed in filling large bags of corn, to be carried upon
bullocks, to serve as provisions for Daman's family on the road.

June 28th. At daybreak, we departed from Kadeeja; and,
having passed Troongoomba, without stopping, arrived in the
afternoon at Queira. I remained here two days, in order to recruit my horse, which the Moors had reduced to a perfect Rosi-
nante, and to wait for the arrival of some Mandingo Negroes,
who were going for Bambarra in the course of a few days.

On the afternoon of the 1st of July, as I was tending my horse
in the fields, Ali's chief slave and four Moors arrived at Queira,
and took up their lodging at the Dooty's house. My interpreter,
Johnson, who suspected the nature of this visit, sent two boys
to overhear their conversation; from which he learnt that they
were sent to convey me back to Bubaker. The same evening,
two of the Moors came privately to look at my horse, and one
of them proposed taking it to the Dooty's hut, but the other
observed that such a precaution was unnecessary, as I could
never escape upon such an animal. They then inquired where
I slept, and returned to their companions.

All this was like a stroke of thunder to me, for I dreaded
nothing so much as confinement again among the Moors; from
whose barbarity I had nothing but death to expect. I therefore
determined to set off immediately for Bambarra; a measure which
I thought offered almost the only chance of saving my life, and
gaining the object of my mission. I communicated the design
to Johnson, who, altho' he applauded my resolution, was so far
from shewing any inclination to accompany me, that he solemnly

protested, he would rather forfeit his wages, than go any farther. He told me that Daman had agreed to give him half the
price of a slave for his service, to assist in conducting a coffle
of slaves to Gambia, and that he was determined to embrace
the opportunity of returning to his wife and family.

Having no hopes therefore of persuading him to accompany
me, I resolved to proceed by myself. About midnight I got
my clothes in readiness, which consisted of two shirts, two pair
of trowsers, two pocket-handkerchiefs, an upper and under
waistcoat, a hat, and a pair of half boots ; these, with a cloak,
constituted my whole wardrobe. And I had not one single bead,
nor any other article of value in my possession, to purchase victuals for myself, or corn for my horse.

About daybreak, Johnson, who had been listening to the
Moors all night, came and whispered to me that they were
asleep. The awful crisis was now arrived, when I was again
either to taste the blessing of freedom, or languish out my days
in captivity. A cold sweat moistened my forehead, as I thought
on the dreadful alternative, and reflected, that, one way or the
the other, my fate must be decided in the course of the ensuing
day. But to deliberate, was to lose the only chance of escaping.
So, taking up my bundle, I stepped gently over the Negroes,
who were sleeping in the open air, and having mounted my
horse, I bade Johnson farewell, desiring him to take particular
care of the papers I had entrusted him with, and inform my
friends in Gambia that he had left me in good health, on my
way to Bambarra.

I proceeded with great caution ; surveying each bush, and

frequently listening and looking behind me for the Moorish horsemen, until I was about a mile from the town, when I was surprised to find myself in the neighbourhood of a Korree, belonging to the Moors. The shepherds followed me for about a mile, hooting and throwing stones after me; and when I was out of their reach, and had begun to indulge the pleasing hopes of escaping, I was again greatly alarmed to hear somebody holla behind me; and looking back, I saw three Moors on horseback, coming after me at full speed; hooping and brandishing their double-barrelled guns. I knew it was in vain to think of escaping, and therefore turned back and met them: when two of them caught hold of my bridle, one on each side, and the third, presenting his musket, told me I must go back to Ali. When the human mind has for some time been fluctuating between hope and despair, tortured with anxiety, and hurried from one extreme to another, it affords a sort of gloomy relief to know the worst that can possibly happen: such was my situation. An indifference about life, and all its enjoyments, had completely benumbed my faculties, and I rode back with the Moors with apparent unconcern. But a change took place much sooner than I had any reason to expect. In passing through some thick bushes, one of the Moors ordered me to untie my bundle, and shew them the contents. Having examined the different articles, they found nothing worth taking except my cloak, which they considered as a very valuable acquisition, and one of them pulling it from me, wrapped it about himself. This cloak had been of great use to me; it served to cover me from the rains in the

day, and to protect me from the musketoes in the night; I
therefore earnestly begged him to return it, and followed him
some little way to obtain it; but without paying any attention to my request, he and one of his companions rode off
with their prize. When I attempted to follow them, the third,
who had remained with me, struck my horse over the head,
and presenting his musket, told me I should proceed no further. I now perceived that these men had not been sent by any
authority to apprehend me, but had pursued me solely in the
view to rob and plunder me. Turning my horse's head therefore once more towards the east, and observing the Moor follow
the track of his confederates, I congratulated myself on having
escaped with my life, though in great distress, from such a
horde of barbarians.

I was no sooner out of sight of the Moor, than I struck into
the woods, to prevent being pursued, and kept pushing on, with
all possible speed, until I found myself near some high rocks,
which I remembered to have seen in my former route from
Queira to Deena; and directing my course a little to the northward, I fortunately fell in with the path.

CHAPTER XIV.

The Author feels great Joy at his Deliverance, and proceeds through the Wilderness, E. S. E.; but finds his Situation very deplorable.—Suffers greatly from Thirst, and faints on the Sand:—recovers, and makes another Effort to push forward. —Is providentially relieved by a Fall of Rain.—Arrives at a Foulah Village, where he is refused Relief by the Dooty; but obtains Food from a poor Woman.—Continues his Journey through the Wilderness, and the next Day lights on another Foulah Village, where he is hospitably received by one of the Shepherds.—Arrives on the third Day at a Negro Town called Wawra, tributary to the King of Bambarra.

I⊤ is impossible to describe the joy that arose in my mind, when I looked around and concluded that I was out of danger. I felt like one recovered from sickness; I breathed freer; I found unusual lightness in my limbs; even the Desert looked pleasant; and I dreaded nothing so much as falling in with some wandering parties of Moors, who might convey me back to the land of thieves and murderers, from which I had just escaped.

I soon became sensible, however, that my situation was very deplorable; for I had no means of procuring food, nor prospect of finding water. About ten o'clock, perceiving a herd of goats feeding close to the road, I took a circuitous route to avoid being seen; and continued travelling through the Wilderness, directing my course, by compass, nearly east-south-east, in order to reach, as soon as possible, some town or village of the kingdom of Bambarra.

A little after noon, when the burning heat of the sun was reflected with double violence from the hot sand, and the distant ridges of the hills, seen through the ascending vapour, seemed to wave and fluctuate like the unsettled sea, I became faint with thirst, and climbed a tree in hopes of seeing distant smoke, or some other appearance of a human habitation; but in vain: nothing appeared all around but thick underwood, and hillocks of white sand.

About four o'clock, I came suddenly upon a large herd of goats, and pulling my horse into a bush, I watched to observe if the keepers were Moors or Negroes. In a little time I perceived two Moorish boys, and with some difficulty persuaded them to approach me. They informed me that the herd belonged to Ali, and that they were going to Deena, where the water was more plentiful, and where they intended to stay, until the rain had filled the pools in the Desert. They shewed me their empty water-skins, and told me that they had seen no water in the woods. This account afforded me but little consolation; however, it was in vain to repine, and I pushed on as fast as possible, in hopes of reaching some watering-place in the course of the night. My thirst was by this time become insufferable; my mouth was parched and inflamed; a sudden dimness would frequently come over my eyes, with other symptoms of fainting; and my horse being very much fatigued, I began seriously to apprehend that I should perish of thirst. To relieve the burning pain in my mouth and throat, I chewed the leaves of different shrubs, but found them all bitter, and of no service to me.

A little before sunset, having reached the top of a gentle rising, I climbed a high tree, from the topmost branches of which I cast a melancholy look over the barren Wilderness, but without discovering the most distant trace of a human dwelling. The same dismal uniformity of shrubs and sand every where presented itself, and the horizon was as level and uninterrupted as that of the sea.

Descending from the tree, I found my horse devouring the stubble and brushwood with great avidity; and as I was now too faint to attempt walking, and my horse too much fatigued to carry me, I thought it but an act of humanity, and perhaps the last I should ever have it in my power to perform, to take off his bridle and let him shift for himself; in doing which I was suddenly affected with sickness and giddiness; and falling upon the sand, felt as if the hour of death was fast approaching. " Here then, thought I, after a short but ineffec- " tual struggle, terminate all my hopes of being useful in my " day and generation: here must the short span of my life " come to an end."—I cast (as I believed) a last look on the surrounding scene, and whilst I reflected on the awful change that was about to take place, this world with its enjoyments seemed to vanish from my recollection. Nature, however, at length resumed its functions; and on recovering my senses, I found myself stretched upon the sand, with the bridle still in my hand, and the sun just sinking behind the trees. I now summoned all my resolution, and determined to make another effort to prolong my existence. And as the evening was somewhat cool, I resolved to travel as far as my limbs would carry me, in hopes of reaching (my only resource) a watering-place. With this view, I put the bridle on my horse, and driving him before me, went slowly along for about an hour, when I perceived some lightning from the north-east; a most delightful sight; for it promised rain. The darkness and lightning increased very rapidly; and in less than an hour I heard the wind roaring among the bushes. I had already opened my mouth to receive the refreshing drops which I expected; but I was instantly covered with a cloud of sand, driven with such force by the wind as to give a very disagreeable sensation to my face and arms; and I was obliged to mount my horse, and stop under a bush, to prevent being suffocated. The sand continued to fly in amazing quantities for near an hour, after which I again set forward, and travelled with difficulty, until ten o'clock. About this time I was agreeably surprised by some very vivid flashes of lightning, followed by a few heavy drops of rain. In a little time the sand ceased to fly, and I alighted, and spread out all my clean clothes to collect the rain, which at length I saw would certainly fall. For more than an hour it rained plentifully, and I quenched my thirst, by wringing and sucking my clothes.

There being no moon, it was remarkably dark, so that I was obliged to lead my horse, and direct my way by the compass, which the lightning enabled me to observe. In this manner I travelled, with tolerable expedition, until past midnight; when, the lightning becoming more distant, I was under the necessity of groping along, to the no small danger of my hands and eyes. About two o'clock my horse started at something, and looking round, I was not a little surprised to see a light at a short distance among the trees, and supposing it to be a town, I groped along the sand in hopes of finding corn-stalks, cotton, or other appearances of cultivation, but found none. As I approached, I perceived a number of other lights in different places, and began to suspect that I had fallen upon a party of Moors. However, in my present situation. I was resolved to see who they were, if I could do it with safety. I accordingly led my horse cautiously towards the light, and heard by the lowing of the cattle, and the clamorous tongues of the herdsmen, that it was a watering-place, and most likely belonged to the Moors. Delightful as the sound of the human voice was to me, I resolved once more to strike into the woods, and rather run the risk of perishing of hunger, than trust myself again in their hands; but being still thirsty, and dreading the approach of the burning day, I thought it prudent to search for the wells, which I expected to find at no great distance. In this pursuit, I inadvertently approached so near to one of the tents, as to be perceived by a woman, who immediately screamed out. Two people came running to her assistance from some of the neighbouring tents, and passed so very near to me, that I thought I was discovered; and hastened again into the woods.

About a mile from this place, I heard a loud and confused noise somewhere to the right of my course, and in a short time was happy to find it was the croaking of frogs, which was heavenly

A a 2

music to my ears. I followed the sound, and at daybreak arrived at some shallow muddy pools, so full of frogs, that it was difficult to discern the water. The noise they made frightened my
horse, and I was obliged to keep them quiet, by beating the
water with a branch until he had drank. Having here quenched
my thirst, I ascended a tree, and the morning being calm, I soon
perceived the smoke of the watering-place which I had passed
in the night; and observed another pillar of smoke east-south-
east, distant 12 or 14 miles. Towards this I directed my route,
and reached the cultivated ground a little before eleven o'clock;
where seeing a number of Negroes at work planting corn, I inquired the name of the town; and was informed that it was a
Foulah village, belonging to Ali, called Shrilla. I had now
some doubts about entering it; but my horse being very much
fatigued, and the day growing hot, not to mention the pangs
of hunger which began to assail me, I resolved to venture; and
accordingly rode up to the Dooty's house, where I was unfortunately denied admittance, and could not obtain even a handful of corn, either for myself or horse. Turning from this inhospitable door, I rode slowly out of the town, and perceiving
some low scattered huts without the walls, I directed my route
towards them; knowing that in Africa, as well as in Europe,
hospitality does not always prefer the highest dwellings. At
the door of one of these huts, an old motherly-looking woman
sat, spinning cotton; I made signs to her that I was hungry, and
inquired if she had any victuals with her in the hut. She immediately laid down her distaff, and desired me, in Arabic, to come
in. When I had seated myself upon the floor, she set before

me a dish of kouskous, that had been left the preceding night, of which I made a tolerable meal ; and in return for this kindness I gave her one of my pocket-handkerchiefs ; begging at the same time, a little corn for my horse, which she readily brought me.

Overcome with joy at so unexpected a deliverance, I lifted up my eyes to heaven, and whilst my heart swelled with gratitude, I returned thanks to that gracious and bountiful Being, whose power had supported me under so many dangers, and had now spread for me a table in the Wilderness.

Whilst my horse was feeding, the people began to assemble, and one of them whispered something to my hostess, which very much excited her surprise. Though I was not well acquainted with the Foulah language, I soon discovered that some of the men wished to apprehend and carry me back to Ali ; in hopes, I suppose, of receiving a reward. I therefore tied up the corn; and lest any one should suspect I had ran away from the Moors, I took a northerly direction, and went cheerfully along, driving my horse before me, followed by all the boys and girls of the town. When I had travelled about two miles, and got quit of all my troublesome attendants, I struck again into the woods, and took shelter under a large tree ; where I found it necessary to rest myself; a bundle of twigs serving me for a bed, and my saddle for a pillow.

I was awakened about two o'clock by three Foulahs, who, taking me for a Moor, pointed to the sun, and told me it was time to pray. Without entering into conversation with them,

I saddled my horse and continued my journey. I travelled over a level, but more fertile country, than I had seen for some time, until sunset, when, coming to a path that took a southerly direction, I followed it until midnight, at which time I arrived at a small pool of rain-water, and the wood being open, I determined to rest by it for the night. Having given my horse the remainder of the corn, I made my bed as formerly : but the musketoes and flies from the pool prevented sleep for some time, and I was twice disturbed in the night by wild beasts, which came very near, and whose howlings kept the horse in continual terror.

July 4th.   At daybreak I pursued my course through the woods as formerly: saw numbers of antelopes, wild hogs, and ostriches; but the soil was more hilly, and not so fertile as I had found it the preceding day. About eleven o'clock I ascended an eminence, where I climbed a tree, and discovered at about eight miles distance, an open part of the country, with several red spots, which I concluded were cultivated land ; and directing my course that way, came to the precincts of a watering-place, about one o'clock. From the appearance of the place, I judged it to belong to the Foulahs, and was hopeful that I should meet a better reception than I had experienced at Shrilla. In this I was not deceived ; for one of the shepherds invited me to come into his tent, and partake of some dates. This was one of those low Foulah tents in which there is room just sufficient to sit upright, and in which the family, the furniture, &c. seem huddled together like so many articles in a chest. When I had crept upon my hands and knees into this humble habitation, I found that it contained a woman and three children; who, together with the shepherd and myself, completely occupied the floor. A dish of boiled corn and dates was produced, and the master of the family, as is customary in this part of the country, first tasted it himself, and then desired me to follow his example. Whilst I was eating, the children kept their eyes fixed upon me; and no sooner did the shepherd pronounce the word *Nazarani*, than they began to cry, and their mother crept slowly towards the door, out of which she sprang like a greyhound, and was instantly followed by her children. So frightened were they at the very name of a Christian, that no entreaties could induce them to approach the tent. Here I purchased some corn for my horse in exchange for some brass buttons; and having thanked the shepherd for his hospitality, struck again into the woods. At sunset, I came to a road that took the direction for Bambarra, and resolved to follow it for the night; but about eight o'clock, hearing some people coming from the southward, I thought it prudent to hide myself among some thick bushes near the road. As these thickets are generally full of wild beasts, I found my situation rather unpleasant; sitting in the dark, holding my horse by the nose, with both hands, to prevent him from neighing, and equally afraid of the natives without, and the wild beasts within. My fears, however, were soon dissipated; for the people, after looking round the thicket, and perceiving nothing, went away; and I hastened to the more open parts of the wood, where I pursued my journey E. S. E, until past midnight; when the joyful cry of frogs induced me once more to deviate a little from my route, in order to quench my thirst. Having accomplished this, from a large pool of rain water, I sought for an open place, with a single tree in the midst, under which I made my bed for the night. I was disturbed by some wolves towards morning, which induced me to set forward a little before day; and having passed a small village called Wassalita, I came about ten o'clock (July 5th,) to a Negro town called Wawra, which properly belongs to Kaarta, but was at this time tributary to Mansong, King of Bambarra.

CHAPTER XV.

The Author proceeds to Wassiboo—is joined by some fugitive Kaartans, who accompany him in his Route through Bambarra. —Discovers the Niger.—Some Account of Sego, the Capital of Bambarra.—Mansong, the King, refuses to see the Author, but sends him a Present.—Great Hospitality of a Negro Woman.

WAWRA is a small town surrounded with high walls, and inhabited by a mixture of Mandingoes and Foulahs. The inhabitants employ themselves chiefly in cultivating corn, which they exchange with the Moors for salt. Here, being in security from the Moors, and very much fatigued, I resolved to rest myself; and meeting with a hearty welcome from the Dooty, whose name was Flancharee, I laid myself down upon a bullock's hide, and slept soundly for about two hours. The curiosity of the people would not allow me to sleep any longer. They had seen my saddle and bridle, and were assembled in great number to learn who I was, and whence I came. Some were of opinion that I was an Arab: others insisted that I was some Moorish Sultan; and they continued to debate the matter with such warmth, that the noise awoke me. The Dooty (who had formerly been at Gambia) at last interposed in my behalf, and

B b

assured them that I was certainly a white man; but he was convinced, from my appearance, that I was a very poor one.

In the course of the day, several women, hearing that I was going to Sego, came and begged me to inquire of Mansong, the king, what was become of their children. One woman, in particular, told me that her son's name was Mamadee; that he was no Heathen, but prayed to God morning and evening, and had been taken from her about three years ago, by Mansong's army; since which she had never heard of him. She said, she often dreamed about him; and begged me, if I should see him, either in Bambarra, or in my own country, to tell him, that his mother and sister were still alive. In the afternoon, the Dooty examined the contents of the leather bag, in which I had packed up my clothes; but finding nothing that was worth taking, he returned it, and told me to depart in the morning.

July 6th. It rained very much in the night, and at day-light I departed, in company with a Negro, who was going to a town called Dingyee for corn; but we had not proceeded above a mile, before the ass upon which he rode kicked him off, and he returned, leaving me to prosecute the journey by myself.

I reached Dingyee about noon; but the Dooty and most of the inhabitants had gone into the fields to cultivate corn. An old Foulah, observing me wandering about the town, desired me to come to his hut, where I was well entertained; and the Dooty, when he returned, sent me some victuals for myself, and corn for my horse.

July 7th. In the morning, when I was about to depart, my landlord, with a great deal of diffidence, begged me to give him a lock of my hair. He had been told, he said, that white men's hair made a saphie, that would give to the possessor all the knowledge of white men. I had never before heard of so simple a mode of education, but instantly complied with the request; and my landlord's thirst for learning was such, that, with cutting and pulling, he cropped one side of my head pretty closely; and would have done the same with the other, had I not signified my disapprobation, by putting on my hat, and assuring him, that I wished to reserve some of this precious merchandize for a future occasion.

I reached a small town called Wassiboo, about twelve o'clock, where I was obliged to stop until an opportunity should offer of procuring a guide to Satilé, which is distant a very long day's journey, through woods without any beaten path. I accordingly took up my residence at the Dooty's house, where I staid four days; during which time I amused myself by going to the fields with the family to plant corn. Cultivation is carried on here on a very extensive scale; and, as the natives themselves express it, " hunger is never known." In cultivating the soil, the men and women work together. They use a large sharp paddle, much superior to the paddle used in Gambia; but they are obliged, for fear of the Moors, to carry their arms with them to the field. The master, with the handle of his spear, marks the field into regular plats, one of which is assigned to every three slaves.

On the evening of the 11th, eight of the fugitive Kaartans arrived at Wassiboo. They had found it impossible to live under the tyrannical government of the Moors, and were now going to transfer their allegiance to the King of Bambarra. They offered to take me along with them as far as Satilé; and I accepted the offer.

July 12th. At daybreak we set out, and travelled with uncommon expedition until sunset: we stopped only twice in the course of the day; once at a watering-place in the woods, and another time at the ruins of a town, formerly belonging to Daisy, called *Illa-Compe* (the corn town). When we arrived in the neighbourhood of Satilé, the people who were employed in the corn fields, seeing so many horsemen, took us for a party of Moors, and ran screaming away from us. The whole town was instantly alarmed, and the slaves were seen, in every direction, driving the cattle and horses towards the town. It was in vain that one of our company galloped up to undeceive them: it only frightened them the more; and when we arrived at the town, we found the gates shut, and the people all under arms. After a long parley, we were permitted to enter; and, as there was every appearance of a heavy tornado, the Dooty allowed us to sleep in his baloon, and gave us each a bullock's hide for a bed.

July 13th. Early in the morning we again set forward. The roads were wet and slippery, but the country was very beautiful, abounding with rivulets, which were increased by the rain into rapid streams. About ten o'clock, we came to the ruins of a village, which had been destroyed by war about six months before; and in order to prevent any town from being built there in future, the large Bentang tree, under which the natives spent the day, had been burnt down; the wells filled up; and every thing that could make the spot desirable completely destroyed.

About noon, my horse was so much fatigued that I could not keep up with my companions; I therefore dismounted, and desired them to ride on, telling them, that I would follow as soon as my horse had rested a little. But I found them unwilling to leave me: the lions, they said, were very numerous in those parts, and though they might not so readily attack a body of people, they would soon find out an individual: it was therefore agreed, that one of the company should stay with me, to assist in driving my horse, while the others passed on to Galloo, to procure lodgings, and collect grass for the horses before night. Accompanied by this worthy Negro, I drove my horse before me until about four o'clock, when we came in sight of Galloo; a considerable town, standing in a fertile and beautiful valley, surrounded with high rocks.

As my companions had thoughts of settling in this neighbourhood, they had a fine sheep given them by the Dooty; and I was fortunate enough to procure plenty of corn for my horse. Here they blow upon elephants' teeth when they announce evening prayers, in the same manner as at Kemmoo.

Early next morning, (July 14th,) having first returned many thanks to our landlord for his hospitality, while my fellow-travellers offered up their prayers that he might never want, we set forward; and about three o'clock arrived at Moorja; a large town, famous for its trade in salt, which the Moors bring here in great quantities, to exchange for corn and cotton-cloth.

As most of the people here are Mahomedans, it is not allowed to the Kafirs to drink beer, which they call *Neo-dollo* (corn spirit,) except in certain houses. In one of these I saw about twenty people sitting round large vessels of this beer, with the greatest conviviality; many of them in a state of intoxication. As corn is plentiful, the inhabitants are very liberal to strangers: I believe we had as much corn and milk sent us by different people, as would have been sufficient for three times our number; and though we remained here two days, we experienced no diminution of their hospitality.

On the morning of the 16th, we again set forward, accompanied by a coffle of fourteen asses, loaded with salt, bound for Sansanding. The road was particularly romantic, between two rocky hills; but the Moors sometimes lie in wait here to plunder strangers. As soon as we had reached the open country, the master of the salt coffle thanked us for having staid with him so long, and now desired us to ride on. The sun was almost set before we reached Datliboo. In the evening we had a most tremendous tornado. The house in which we lodged, being flat roofed, admitted the rain in streams; the floor was soon ankle deep, the fire extinguished, and we were left to pass the night upon some bundles of fire wood, that happened to lie in a corner.

July 17th. We departed from Datliboo; and about ten o'clock passed a large coffle returning from Sego, with corn paddles, mats, and other household utensils. At five o'clock we came to a large village, where we intended to pass the night; but the Dooty would not receive us. When we departed from this place, my horse was so much fatigued that I was under the necessity of driving him, and it was dark before we reached Fanimboo, a small village; the Dooty of which no sooner heard that I was a white man, than he brought out three old muskets, and was much disappointed when he was told that I could not repair them.

July 18th. We continued our journey; but, owing to a light supper the preceding night, we felt ourselves rather hungry this morning, and endeavoured to procure some corn at a village; but without success. The towns were now more numerous, and the land that is not employed in cultivation affords excellent pasturage for large herds of cattle; but, owing to the great concourse of people daily going to and returning from Sego, the inhabitants are less hospitable to strangers.

My horse becoming weaker and weaker every day, was now of very little service to me: I was obliged to drive him before me for the greater part of the day; and did not reach Geosorro until eight o'clock in the evening. I found my companions wrangling with the Dooty, who had absolutely refused to give or sell them any provisions; and as none of us had tasted victuals for the last twenty-four hours, we were by no means disposed to fast another day, if we could help it. But finding our entreaties without effect, and being very much fatigued, I fell asleep, from which I was awakened, about midnight, with the joyful information " *kinne-nata*" (the victuals is come.) This made the remainder of the night pass away pleasantly; and at daybreak, July 19th, we resumed our journey, proposing to stop at a village called Doolinkeaboo, for the night following. My fellow-travellers, having better horses than myself, soon left me; and I was walking barefoot, driving my horse, when I was met by a coffle of slaves, about seventy in number, coming from Sego. They were tied together by their necks with thongs of a bullock's hide, twisted like a rope; seven slaves upon a thong; and a man with a musket between every seven. Many of the slaves were ill conditioned, and a great number of them women. In the rear came Sidi Mahomed's servant, whom I remembered to have seen at the camp of Benowm: he presently knew me, and told me that these slaves were going to Morocco, by the way of Ludamar, and the Great Desert.

In the afternoon, as I approached Doolinkeaboo, I met about twenty Moors on horseback, the owners of the slaves I had seen in the morning; they were well armed with muskets, and were very inquisitive concerning me, but not so rude as their countrymen generally are. From them I learned that Sidi Mahomed was not at Sego, but had gone to Cancaba for gold-dust.

When I arrived at Doolinkeaboo, I was informed that my fellow-travellers had gone on; but my horse was so much fatigued that I could not possibly proceed after them. The Dooty of the town, at my request, gave me a draught of water, which is generally looked upon as an earnest of greater hospitality; and I had no doubt of making up for the toils of the day, by a good supper and a sound sleep: unfortunately, I had neither one nor the other. The night was rainy and tempestuous, and the Dooty limited his hospitality to the draught of water.

July 20th. In the morning, I endeavoured, both by entreaties and threats, to procure some victuals from the Dooty, but in vain. I even begged some corn from one of his female slaves, as she was washing it at the well, and had the mortification to be refused. However, when the Dooty was gone to the fields, his wife sent me a handful of meal, which I mixed with water, and drank for breakfast. About eight o'clock, I departed from Doolinkeaboo, and at noon stopped a few minutes at a large Korree; where I had some milk given me by the Foulahs. And hearing that two Negroes were going from thence to Sego, I was happy to have their company, and we set out immediately. About four o'clock, we stopped at a small village, where one of the Negroes met with an acquaintance, who invited us to a sort of public entertainment, which was conducted with more than common propriety. A dish, made of sour milk and meal, called *Sinkatoo*, and beer made from their corn, was distributed with great liberality; and the women were admitted into the society; a circumstance I had never before observed in Africa. There was no compulsion; every one was at liberty to drink as he pleased: they nodded to each other when about to drink, and on setting down the calabash, commonly said *berka*, (thank you). Both men and women, appeared to be somewhat intoxicated, but they were far from being quarrelsome.

Departing from thence, we passed several large villages, where I was constantly taken for a Moor, and became the subject of much merriment to the Bambarrans; who, seeing me drive my horse before me, laughed heartily at my appearance. —He has been at Mecca, says one; you may see that by his

C c

clothes: another asked me if my horse was sick; a third wished to purchase it, &c.; so that I believe the very slaves were ashamed to be seen in my company. Just before it was dark, we took up our lodging for the night at a small village, where I procured some victuals for myself, and some corn for my horse, at the moderate price of a button; and was told that I should see the Niger (which the Negroes call Joliba, or *the great water*), early the next day. The lions are here very numerous: the gates are shut a little after sunset, and nobody allowed to go out. The thoughts of seeing the Niger in the morning, and the troublesome buzzing of musketoes, prevented me from shutting my eyes during the night; and I had saddled my horse, and was in readiness before daylight; but, on account of the wild beasts, we were obliged to wait until the people were stirring, and the gates opened. This happened to be a market-day at Sego, and the roads were every where filled with people, carrying different articles to sell. We passed four large villages, and at eight o'clock saw the smoke over Sego.

As we approached the town, I was fortunate enough to over-take the fugitive Kaartans, to whose kindness I had been so much indebted in my journey through Bambarra. They readily agreed to introduce me to the king; and we rode together through some marshy ground, where, as I was anxi-ously looking around for the river, one of them called out, *geo affilli*, (see the water); and looking forwards, I saw with infinite pleasure the great object of my mission; the long sought for, majestic Niger, glittering to the morning sun, as broad as the Thames at Westminster, and flowing slowly *to the eastward*.

I hastened to the brink, and, having drank of the water, lifted up my fervent thanks in prayer, to the Great Ruler of all things, for having thus far crowned my endeavours with success.

The circumstance of the Niger's flowing towards the east, and its collateral points, did not, however, excite my surprise; for although I had left Europe in great hesitation on this subject, and rather believed that it ran in the contrary direction, I had made such frequent inquiries during my progress, concerning this river; and received from Negroes of different nations, such clear and decisive assurances that its general course was *towards the rising sun*, as scarce left any doubt on my mind; and more especially as I knew that Major Houghton, had collected similar information, in the same manner.

Sego, the capital of Bambarra, at which I had now arrived, consists, properly speaking, of four distinct towns; two on the northern bank of the Niger, called Sego Korro, and Sego Boo; and two on the southern bank, called Sego Soo Korro, and Sego See Korro. They are all surrounded with high mud-walls; the houses are built of clay, of a square form, with flat roofs; some of them have two stories, and many of them are whitewashed. Besides these buildings, Moorish mosques are seen in every quarter; and the streets, though narrow, are broad enough for every useful purpose, in a country where wheel carriages are entirely unknown. From the best inquiries I could make, I have reason to believe that Sego contains altogether about thirty thousand inhabitants. The King of Bambarra constantly resides at Sego See Korro; he employs

C c 2

a great many slaves in conveying people over the river, and
the money they receive (though the fare is only ten Kowrie
shells for each individual) furnishes a considerable revenue
to the king, in the course of a year. The canoes are of a singular construction, each of them being formed of the trunks of
two large trees, rendered concave, and joined together, not side
by side, but end ways; the junction being exactly across the
middle of the canoe: they are therefore very long and dispro-
portionably narrow, and have neither decks nor masts; they
are, however, very roomy; for I observed in one of them four
horses, and several people, crossing over the river. When
we arrived at this ferry, we found a great number waiting
for a passage; they looked at me with silent wonder, and I distinguished, with concern, many Moors among them. There
were three different places of embarkation, and the ferrymen
were very diligent and expeditious; but, from the crowd of
people, I could not immediately obtain a passage; and sat down
upon the bank of the river, to wait for a more favourable
opportunity. The view of this extensive city; the numerous
canoes upon the river; the crowded population, and the cultivated state of the surrounding country, formed altogether a
prospect of civilization and magnificence, which I little expected to find in the bosom of Africa.

I waited more than two hours, without having an opportunity of crossing the river; during which time the people
who had crossed, carried information to Mansong the King,
that a white man was waiting for a passage, and was coming
to see him. He immediately sent over one of his chief men,

who informed me that the king could not possibly see me, until he knew what had brought me into his country; and that I must not presume to cross the river without the king's permission. He therefore advised me to lodge at a distant village, to which he pointed, for the night; and said that in the morning he would give me further instructions how to conduct myself. This was very discouraging. However, as there was no remedy, I set off for the village; where I found, to my great mortification, that no person would admit me into his house. I was regarded with astonishment and fear, and was obliged to sit all day without victuals, in the shade of a tree; and the night threatened to be very uncomfortable, for the wind rose, and there was great appearance of a heavy rain; and the wild beasts are so very numerous in the neighbourhood, that I should have been under the necessity of climbing up the tree, and resting amongst the branches. About sunset, however, as I was preparing to pass the night in this manner, and had turned my horse loose, that he might graze at liberty, a woman, returning from the labours of the field, stopped to observe me, and perceiving that I was weary and dejected, inquired into my situation, which I briefly explained to her; whereupon, with looks of great compassion, she took up my saddle and bridle, and told me to follow her. Having conducted me into her hut, she lighted up a lamp, spread a mat on the floor, and told me I might remain there for the night. Finding that I was very hungry, she said she would procure me something to eat. She accordingly went out, and returned in a short time with a very fine fish; which, having caused to be half broiled upon some embers, she gave me for supper. The rites of hospitality being thus performed towards a stranger in distress; my worthy benefactress (pointing to the mat, and telling me I might sleep there without apprehension) called to the female part of her family, who had stood gazing on me all the while in fixed astonishment, to resume their task of spinning cotton; in which they continued to employ themselves great part of the night. They lightened their labour by songs, one of which was composed extempore; for I was myself the subject of it. It was sung by one of the young women, the rest joining in a sort of chorus. The air was sweet and plaintive, and the words, literally translated, were these.—" The winds roared, and the rains fell. " —The poor white man, faint and weary, came and sat under " our tree.—He has no mother to bring him milk; no wife to " grind his corn. *Chorus.* Let us pity the white man; no mother " has he, &c. &c." Trifling as this recital may appear to the reader, to a person in my situation, the circumstance was affecting in the highest degree. I was oppressed by such unexpected kindness; and sleep fled from my eyes. In the morning I presented my compassionate landlady with two of the four brass buttons which remained on my waistcoat; the only recompence I could make her.

July 21st. I continued in the village all this day, in conversation with the natives, who came in crowds to see me; but was rather uneasy towards evening, to find that no message had arrived from the king; the more so, as the people began to whisper, that Mansong had received some very unfavourable accounts of me, from the Moors and Slatees residing at Sego;

who it seems were exceedingly suspicious concerning the motives of my journey. I learnt that many consultations had been held with the king, concerning my reception and disposal; and some of the villagers frankly told me, that I had many enemies, and must expect no favour.

July 22d. About eleven o'clock, a messenger arrived from the king; but he gave me very little satisfaction. He inquired particularly if I had brought any present; and seemed much disappointed when he was told that I had been robbed of every thing by the Moors. When I proposed to go along with him, he told me to stop until the afternoon, when the king would send for me.

July 23d. In the afternoon, another messenger arrived from Mansong, with a bag in his hands. He told me, it was the king's pleasure that I should depart forthwith from the vicinage of Sego; but that Mansong, wishing to relieve a white man in distress, had sent me five thousand Kowries.* to enable me to purchase provisions in the course of my journey: the messenger added, that if my intentions were really to proceed to Jenné, he had orders to accompany me as a guide to Sansanding. I was at first puzzled to account for this behaviour of the king; but, from the conversation I had with the guide, I had after-

---

* Mention has already been made of these little shells, (p. 27) which pass current as money, in many parts of the East-Indies, as well as Africa. In Bambarra, and the adjacent countries, where the necessaries of life are very cheap, one hundred of them would commonly purchase a day's provisions for myself, and corn for my horse. I reckoned about two hundred and fifty Kowries, equal to one shilling.

ward reason to believe, that Mansong would willingly have
admitted me into his presence at Sego; but was apprehensive
he might not be able to protect me, against the blind and
inveterate malice of the Moorish inhabitants. His conduct,
therefore, was at once prudent and liberal. The circumstances
under which I made my appearance at Sego, were undoubtedly
such as might create in the mind of the king, a well warranted
suspicion that I wished to conceal the true object of my journey.
He argued, probably, as my guide argued; who, when he was
told, that I had come from a great distance, and through many
dangers, to behold the Joliba river, naturally inquired, if
there were no rivers in my own country, and whether one
river was not like another. Notwithstanding this, and in spite
of the jealous machinations of the Moors, this benevolent
prince thought it sufficient, that a white man was found in
his dominions, in a condition of extreme wretchedness; and
that no other plea was necessary to entitle the sufferer to his
bounty.

CHAPTER XVI.

Departure from Sego, and Arrival at Kabba.—Description of the Shea, or vegetable Butter Tree.—The Author and his Guide arrive at Sansanding. Behaviour of the Moors at that Place.—The Author pursues his Journey to the Eastward. —Incidents on the Road.—Arrives at Modiboo, and proceeds for Kea; but obliged to leave his Horse by the Way.—Embarks at Kea in a Fisherman's Canoe for Moorzan; is conveyed from thence across the Niger to Silla.—Determines to proceed no further Eastward.—Some Account of the further Course of the Niger, and the Towns in its Vicinage, towards the East.

BEING, in the manner that has been related, compelled to leave Sego, I was conducted the same evening to a village about seven miles to the eastward, with some of the inhabitants of which my guide was acquainted, and by whom we were well received.* He was very friendly and communicative, and spoke highly of the hospitality of his countrymen; but withal told me, that if Jenné was the place of my destination, which he seemed to have hitherto doubted, I had undertaken an enter-

* I should have before observed, that I found the language of Bambarra, a sort of corrupted Mandingo. After a little practice, I understood, and spoke it without difficulty.

D d

prize of greater danger than probably I was apprized of; for, although the town of Jenné was, nominally, a part of the King of Bambarra's dominions, it was in fact, he said, a city of the Moors; the leading part of the inhabitants being Bushreens, and even the governor himself, though appointed by Mansong, of the same sect. Thus was I in danger of falling a second time into the hands of men who would consider it not only justifiable, but meritorious, to destroy me; and this reflection was aggravated by the circumstance that the danger increased, as I advanced in my journey; for I learned that the places beyond Jenné were under the Moorish influence, in a still greater degree than Jenné itself; and Tombuctoo, the great object of my search, altogether in possession of that savage and merciless people, who allow no Christian to live there. But I had now advanced too far to think of returning to the westward, on such vague and uncertain information, and determined to proceed; and being accompanied by the guide, I departed from the village on the morning of the 24th. About eight o'clock, we passed a large town called Kabba, situated in the midst of a beautiful and highly cultivated country; bearing a greater re-semblance to the centre of England, than to what I should have supposed had been the middle of Africa. The people were every where employed in collecting the fruit of the Shea trees, from which they prepare the vegetable butter, mentioned in former parts of this work. These trees grow in great abun-dance all over this part of Bambarra. They are not planted by the natives, but are found growing naturally in the woods; and, in clearing wood land for cultivation, every tree is cut down but the Shea. The tree itself, very much resembles the American oak; and the fruit, from the kernel of which, being first dried in the sun, the butter is prepared, by boiling the kernel in water, has somewhat the appearance of a Spanish olive. The kernel is enveloped in a sweet pulp, under a thin green rind; and the butter produced from it, besides the advantage of its keeping the whole year without salt; is whiter, firmer, and, to my palate, of a richer flavour, than the best butter I ever tasted made from cows' milk. The growth and preparation of this commodity, seem to be among the first objects of African industry in this and the neighbouring states; and it constitutes a main article of their inland commerce.

We passed, in the course of the day, a great many villages, inhabited chiefly by fishermen; and in the evening about five o'clock arrived at Sansanding; a very large town, containing, as I was told, from eight to ten thousand inhabitants. This place is much resorted to by the Moors, who bring salt from Beeroo, and beads and coral from the Mediterranean, to exchange here for gold–dust, and cotton-cloth. This cloth they sell to great advantage in Beeroo, and other Moorish countries, where, on account of the want of rain, no cotton is cultivated.

I desired my guide to conduct me to the house in which we were to lodge, by the most private way possible. We accordingly rode along between the town and the river, passing by a creek or harbour, in which I observed twenty large canoes, most of them fully loaded, and covered with mats, to prevent the rain from injuring the goods. As we proceeded, three other canoes arrived, two with passengers, and one with goods.

I was happy to find, that all the Negro inhabitants took me for a Moor; under which character I should probably have passed unmolested, had not a Moor, who was sitting by the river side, discovered the mistake, and setting up a loud exclamation, brought together a number of his countrymen.

When I arrived at the house of Counti Mamadi, the Dooty of the town, I was surrounded with hundreds of people, speaking a variety of different dialects, all equally unintelligible to me. At length, by the assistance of my guide, who acted as interpreter, I understood that one of the spectators pretended to have seen me at one place, and another at some other place; and a Moorish woman, absolutely swore that she had kept my house three years at Gallam, on the river Senegal. It was plain that they mistook me for some other person; and I desired two of the most confident, to point towards the place where they had seen me. They pointed due south; hence I think it probable that they came from Cape Coast, where they might have seen many white men. Their language was different from any I had yet heard. The Moors now assembled in great number; with their usual arrogance, compelling the Negroes to stand at a distance. They immediately began to question me concerning my religion; but finding that I was not master of the Arabic, they sent for two men, whom they call *Ilbuidi* (Jews), in hopes that they might be able to converse with me. These Jews, in dress and appearance, very much resemble the Arabs; but though they so far conform to the religion of Mahomet, as to recite, in public, prayers from the Koran; they are but little respected by the Negroes; and even the Moors themselves allowed, that though I was a Christian, I was a better man than a Jew. They, however, insisted that, like the Jews, I must conform so far as to repeat the Mahomedan prayers; and when I attempted to wave the subject, by telling them that I could not speak Arabic, one of them, a Shereef from Tuat, in the Great Desert, started up and swore by the Prophet, that if I refused to go to the mosque, he would be one that would assist in carrying me thither. And there is no doubt but this threat would have been immediately executed, had not my landlord interposed in my behalf. He told them, that I was the king's stranger, and he could not see me ill treated, whilst I was under his protection. He therefore advised them to let me alone for the night; assuring them, that, in the morning, I should be sent about my business. This somewhat appeased their clamour; but they compelled me to ascend a high seat, by the door of the mosque, in order that every body might see me; for the people had assembled in such numbers as to be quite ungovernable; climbing upon the houses, and squeezing each other, like the spectators at an execution. Upon this seat I remained until sunset, when I was conducted into a neat little hut, with a small court before it; the door of which Counti Mamadi shut, to prevent any person from disturbing me. But this precaution could not exclude the Moors. They climbed over the top of the mud-wall, and came in crowds into the court, in order, they said, to see me *perform my evening devotions, and eat eggs.* The former of these ceremonies, I did not think proper to comply with; but I told them I had no objection to eat eggs, provided they would bring me eggs to eat. My landlord immediately brought me seven hen's eggs, and was much surprised to find that I could not eat them raw; for it seems to be a prevalent opinion among the inhabitants of the interior, that Europeans subsist almost entirely on this diet. When I had succeeded, in persuading my landlord that this opinion was without foundation, and that I would gladly partake of any victuals which he might think proper to send me; he ordered a sheep to be killed, and part of it to be dressed for my supper. About midnight, when the Moors had left me, he paid me a visit, and with much earnestness, desired me to write him a saphie. "If a Moor's saphie is good, (said this hospitable old man), a white man's must needs be better." I readily furnished him with one, possessed of all the virtues I could concentrate; for it contained the Lord's prayer. The pen with which it was written was made of a reed; a little charcoal and gum-water made very tolerable ink, and a thin board answered the purpose of paper.

July 25th. Early in the morning, before the Moors were assembled, I departed from Sansanding, and slept the ensuing night at a small town called Sibili; from whence, on the day following, I reached Nyara, a large town at some distance from the river, where I halted the 27th, to have my clothes washed, and recruit my horse. The Dooty there has a very commodious house, flat roofed, and two stories high. He shewed me some gunpowder of his own manufacturing: and pointed out as a great curiosity, a little brown monkey, that was tied to a stake by the door, telling me that it came from a far distant country, called Kong.

July 28th. I departed from Nyara, and reached Nyamee about noon. This town is inhabited chiefly by Foulahs, from the kingdom of Masina. The Dooty (I know not why), would not receive me, but civilly sent his son on horseback, to conduct me to Modiboo; which he assured me was at no great distance.

We rode nearly in a direct line, through the woods; but in general went forwards with great circumspection. I observed that my guide frequently stopped, and looked under the bushes. On inquiring the reason of this caution, he told me that lions were very numerous in that part of the country, and frequently attacked people travelling through the woods. While he was speaking, my horse started, and looking round, I observed a large animal of the camelopard kind, standing at a little distance. The neck and fore legs were very long; the head was furnished with two short black horns, turning backwards; the tail, which reached down to the ham joint, had a tuft of hair at the end. The animal was of a mouse colour; and it trotted away from us in a very sluggish manner; moving its head from side to side, to see if we were pursuing it. Shortly after this, as we were crossing a large open plain, where there were a few scattered bushes, my guide, who was a little way before me, wheeled his horse round in a moment, calling out something in the Foulah language, which I did not understand. I inquired in Mandingo what he meant; *Wara billi billi*, a very large lion, said he; and made signs for me to ride away. But my horse was too much fatigued: so we rode slowly past the bush, from which the animal had given us the alarm. Not seeing any thing myself, however, I thought my guide had been mistaken, when the Foulah suddenly put his hand to his mouth, exclaiming, *Soubah an allahi*, (God preserve us!) and to my great surprise, I then perceived a large red lion, at a short distance from the bush, with his head couched between his fore paws. I expected he would instantly spring upon me, and instinctively pulled my feet from my stirrups, to throw myself on the ground, that my horse might become the victim, rather than myself. But it is probable the lion was not hungry; for he quietly suffered us to pass, though we were fairly within his reach. My eyes were so riveted upon this sovereign of the beasts, that I found it impossible to remove them, until we were at a considerable distance. We now took a circuitous route, through some swampy ground, to avoid any more of these disagreeable rencounters. At sunset we arrived at Modi-boo; a delightful village on the banks of the Niger, command-ing a view of the river for many miles, both to the east and west. The small green islands (the peaceful retreat of some industrious Foulahs, whose cattle are here secure from the depredations of wild beasts), and the majestic breadth of the river, which is here much larger than at Sego, render the situation one of the most enchanting in the world. Here are caught great plenty of fish, by means of long cotton nets, which the natives make themselves; and use nearly in the same manner as nets are used in Europe. I observed the head of a crocodile lying upon one of the houses, which they told me had been killed by the shepherds, in a swamp near the town. These animals are not uncommon in the Niger; but I believe they are not oftentimes found dangerous. They are of little account to the traveller, when compared with the amazing swarms of musketoes, which rise from the swamps and creeks, in such numbers as to harass even the most torpid of the natives; and as my clothes were now almost worn to rags, I was but ill prepared to resist their attacks. I usually passed the night, without shutting my eyes, walking backwards and forwards, fanning myself with my hat; their stings raised numerous blisters on my legs and arms; which, together with the want of rest, made me very feverish and uneasy.

July 29th. Early in the morning, my landlord observing that I was sickly, hurried me away; sending a servant with me as a guide to Kea. But though I was little able to walk, my horse was still less able to carry me; and about six miles to the east of Modiboo, in crossing some rough clayey ground, he fell; and the united strength of the guide and myself, could not place him again upon his legs. I sat down for some time, beside this worn-out associate of my adventures; but finding him still unable to rise, I took off the saddle and bridle, and placed a quantity of grass before him. I surveyed the poor animal, as he lay panting on the ground, with sympathetic emotion; for I could not suppress the sad apprehension, that I should myself, in a short time, lie down and perish in the same manner, of fatigue and hunger. With this foreboding, I left my poor horse; and with great reluctance followed my

E e

guide on foot, along the bank of the river, until about noon; when we reached Kea, which I found to be nothing more than a small fishing village. The Dooty, a surly old man, who was sitting by the gate, received me very coolly; and when I informed him of my situation, and begged his protection, told me, with great indifference, that he paid very little attention to fine speeches, and that I should not enter his house. My guide remonstrated in my favour, but to no purpose; for the Dooty remained inflexible in his determination. I knew not where to rest my wearied limbs, but was happily relieved by a fishing canoe belonging to Silla, which was at that moment coming down the river. The Dooty waved to the fisherman to come near, and desired him to take charge of me as far as Moorzan. The fisherman, after some hesitation, consented to carry me; and I embarked in the canoe, in company with the fisherman, his wife, and a boy. The Negro, who had conducted me from Modiboo, now left me; I requested him to look to my horse on his return, and take care of him if he was still alive, which he promised to do.

Departing from Kea, we proceeded about a mile down the river, when the fisherman paddled the canoe to the bank, and desired me to jump out. Having tied the canoe to a stake, he stripped off his clothes, and dived for such a length of time, that I thought he had actually drowned himself, and was surprised to see his wife behave with so much indifference upon the occasion; but my fears were over when he raised up his head astern of the canoe, and called for a rope. With this rope he dived a second time; and then got into the canoe, and ordered the boy to assist him in pulling. At length, they brought up a large basket, about ten feet in diameter, containing two fine fish, which the fisherman (after returning the basket into the water), immediately carried ashore, and hid in the grass. We then went a little farther down, and took up another basket, in which was one fish. The fisherman now left us, to carry his prizes to some neighbouring market; and the woman and boy proceeded with me in the canoe, down the river.

About four o'clock, we arrived at Moorzan, a fishing town on the northern bank; from whence I was conveyed across the river to Silla, a large town; where I remained until it was quite dark, under a tree, surrounded by hundreds of people. But their language was very different from the other parts of Bambarra; and I was informed that, in my progress eastward, the Bambarra tongue was but little understood, and that when I reached Jenné, I should find that the majority of the inhabitants spoke a different language, called *Jenné Kummo* by the Negroes; and *Kalam Soudan*, by the Moors.

With a great deal of entreaty, the Dooty allowed me to come into his baloon, to avoid the rain; but the place was very damp, and I had a smart paroxysm of fever, during the night. Worn down by sickness, exhausted with hunger and fatigue; half naked, and without any article of value, by which I might procure provisions, clothes, or lodging; I began to reflect seriously on my situation. I was now convinced, by painful experience, that the obstacles to my further progress were insurmountable. The tropical rains were already

set in, with all their violence; the rice grounds and swamps,
were every where overflowed; and, in a few days more, travelling of every kind, unless by water, would be completely obstructed. The Kowries which remained of the King of Bambarra's present, were not sufficient to enable me to hire a canoe
for any great distance; and I had but little hopes of subsisting
by charity, in a country where the Moors have such influence.
But above all, I perceived that I was advancing, more and
more, within the power of those merciless fanatics; and from
my reception both at Sego and Sansanding, I was apprehensive
that, in attempting to reach even Jenné (unless under the protection of some man of consequence amongst them, which I
had no means of obtaining), I should sacrifice my life to no
purpose; for my discoveries would perish with me. The prospect either way was gloomy. In returning to the Gambia, a
journey on foot of many hundred miles, presented itself to my
contemplation, through regions and countries unknown. Nevertheless, this seemed to be the only alternative; for I saw inevitable destruction in attempting to proceed to the eastward.
With this conviction on my mind, I hope my readers will
acknowledge, that I did right in going no farther. I had
made every effort to execute my mission in its fullest extent,
which prudence could justify. Had there been the most distant
prospect of a successful termination, neither the unavoidable
hardships of the journey, nor the dangers of a second captivity,
should have forced me to desist. This, however, necessity
compelled me to do; and whatever may be the opinion of
my general readers on this point, it affords me inexpressible

satisfaction, that my honourable employers have been pleased, since my return, to express their full approbation of my
conduct.

Having thus brought my mind, after much doubt and perplexity, to a determination to return westward; I thought it
incumbent on me, before I left Silla, to collect from the
Moorish and Negro traders, all the information I could, concerning the further course of the Niger eastward; and the
situation and extent of the kingdoms in its vicinage; and the
following few notices I received from such various quarters,
as induce me to think they are authentic.

Two short days' journey to the eastward of Silla, is the town
of Jenné, which is situated on a small island in the river; and
is said to contain a greater number of inhabitants than Sego
itself, or any other town in Bambarra. At the distance of two
days more, the river spreads into a considerable lake, called
Dibbie (or the dark lake), concerning the extent of which, all
the information I could obtain was, that in crossing it, from
west to east, the canoes lose sight of land one whole day.
From this lake, the water issues in many different streams,
which terminate in two large branches, one whereof flows
towards the north-east, and the other to the east; but these
branches join at Kabra, which is one day's journey to the
southward of Tombuctoo, and is the port or shipping-place of
that city. The tract of land which the two streams encircle, is
called Jinbala, and is inhabited by Negroes; and the whole
distance, by land, from Jenné to Tombuctoo, is twelve days'
journey.

From Kabra, at the distance of eleven days' journey, down the stream, the river passes to the southward of Houssa, which is two days' journey distant from the river. Of the further progress of this great river, and its final exit, all the natives with whom I conversed, seem to be entirely ignorant. Their commercial pursuits seldom induce them to travel further than the cities of Tombuctoo and Houssa; and as the sole object of those journies is the acquirement of wealth, they pay but little attention to the course of rivers, or the geography of countries. It is, however, highly probable that the Niger affords a safe and easy communication between very remote nations. All my informants agreed, that many of the Negro merchants who arrive at Tombuctoo and Houssa, from the eastward, speak a different language from that of Bambarra, or any other kingdom with which they are acquainted. But even these merchants, it would seem, are ignorant of the termination of the river, for such of them as can speak Arabic, describe the amazing length of its course in very general terms; saying only, that they believe *it runs to the world's end*.

The names of many kingdoms to the eastward of Houssa, are familiar to the inhabitants of Bambarra. I was shewn quivers and arrows of very curious workmanship, which I was informed came from the kingdom of Kassina.

On the northern bank of the Niger, at a short distance from Silla, is the kingdom of Masina, which is inhabited by Foulahs. They employ themselves there, as in other places, chiefly in pasturage, and pay an annual tribute to the King of Bambarra, for the lands which they occupy.

To the north-east of Masina, is situated the kingdom of Tombuctoo, the great object of European research; the capital of this kingdom being one of the principal marts for that extensive commerce which the Moors carry on with the Negroes. The hopes of acquiring wealth in this pursuit, and zeal for propagating their religion, have filled this extensive city with Moors and Mahomedan converts; the king himself, and all the chief officers of state are Moors; and they are said to be more severe and intolerant in their principles than any other of the Moorish tribes in this part of Africa. I was informed by a venerable old Negro, that when he first visited Tombuctoo, he took up his lodging at a sort of public inn, the landlord of which, when he conducted him into his hut, spread a mat on the floor, and laid a rope upon it; saying " if you are a Mussulman, " you are my friend, sit down; but if you are a Kafir, you are " my slave; and with this rope, I will lead you to market." The present King of Tombuctoo is named *Abu Abrahima;* he is reported to possess immense riches. His wives and concubines are said to be clothed in silk, and the chief officers of state live in considerable splendour. The whole expence of his government is defrayed, as I was told, by a tax upon merchandize, which is collected at the gates of the city.

The city of Houssa, (the capital of a large kingdom of the same name, situated to the eastward of Tombuctoo,) is another great mart for Moorish commerce. I conversed with many merchants who had visited that city; and they all agreed that it is larger, and more populous, than Tombuctoo. The trade, police, and government, are nearly the same in both; but in Houssa, the Negroes are in greater proportion to the Moors, and have some share in the government.

Concerning the small kingdom of Jinbala, I was not able to collect much information. The soil is said to be remarkably fertile, and the whole country so full of creeks and swamps, that the Moors have hitherto been baffled in every attempt to subdue it. The inhabitants are Negroes, and some of them are said to live in considerable affluence, particularly those near the capital; which is a resting-place for such merchants as transport goods from Tombuctoo to the western parts of Africa.

To the southward of Jinbala, is situated the Negro kingdom of Gotto, which is said to be of great extent. It was formerly divided into a number of petty states, which were governed by their own chiefs; but their private quarrels invited invasion from the neighbouring kingdoms. At length a politic chief, of the name of Moossee, had address enough to make them unite in hostilities against Bambarra; and on this occasion he was unanimously chosen general; the different chiefs consenting for a time to act under his command. Moossee immediately dispatched a fleet of canoes, loaded with provisions, from the banks of the lake Dibbie up the Niger, towards Jenné, and with the whole of his army pushed forwards into Bambarra. He arrived on the bank of the Niger opposite to Jenné, before the townspeople had the smallest intimation of his approach; his fleet of canoes joined him the same day, and having landed the provisions, he embarked part of his army, and in the night took Jenné by storm. This event so terrified the King of

Bambarra, that he sent messengers to sue for peace, and in order to obtain it, consented to deliver to Moossee a certain number of slaves every year; and return every thing that had been taken from the inhabitants of Gotto. Moossee, thus triumphant, returned to Gotto, where he was declared king, and the capital of the country is called by his name.

On the west of Gotto, is the kingdom of Baedoo, which was conquered by the present King of Bambarra about seven years ago, and has continued tributary to him ever since.

West of Baedoo, is Maniana; the inhabitants of which, according to the best information I was able to collect, are cruel and ferocious; carrying their resentment towards their enemies, so far as never to give quarter; and even to indulge themselves with unnatural and disgusting banquets of human flesh.

I am well aware that the accounts which the Negroes give of their enemies, ought to be received with great caution; but I heard the same account in so many different kingdoms, and from such variety of people, whose veracity I had no occasion to suspect, that I am disposed to allow it some degree of credit. The inhabitants of Bambarra, in the course of a long and bloody war, must have had frequent opportunities of satisfying themselves as to the fact: and if the report had been entirely without foundation, I cannot conceive why the term *Ma dummulo*, (man eaters), should be applied exclusively to the inhabitants of Maniana.

F f

CHAPTER XVII.

The Author returns Westward—arrives at Modiboo, and recovers his Horse—finds great Difficulty in travelling, in consequence of the Rains, and the overflowing of the River;—is informed that the King of Bambarra had sent Persons to apprehend him:— avoids Sego, and prosecutes his Journey along the Banks of the Niger.—Incidents on the Road.—Cruelties attendant on African Wars.—The Author crosses the River Frina, and arrives at Taffara.

Having, for the reasons assigned in the last Chapter, determined to proceed no farther eastward than Silla, I acquainted the Dooty with my intention of returning to Sego, proposing to travel along the southern side of the river; but he informed me, that, from the number of creeks and swamps on that side, it was impossible to travel by any other route than along the northern bank ; and even that route, he said, would soon be impassable, on account of the overflowing of the river. However, as he commended my determination to return westward, he agreed to speak to some one of the fishermen to carry me over to Moorzan. I accordingly stepped into a canoe about eight o'clock in the morning of July 30th, and in about an hour was landed at Moorzan. At this place I hired a canoe for sixty Kowries, and in the afternoon arrived at Kea; where, for forty Kowries more, the Dooty permitted me to sleep in the same hut with one of his slaves. This poor Negro, perceiving that I was sickly, and that my clothes were very ragged, humanely lent me a large cloth to cover me for the night.

July 31st. The Dooty's brother being going to Modiboo, I embraced the opportunity of accompanying him thither, there being no beaten road. He promised to carry my saddle, which I had left at Kea when my horse fell down in the woods, as I now proposed to present it to the King of Bambarra.

We departed from Kea at eight o'clock, and about a mile to the westward observed, on the bank of the river, a great number of earthen jars, piled up together. They were very neatly formed, but not glazed; and were evidently of that sort of pottery which is manufactured at Downie (a town to the west of Tombuctoo), and sold to great advantage in different parts of Bambarra. As we approached towards the jars, my companion plucked up a large handful of herbage, and threw it upon them; making signs for me to do the same, which I did. He then, with great seriousness, told me that these jars belonged to some supernatural power; that they were found in their present situation about two years ago; and as no person had claimed them, every traveller as he passed them, from respect to the invisible proprietor, threw some grass, or the branch of a tree, upon the heap, to defend the jars from the rain.

Thus conversing, we travelled in the most friendly manner until, unfortunately, we perceived the footsteps of a lion, quite fresh in the mud, near the river side. My companion now proceeded with great circumspection; and at last, coming to some thick underwood, he insisted that I should walk before him. I endeavoured to excuse myself, by alleging that I did not know the road ; but he obstinately persisted ; and after a few high words and menacing looks, threw down the saddle and went away. This very much disconcerted me ; but as I had given up all hopes of obtaining a horse, I could not think of encumbering myself with the saddle ; and taking off the stirrups and girths, I threw the saddle into the river. The Negro no sooner saw me throw the saddle into the water, than he came running from among the bushes where he had concealed himself, jumped into the river, and by help of his spear brought out the saddle, and ran away with it. I continued my course along the bank ; but as the wood was remarkably thick, and I had reason to believe that a lion was at no great distance, I became much alarmed, and took a long circuit through the bushes to avoid him.

About four in the afternoon I reached Modiboo, where I found my saddle. The guide, who had got there before me, being afraid that I should inform the king of his conduct, had brought the saddle with him in a canoe.

While I was conversing with the Dooty, and remonstrating against the guide for having left me in such a situation, I heard a horse neigh in one of the huts ; and the Dooty inquired, with a smile, if I knew who was speaking to me ? He explained himself, by telling me that my horse was still alive, and somewhat recovered from his fatigue ; but he insisted that I should take him along with me ; adding, that he had once kept a Moor's horse for four months, and when the horse had recovered and got into good condition, the Moor returned and claimed it, and refused to give him any reward for his trouble.

August 1st. I departed from Modiboo, driving my horse before me; and in the afternoon reached Nyamee, where I remained three days; during which time it rained without intermission, and with such violence, that no person could venture out of doors.

Aug. 5th. I departed from Nyamee; but the country was so deluged, that I was frequently in danger of losing the road, and had to wade across the savannahs for miles together, knee deep in water. Even the corn ground, which is the driest land in the country, was so completely flooded, that my horse twice stuck fast in the mud, and was not got out without the greatest difficulty.

In the evening of the same day, I arrived at Nyara, where I was well received by the Dooty; and as the 6th was rainy, I did not depart until the morning of the 7th; but the water had swelled to such a height, that in many places the road was scarcely passable; and though I waded breast deep across the swamps, I could only reach a small village called Nemaboo, where, however, for an hundred Kowries, I procured from some Foulahs, plenty of corn for my horse, and milk for myself.

Aug. 8th. The difficulties I had experienced the day before, made me anxious to engage a fellow-traveller; particularly as I was assured, that, in the course of a few days, the country would be so completely overflowed, as to render the road utterly impassable; but though I offered two hundred Kowries for a guide, nobody would accompany me. However, on the morning following, (August 9th,) a Moor and his wife, riding upon two bullocks, and bound for Sego with salt, passed the village, and agreed to take me along with them ; but I found them of little service ; for they were wholly unacquainted with the road, and being accustomed to a sandy soil, were very bad travellers. Instead of wading before the bullocks, to feel if the ground was solid, the woman boldly entered the first swamp, riding upon the top of the load ; but when she had proceeded about two hundred yards, the bullock sunk into a hole, and threw both the load and herself among the reeds. The frightened husband stood for some time seemingly petrified with horror, and suffered his wife to be almost drowned before he went to her assistance.

About sunset we reached Sibity ; but the Dooty received me very coolly : and when I solicited for a guide to Sansanding, he told me his people were otherwise employed. I was shewn into a damp old hut, where I passed a very uncomfortable night ; for when the walls of the huts are softened by the rain, they frequently become too weak to support the weight of the roof. I heard three huts fall during the night, and was apprehensive that the hut I lodged in would be the fourth. In the morning, as I went to pull some grass for my horse, I counted fourteen huts which had fallen in this manner, since the commencement of the rainy season.

It continued to rain with great violence all the 10th ; and as the Dooty refused to give me any provisions, I purchased some corn, which I divided with my horse.

Aug. 11th. The Dooty compelled me to depart from the town, and I set out for Sansanding, without any great hopes of faring better there than I had done at Sibity; for I learned, from people who came to visit me, that a report prevailed, and was universally believed, that I had come to Bambarra as a spy; and as Mansong had not admitted me into his presence, the Dooties of the different towns were at liberty to treat me in what manner they pleased. From repeatedly hearing the same story, I had no doubt of the truth of it; but as there was no alternative, I determined to proceed, and a little before sunset I arrived at Sansanding. My reception was what I expected. Counti Mamadi, who had been so kind to me formerly, scarcely gave me welcome. Every one wished to shun me; and my landlord sent a person to inform me, that a very unfavourable report was received from Sego concerning me, and that he wished me to depart early in the morning. About ten o'clock at night Counti Mamadi himself came privately to me, and informed me, that Mansong had dispatched a canoe to Jenné to bring me back; and he was afraid I should find great difficulty in going to the west country. He advised me, therefore, to depart from Sansanding before daybreak; and cautioned me against stopping at Diggani, or any town near Sego.

Aug. 12th. I departed from Sansanding, and reached Kabba in the afternoon. As I approached the town, I was surprised to see several people assembled at the gate; one of whom, as I advanced, came running towards me, and taking my horse by the bridle, led me round the walls of the town; and then pointing to the west, told me to go along, or it would fare worse with me. It was in vain that I represented the danger of being benighted in the woods, exposed to the inclemency of the weather, and the fury of wild beasts. " Go along," was all the answer; and a number of people coming up, and urging me in the same manner, with great earnestness, I suspected that some of the king's messengers, who were sent in search of me, were in the town; and that these Negroes, from mere kindness, conducted me past it, with a view to facilitate my escape. I accordingly took the road for Sego, with the uncomfortable prospect of passing the night on the branches of a tree. After travelling about three miles, I came to a small village near the road. The Dooty was splitting sticks by the gate; but I found I could have no admittance; and when I attempted to enter, he jumped up, and with the stick he held in his hand threatened to strike me off the horse, if I presumed to advance another step.

At a little distance from this village (and farther from the road), is another small one. I conjectured, that being rather out of the common route, the inhabitants might have fewer objections to give me house room for the night; and having crossed some corn fields, I sat down under a tree by the well. Two or three women came to draw water; and one of them perceiving I was a stranger, inquired whither I was going. I told her I was going for Sego, but being benighted on the road, I wished to stay at the village until morning; and begged she would acquaint the Dooty with my situation. In a little time the Dooty sent for me, and permitted me to sleep in a large baloon, in one corner of which was constructed a kiln for drying the fruit of the Shea trees: it contained about half a cartload of fruit, under which was kept up a clear wood fire. I was

informed, that in three days the fruit would be ready for pounding and boiling; and that the butter thus manufactured, is preferable to that which is prepared from fruit dried in the sun;
especially in the rainy season; when the process by insolation
is always tedious, and oftentimes ineffectual.

Aug. 13. About ten o'clock I reached a small village within
half a mile of Sego, where I endeavoured, but in vain, to procure some provisions. Every one seemed anxious to avoid me;
and I could plainly perceive, by the looks and behaviour of the
inhabitants, that some very unfavourable accounts had been
circulated concerning me. I was again informed, that Mansong
had sent people to apprehend me; and the Dooty's son told
me I had no time to lose, if I wished to get safe out of Bambarra. I now fully saw the danger of my situation, and determined to avoid Sego altogether. I accordingly mounted my
horse, and taking the road for Diggani, travelled as fast as I
could, until I was out of sight of the villagers, when I struck to
the westward, through high grass and swampy ground. About
noon, I stopped under a tree, to consider what course to take; for
I had now no doubt that the Moors and Slatees had misinformed
the king respecting the object of my mission, and that people
were absolutely in search of me, to convey me a prisoner to Sego.
Sometimes I had thoughts of swimming my horse across the
Niger, and going to the southward, for Cape Coast; but reflecting that I had ten days to travel before I should reach Kong,
and afterward an extensive country to traverse, inhabited by
various nations, with whose language and manners I was totally
unacquainted, I relinquished this scheme, and judged, that I

G g

should better answer the purpose of my mission, by proceeding to the westward along the Niger, endeavouring to ascertain how far the river was navigable in that direction. Having resolved upon this course, I proceeded accordingly; and a little before sunset arrived at a Foulah village called Sooboo, where, for two hundred Kowries, I procured lodging for the night.

Aug. 14th. I continued my course along the bank of the river, through a populous and well cultivated country. I passed a walled town called Kamalia,* without stopping; and at noon rode through a large town called Samee, where there happened to be a market, and a number of people assembled in an open place in the middle of the town, selling cattle, cloth, corn, &c. I rode through the midst of them without being much observed; every one taking me for a Moor. In the afternoon I arrived at a small village called Binni, where I agreed with the Dooty's son, for one hundred Kowries, to allow me to stay for the night; but when the Dooty returned, he insisted that I should instantly leave the place; and if his wife and son had not interceded for me, I must have complied.

Aug. 15th. About nine o'clock I passed a large town called Sai, which very much excited my curiosity. It is completely surrounded by two very deep trenches, at about two hundred yards distant from the walls. On the top of the trenches are a number of square towers; and the whole has the appearance of a regular fortification. Inquiring into the origin of this extraordinary entrenchment, I learned from two of the towns-

---

* There is another town of this name, hereafter to be mentioned.

people the following particulars; which, if true, furnish a mournful picture of the enormities of African wars. About fifteen years ago, when the present King of Bambarra's father desolated Maniana, the Dooty of Sai had two sons slain in battle, fighting in the king's cause. He had a third son living; and when the king demanded a further reinforcement of men, and this youth among the rest, the Dooty refused to send him. This conduct so enraged the king, that when he returned from Maniana, about the beginning of the rainy season, and found the Dooty protected by the inhabitants, he sat down before Sai, with his army, and surrounded the town with the trenches I had now seen. After a siege of two months, the townspeople became involved in all the horrors of famine; and whilst the king's army were feasting in their trenches, they saw with pleasure, the miserable inhabitants of Sai devour the leaves and bark of the Bentang tree that stood in the middle of the town. Finding, however, that the besieged would sooner perish than surrender, the king had recourse to treachery. He promised, that if they would open the gates, no person should be put to death, nor suffer any injury, but the Dooty alone. The poor old man determined to sacrifice himself, for the sake of his fellow-citizens, and immediately walked over to the king's army, where he was put to death. His son, in attempting to escape, was caught and massacred in the trenches; and the rest of the townspeople were carried away captives, and sold as slaves to the different Negro traders.

About noon I came to the village of Kaimoo, situated upon the bank of the river; and as the corn I had purchased at Sibili,

G g 2

was exhausted, I endeavoured to purchase a fresh supply; but was informed that corn was become very scarce all over the country; and though I offered fifty Kowries for a small quantity, no person would sell me any. As I was about to depart, however, one of the villagers (who probably mistook me for some Moorish shereef) brought me some as a present; only desiring me in return, to bestow my blessing upon him; which I did in plain English, and he received it with a thousand acknowledgments. Of this present I made my dinner; and it was the third successive day that I had subsisted entirely upon raw corn.

In the evening I arrived at a small village called Song, the surly inhabitants of which would not receive me, nor so much as permit me to enter the gate; but as lions were very numerous in this neighbourhood, and I had frequently, in the course of the day, observed the impression of their feet on the road, I resolved to stay in the vicinity of the village. Having collected some grass for my horse, I accordingly lay down under a tree by the gate. About ten o'clock I heard the hollow roar of a lion at no great distance, and attempted to open the gate; but the people from within told me, that no person must attempt to enter the gate without the Dooty's permission. I begged them to inform the Dooty that a lion was approaching the village, and I hoped he would allow me to come within the gate. I waited for an answer to this message with great anxiety; for the lion kept prouling round the village, and once advanced so very near me, that I heard him rustling among the grass, and climbed the tree for safety. About midnight the Dooty with some of his people, opened the gate, and desired me to come in. They were convinced, they said, that I was not a Moor; for no Moor ever waited any time at the gate of a village, without cursing the inhabitants.

Aug. 16th. About ten o'clock I passed a considerable town, with a mosque, called Jabbee. Here the country begins to rise into hills, and I could see the summits of high mountains to the westward. I had very disagreeable travelling all this day, on account of the swampiness of the roads; for the river was now risen to such a height, as to overflow great part of the flat land on both sides; and from the muddiness of the water, it was difficult to discern its depth. In crossing one of these swamps, a little to the westward of a town called Gangu, my horse being up to the belly in water, slipt suddenly into a deep pit, and was almost drowned before he could disengage his feet from the stiff clay at the bottom. Indeed, both the horse and his rider were so completely covered with mud, that in passing the village of Callimana, the people compared us to two dirty elephants. About noon I stopped at a small village near Yamina, where I purchased some corn, and dried my papers and clothes.

The town of Yamina, at a distance, has a very fine appearance. It covers nearly the same extent of ground as Sansanding; but having been plundered by Daisy, King of Kaarta, about four years ago, it has not yet resumed its former prosperity; nearly one half of the town being nothing but a heap of ruins: however, it is still a considerable place, and is so much frequented by the Moors, that I did not think it safe to lodge in it; but, in order to satisfy myself respecting its population and extent, I resolved to ride through it; in doing which I observed a great many Moors sitting upon the Bentangs, and other places of public resort. Every body looked at me with astonishment; but as I rode briskly along, they had no time to ask questions.

I arrived in the evening at Farra, a walled village; where, without much difficulty, I procured a lodging for the night.

Aug. 17th. Early in the morning I pursued my journey, and at eight o'clock passed a considerable town called Balaba; after which the road quits the plain, and stretches along the side of the hill. I passed in the course of this day, the ruins of three towns; the inhabitants of which were all carried away by Daisy, King of Kaarta, on the same day that he took and plundered Yamina. Near one of these ruins I climbed a tamarind tree, but found the fruit quite green and sour; and the prospect of the country was by no means inviting; for the high grass and bushes seemed completely to obstruct the road, and the low lands were all so flooded by the river, that the Niger had the appearance of an extensive lake. In the evening I arrived at Kanika, where the Dooty, who was sitting upon an elephant's hide at the gate, received me kindly; and gave me for supper, some milk and meal; which I considered (as to a person in my situation it really was) a very great luxury.

Aug. 18th. By mistake, I took the wrong road, and did not discover my error until I had travelled near four miles; when coming to an eminence, I observed the Niger considerably to the left. Directing my course towards it, I

travelled through long grass and bushes, with great difficulty, until two o'clock in the afternoon; when I came to a
comparatively small, but very rapid river; which I took at first
for a creek, or one of the streams of the Niger. However,
after I had examined it with more attention, I was convinced
that it was a distinct river; and as the road evidently crossed it (for I could see the pathway on the opposite side), I
sat down upon the bank, in hopes that some traveller might
arrive, who would give me the necessary information concerning the fording place; for the banks were so covered
with reeds and bushes, that it would have been almost impossible to land on the other side, except at the pathway; which,
on account of the rapidity of the stream, it seemed very difficult to reach. No traveller, however, arriving, and there being
a great appearance of rain, I examined the grass and bushes,
for some way up the bank, and determined upon entering the
river considerably above the pathway, in order to reach the
other side before the stream had swept me too far down. With
this view I fastened my clothes upon the saddle, and was
standing up to the neck in water, pulling my horse by the
bridle to make him follow me, when a man came accidentally
to the place, and seeing me in the water, called to me with
great vehemence to come out. The alligators, he said, would
devour both me and my horse, if we attempted to swim over.
When I had got out, the stranger, who had never before seen a
European, seemed wonderfully surprised. He twice put his
hand to his mouth, exclaiming in a low tone of voice, " God
preserve me! who is this?" but when he heard me speak the

Bambarra tongue, and found that I was going the same way as himself, he promised to assist me in crossing the river; the name of which he told me was Frina. He then went a little way along the bank, and called to some person, who answered from the other side. In a short time, a canoe with two boys, came paddling from among the reeds: these boys agreed for fifty Kowries, to transport me and my horse over the river, which was effected without much difficulty; and I arrived in the evening at Taffara, a walled town; and soon discovered that the language of the natives was improved, from the corrupted dialect of Bambarra, to the pure Mandingo.

CHAPTER XVIII.

Inhospitable Reception at Taffara.—A Negro Funeral at Sooha.—
The Author continues his Route through several Villages along
the Banks of the Niger, until he comes to Koolikorro.—Supports
himself by writing Saphies—*reaches Maraboo—loses the Road;*
and after many Difficulties arrives at Bammakoo.—Takes the
Road for Sibidooloo—meets with great Kindness at a Village
called Kooma ;—is afterwards robbed, stripped, and plundered by
Banditti.—The Author's Resource and Consolation under exqui-
site Distress.—He arrives in Safety at Sibidooloo.

On my arrival at Taffara, I inquired for the Dooty, but was
informed that he had died a few days before my arrival, and
that there was, at that moment, a meeting of the chief men for
electing another ; there being some dispute about the succession. It was probably owing to this unsettled state of the town,
that I experienced such a want of hospitality in it ; for though
I informed the inhabitants that I should only remain with them
for one night, and assured them that Mansong had given me
some Kowries to pay for my lodging, yet no person invited me
to come in ; and I was forced to sit alone, under the Bentang tree, exposed to the rain and wind of a tornado, which
lasted with great violence until midnight. At this time the
stranger, who had assisted me in crossing the river, paid me a

H h

visit, and observing that I had not found a lodging, invited me to take part of his supper, which he had brought to the door of his hut; for, being a guest himself, he could not, without his landlord's consent, invite me to come in. After this, I slept upon some wet grass in the corner of a court. My horse fared still worse than myself; the corn I had purchased being all expended, and I could not procure a supply.

Aug. 20. I passed the town of Jaba, and stopped a few minutes at a village called Somino, where I begged and obtained some coarse food, which the natives prepare from the husks of corn, and call *Boo*. About two o'clock I came to the village of Sooha, and endeavoured to purchase some corn from the Dooty, who was sitting by the gate; but without success. I then requested a little food by way of charity, but was told he had none to spare. Whilst I was examining the countenance of this inhospitable old man, and endeavouring to find out the cause of the sullen discontent, which was visible in his eye, he called to a slave who was working in the corn-field at a little distance, and ordered him to bring his paddle along with him. The Dooty then told him to dig a hole in the ground; pointing to a spot at no great distance. The slave, with his paddle, began to dig a pit in the earth; and the Dooty, who appeared to be a man of a very fretful disposition, kept muttering and talking to himself until the pit was almost finished, when he repeatedly pronounced the words *dankatoo* (good for nothing); *jankra lemen* (a real plague); which expressions I thought could be applied to nobody but myself; and as the pit had very much the appearance of a grave, I thought it prudent to mount my horse, and was about to decamp, when the slave, who had before gone into the village, to my surprise, returned with the corpse of a boy about nine or ten years of age, quite naked. The Negro carried the body by a leg and an arm, and threw it into the pit with a savage indifference, which I had never before seen. As he covered the body with earth, the Dooty often expressed himself, *naphula attiniata* (money lost); whence I concluded that the boy had been one of his slaves.

Departing from this shocking scene, I travelled by the side of the river until sunset, when I came to Koolikorro; a considerable town, and a great market for salt. Here I took up my lodging at the house of a Bambarran, who had formerly been the slave of a Moor, and in that character had travelled to Aroan, Towdinni, and many other places in the Great Desert; but turning Mussulman, and his master dying at Jenné, he obtained his freedom, and settled at this place, where he carries on a considerable trade in salt, cotton-cloth, &c. His knowledge of the world had not lessened that superstitious confidence in saphies and charms, which he had imbibed in his earlier years; for when he heard that I was a Christian, he immediately thought of procuring a saphie; and for this purpose brought out his *walha*, or writing board; assuring me, that he would dress me a supper of rice, if I would write him a saphie to protect him from wicked men. The proposal was of too great consequence to me to be refused; I therefore wrote the board full, from top to bottom, on both sides; and my landlord, to be certain of having the whole force of the charm, washed the writing from the board into a calabash with a little water, and having said a

H h 2

few prayers over it, drank this powerful draught ; after which, lest a single word should escape, he licked the board until it was quite dry. A saphie writer was a man of too great consequence to be long concealed : the important information was carried to the Dooty, who sent his son with half a sheet of writing-paper, desiring me to write him a *naphula saphie* (a charm to procure wealth). He brought me, as a present, some meal and milk ; and when I had finished the saphie, and read it to him with an audible voice, he seemed highly satisfied with his bargain, and promised to bring me in the morning some milk for my breakfast. When I had finished my supper of rice and salt, I laid myself down upon a bullock's hide, and slept very quietly until morning ; this being the first good meal and refreshing sleep that I had enjoyed for a long time.

Aug. 21st. At daybreak I departed from Koolikorro, and about noon passed the villages of Kayoo and Toolumbo. In the afternoon I arrived at Marraboo ; a large town, and, like Koolikorro, famous for its trade in salt. I was conducted to the house of a Kaartan, of the tribe of Jower, by whom I was well received. This man had acquired a considerable property in the slave trade ; and from his hospitality to strangers, was called, by way of pre-eminence, *Jatee* (the landlord); and his house was a sort of public inn for all travellers. Those who had money were well lodged, for they always made him some return for his kindness; but those who had nothing to give, were content to accept whatever he thought proper ; and as I could not rank myself among the monied men, I was happy to take up my lodging in the same hut with seven poor fellows who had come from Kancaba in a canoe. But our landlord sent us some victuals.

Aug. 22d. One of the landlord's servants went with me a little way from the town, to shew me what road to take ; but, whether from ignorance or design I know not, he directed me wrong ; and I did not discover my mistake until the day was far advanced ; when, coming to a deep creek, I had some thoughts of turning back ; but as, by that means, I foresaw that I could not possibly reach Bammakoo before night, I resolved to cross it ; and leading my horse close to the brink, I went behind him, and pushed him headlong into the water ; and then taking the bridle in my teeth, swam over to the other side. This was the third creek I had crossed in this manner, since I had left Sego; but having secured my notes and memorandums in the crown of my hat, I received little or no inconvenience from such adventures. The rain and heavy dew kept my clothes constantly wet; and the roads being very deep, and full of mud, such a washing was sometimes pleasant, and oftentimes necessary. I continued travelling, through high grass, without any beaten road, and about noon came to the river; the banks of which are here very rocky, and the force and roar of the water were very great. The King of Bambarra's canoes, however, frequently pass these rapids, by keeping close to the bank; persons being stationed on the shore with ropes fastened to the canoe, while others push it forward with long poles. At this time, however, it would, I think, have been a matter of great difficulty for any European boat to have crossed the stream. About four o'clock in the afternoon, having altered my course from the river towards the mountains,

I came to a small pathway, which led to a village called Froo-
kaboo, where I slept.

Aug. 23d. Early in the morning I set out for Bammakoo, at
which place I arrived about five o'clock in the afternoon. I had
heard Bammakoo much talked of as a great market for salt,
and I felt rather disappointed to find it only a middling town,
not quite so large as Marraboo : however, the smallness of its
size, is more than compensated by the richness of its inhabitants ; for when the Moors bring their salt through Kaarta
or Bambarra, they constantly rest a few days at this place ; and
the Negro merchants here, who are well acquainted with the
value of salt in different kingdoms, frequently purchase by
wholesale, and retail it to great advantage. Here I lodged at
the house of a Sera-Woolli Negro, and was visited by a number of Moors. They spoke very good Mandingo, and were
more civil to me than their countrymen had been. One of them
had travelled to Rio Grande, and spoke very highly of the Christians. He sent me in the evening some boiled rice and milk.
I now endeavoured to procure information concerning my route
to the westward, from a slave merchant who had resided some
years on the Gambia. He gave me some imperfect account of
the distance, and enumerated the names of a great many places
that lay in the way ; but withal told me, that the road was impassable at this season of the year : he was even afraid, he said,
that I should find great difficulty in proceeding any farther ; as
the road crossed the Joliba at a town about half a day's journey
to the westward of Bammakoo ; and there being no canoes at
that place large enough to receive my horse, I could not pos-

sibly get him over for some months to come. This was an obstruction of a very serious nature; but as I had no money to maintain myself even for a few days, I resolved to push on, and if I could not convey my horse across the river, to abandon him, and swim over myself. In thoughts of this nature I passed the night, and in the morning consulted with my landlord, how I should surmount the present difficulty. He informed me that one road still remained, which was indeed very rocky, and scarcely passable for horses; but that if I had a proper guide over the hills to a town called Sibidooloo, he had no doubt, but with patience and caution, I might travel forwards through Manding. I immediately applied to the Dooty, and was informed that a *Jilli kea* (singing man) was about to depart for Sibidooloo, and would shew me the road over the hills. With this man, who undertook to be my conductor, I travelled up a rocky glen about two miles, when we came to a small village; and here my musical fellow-traveller found out that he had brought me the wrong road. He told me that the horse-road lay on the other side of the hill, and throwing his drum upon his back, mounted up the rocks, where indeed no horse could follow him, leaving me to admire his agility, and trace out a road for myself. As I found it impossible to proceed, I rode back to the level ground, and directing my course to the eastward, came about noon to another glen, and discovered a path on which I observed the marks of horses' feet: following this path, I came in a short time to some shepherds' huts, where I was informed that I was in the right road. but that I could not possibly reach Sibidooloo before night. Soon after this I gained the summit of a hill, from whence I had an extensive view of the country. Towards the south-east, appeared some very distant mountains, which I had formerly seen from an eminence near Marraboo, where the people informed me, that these mountains were situated in a large and powerful kingdom called Kong; the sovereign of which could raise a much greater army than the King of Bambarra. Upon this height the soil is shallow; the rocks are iron-stone and schistus, with detached pieces of white quartz.

A little before sunset, I descended on the north-west side of this ridge of hills, and as I was looking about for a convenient tree, under which to pass the night (for I had no hopes of reaching any town), I descended into a delightful valley, and soon afterwards arrived at a romantic village called Kooma. This village is surrounded by a high wall, and is the sole property of a Mandingo merchant, who fled hither with his family, during a former war. The adjacent fields yield him plenty of corn, his cattle roam at large in the valley, and the rocky hills secure him from the depredations of war. In this obscure retreat he is seldom visited by strangers, but whenever this happens he makes the weary traveller welcome. I soon found myself surrounded by a circle of the harmless villagers. They asked a thousand questions about my country; and, in return for my information, brought corn and milk for myself, and grass for my horse; kindled a fire in the hut where I was to sleep, and appeared very anxious to serve me.

Aug. 25th. I departed from Kooma, accompanied by two shepherds, who were going towards Sibidooloo. The road was very steep and rocky, and as my horse had hurt his feet much in coming from Bammakoo, he travelled slowly and with great difficulty; for in many places the ascent was so sharp, and the declivities so great, that if he had made one false step, he must inevitably have been dashed to pieces. The shepherds being anxious to proceed, gave themselves little trouble about me or my horse, and kept walking on at a considerable distance. It was about eleven o'clock, as I stopped to drink a little water at a rivulet (my companions being near a quarter of a mile before me), that I heard some people calling to each other, and presently a loud screaming, as from a person in great distress. I immediately conjectured that a lion had taken one of the shepherds, and mounted my horse to have a better view of what had happened. The noise, however, ceased; and I rode slowly towards the place from whence I thought it had proceeded, calling out; but without receiving any answer. In a little time, however, I perceived one of the shepherds lying among the long grass near the road; and though I could see no blood upon him, I concluded he was dead. But when I came close to him, he whispered to me to stop; telling me that a party of armed men had seized upon his companion, and shot two arrows at himself, as he was making his escape. I stopped to consider what course to take, and looking round, saw at a little distance a man sitting upon the stump of a tree: I distinguished also the heads of six or seven more, sitting among the grass, with muskets in their hands. I had now no hopes of escaping, and therefore determined to ride forward towards them. As I approached them, I was in hopes they were elephant hunters;

and by way of opening the conversation, inquired if they had shot any thing; but without returning an answer, one of them ordered me to dismount; and then, as if recollecting himself, waved with his hand for me to proceed. I accordingly rode past, and had with some difficulty crossed a deep rivulet, when I heard somebody holloa; and looking behind, saw those I had taken for elephant hunters, running after me, and calling out to me to turn back. I stopped until they were all come up; when they informed me, that the King of the Foulahs had sent them on purpose to bring me, my horse, and every thing that belonged to me, to Fooladoo; and that therefore I must turn back, and go along with them. Without hesitating a moment, I turned round and followed them, and we travelled together near a quarter of a mile, without exchanging a word; when coming to a dark place in the wood, one of them said, in the Mandingo language, " this place will do;" and immediately snatched my hat from my head. Though I was by no means free of apprehension, yet I resolved to shew as few signs of fear as possible, and therefore told them, that unless my hat was returned to me, I should proceed no further. But before I had time to receive an answer, another drew his knife, and seizing upon a metal button which remained upon my waistcoat, cut it off, and put it into his pocket. Their intentions were now obvious; and I thought that the easier they were permitted to rob me of every thing, the less I had to fear. I therefore allowed them to search my pockets without resistance, and examine every part of my apparel, which they did with the most scrupulous exactness. But observing that I had one waistcoat under another, they insisted that I should cast them both off; and at last, to make sure work, they stripped me quite naked. Even my half boots (though the sole of one of them was tied on to my foot with a broken bridle-rein), were minutely inspected. Whilst they were examining the plunder, I begged them, with great earnestness, to return my pocket compass; but when I pointed it out to them, as it was lying on the ground, one of the banditti, thinking I was about to take it up, cocked his musket and swore that he would lay me dead upon the spot, if I presumed to put my hand upon it. After this, some of them went away with my horse, and the remainder stood considering whether they should leave me quite naked, or allow me something to shelter me from the sun. Humanity at last prevailed: they returned me the worst of the two shirts, and a pair of trowsers; and, as they went away, one of them threw back my hat, in the crown of which I kept my memorandums; and this was probably the reason they did not wish to keep it. After they were gone, I sat for some time, looking around me with amazement and terror. Which ever way I turned, nothing appeared but danger and difficulty. I saw myself in the midst of a vast wilderness, in the depth of the rainy season; naked and alone; surrounded by savage animals, and men still more savage. I was five hundred miles from the nearest European settlement. All these circumstances crowded at once on my recollection; and I confess that my spirits began to fail me. I considered my fate as certain, and that I had no alternative, but to lie down and perish. The influence of religion, however, aided and supported me. I reflected that no human prudence or foresight, could possibly have averted my present sufferings. I was indeed a stranger in a strange land, yet I was still under the protecting eye of that Providence who has condescended to call himself the stranger's friend. At this moment, painful as my reflections were, the extraordinary beauty of a small moss, in fructification, irresistibly caught my eye. I mention this to shew from what trifling circumstances the mind will sometimes derive consolation; for though the whole plant was not larger than the top of one of my fingers, I could not contemplate the delicate conformation of its roots, leaves, and capsula, without admiration. Can that Being (thought I), who planted, watered, and brought to perfection, in this obscure part of the world, a thing which appears of so small importance, look with unconcern upon the situation and sufferings of creatures formed after his own image?—surely not! Reflections like these, would not allow me to despair. I started up, and disregarding both hunger and fatigue, travelled forwards, assured that relief was at hand; and I was not disappointed. In a short time I came to a small village, at the entrance of which I overtook the two shepherds who had come with me from Kooma. They were much surprised to see me; for they said, they never doubted that the Foulahs, when they had robbed, had murdered me. Departing from this village, we travelled over several rocky ridges, and at sunset, arrived at Sibidooloo; the frontier town of the kingdom of Manding.

CHAPTER XIX.

Government of Manding.—The Author's Reception by the Mansa, or chief Man of Sibidooloo, who takes Measures for the Recovery of his Horse and Effects.—The Author removes to Wanda;—great Scarcity, and its afflicting Consequences.—The Author recovers his Horse and Clothes—presents his Horse to the Mansa; and prosecutes his Journey to Kamalia—some Account of that Town.—The Author's kind Reception by Karfa Taura, a Slatee, who proposes to go to the Gambia in the next dry Season, with a Caravan of Slaves.—The Author's Sickness, and Determination to remain and accompany Karfa.

THE town of Sibidooloo is situated in a fertile valley, surrounded with high rocky hills. It is scarcely accessible for horses, and during the frequent wars between the Bambarrans, Foulahs, and Mandingoes, has never once been plundered by an enemy. When I entered the town, the people gathered round me, and followed me into the baloon; where I was presented to the Dooty or chief man, who is here called Mansa, which usually signifies king. Nevertheless, it appeared to me that the government of Manding was a sort of republic, or rather an oligarchy; every town having a particular Mansa, and the chief power of the state, in the last resort, being lodged in the assembly of the whole body. I related to the Mansa, the circumstances of my having been robbed of my horse and apparel; and my story was confirmed by the two shepherds. He continued smoking his pipe all the time I was speaking; but I had no sooner finished, than taking his pipe from his mouth, and tossing up the sleeve of his cloak with an indignant air, " sit down (said he), you shall have every thing restored " to you; I have sworn it:"—and then turning to an attendant, " give the white man (said he) a draught of water; and with " the first light of the morning, go over the hills, and inform " the Dooty of Bammakoo, that a poor white man, the King " of Bambarra's stranger, has been robbed by the King of " Fooladoo's people."

I little expected, in my forlorn condition, to meet with a man who could thus feel for my sufferings. I heartily thanked the Mansa for his kindness, and accepted his invitation to remain with him until the return of the messenger. I was conducted into a hut, and had some victuals sent me; but the crowd of people which assembled to see me, all of whom commiserated my misfortunes, and vented imprecations against the Foulahs, prevented me from sleeping until past midnight. Two days I remained without hearing any intelligence of my horse or clothes; and as there was at this time a great scarcity of provisions, approaching even to famine, all over this part of the country, I was unwilling to trespass any farther on the Mansa's generosity, and begged permission to depart to the next village. Finding me very anxious to proceed, he told me that I might go as far as a town called Wonda, where he hoped

I would remain a few days, until I heard some account of my horse, &c.

I departed accordingly on the next morning of the 28th, and stopped at some small villages for refreshment. I was presented at one of them with a dish which I had never before seen. It was composed of the blossoms or *antheræ* of the maize, stewed in milk and water. It is eaten only in time of great scarcity. On the 30th, about noon, I arrived at Wonda; a small town with a mosque, and surrounded by a high wall. The Mansa, who was a Mahomedan, acted in two capacities; as chief magistrate of the town, and schoolmaster to the children. He kept his school in an open shed, where I was desired to take up my lodging, until some account should arrive from Sibidooloo, concerning my horse and clothes; for though the horse was of little use to me, yet the few clothes were essential. The little raiment upon me could neither protect me from the sun by day, nor the dews and musketoes by night: indeed, my shirt was not only worn thin, like a piece of muslin, but withal was so very dirty, that I was happy to embrace an opportunity of washing it; which having done, and spread it upon a bush, I sat down naked, in the shade, until it was dry.

Ever since the commencement of the rainy season, my health had been greatly on the decline. I had often been affected with slight paroxysms of fever; and from the time of leaving Bammakoo, the symptoms had considerably increased. As I was sitting in the manner described, the fever returned with such violence, that it very much alarmed me: the more so, as I had no medicine to stop its progress, nor any hope of obtaining that care and attention which my situation required.

I remained at Wonda nine days; during which time I experienced the regular return of the fever every day. And though I endeavoured as much as possible to conceal my distress from my landlord, and frequently lay down the whole day, out of his sight, in a field of corn; conscious how burthensome I was to him and his family, in a time of such great scarcity; yet I found that he was apprized of my situation; and one morning, as I feigned to be asleep by the fire, he observed to his wife, that they were likely to find me a very troublesome and chargeable guest; for that, in my present sickly state, they should be obliged, for the sake of their good name, to maintain me until I recovered, or died.

The scarcity of provisions was certainly felt at this time most severely by the poor people, as the following circumstance most painfully convinced me. Every evening, during my stay, I observed five or six women come to the Mansa's house, and receive each of them a certain quantity of corn. As I knew how valuable this article was at this juncture, I inquired of the Mansa, whether he maintained these poor women from pure bounty, or expected a return when the harvest should be gathered in. " Observe that boy said he, (pointing to a fine child, about five years of age); " his mother has sold him to me, " for forty days' provision for herself, and the rest of her family. " I have bought another boy in the same manner." Good God, thought I, what must a mother suffer, before she sells her own child! I could not get this melancholy subject out of my mind, and the next night, when the women returned for their allowance, I desired the boy to point out to me his mother, which he did. She was much emaciated, but had nothing cruel or savage in her countenance; and when she had received her corn, she came and talked to her son, with as much cheerfulness as if he had still been under her care.

Sept. 6th. Two people arrived from Sibidooloo, bringing with them my horse and clothes; but I found that my pocket compass was broken to pieces. This was a great loss, which I could not repair.

Sept. 7th. As my horse was grazing near the brink of a well, the ground gave way, and he fell in. The well was about ten feet diameter, and so very deep, that when I saw my horse snorting in the water, I thought it was impossible to save him. The inhabitants of the village, however, immediately assembled, and having tied together a number of withes,* they lowered a man down into the well, who fastened those withes round the body of the horse; and the people, having first drawn up the man, took hold of the withes, and to my surprise pulled the horse out with the greatest facility. The poor animal was now reduced to a mere skeleton, and the roads were scarcely passable, being either very rocky, or else full of mud and water; I therefore found it impracticable to travel with him any farther, and was happy to leave him in the hands of one who I thought would take care of him. I accordingly presented him to my landlord; and desired him to send

* From a plant called *kabba*, that climbs like a vine upon the trees.

K k

my saddle and bridle, as a present, to the Mansa of Sibidooloo; being the only return I could make him, for having taken so much trouble in procuring my horse and clothes.

I now thought it necessary, sick as I was, to take leave of my hospitable landlord. On the morning of Sept. 8th, when I was about to depart, he presented me with his spear, as a token of remembrance, and a leather bag to contain my clothes. Having converted my half boots into sandals, I travelled with more ease, and slept that night at a village called Ballanti. On the 9th, I reached Nemacoo; but the Mansa of the village thought fit to make me sup upon the camelion's dish. By way of apology, however, he assured me the next morning, that the scarcity of corn was such, that he could not possibly allow me any. I could not accuse him of unkindness, as all the people actually appeared to be starving.

Sept. 10th. It rained hard all day, and the people kept themselves in their huts. In the afternoon, I was visited by a Negro, named Modi Lemina Taura, a great trader, who, suspecting my distress, brought me some victuals; and promised to conduct me to his own house at Kinyeto the day following.

Sept. 11th. I departed from Nemacoo, and arrived at Kinyeto in the evening; but having hurt my ankle in the way, it swelled and inflamed so much that I could neither walk, nor set my foot to the ground, the next day, without great pain. My landlord observing this, kindly invited me to stop with him a few days; and I accordingly remained at his house until the 14th; by which time I felt much relieved, and could walk with the help of a staff. I now set out, thanking my landlord for his great care and attention; and being accompanied by a young man, who was travelling the same way, I proceeded for Jerijang, a beautiful and well cultivated district, the Mansa of which is reckoned the most powerful chief of any in Manding.

On the 15th, I reached Dosita, a large town, where I stayed one day on account of the rain; but I continued very sickly, and was slightly delirious in the night. On the 17th, I set out for Mansia, a considerable town, where small quantities of gold are collected. The road led over a high rocky hill, and my strength and spirits were so much exhausted, that before I could reach the top of the hill, I was forced to lie down three times, being very faint and sickly. I reached Mansia in the afternoon. The Mansa of this town had the character of being very inhospitable; he, however, sent me a little corn for my supper, but demanded something in return: and when I assured him that I had nothing of value in my possession, he told me (as if in jest), that my white skin should not defend me, if I told him lies. He then shewed me the hut wherein I was to sleep; but took away my spear, saying that it should be returned to me in the morning. This trifling circumstance, when joined to the character I had heard of the man, made me rather suspicious of him; and I privately desired one of the inhabitants of the place, who had a bow and quiver, to sleep in the same hut with me. About midnight, I heard somebody approach the door, and observing the moonlight strike suddenly into the hut, I started up, and saw a man stepping cautiously over the threshold. I immediately snatched

up the Negro's bow and quiver, the rattling of which made
the man withdraw: and my companion looking out, assured me
that it was the Mansa himself, and advised me to keep awake
until the morning. I closed the door, and placed a large piece
of wood behind it; and was wondering at this unexpected visit,
when somebody pressed so hard against the door, that the
Negro could scarcely keep it shut. But when I called to him to
open the door, the intruder ran off, as before.

Sept. 16th. As soon as it was light, the Negro, at my request, went to the Mansa's house and brought away my spear.
He told me that the Mansa was asleep, and lest this inhospitable chief should devise means to detain me, he advised me
to set out before he was awake; which I immediately did; and
about two o'clock reached Kamalia, a small town, the appearance of which is represented in the annexed Plate, situated at
the bottom of some rocky hills, where the inhabitants collect
gold in considerable quantities. The Bushreens here live
apart from the Kafirs, and have built their huts in a scattered
manner, at a short distance from the town. They have a place
set apart for performing their devotions in, to which they give
the name of *missura*, or mosque; but it is in fact nothing more
than a square piece of ground made level, and surrounded with
the trunks of trees, having a small projection towards the east,
where the Marraboo, or priest, stands, when he calls the people
to prayers. Mosques of this construction are very common
among the converted Negroes; but having neither walls nor
roof, they can only be used in fine weather. When it rains,
the Bushreens perform their devotions in their huts.

A VIEW of KAMALIA.

J C Barrow del from a sketch by M Park.

Published June 1 1799 by G Nicol & W Vol.

W C Wilson, Sculp.

On my arrival at Kamalia, I was conducted to the house of a Bushreen named Karfa Taura, the brother of him to whose hospitality I was indebted at Kinyeto. He was collecting a coffle of slaves, with a view to sell them to the Europeans on the Gambia, as soon as the rains should be over. I found him sitting in his baloon, surrounded by several Slatees, who proposed to join the coffle. He was reading to them from an Arabic book; and inquired, with a smile, if I understood it? Being answered in the negative, he desired one of the Slatees to fetch the little curious book, which had been brought from the west country. On opening this small volume, I was surprised, and delighted, to find it our *Book of Common Prayer;* and Karfa expressed great joy to hear that I could read it: for some of the Slatees, who had seen the Europeans upon the Coast, observing the colour of my skin (which was now become very yellow from sickness), my long beard, ragged clothes, and extreme poverty; were unwilling to admit that I was a white man, and told Karfa, that they suspected I was some Arab in disguise. Karfa, however, perceiving that I could read this book, had no doubt concerning me; and kindly promised me every assistance in his power. At the same time he informed me, that it was impossible to cross the Jallonka wilderness for many months yet to come, as no less than eight rapid rivers, he said, lay in the way. He added, that he intended to set out himself for Gambia as soon as the rivers were fordable, and the grass burnt; and advised me to stay and accompany him. He remarked, that when a caravan of the natives could not travel through the country, it was idle for a single white man to attempt it. I readily admitted that such an attempt was an act of rashness, but I assured him that I had now no alternative; for having no money to support myself, I must either beg my subsistence, by travelling from place to place, or perish for want. Karfa now looked at me with great earnestness, and inquired if I could eat the common victuals of the country; assuring me he had never before seen a white man. He added, that if I would remain with him until the rains were over, he would give me plenty of victuals in the meantime, and a hut to sleep in; and that after he had conducted me in safety to the Gambia, I might then make him what return I thought proper. I asked him, if the value of one prime slave would satisfy him. He answered in the affirmative; and immediately ordered one of the huts to be swept for my accommodation. Thus was I delivered, by the friendly care of this benevolent Negro, from a situation truly deplorable. Distress and famine pressed hard upon me; I had, before me, the gloomy wilds of Jallonkadoo, where the traveller sees no habitation for five successive days. I had observed at a distance, the rapid course of the river Kokoro. I had almost marked out the place, where I was doomed, I thought, to perish, when this friendly Negro stretched out his hospitable hand for my relief.

In the hut which was appropriated for me, I was provided with a mat to sleep on, an earthen jar for holding water, and a small calabash to drink out of; and Karfa sent me from his own dwelling, two meals a day; and ordered his slaves to supply me with fire-wood and water. But I found that neither the kindness of Karfa, nor any sort of accommodation could put a stop to the fever which weakened me, and which became every day more alarming. I endeavoured as much as possible to conceal my distress; but on the third day after my arrival, as I was going with Karfa to visit some of his friends, I found myself so faint that I could scarcely walk, and before we reached the place, I staggered, and fell into a pit from which the clay had been taken to build one of the huts. Karfa endeavoured to console me with the hopes of a speedy recovery; assuring me, that if I would not walk out in the wet, I should soon be well. I determined to follow his advice, and confine myself to my hut: but was still tormented with the fever, and my health continued to be in a very precarious state, for five ensuing weeks. Sometimes I could crawl out of the hut, and sit a few hours in the open air; at other times I was unable to rise, and passed the lingering hours in a very gloomy and solitary manner. I was seldom visited by any person except my benevolent landlord, who came daily to inquire after my health. When the rains became less frequent, and the country began to grow dry, the fever left me; but in so debilitated a condition, that I could scarcely stand upright, and it was with great difficulty that I could carry my mat to the shade of a tamarind tree, at a short distance, to enjoy the refreshing smell of the corn-fields, and delight my eyes with a prospect of the country. I had the pleasure, at length, to find myself in a state of convalescence; towards which, the benevolent and simple manners of the Negroes, and the perusal of Karfa's little volume, greatly contributed.

In the meantime, many of the Slatees who resided at Kamalia, having spent all their money, and become in a great measure dependent upon Karfa's hospitality, beheld me with an eye of envy, and invented many ridiculous and trifling stories to lessen me in Karfa's esteem. And in the beginning of December, a Sera-Woolli Slatee, with five slaves, arrived from Sego: this man too, spread a number of malicious reports concerning me ; but Karfa paid no attention to them, and continued to shew me the same kindness as formerly. As I was one day conversing with the slaves which this Slatee had brought, one of them begged me to give him some victuals. I told him I was a stranger, and had none to give. He replied, " I gave *you* victuals when you was hungry.—Have you forgot " the man who brought you milk at Karrankalla? But (added " he, with a sigh) *the irons were not then upon my legs!*" I immediately recollected him, and begged some ground-nuts from Karfa to give him, as a return for his former kindness. He told me that he had been taken by the Bambarrans, the day after the battle at Joka, and sent to Sego; where he had been purchased by his present master, who was carrying him down to Kajaaga. Three more of these slaves were from Kaarta, and one from Wassela, all of them prisoners of war. They stopped four days at Kamalia, and were then taken to Bala, where they remained until the river Kokoro was fordable, and the grass burnt.

In the beginning of December, Karfa proposed to complete his purchase of slaves; and for this purpose, collected all the debts which were owing to him in his own country. And on the 19th, being accompanied by three Slatees, he departed for

Kancaba, a large town on the banks of the Niger; and a great slave-market. Most of the slaves, who are sold at Kancaba, come from Bambarra; for Mansong, to avoid the expence and danger of keeping all his prisoners at Sego, commonly sends them in small parties, to be sold at the different trading towns; and as Kancaba is much resorted to by merchants, it is always well supplied with slaves, which are sent thither up the Niger in canoes. When Karfa departed from Kamalia, he proposed to return in the course of a month; and during his absence I was left to the care of a good old Bushreen, who acted as schoolmaster to the young people of Kamalia.

Being now left alone, and at leisure to indulge my own reflections; it was an opportunity not to be neglected of augmenting and extending the observations I had already made, on the climate and productions of the country; and of acquiring a more perfect knowledge of the natives, than it was possible for me to obtain, in the course of a transient and perilous journey through the country. I endeavoured likewise to collect all the information I could, concerning those important branches of African commerce, the trade for gold, ivory, and slaves. Such was my employment, during the remainder of my stay at Kamalia; and I shall now proceed to lay before my readers the result of my researches and inquiries; avoiding, as far as I can, a repetition of those circumstances and observations, which were related, as occasion arose, in the narrative of my journey.

CHAPTER XX.

Of the Climate and Seasons.—Winds.—Vegetable Productions.—
Population.—General Observations on the Character and Dis-
position of the Mandingoes; and a summary Account of their
Manners and Habits of Life, their Marriages, &c.

THE whole of my route, both in going and returning, having
been confined to a tract of country bounded nearly by the 12th
and 15th parallels of latitude, the reader must imagine that
I found the climate in most places extremely hot; but no where
did I feel the heat so intense and oppressive as in the camp at
Benowm, of which mention has been made in a former place.
In some parts, where the country ascends into hills, the air is
at all times comparatively cool; yet none of the districts which
I traversed, could properly be called mountainous. About the
middle of June, the hot and sultry atmosphere is agitated by
violent gusts of wind, (called *tornadoes*) accompanied with
thunder and rain. These usher in what is denominated *the*
rainy season; which continues until the month of November.
During this time, the diurnal rains are very heavy; and the
prevailing winds are from the south-west. The termination of
the rainy season, is likewise attended with violent tornadoes;
after which the wind shifts to the north-east, and continues to
blow from that quarter, during the rest of the year.

When the wind sets in from the north-east, it produces a wonderful change in the face of the country. The grass soon becomes dry and withered; the rivers subside very rapidly, and many of the trees shed their leaves. About this period is commonly felt the *harmattan*, a dry and parching wind, blowing from the north-east, and accompanied by a thick smoky haze; through which the sun appears of a dull red colour. This wind, in passing over the great desert of Sahara, acquires a very strong attraction for humidity, and parches up every thing exposed to its current. It is, however, reckoned very salutary, particularly to Europeans, who generally recover their health during its continuance. I experienced immediate relief from sickness, both at Dr. Laidley's, and at Kamalia, during the harmattan. Indeed, the air during the rainy season is so loaded with moisture, that clothes, shoes, trunks, and every thing that is not close to the fire, become damp and mouldy; and the inhabitants may be said to live in a sort of vapour bath: but this dry wind braces up the solids, which were before relaxed, gives a cheerful flow of spirits, and is even pleasant to respiration. Its ill effects are, that it produces chaps in the lips, and afflicts many of the natives with sore eyes.

Whenever the grass is sufficiently dry, the Negroes set it on fire; but in Ludamar, and other Moorish countries, this practice is not allowed; for it is upon the withered stubble that the Moors feed their cattle, until the return of the rains. The burning the grass in Manding exhibits a scene of terrific grandeur. In the middle of the night, I could see the plains and mountains, as far as my eye could reach, variegated with lines of fire; and the light reflected on the sky, made the heavens appear in a blaze. In the day time, pillars of smoke were seen in every direction; while the birds of prey were observed hovering round the conflagration, and pouncing down upon the snakes, lizards, and other reptiles, which attempted to escape from the flames. This annual burning is soon followed by a fresh and sweet verdure, and the country is thereby rendered more healthful and pleasant.

Of the most remarkable and important of the vegetable productions, mention has already been made; and they are nearly the same in all the districts through which I passed. It is observable, however, that although many species of the edible roots, which grow in the West-India Islands, are found in Africa, yet I never saw, in any part of my journey, either the sugar-cane, the coffee, or the cacao tree; nor could I learn, on inquiry, that they were known to the natives. The pine-apple, and the thousand other delicious fruits, which the industry of civilized man (improving the bounties of nature), has brought to so great perfection in the tropical climates of America, are here equally unknown. I observed, indeed, a few orange and banana trees, near the mouth of the Gambia; but whether they were indigenous, or were formerly planted there by some of the white traders, I could not positively learn. I suspect, that they were originally introduced by the Portuguese.

Concerning property in the soil; it appeared to me that the lands in native woods, were considered as belonging to the king, or (where the government was not monarchical) to the state. When any individual of free condition, had the means of cultivating more land than he actually possessed, he applied to the chief man of the district, who allowed him an extension of territory, on condition of forfeiture if the lands were not brought into cultivation by a given period. The condition being fulfilled, the soil became vested in the possessor; and, for aught that appeared to me, descended to his heirs.

The population, however, considering the extent and fertility of the soil, and the ease with which lands are obtained, is not very great, in the countries which I visited. I found many extensive and beautiful districts, entirely destitute of inhabitants; and in general, the borders of the different kingdoms, were either very thinly peopled, or entirely deserted. Many places are likewise unfavourable to population, from being unhealthful. The swampy banks of the Gambia, the Senegal, and other rivers towards the Coast, are of this description. Perhaps, it is on this account chiefly, that the interior countries abound more with inhabitants, than the maritime districts; for all the Negro nations that fell under my observation, though divided into a number of petty independent states, subsist chiefly by the same means, live nearly in the same temperature, and possess a wonderful similarity of disposition. The Mandingoes, in particular, are a very gentle race; cheerful in their dispositions, inquisitive, credulous, simple, and fond of flattery. Perhaps, the most prominent defect in their character, is that insurmountable propensity, which the reader must have observed to prevail in all classes of them, to steal from me the few effects I was possessed of. For this part

of their conduct, no complete justification can be offered, because theft is a crime in their own estimation; and it must be
observed, that they are not habitually and generally guilty of
it towards each other. This, however, is an important circumstance in mitigation; and, before we pronounce them a more
depraved people than any other, it were well to consider
whether the lower order of people in any part of Europe, would
have acted, under similar circumstances, with greater honesty
towards a stranger, than the Negroes acted towards me. It
must not be forgotten, that the laws of the country afforded
me no protection; that every one was at liberty to rob me with
impunity; and finally, that some part of my effects were of as
great value, in the estimation of the Negroes, as pearls and
diamonds would have been in the eyes of a European. Let us
suppose, a black merchant of Hindostan to have found his way
into the centre of England, with a box of jewels at his back;
and that the laws of the kingdom afforded him no security; in
such a case, the wonder would be, not that the stranger was
robbed of any part of his riches, but that any part was left for
a second depredator. Such, on sober reflection, is the judgment I have formed concerning the pilfering disposition of the
Mandingo Negroes towards myself. Notwithstanding I was so
great a sufferer by it, I do not consider that their natural
sense of justice was perverted or extinguished: it was overpowered only, for the moment, by the strength of a temptation
which it required no common virtue to resist.

On the other hand, as some counterbalance to this depravity
in their nature, allowing it to be such, it is impossible for me

to forget the disinterested charity, and tender solicitude, with which many of these poor heathens (from the sovereign of Sego, to the poor women who received me at different times into their cottages, when I was perishing of hunger) sympathized with me in my sufferings; relieved my distresses; and contributed to my safety. This acknowledgment, however, is perhaps more particularly due to the female part of the nation. Among the men, as the reader must have seen, my reception, though generally kind, was sometimes otherwise. It varied according to the various tempers of those to whom I made application. The hardness of avarice in some, and the blindness of bigotry in others, had closed up the avenues to compassion : but I do not recollect a single instance of hard-heartedness towards me in the women. In all my wanderings and wretchedness, I found them uniformly kind and compassionate; and I can truly say, as my predecessor Mr. Ledyard, has eloquently said before me; " To a woman, I never ad-" dressed myself in the language of decency and friendship, " without receiving a decent and friendly answer. If I was " hungry, or thirsty, wet, or sick, they did not hesitate, like " the men, to perform a generous action. In so free, and so " kind a manner did they contribute to my relief; that if I " was dry, I drank the sweetest draught, and if hungry, I eat " the coarsest morsel with a double relish."

It is surely reasonable to suppose, that the soft and amiable sympathy of nature, which was thus spontaneously manifested towards me, in my distress, is displayed by these poor people, as occasion requires, much more strongly towards persons of their own nation and neighbourhood, and especially when the objects of their compassion are endeared to them by the ties of consanguinity. Accordingly, the maternal affection (neither suppressed by the restraints, nor diverted by the solicitudes of civilized life) is every where conspicuous among them; and creates a correspondent return of tenderness in the child. An illustration of this has been given in p. 47. " Strike me," said my attendant, " but do not curse my mother." The same sentiment I found universally to prevail, and observed in all parts of Africa, that the greatest affront which could be offered to a Negro, was to reflect on her who gave him birth.

It is not strange, that this sense of filial duty and affection among the Negroes, should be less ardent towards the father than the mother. The system of polygamy, while it weakens the father's attachment, by dividing it among the children of different wives, concentrates all the mother's jealous tenderness to one point, the protection of her own offspring. I perceived with great satisfaction too, that the maternal solicitude extended not only to the growth and security of the person, but also, in a certain degree, to the improvement of the mind of the infant; for one of the first lessons, in which the Mandingo women instruct their children, is *the practice of truth*. The reader will probably recollect the case of the unhappy mother, whose son was murdered by the Moorish banditti, at Funingkedy, p. 102.—Her only consolation, in her uttermost distress, was the reflection that the poor boy, in the course of his blameless life, *had never told a lie*. Such testimony, from a fond mother, on such an occasion, must have operated powerfully on the youthful part of the surrounding spectators. It was at once a tribute of praise to the deceased, and a lesson to the living.

The Negro women suckle their children, until they are able to walk of themselves. Three years nursing is not uncommon; and during this period the husband devotes his whole attention to his other wives. To this practice it is owing, I presume, that the family of each wife is seldom very numerous. Few women have more than five or six children. As soon as an infant is able to walk, it is permitted to run about with great freedom. The mother is not over solicitous to preserve it from slight falls, and other trifling accidents. A little practice soon enables a child to take care of itself, and experience acts the part of a nurse. As they advance in life, the girls are taught to spin cotton, and to beat corn, and are instructed in other domestic duties; and the boys are employed in the labours of the field. Both sexes, whether Bushreens or Kafirs, on attaining the age of puberty, are circumcised. This painful operation is not considered by the Kafirs, so much in the light of a religious ceremony, as a matter of convenience and utility. They have, indeed, a superstitious notion that it contributes to render the marriage state prolific. The operation is performed upon several young people at the same time; all of whom are exempted from every sort of labour, for two months afterwards. During this period, they form a society called *Solimana*. They visit the towns and villages in the neighbourhood, where they dance and sing, and are well treated by the inhabitants. I had frequently, in the course of my journey, observed parties of

M m

this description, but they were all males. I had, however, an opportunity of seeing a female *Solimana*, at Kamalia.

In the course of this celebration, it frequently happens that some of the young women get married. If a man takes a fancy to any one of them, it is not considered as absolutely necessary, that he should make an overture to the girl herself. The first object is to agree with the parents, concerning the recompence to be given them, for the loss of the company and services of their daughter. The value of two slaves is a common price, unless the girl is thought very handsome; in which case, the parents will raise their demand very considerably. If the lover is rich enough, and willing to give the sum demanded, he then communicates his wishes to the damsel; but her consent is by no means necessary to the match; for if the parents agree to it, and eat a few *kolla-nuts*, which are presented by the suitor as an earnest of the bargain, the young lady must either have the man of their choice, or continue unmarried, for she cannot afterwards be given to another. If the parents should attempt it, the lover is then authorized, by the laws of the country, to seize upon the girl as his slave. When the day for celebrating the nuptials is fixed on, a select number of people are invited to be present at the wedding: a bullock or goat is killed, and great plenty of victuals dressed for the occasion. As soon as it is dark, the bride is conducted into a hut, where a company of matrons assist in arranging the wedding dress, which is always white cotton, and is put on in such a manner as to conceal the bride from head to foot. Thus arrayed, she is seated upon a mat, in the middle of the floor, and the old women place themselves in a circle round her. They then give her a series of instructions, and point out, with great propriety, what ought to be her future conduct in life. This scene of instruction, however, is frequently interrupted by girls, who amuse the company with songs and dances, which are rather more remarkable for their gaiety than delicacy. While the bride remains within the hut with the women, the bridegroom devotes his attention to the guests of both sexes, who assemble without doors, and by distributing among them small presents of kolla-nuts, and seeing that every one partakes of the good cheer which is provided, he contributes much to the general hilarity of the evening. When supper is ended, the company spend the remainder of the night in singing and dancing, and seldom separate until daybreak. About midnight, the bride is privately conducted by the women into the hut which is to be her future residence; and the bridegroom, upon a signal given, retires from his company. The new married couple, however, are always disturbed towards morning by the women, who assemble to inspect the nuptial sheet, (according to the manners of the ancient Hebrews, as recorded in Scripture,) and dance round it. This ceremony is thought indispensably necessary; nor is the marriage considered as valid without it.

The Negroes, as hath been frequently observed, whether Mahomedan or Pagan, allow a plurality of wives. The Mahomedans alone, are by their religion confined to four; and as the husband commonly pays a great price for each, he requires from all of them the utmost deference and submission, and treats them more like hired servants, than companions. They

have, however, the management of domestic affairs, and each in
rotation is mistress of the household, and has the care of dressing
the victuals, overlooking the female slaves, &c. But though the
African husbands are possessed of great authority over their
wives, I did not observe, that in general they treat them with
cruelty; neither did I perceive that mean jealousy in their dispositions, which is so prevalent among the Moors. They permit their wives to partake of all public diversions, and this
indulgence is seldom abused; for though the Negro women
are very cheerful and frank in their behaviour, they are by
no means given to intrigue: I believe that instances of con-
jugal infidelity are not common. When the wives quarrel
among themselves, a circumstance which, from the nature of
their situation, must frequently happen, the husband decides
between them; and sometimes finds it necessary to administer
a little corporal chastisement, before tranquillity can be restored.
But if any one of the ladies complains to the chief of the
town, that her husband has unjustly punished her, and shewn
an undue partiality to some other of his wives, the affair is
brought to a public trial. In these *palavers*, however, which are
conducted chiefly by married men, I was informed that the
complaint of the wife, is not always considered in a very serious
light; and the complainant herself, is sometimes convicted of
strife and contention, and left without remedy. If she murmurs
at the decision of the court, the magic rod of *Mumbo Jumbo*
soon puts an end to the business.

The children of the Mandingoes are not always named after
their relations; but frequently in consequence of some remark-

able occurrence. Thus, my landlord at Kamalia, was called *Karfa*, a word signifying *to replace;* because he was born shortly after the death of one of his brothers. Other names are descriptive of good or bad qualities; as *Modi*, " a good man ;" *Fadibba*, " father of the town," &c. : indeed, the very names of their towns have something descriptive in them; as *Sibidooloo*, " the town of ciboa trees ;" *Kenneyetoo*, " victuals here ;" *Dosita*, " lift your spoon." Others appear to be given by way of reproach, as *Bammakoo*, " wash a crocodile ;" *Karrankalla*, " no cup to drink from, &c." A child is named, when it is seven or eight days old. The ceremony commences by shaving the infant's head; and a dish called *Dega,* made of pounded corn and sour milk, is prepared for the guests. If the parents are rich, a sheep or a goat is commonly added. This feast is called *Ding koon lee*, " the child's head shaving." During my stay at Kamalia, I was present at four different feasts of this kind, and the ceremony was the same in each, whether the child belonged to a Bushreen or a Kafir. The schoolmaster, who officiated as priest on those occasions, and who is necessarily a Bushreen, first said a long prayer over the *dega;* during which every person present took hold of the brim of the calabash with his right hand. After this, the schoolmaster took the child in his arms, and said a second prayer; in which he repeatedly solicited the blessing of God upon the child, and upon all the company. When this prayer was ended, he whispered a few sentences in the child's ear, and spit three times in its face; after which he pronounced its name aloud, and returned the infant to the mother. This part of the ceremony being ended, the father of the child divided the *dega* into a number of balls, one of which he distributed to every person present. And inquiry was then made, if any person in the town was dangerously sick, it being usual, in such cases, to send the party a large portion of the *dega;* which is thought to possess great medical virtues.*

Among the Negroes every individual, besides his own proper name, has likewise a *kontong*, or surname, to denote the family or clan to which he belongs. Some of these families are very numerous and powerful. It is impossible to enumerate the various *kontongs* which are found in different parts of the country; though the knowledge of many of them is of great service to the traveller; for as every Negro plumes himself upon the importance, or the antiquity of his clan, he is much flattered when he is addressed by his *kontong*.

Salutations, among the Negroes to each other, when they meet, are always observed; but those in most general use among the Kafirs, are *Abbe baeretto,—E ning seni,—Anawari, &c.* all of which have nearly the same meaning, and signify, *are you well*, or to that effect. There are likewise salutations which are used at different times of the day, as *E ning somo*, good morning, &c. The general answer to all salutations, is to repeat the *kontong* of the person who salutes, or else to repeat the salutation itself, first pronouncing the word *marhaba*, my friend.

* Soon after baptism, the children are marked in different parts of the skin, in a manner resembling what is called *tatowing* in the South-sea Islands.

CHAPTER XXI.

The Account of the Mandingoes continued.—Their Notions in respect of the Planetary Bodies, and the Figure of the Earth. —Their religious Opinions, and Belief in a Future State.— Their Diseases and Methods of Treatment.—Their Funeral Ceremonies, Amusements, Occupations, Diet, Arts, Manufactures, &c.

THE Mandingoes, and I believe the Negroes in general, have no artificial method of dividing time. They calculate the years by the number of *rainy seasons*. They portion the year into *moons*, and reckon the days by so many *suns*. The day, they divide into morning, mid-day, and evening; and further subdivide it, when necessary, by pointing to the sun's place in the Heavens. I frequently inquired of some of them, what became of the sun during the night, and whether we should see the same sun, or a different one, in the morning: but I found that they considered the question as very childish. The subject appeared to them, as placed beyond the reach of human investigation: they had never indulged a conjecture, nor formed any hypothesis about the matter. The moon, by varying her form, has more attracted their attention. On the first appearance of the new moon, which they look upon to be newly created, the Pagan natives, as well as Mahomedans, say a short prayer; and this seems to be the only visible adoration which the Kafirs offer up to the Supreme Being. This prayer is pronounced in a whisper; the party holding up his hands before his face: its purport (as I have been assured by many different people) is to return thanks to God for his kindness through the existence of the past moon, and to solicit a continuation of his favour during that of the new one. At the conclusion, they spit upon their hands, and rub them over their faces. This seems to be nearly the same ceremony, which prevailed among the Heathens in the days of Job.*

Great attention, however, is paid to the changes of this luminary, in its monthly course; and it is thought very unlucky to begin a journey, or any other work of consequence, in the last quarter. An eclipse, whether of the sun or moon, is supposed to be effected by witchcraft. The stars are very little regarded; and the whole study of astronomy appears to them as a useless pursuit, and attended to by such persons only as deal in magic.

Their notions of geography, are equally puerile. They imagine that the world is an extended plain, the termination of which no eye has discovered; it being, they say, overhung with clouds and darkness. They describe the sea as a large river of salt water, on the farther shore of which is situated a country called *Tobaubo doo;* " the land of the white people." At a distance from Tobaubo doo, they describe another country,

* Chap. xxxi. ver. 26, 27, 28.

which they allege is inhabited by cannibals of gigantic size, called *Koomi*. This country they call *Jong sang doo* " the " land where the slaves are sold." But of all countries in the world their own appears to them as the best, and their own people as the happiest; and they pity the fate of other nations, who have been placed by Providence in less fertile and less fortunate districts.

Some of the religious opinions of the Negroes, though blended with the weakest credulity and superstition, are not unworthy attention. I have conversed with all ranks and conditions, upon the subject of their faith, and can pronounce, without the smallest shadow of doubt, that the belief of one God, and of a future state of reward and punishment, is entire and universal among them. It is remarkable, however, that, except on the appearance of a new moon, as before related, the Pagan natives do not think it necessary to offer up prayers and supplications to the Almighty. They represent the Deity, indeed, as the creator and preserver of all things; but in general they consider him as a Being so remote, and of so exalted a nature, that it is idle to imagine the feeble supplications of wretched mortals can reverse the decrees, and change the purposes of unerring Wisdom. If they are asked, for what reason then do they offer up a prayer on the appearance of the new moon; the answer is, that custom has made it necessary: they do it, because their fathers did it before them. Such is the blindness of unassisted nature! The concerns of this world, they believe, are committed by the Almighty to the superintendance and direction of subordinate spirits, over whom they suppose

N n

that certain magical ceremonies have great influence. A white
fowl, suspended to the branch of a particular tree; a snake's
head, or a few handfuls of fruit, are offerings which ignorance
and superstition frequently present, to deprecate the wrath, or
to conciliate the favour, of these tutelary agents. But it is not
often that the Negroes make their religious opinions the subject of conversation: when interrogated, in particular, concerning their ideas of a future state, they express themselves with
great reverence, but endeavour to shorten the discussion by
observing—*mo o mo inta allo,* " no man knows any thing about
it." They are content, they say, to follow the precepts and examples of their forefathers, through the various vicissitudes of
life; and when this world presents no objects of enjoyment or of
comfort, they seem to look with anxiety towards another, which
they believe will be better suited to their natures; but concerning
which they are far from indulging vain and delusive conjectures.

The Mandingoes seldom attain extreme old age. At forty,
most of them become gray haired, and covered with wrinkles;
and but few of them survive the age of fifty-five, or sixty.
They calculate the years of their lives, as I have already observed, by the number of rainy seasons (there being but one
such in the year); and distinguish each year by a particular
name, founded on some remarkable occurrence which happened in that year. Thus they say the year of the *Farbanna
war;* the year of the *Kaarta war;* the year on which *Gadou
   plundered, &c. &c.;* and I have no doubt that the year
1796, will in many places be distinguished by the name of
Tobaubo tambi sang, " the year the white man passed;" as such

an occurrence would naturally form an epoch in their tradi-
tional history.

But, notwithstanding that longevity is uncommon among
them, it appeared to me that their diseases are but few in
number. Their simple diet, and active way of life, preserve
them from many of those disorders, which embitter the days
of luxury and idleness. Fevers and fluxes are the most common,
and the most fatal. For these, they generally apply saphies
to different parts of the body, and perform a great many other
superstitious ceremonies; some of which are, indeed, well calculated to inspire the patient with the hope of recovery, and
divert his mind from brooding over his own danger. But I
have sometimes observed among them, a more systematic mode
of treatment. On the first attack of a fever, when the patient
complains of cold, he is frequently placed in a sort of vapour
bath: this is done by spreading branches of the *nauclea orien-
talis* upon hot wood embers, and laying the patient upon them,
wrapped up in a large cotton cloth. Water is then sprinkled
upon the branches, which descending to the hot embers, soon
covers the patient with a cloud of vapour, in which he is
allowed to remain until the embers are almost extinguished.
This practice commonly produces a profuse perspiration, and
wonderfully relieves the sufferer.

For the dysentery, they use the bark of different trees
reduced to powder, and mixed with the patient's food; but this
practice is in general very unsuccessful.

The other diseases which prevail among the Negroes, are
the *yaws;* the *elephantiasis;* and a *leprosy* of the very worst kind.

This last mentioned complaint appears, at the beginning, in scurfy spots upon different parts of the body; which finally settle upon the hands or feet, where the skin becomes withered, and cracks in many places. At length, the ends of the fingers swell and ulcerate; the discharge is acrid and fetid; the nails drop off, and the bones of the fingers become carious, and separate at the joints. In this manner the disease continues to spread, frequently until the patient loses all his fingers and toes. Even the hands and feet are sometimes destroyed by this inveterate malady, to which the Negroes give the name of *balla jou*, " incurable."

The *Guinea worm* is likewise very common in certain places, especially at the commencement of the rainy season. The Negroes attribute this disease, which has been described by many writers, to bad water; and allege that the people who drink from wells, are more subject to it than those who drink from streams. To the same cause, they attribute the swelling of the glands of the neck (goitres), which are very common in some parts of Bambarra. I observed also, in the interior countries, a few instances of simple gonorrhœa; but never the confirmed lues. On the whole, it appeared to me that the Negroes are better surgeons than physicians. I found them very successful in their management of fractures and dislocations, and their splints and bandages are simple, and easily removed. The patient is laid upon a soft mat, and the fractured limb is frequently bathed with cold water. All abscesses they open with the actual cautery; and the dressings are composed of either soft leaves, Shea butter, or cows' dung, as the case seems, in their judgment, to require. Towards the Coast, where a supply of European lancets can be procured, they sometimes perform phlebotomy; and in cases of local inflammation, a curious sort of cupping is practised. This operation is performed by making incisions in the part, and applying to it a bullock's horn, with a small hole in the end. The operator then takes a piece of bees-wax in his mouth, and putting his lips to the hole, extracts the air from the horn; and by a dexterous use of his tongue, stops up the hole with the wax. This method is found to answer the purpose, and in general produces a plentiful discharge.

When a person of consequence dies, the relations and neighbours meet together, and manifest their sorrow by loud and dismal howlings. A bullock or goat is killed for such persons as come to assist at the funeral; which generally takes place in the evening of the same day on which the party died. The Negroes have no appropriate burial places, and frequently dig the grave in the floor of the deceased's hut, or in the shade of a favourite tree. The body is dressed in white cotton, and wrapped up in a mat. It is carried to the grave, in the dusk of the evening, by the relations. If the grave is without the walls of the town, a number of prickly bushes are laid upon it, to prevent the wolves from digging up the body; but I never observed that any stone was placed over the grave, as a monument or memorial.

Hitherto I have considered the Negroes chiefly in a moral light; and confined myself to the most prominent features in their mental character: their domestic amusements, occupa-

tions, and diet; their arts and manufactures, with some other
subordinate objects, are now to be noticed.

Of their music and dances, some account has incidentally
been given in different parts of my Journal. On the first of
these heads, I have now to add a list of their musical instruments, the principal of which are,—the *koonting*, a sort of
guitar with three strings;—the *korro*, a large harp, with eighteen strings;—the *simbing*, a small harp, with seven strings;—
the *balafou*, an instrument composed of twenty pieces of hard
wood of different lengths, with the shells of gourds hung under-
neath, to increase the sound;—the *tangtang*, a drum, open at the
lower end; and lastly, the *tabala*, a large drum, commonly used
to spread an alarm through the country. Besides these, they
make use of small flutes, bowstrings, elephants' teeth, and
bells; and at all their dances and concerts, *clapping of hands*
appears to constitute a necessary part of the chorus.

With the love of music is naturally connected a taste for
poetry; and, fortunately for the poets of Africa, they are in a
great measure exempted from that neglect and indigence,
which in more polished countries commonly attend the votaries
of the Muses. They consist of two classes; the most numerous
are the *singing men*, called *Jilli kea*, mentioned in a former
part of my narrative. One or more of these may be found in
every town. They sing extempore songs, in honour of their
chief men, or any other persons who are willing to give " solid
" pudding for empty praise." But a nobler part of their office
is to recite the historical events of their country: hence, in war,
they accompany the soldiers to the field; in order, by reciting

the great actions of their ancestors, to awaken in them a spirit of glorious emulation. The other class, are devotees of the Mahomedan faith, who travel about the country, singing devout hymns, and performing religious ceremonies, to conciliate the favour of the Almighty; either in averting calamity, or insuring success to any enterprize. Both descriptions of these itinerant bards are much employed and respected by the people, and very liberal contributions are made for them.

The usual diet of the Negroes is somewhat different in different districts; in general, the people of free condition breakfast about daybreak, upon gruel made of meal and water, with a little of the fruit of the tamarind to give it an acid taste. About two o'clock in the afternoon, a sort of hasty pudding, with a little Shea butter, is the common meal; but the supper constitutes the principal repast, and is seldom ready before midnight. This consists almost universally of kouskous, with a small portion of animal food. or Shea butter, mixed with it. In eating, the Kafirs, as well as Mahomedans, use the right hand only.

The beverage of the Pagan Negroes, are beer and mead; of each of which they frequently drink to excess. The Maho--medan converts drink nothing but water. The natives of all descriptions take snuff and smoke tobacco; their pipes are made of wood, with an earthen bowl of curious workmanship. But in the interior countries, the greatest of all luxuries is salt. It would appear strange to an European, to see a child suck a piece of rock-salt, as if it were sugar. This, however, I have frequently seen; although, in the inland parts, the poorer class of inhabitants are so very rarely indulged with this precious article, that to say *a man eats salt with his victuals,* is the same as saying, *he is a rich man.* I have myself suffered great inconvenience from the scarcity of this article. The long use of vegetable food, creates so painful a longing for salt, that no words can sufficiently describe it.

The Negroes in general, and the Mandingoes in particular, are considered by the whites on the Coast as an indolent and inactive people; I think, without reason. The nature of the climate is, indeed, unfavourable to great exertion; but surely a people cannot justly be denominated habitually indolent, whose wants are supplied, not by the spontaneous productions of nature, but by their own exertions. Few people work harder, when occasion requires, than the Mandingoes; but not having many opportunities of turning to advantage, the superfluous produce of their labour, they are content with cultivating as much ground only, as is necessary for their own support. The labours of the field give them pretty full employment during the rains; and in the dry season, the people who live in the vicinity of large rivers, employ themselves chiefly in fishing. The fish are taken in wicker baskets, or with small cotton nets; and are preserved by being first dried in the sun, and afterwards rubbed with Shea butter, to prevent them from contracting fresh moisture. Others of the natives employ themselves in hunting. Their weapons are bows and arrows; but the arrows in common use are not poisoned.* They are

* Poisoned arrows are used chiefly in war. The poison, which is said to be very deadly, is prepared from a shrub called *koona,* (a species of *echites*) which is

very dexterous marksmen, and will hit a lizard on a tree, or any other small object, at an amazing distance. They likewise kill Guinea-fowls, partridges, and pigeons, but never on the wing. While the men are occupied in these pursuits, the women are very diligent in manufacturing cotton-cloth. They prepare the cotton for spinning, by laying it in small quantities at a time, upon a smooth stone, or piece of wood, and rolling the seeds out with a thick iron spindle; and they spin it with the distaff. The thread is not fine, but well twisted, and makes a very durable cloth. A woman with common diligence, will spin from six to nine garments of this cloth in one year; which, according to its fineness, will sell for a minkalli and a half, or two minkallies each.* The weaving is performed by the men. The loom is made exactly upon the same principle as that of Europe; but so small and narrow, that the web is seldom more than four inches broad. The shuttle is of the common construction; but as the thread is coarse, the chamber is somewhat larger than the European.

The women die this cloth of a rich and lasting blue colour, by the following simple process: the leaves of the indigo when fresh gathered, are pounded in a wooden mortar, and mixed in a large earthen jar, with a strong ley of wood ashes; chamber-

---

very common in the woods. The leaves of this shrub, when boiled with a small quantity of water, yield a thick black juice, into which the Negroes dip a cotton thread; this thread they fasten round the iron of the arrow, in such a manner that it is almost impossible to extract the arrow, when it has sunk beyond the barbs, without leaving the iron point, and the poisoned thread, in the wound.

* A minkalli is a quantity of gold, nearly equal in value to ten shillings sterling.

ley is sometimes added. The cloth is steeped in this mixture, and allowed to remain until it has aquired the proper shade. In Kaarta and Ludamar, where the indigo is not plentiful, they collect the leaves, and dry them in the sun; and when they wish to use them, they reduce a sufficient quantity to powder, and mix it with the ley as before mentioned. Either way, the colour is very beautiful, with a fine purple gloss; and equal, in my opinion, to the best Indian or European blue. This cloth is cut into various pieces, and sewed into garments, with needles of the natives' own making.

As the arts of weaving, dying, sewing, &c. may easily be acquired, those who exercise them are not considered in Africa as following any particular profession; for almost every slave can weave, and every boy can sew. The only artists which are distinctly acknowledged as such by the Negroes, and who value themselves on exercising appropriate and peculiar trades, are the manufacturers of *leather* and of *iron*. The first of these, are called *Karrankea* (or as the word is sometimes pronounced *Gaungay*). They are to be found in almost every town, and they frequently travel through the country in the exercise of their calling. They tan and dress leather with very great expedition, by steeping the hide first in a mixture of wood-ashes and water, until it parts with the hair; and afterwards by using the pounded leaves of a tree called *goo*, as an astringent. They are at great pains to render the hide as soft and pliant as possible, by rubbing it frequently between their hands, and beating it upon a stone. The hides of bullocks are converted chiefly into sandals, and therefore require less care in dressing than the skins of sheep and goats, which are used for covering quivers and saphies, and in making sheaths for swords and knives, belts, pockets, and a variety of ornaments. These skins are commonly dyed of a red or yellow colour; the red, by means of millet stalks reduced to powder; and the yellow, by the root of a plant, the name of which I have forgotten.

The manufacturers in iron are not so numerous as the *Karrankeas;* but they appear to have studied their business with equal diligence. The Negroes on the Coast being cheaply supplied with iron from the European traders, never attempt the manufacturing of this article themselves; but in the inland parts, the natives smelt this useful metal in such quantities, as not only to supply themselves from it with all necessary weapons and instruments, but even to make it an article of commerce with some of the neighbouring states. During my stay at Kamalia, there was a smelting furnace at a short distance from the hut where I lodged, and the owner and his workmen made no secret about the manner of conducting the operation; and readily allowed me to examine the furnace, and assist them in breaking the iron-stone. The furnace was a circular tower of clay, about ten feet high, and three feet in diameter; surrounded in two places with withes, to prevent the clay from cracking and falling to pieces by the violence of the heat. Round the lower part, on a level with the ground (but not so low as the bottom of the furnace, which was somewhat concave), were made seven openings, into every one of which were placed three tubes of clay, and the openings again plastered up in such a manner that no air could enter the

furnace, but through the tubes; by the opening and shutting
of which they regulated the fire. These tubes were formed by
plastering a mixture of clay and grass round a smooth roller
of wood, which as soon as the clay began to harden was withdrawn, and the tube left to dry in the sun. The iron-stone
which I saw was very heavy, of a dull red colour, with greyish
specks; it was broken into pieces about the size of a hen's egg.
A bundle of dry wood was first put into the furnace, and
covered with a considerable quantity of charcoal, which was
brought, ready burnt, from the woods. Over this was laid a
stratum of iron-stone, and then another of charcoal, and so on,
until the furnace was quite full. The fire was applied through
one of the tubes, and blown for some time with bellows made
of goats' skins. The operation went on very slowly at first, and
it was some hours before the flame appeared above the furnace;
but after this, it burnt with great violence all the first night;
and the people who attended put in at times more charcoal.
On the day following the fire was not so fierce, and on the
second night, some of the tubes were withdrawn, and the air
allowed to have freer access to the furnace; but the heat was
still very great, and a bluish flame rose some feet above the
top of the furnace. On the third day from the commencement
of the operation, all the tubes were taken out, the ends of
many of them being vitrified with the heat; but the metal was
not removed until some days afterwards, when the whole was
perfectly cool. Part of the furnace was then taken down, and
the iron appeared in the form of a large irregular mass, with
pieces of charcoal adhering to it. It was sonorous; and when

any portion was broken off, the fracture exhibited a granulated appearance, like broken steel. The owner informed me that many parts of this cake were useless, but still there was good iron enough to repay him for his trouble. This iron, or rather steel, is formed into various instruments, by being repeatedly heated in a forge, the heat of which is urged by a pair of double bellows, of a very simple construction, being made of two goats' skins; the tubes from which unite, before they enter the forge, and supply a constant and very regular blast. The hammer, forceps, and anvil, are all very simple, and the workmanship (particularly in the formation of knives and spears) is not destitute of merit. The iron, indeed, is hard and brittle; and requires much labour before it can be made to answer the purpose.

Most of the African blacksmiths are acquainted also with the method of smelting gold, in which process they use an alkaline salt, obtained from a ley of burnt corn-stalks evaporated to dryness. They likewise draw the gold into wire, and form it into a variety of ornaments, some of which are executed with a great deal of taste and ingenuity.

Such is the chief information I obtained, concerning the present state of arts and manufactures in those regions of Africa which I explored in my journey. I might add, though it is scarce worthy observation, that in Bambarra and Kaarta, the natives make very beautiful baskets, hats, and other articles, both for use and ornament, from *rushes*, which they stain of different colours; and they contrive also to cover their calabashes with interwoven cane, dyed in the same manner.

In all the laborious occupations above described, the master and his slaves work together, without any distinction of superiority. Hired servants, by which I mean persons of free condition, voluntarily working for pay, are unknown in Africa; and this observation naturally leads me to consider the condition of the slaves, and the various means by which they are reduced to so miserable a state of servitude. This unfortunate class are found, I believe, in all parts of this extensive country, and constitute a considerable branch of commerce, with the states on the Mediterranean, as well as with the nations of Europe.

CHAPTER XXII.

Observations concerning the State and Sources of Slavery in Africa.

A STATE of subordination, and certain inequalities of rank and condition, are inevitable in every stage of civil society; but when this subordination is carried to so great a length, that the persons and services of one part of the community are entirely at the disposal of another part, it may then be denominated a state of slavery; and in this condition of life, a great body of the Negro inhabitants of Africa have continued from the most early period of their history; with this aggravation, that their children are born to no other inheritance.

The slaves in Africa, I suppose, are nearly in the proportion of three to one to the freemen. They claim no reward for their services, except food and clothing; and are treated with kindness, or severity, according to the good or bad disposition of their masters. Custom, however, has established certain rules with regard to the treatment of slaves, which it is thought dishonourable to violate. Thus, the domestic slaves, or such as are born in a man's own house, are treated with more lenity than those which are purchased with money. The authority of the master over the domestic slave, as I have elsewhere observed, extends only to reasonable correction; for the master cannot sell his domestic, without having first brought him to a public trial, before the chief men of the place.* But these restrictions on the power of the master, extend not to the case of prisoners taken in war, nor to that of slaves purchased with money. All these unfortunate beings are considered as strangers and foreigners, who have no right to the protection of the law, and may be treated with severity, or sold to a stranger, according to the pleasure of their owners. There are, indeed, regular markets, where slaves of this description are bought and sold; and the value of a slave in the eye of an African purchaser, increases in proportion to his distance from his native kingdom: for when slaves are only a few days' journey from the place of their nativity, they frequently effect their escape; but when one or more kingdoms intervene, escape being more difficult, they are more readily reconciled to their situation. On this account, the unhappy slave is frequently transferred from one dealer to another, until he has lost all hopes of returning to his native kingdom. The slaves which are purchased by the Europeans on the Coast, are chiefly of this description; a few of them are collected in the petty wars, hereafter to be described, which take place near the Coast; but by far the greater number are brought down in large caravans

* In time of famine, the master is permitted to sell one or more of his domestics, to purchase provisions for his family; and in case of the master's insolvency, the domestic slaves are sometimes seized upon by the creditors; and if the master cannot redeem them, they are liable to be sold for payment of his debts. These are the only cases that I recollect, in which the domestic slaves are liable to be sold, without any misconduct or demerit of their own.

from the inland countries, of which many are unknown, even
by name, to the Europeans. The slaves which are thus brought
from the interior, may be divided into two distinct classes;
first, such as were slaves from their birth, having been born of
enslaved mothers; *secondly*, such as were born free, but who
afterwards, by whatever means, became slaves. Those of the
first description, are by far the most numerous; for prisoners
taken in war (at least such as are taken in open and declared
war, when one kingdom avows hostilities against another) are
generally of this description. The comparatively small proportion of free people, to the enslaved, throughout Africa, has
already been noticed; and it must be observed, that men of free
condition, have many advantages over the slaves, even in war
time. They are in general better armed, and well mounted;
and can either fight or escape, with some hopes of success; but
the slaves, who have only their spears and bows, and of whom
great numbers are loaded with baggage, become an easy
prey. Thus, when Mansong, King of Bambarra, made war
upon Kaarta (as I have related in a former Chapter), he took
in one day nine hundred prisoners, of which number not more
than seventy were free men. This account I received from
Daman Jumma, who had thirty slaves at Kemmoo, all of whom
were made prisoners by Mansong. Again, when a freeman is
taken prisoner, his friends will sometimes ransom him, by
giving two slaves in exchange; but when a slave is taken, he
has no hopes of such redemption. To these disadvantages, it
is to be added, that the Slatees, who purchase slaves in the
interior countries, and carry them down to the Coast for sale,

P p

constantly prefer such as have been in that condition of life from their infancy, well knowing that these have been accustomed to hunger and fatigue, and are better able to sustain the hardships of a long and painful journey, than free men; and on their reaching the Coast, if no opportunity offers of selling them to advantage, they can easily be made to maintain themselves by their labour; neither are they so apt to attempt making their escape, as those who have once tasted the blessings of freedom.

Slaves of the second description, generally become such by one or other of the following causes, 1. *Captivity.* 2. *Famine.* 3. *Insolvency.* 4. *Crimes.* A freeman may, by the established customs of Africa, become a slave, by being taken in war. War, is of all others, the most productive source, and was probably the origin, of slavery; for when one nation had taken from another, a greater number of captives than could be exchanged on equal terms, it is natural to suppose that the conquerors, finding it inconvenient to maintain their prisoners, would compel them to labour; at first, perhaps, only for their own support; but afterwards to support their masters. Be this as it may, it is a known fact, that prisoners of war in Africa, are the slaves of the conquerors; and when the weak or unsuccessful warrior, begs for mercy beneath the uplifted spear of his opponent, he gives up at the same time his claim to liberty; and purchases his life at the expence of his freedom.

In a country, divided into a thousand petty states, mostly independent and jealous of each other; where every freeman is accustomed to arms, and fond of military achievements; where the youth who has practised the bow and spear from his infancy, longs for nothing so much as an opportunity to display his valour, it is natural to imagine that wars frequently originate from very frivolous provocation. When one nation is more powerful than another, a pretext is seldom wanting for commencing hostilities. Thus the war between Kajaaga and Kasson was occasioned by the detention of a fugitive slave; that between Bambarra and Kaarta by the loss of a few cattle. Other cases of the same nature perpetually occur, in which the folly or mad ambition of their princes, and the zeal of their religious enthusiasts, give full employment to the scythe of desolation.

The wars of Africa are of two kinds, which are distinguished by different appellations: that species which bears the greatest resemblance to our European contests, is denominated *killi*, a word signifying " to call out," because such wars are openly avowed, and previously declared. Wars of this description in Africa, commonly terminate, however, in the course of a single campaign. A battle is fought; the vanquished seldom think of rallying again; the whole inhabitants become panic struck; and the conquerors have only to bind the slaves, and carry off their plunder and their victims. Such of the prisoners as, through age or infirmity, are unable to endure fatigue, or are found unfit for sale, are considered as useless; and I have no doubt are frequently put to death. The same fate commonly awaits a chief, or any other person who has taken a very distinguished part in the war. And here it may be observed that, notwithstanding this exterminating system, it is surprising to behold how soon an African town is rebuilt and repeopled. The circumstance arises probably from this; that their pitched battles are few; the weakest know their own situation, and seek safety in flight. When their country has been desolated, and their ruined towns and villages deserted by the enemy, such of the inhabitants as have escaped the *sword*, and the *chain*, generally return, though with cautious steps, to the place of their nativity; for it seems to be the universal wish of mankind, to spend the evening of their days where they passed their infancy. The poor Negro feels this desire in its full force. To him, no water is sweet but what is drawn from his own well; and no tree has so cool and pleasant a shade as the *tabba* tree* of his native village. When war compels him to abandon the delightful spot in which he first drew his breath, and seek for safety in some other kingdom, his time is spent in talking about the country of his ancestors; and no sooner is peace restored than he turns his back upon the land of strangers, rebuilds with haste his fallen walls, and exults to see the smoke ascend from his native village.

The other species of African warfare, is distinguished by the appellation of *tegria*, " plundering or stealing." It arises from a sort of hereditary feud, which the inhabitants of one nation or district bear towards another. No immediate cause of hostility is assigned, or notice of attack given; but the inhabitants of each, watch every opportunity to plunder and distress the objects of their animosity by predatory excursions. These, are very common, particularly about the beginning of the dry

---

* This is a large spreading tree (a species of *sterculia*) under which the Bentang is commonly placed.

season, when the labour of the harvest is over and provisions are plentiful. Schemes of vengeance are then meditated. The chief man surveys the number and activity of his vassals, as they brandish their spears at festivals; and elated with his own importance, turns his whole thoughts towards revenging some depredation or insult, which either he or his ancestors may have received from a neighbouring state.

Wars of this description are generally conducted with great secrecy. A few resolute individuals, headed by some person of enterprise and courage, march quietly through the woods, surprize in the night some unprotected village, and carry off the inhabitants and their effects, before their neighbours can come to their assistance. One morning, during my stay at Kamalia, we were all much alarmed by a party of this kind. The king of Fooladoo's son, with five hundred horsemen, passed secretly through the woods, a little to the southward of Kamalia, and on the morning following, plundered three towns belonging to Madigai, a powerful chief in Jallonkadoo.

The success of this expedition encouraged the governor of Bangassi, a town in Fooladoo, to make a second inroad upon another part of the same country. Having assembled about two hundred of his people, he passed the river Kokoro in the night, and carried off a great number of prisoners. Several of the inhabitants who had escaped these attacks, were afterwards seized by the Mandingoes, as they wandered about in the woods, or concealed themselves in the glens and strong places of the mountains.

These plundering excursions, always produce speedy retaliation; and when large parties cannot be collected for this purpose, a few friends will combine together, and advance into the enemy's country, with a view to plunder, or carry off the inhabitants. A single individual has been known to take his bow and quiver, and proceed in like manner. Such an attempt is doubtless in him an act of rashness; but when it is considered that, in one of these predatory wars, he has probably been deprived of his child or his nearest relation, his situation will rather call for pity than censure. The poor sufferer, urged on by the feelings of domestic or paternal attachment, and the ardour of revenge, conceals himself among the bushes, until some young or unarmed person passes by. He then, tyger-like, springs upon his prey; drags his victim into the thicket, and in the night carries him off as a slave.

When a Negro has, by means like these, once fallen into the hands of his enemies, he is either retained as the slave of his conqueror, or bartered into a distant kingdom; for an African, when he has once subdued his enemy, will seldom give him an opportunity of lifting up his hand against him at a future period. A conqueror commonly disposes of his captives according to the rank which they held in their native kingdom. Such of the domestic slaves as appear to be of a mild disposition, and particularly the young women, are retained as his own slaves. Others that display marks of discontent, are disposed of in a distant country; and such of the freemen or slaves, as have taken an active part in the war, are either sold to the Slatees, or put to death. War, therefore, is certainly the most general, and most productive source of slavery; and the desolations of war often (but not always) produce the second cause of slavery, *famine;* in which case a freeman becomes a slave, to avoid a greater calamity.

Perhaps, by a philosophic and reflecting mind, death itself would scarcely be considered as a greater calamity than slavery; but the poor Negro, when fainting with hunger, thinks like Esau of old; " *behold I am at the point to die, and what* " *profit shall this birthright do to me?"* There are many instances of free men voluntarily surrendering up their liberty to save their lives. During a great scarcity which lasted for three years, in the countries of the Gambia great numbers of people became slaves in this manner. Dr. Laidley assured me that, at that time, many free men came and begged, with great earnestness, *to be put upon his slave-chain,* to save them from perishing of hunger. Large families are very often exposed to absolute want; and as the parents have almost unlimited authority over their children, it frequently happens, in all parts of Africa, that some of the latter are sold to purchase provisions for the rest of the family. When I was at Jarra, Daman Jumma pointed out to me three young slaves which he had purchased in this manner. I have already related another instance which I saw at Wonda; and I was informed that in Fooladoo, at that time, it was a very common practice.

The third cause of slavery, is *insolvency.* Of all the offences (if insolvency may be so called), to which the laws of Africa have affixed the punishment of slavery, this is the most common. A Negro trader commonly contracts debts on some mercantile speculation, either from his neighbours, to purchase such articles as will sell to advantage in a distant market, or from the European traders on the Coast ; payment to be made in a given time. In both cases, the situation of the adventurer is exactly the same. If he succeeds, he may secure an independency. If he is unsuccessful, his person and services are at the disposal of another ; for in Africa, not only the effects of the insolvent, but even the insolvent himself, is sold to satisfy the lawful demands of his creditors. *

The fourth cause above enumerated, is *the commission of crimes, on which the laws of the country affix slavery as a punishment.* In Africa, the only offences of this class, are murder, adultery, and witchcraft; and I am happy to say, that they did not appear to me to be common. In cases of murder, I was informed, that the nearest relation of the deceased had it in his power, after conviction, either to kill the offender with his own hand, or sell him into slavery. When adultery occurs, it is generally left to the option of the person injured, either to sell the culprit, or accept such a ransom for him, as he may think

* When a Negro takes up goods on credit from any of the Europeans on the Coast, and does not make payment at the time appointed, the European is authorized, by the laws of the country, to seize upon the debtor himself, if he can find him ; or if he cannot be found, on any person of his family ; or, in the last resort, on *any native of the same kingdom.* The person thus seized on, is detained while his friends are sent in quest of the debtor. When he is found, a meeting is called of the chief people of the place, and the debtor is compelled to ransom his friend by fulfilling his engagements. If he is unable to do this, his person is immediately secured and sent down to the Coast, and the other released. If the debtor cannot be found, the person seized on is obliged to pay double the amount of the debt, or is himself sold into slavery. I was given to understand, however, that this part of the law is seldom enforced.

equivalent to the injury he has sustained. By witchcraft, is meant pretended magic, by which the lives or healths of persons are affected: in other words, it is the administering of poison. No trial for this offence, however, came under my observation while I was in Africa; and I therefore suppose that the crime, and its punishment, occur but very seldom.

When a free man has become a slave by any one of the causes before mentioned, he generally continues so for life, and his children (if they are born of an enslaved mother) are brought up in the same state of servitude. There are however a few instances of slaves obtaining their freedom, and sometimes even with the consent of their masters ; as by performing some singular piece of service, or by going to battle, and bringing home two slaves as a ransome ; but the common way of regaining freedom is by escape, and when slaves have once set their minds on running away, they often succeed. Some of them will wait for years before an opportunity presents itself, and during that period shew no signs of discontent. In general, it may be remarked, that slaves who come from a hilly country, and have been much accustomed to hunting and travel, are more apt to attempt their escape, than such as are born in a flat country, and have been employed in cultivating the land.

Such are the general outlines of that system of slavery which prevails in Africa; and it is evident, from its nature and extent, that it is a system of no modern date. It probably had its origin in the remote ages of antiquity, before the Mahomedans explored a path across the Desert. How far it is maintained and supported by the slave traffic, which, for two hundred years, the nations of Europe have carried on with the natives of the Coast, it is neither within my province, nor in my power, to explain. If my sentiments should be required concerning the effect which a discontinuance of that commerce would produce on the manners of the natives, I should have no hesitation in observing, that, in the present unenlightened state of their minds, my opinion is, the effect would neither be so extensive or beneficial, as many wise and worthy persons fondly expect.

CHAPTER XXIII.

Of Gold-dust, and the Manner in which it is collected.—Process of Washing it.—Its Value in Africa.—Of Ivory.—Surprise of the Negroes at the Eagerness of the Europeans for this Commodity.—Scattered Teeth frequently picked up in the Woods.—Mode of Hunting the Elephant.—Some Reflections on the unimproved State of the Country, &c.

THOSE valuable commodities, gold and ivory (the next objects of our inquiry) have probably been found in Africa from the first ages of the world. They are reckoned among its most important productions in the earliest records of its history.

It has been observed, that gold is seldom or never discovered, except in *mountainous* and *barren* countries: Nature, it is said, thus making amends in one way, for her penuriousness in the other. This, however, is not wholly true. Gold is found in considerable quantities throughout every part of Manding; a country which is indeed hilly, but cannot properly be called *mountainous*, much less *barren*. It is also found in great plenty in Jallonkadoo (particularly about Boori), another hilly, but by no means an infertile country. It is remarkable, that in the place last mentioned (Boori), which is situated about four days' journey to the south-west of Kamalia, the salt market is often supplied, at the same time, with rock-salt from the Great

Q q 2

Desert, and sea-salt from the Rio Grande; the price of each, at this distance from its source, being nearly the same; and the dealers in each, whether Moors from the north, or Negroes from the west, are invited thither by the same motives, that of bartering their salt for gold.

The gold of Manding, so far as I could learn, is never found in any matrix or vein, but always in small grains, nearly in a pure state, from the size of a pin's head, to that of a pea; scattered through a large body of sand or clay; and in this state, it is called by the Mandingoes *sanoo munko*, "gold powder." It is, however, extremely probable, by what I could learn of the situation of the ground, that most of it has originally been washed down by repeated torrents from the neighbouring hills. The manner in which it is collected, is nearly as follows:

About the beginning of December, when the harvest is over, and the streams and torrents have greatly subsided, the Mansa, or chief of the town, appoints a day to begin *sanoo koo*, " gold " washing;" and the women are sure to have themselves in readiness by the time appointed. A paddle, or spade, for digging up the sand, two or three calabashes for washing it in, and a few quills for containing the gold dust, are all the implements necessary for the purpose. On the morning of their departure, a bullock is killed for the first day's entertainment, and a number of prayers and charms are used to ensure success; for a failure on that day, is thought a bad omen. The Mansa of Kamalia, with fourteen of his people, were I remember so much disappointed in their first day's washing, that very few of them had resolution to persevere ; and the few that did, had but very indifferent success ; which indeed, is not much to be wondered at ; for instead of opening some untried place, they continued to dig and wash in the same spot where they had dug and washed for years ; and where, of course, but few large grains could be left.

The washing the sands of the streams, is by far the easiest way of obtaining the gold-dust ; but in most places the sands have been so narrowly searched before, that unless the stream takes some new course, the gold is found but in small quantities. While some of the party are busied in washing the sands, others employ themselves farther up the torrent, where the rapidity of the stream has carried away all the clay, sand, &c. and left nothing but small pebbles. The search among these is a very troublesome task. I have seen women who have had the skin worn off the tops of their fingers in this employment. Sometimes, however, they are rewarded by finding pieces of gold, which they call *sanoo birro*, " gold " stones," that amply repay them for their trouble. A woman and her daughter, inhabitants of Kamalia, found in one day two pieces of this kind ; one of five drachms, and the other of three drachms weight. But the most certain and profitable mode of washing, is practised in the height of the dry season, by digging a deep pit, like a draw-well, near some hill which has previously been discovered to contain gold. The pit is dug with small spades or corn paddles, and the earth is drawn up in large calabashes. As the Negroes dig through the different strata of clay or sand, a calabash or two of each is washed, by way of experiment; and in this manner the labourers proceed, until they come to a stratum containing gold; or until they are obstructed by rocks, or inundated by water. In general, when they come to a stratum of fine reddish sand, with small black specks therein, they find gold, in some proportion or other, and send up large calabashes full of the sand, for the women to wash; for though the pit is dug by the men, the gold is always washed by the women, who are accustomed from their infancy to a similar operation, in separating the husks of corn from the meal.

As I never descended into any one of these pits, I cannot say in what manner they are worked under ground. Indeed, the situation in which I was placed, made it necessary for me to be cautious not to incur the suspicion of the natives, by examining too far into the riches of their country; but the manner of separating the gold from the sand, is very simple, and is frequently performed by the women in the middle of the town; for when the searchers return from the valleys in the evening, they commonly bring with them each a calabash or two of sand, to be washed by such of the females as remain at home. The operation is simply as follows.

A portion of sand or clay (for the gold is sometimes found in a brown coloured clay), is put into a large calabash, and mixed with a sufficient quantity of water. The woman, whose office it is, then shakes the calabash in such a manner, as to mix the sand and water together, and give the whole a rotatory motion; at first gently, but afterwards more quick, until a small portion of sand and water, at every revolution, flies over the brim of the calabash. The sand thus separated, is only the coarsest particles mixed with a little muddy water. After the operation has been continued for some time, the sand is allowed to subside, and the water poured off; a portion of coarse sand which is now uppermost in the calabash, is removed by the hand, and fresh water being added, the operation is repeated until the water comes off almost pure. The woman now takes a second calabash, and shakes the sand and water gently from the one to the other, reserving that portion of sand which is next the bottom of the calabash, and which is most likely to contain the gold. This small quantity is mixed with some pure water, and being moved about in the calabash, is carefully examined. If a few particles of gold are picked out, the contents of the other calabash are examined in the same manner; but, in general, the party is well contented, if she can obtain three or four grains from the contents of both calabashes. Some women, however, by long practice, become so well acquainted with the nature of the sand, and the mode of washing it, that they will collect gold, where others cannot find a single particle. The gold dust is kept in quills, stopt up with cotton; and the washers are fond of displaying a number of these quills in their hair. Generally speaking, if a person uses common diligence, in a proper soil, it is supposed that as much gold may be collected by him in the course of the dry season, as is equal to the value of two slaves.

Thus simple is the process by which the Negroes obtain gold in Manding; and it is evident, from this account, that the country contains a considerable portion of this precious metal; for many of the smaller particles must necessarily escape the observation of the naked eye; and as the natives generally search the sands of streams at a considerable distance from the hills, and consequently far removed from the mines where the gold was originally produced, the labourers are sometimes but ill paid for their trouble. Minute particles only, of this heavy metal, can be carried by the current to any considerable distance; the larger must remain deposited near the original source from whence they came. Were the gold-bearing streams to be traced to their fountains; and the hills from whence they spring, properly examined, the sand in which the gold is there deposited would, no doubt, be found to contain particles of a much larger size; * and even the small grains might be collected to considerable advantage by the use of quicksilver, and other improvements, with which the natives are at present unacquainted.

Part of this gold is converted into ornaments for the women, but, in general, these ornaments are more to be admired for their weight, than their workmanship. They are massy and inconvenient, particularly the ear-rings, which are commonly so heavy as to pull down and lacerate the lobe of the ear; to avoid which they are supported by a thong of red leather, which passes over the crown of the head from one ear to the other. The necklace displays greater fancy; and the proper

---

* I am informed that the gold mine, as it is called, in Wicklow, in Ireland, which was discovered in the year 1795, is near the top, and upon the steep slope, of a mountain. Here, pieces of gold of several ounces weight were frequently found. What would have been gold-dust two miles below, was here golden gravel; that is, each grain was like a small pebble in size, and one piece was found which weighed near twenty-two ounces troy.

arrangement of the different beads and plates of gold, is the great criterion of taste and elegance. When a lady of consequence is in full dress, her gold ornaments may be worth altogether, from fifty to eighty pounds sterling.

A small quantity of gold is likewise employed by the Slatees, in defraying the expences of their journies to and from the Coast; but by far the greater proportion is annually carried away by the Moors in exchange for salt, and other merchandize. During my stay at Kamalia, the gold collected by the different traders at that place, for salt alone, was nearly equal to one hundred and ninety-eight pounds sterling; and as Kamalia is but a small town, and not much resorted to by the trading Moors, this quantity must have borne a very small proportion to the gold collected at Kancaba, Kankaree, and some other large towns. The value of salt in this part of Africa is very great. One slab, about two feet and a half in length, fourteen inches in breadth, and two inches in thickness, will sometimes sell for about two pounds ten shillings sterling, and from one pound fifteen shillings, to two pounds, may be considered as the common price. Four of these slabs are considered as a load for an ass, and six for a bullock. The value of European merchandize in Manding varies very much, according to the supply from the Coast, or the dread of war in the country; but the return for such articles is commonly made in slaves. The price of a prime slave when I was at Kamalia, was from *nine* to *twelve* minkallies, and European commodities had then nearly the following value:

R r

18 gun flints,
48 leaves of tobacco,
20 charges of gunpowder,
A cutlass,

} one minkalli.

A musket, from three to four minkallies.

The produce of the country, and the different necessaries of life, when exchanged for gold, sold as follows :

Common provisions for one day, the weight of one *teelee-kissi* (a black bean, six of which make the weight of one minkalli;) —a chicken, one teelee-kissi—a sheep three teelee-kissi—a bullock one minkalli—a horse from ten to seventeen minkallies.

The Negroes weigh the gold in small balances, which they always carry about them. They make no difference in point of value, between gold dust and wrought gold. In bartering one article for another, the person who receives the gold, always weighs it with his own teelee-kissi. These beans are sometimes fraudulently soaked in Shea-butter, to make them heavy; and I once saw a pebble ground exactly into the form of one of them ; but such practices are not very common.

Having now related the substance of what occurs to my recollection concerning the African mode of obtaining gold from the earth, and its value in barter, I proceed to the next article, of which I proposed to treat, namely, *ivory.*

Nothing creates a greater surprise among the Negroes on the sea coast, than the eagerness displayed by the European traders to procure elephants' teeth; it being exceedingly difficult to make them comprehend to what use it is applied. Although they are shewn knives with ivory hafts, combs, and toys of the same material, and are convinced that the ivory thus manufactured, was originally parts of a tooth, they are not satisfied. They suspect that this commodity is more frequently converted in Europe, to purposes of far greater importance; the true nature of which is studiously concealed from them, lest the price of ivory should be enhanced. They cannot, they say, easily persuade themselves, that ships would be built, and voyages undertaken, to procure an article, which had no other value than that of furnishing handles to knives, &c. when pieces of wood would answer the purpose equally well.

Elephants are very numerous in the interior of Africa, but they appear to be a distinct species from those found in Asia. Blumenbach, in his figures of objects of natural history, has given good drawings of a grinder of each; and the variation is evident. M. Cuvier also has given, in the *Magazin Encyclopedique*, a clear account of the difference between them. As I never examined the Asiatic elephant, I have chosen rather to refer to those writers, than advance this as an opinion of my own. It has been said, that the African elephant is of a less docile nature than the Asiatic, and incapable of being tamed. The Negroes certainly do not at present tame them; but when we consider that the Carthaginians had always tame elephants in their armies, and actually transported some of them to Italy in the course of the Punic wars; it seems more likely that they should have possessed the art of taming their own elephants, than have submitted to the expence of bringing such vast animals from Asia. Perhaps, the barbarous practice of hunting the African elephants for the sake of their teeth, has rendered them more untractable and savage, than they were found to be in former times.

The greater part of the ivory which is sold on the Gambia, and Senegal rivers, is brought from the interior country. The lands towards the Coast are too swampy, and too much intersected with creeks and rivers, for so bulky an animal as the elephant to travel through, without being discovered; and when once the natives discern the marks of his feet in the earth, the whole village is up in arms. The thoughts of feasting on his flesh, making sandals of his hide, and selling the teeth to the Europeans, inspire every one with courage; and the animal seldom escapes from his pursuers; but in the plains of Bambarra and Kaarta, and the extensive wilds of Jallonkadoo, the elephants are very numerous; and, from the great scarcity of gunpowder in those districts, they are less annoyed by the natives.

Scattered teeth are frequently picked up in the woods, and travellers are very diligent in looking for them. It is a common practice with the elephant, to thrust his teeth under the roots of such shrubs and bushes as grow in the more dry and elevated parts of the country, where the soil is shallow. These bushes he easily overturns, and feeds on the roots, which are, in general, more tender and juicy than the hard woody branches, or the foliage; but when the teeth are partly decayed by age, and the roots more firmly fixed, the great exertions of the animal, in this practice, frequently causes them to break short. At Kamalia I saw two teeth; one, a very large one; which were found in the woods, and which were evidently broken off in this manner. Indeed it is difficult otherwise to account for such a large proportion of broken ivory, as is daily offered for sale, at the different factories; for when the elephant is killed in hunting, unless he dashes himself over a precipice, the teeth are always extracted entire.

There are certain seasons of the year when the elephants collect into large herds, and traverse the country in quest of food or water; and as all that part of the country to the north of the Niger, is destitute of rivers, whenever the pools in the woods are dried up, the elephants approach towards the banks of that river. Here, they continue until the commencement of the rainy season, in the months of June or July; and during this time they are much hunted by such of the Bambarrans as have gunpowder to spare. The elephant hunters seldom go out singly: a party of four or five join together; and having each furnished himself with powder and ball, and a quantity of corn-meal in a leather bag, sufficient for five or six days provision, they enter the most unfrequented parts of the wood, and examine with great care every thing that can lead to the discovery of the elephants. In this pursuit, notwithstanding the bulk of the animal, very great nicety of observation is required. The broken branches, the scattered dung of the animal, and the marks of his feet, are carefully inspected; and many of the hunters have, by long experience and attentive observation, become so expert in their search, that as soon as they observe the footmarks of an elephant, they will tell almost to a certainty at what time it passed, and at what distance it will be found.

When they discover a herd of elephants, they follow them at

a distance, until they perceive some one stray from the rest, and come into such a situation as to be fired at, with advantage. The hunters then approach with great caution, creeping amongst the long grass, until they have got near enough to be sure of their aim.   They then discharge all their pieces at once, and throw themselves on their faces among the grass.   The wounded elephant immediately applies his trunk to the different wounds, but being unable to extract the balls, and seeing no-body near him, becomes quite furious, and runs about amongst the bushes, until by fatigue and loss of blood he has ex-hausted himself, and affords the hunters an opportunity of firing a second time at him, by which he is generally brought to the ground.

The skin is now taken off, and extended on the ground with pegs, to dry ; and such parts of the flesh as are most esteemed, are cut up into thin slices, and dried in the sun, to serve for provisions on some future occasion.   The teeth are struck out with a light hatchet, which the hunters always carry along with them ; not only for that purpose, but also to enable them to cut down such trees as contain honey ; for though they carry with them only five or six days provisions, they will remain in the woods for months, if they are successful ; and support themselves upon the flesh of such elephants as they kill, and wild honey.

The ivory thus collected, is seldom brought down to the Coast by the hunters themselves.   They dispose of it to the itinerant merchants, who come annually from the Coast with arms and ammunition, to purchase this valuable commodity.

Some of these merchants will collect ivory in the course of one season, sufficient to load four or five asses. A great quantity of ivory is likewise brought from the interior, by the slave coffles; there are, however, some Slatees, of the Mahomedan persuasion, who, from motives of religion, will not deal in ivory; nor eat of the flesh of the elephant, unless it has been killed with a spear.

The quantity of ivory collected in this part of Africa, is not so great, nor are the-teeth in general so large as in the countries nearer the Line: few of them weigh more than eighty, or one hundred pounds; and, upon an average, a bar of European merchandise may be reckoned as the price of a pound of ivory.

I have now, I trust, in this and the preceding Chapters, explained with sufficient minuteness, the nature and extent of the commercial connection which at present prevails, and has long subsisted, between the Negro natives of those parts of Africa which I visited, and the nations of Europe; and it appears, that slaves, gold, and ivory, together with the few articles enumerated in the beginning of my work, *viz.* bees-wax and honey, hides, gums, and dye woods, constitute the whole catalogue of exportable commodities. Other productions, however, have been incidentally noticed as the growth of Africa; such as grain of different kinds, tobacco, indigo, cotton-wool, and perhaps a few others; but of all these (which can only be obtained by cultivation and labour), the natives raise sufficient only for their own immediate expenditure; nor, under the present system of their laws, manners, trade and government. can any thing farther be expected from them. It cannot, however, admit of a doubt, that all the rich and valuable productions, both of the East and West Indies, might easily be naturalized, and brought to the utmost perfection, in the tropical parts of this immense continent. Nothing is wanting to this end, but example, to enlighten the minds of the natives; and instruction, to enable them to direct their industry to proper objects. It was not possible for me to behold the wonderful fertility of the soil, the vast herds of cattle, proper both for labour and food, and a variety of other circumstances favourable to colonization and agriculture; and reflect, withal, on the means which presented themselves of a vast inland navigation, without lamenting that a country, so abundantly gifted and favoured by nature, should remain in its present savage and neglected state. Much more did I lament, that a people of manners and dispositions so gentle and benevolent, should either be left as they now are, immersed in the gross and uncomfortable blindness of pagan superstition, or permitted to become converts to a system of bigotry and fanaticism; which, without enlightening the mind, often debases the heart. On this subject many observations might be made; but the reader will probably think that I have already digressed too largely; and I now, therefore, return to my situation at Kamalia.

CHAPTER XXIV.

Transactions at Kamalia resumed.—Arabic MSS. in Use among the Mahomedan Negroes.—Reflections concerning the Conversion and Education of the Negro Children.—Return of the Author's Benefactor, KARFA.—Further Account of the Purchase and Treatment of Slaves.—Fast of Rhamadan, how observed by the Negroes.—Author's anxiety for the Day of Departure. —The Caravan sets out—Account of it on its Departure, and Proceedings on the Road, until its arrival at Kinytakooro.

THE schoolmaster, to whose care I was entrusted during the absence of Karfa, was a man of a mild disposition, and gentle manners; his name was Fankooma; and although he himself adhered strictly to the religion of Mahomet, he was by no means intolerant in his principles towards others who differed from him. He spent much of his time in reading; and teaching appeared to be his pleasure, as well as employment. His school consisted of seventeen boys, most of whom were sons of Kafirs; and two girls, one of whom was Karfa's own daughter. The girls received their instructions in the day time, but the boys always had their lessons by the light of a large fire before daybreak, and again late in the evening; for being considered, during their scholarship, as the domestic slaves of the master,

S s

they were employed in planting corn, bringing fire-wood, and in other servile offices, through the day.

Exclusive of the Koran, and a book or two of commentaries thereon, the schoolmaster possessed a variety of manuscripts, which had partly been purchased from the trading Moors, and partly borrowed from Bushreens in the neighbourhood, and copied with great care. Other MSS. had been produced to me at different places in the course of my journey; and on recounting those I had before seen, and those which were now shewn to me, and interrogating the schoolmaster on the subject, I discovered that the Negroes are in possession (among others), of an Arabic version of the Pentateuch of Moses, which they call *Taureta la Moosa*. This is so highly esteemed, that it is often sold for the value of one prime slave. They have likewise a version of the Psalms of David (*Zabora Dawidi*); and, lastly, the book of Isaiah, which they call *Lingeeli la Isa*, and it is in very high esteem. I suspect, indeed, that in all these copies, there are interpolations of some of the peculiar tenets of Mahomet, for I could distinguish in many passages the name of the Prophet. It is possible, however, that this circumstance might otherwise have been accounted for, if my knowledge of the Arabic had been more extensive. By means of those books, many of the converted Negroes have acquired an acquaintance with some of the remarkable events recorded in the Old Testament. The account of our first parents; the death of Abel; the deluge; the lives of Abraham, Isaac, and Jacob; the story of Joseph and his brethren; the history of Moses, David, Solomon, &c. All these have been related to me in the Mandingo language, with tolerable exactness, by different people; and my surprise was not greater on hearing these accounts from the lips of the Negroes, than theirs, on finding that I was already acquainted with them; for although the Negroes in general have a very great idea of the wealth and power of the Europeans, I am afraid that the Mahomedan converts among them, think but very lightly of our superior attainments in religious knowledge. The white traders in the maritime districts, take no pains to counteract this unhappy prejudice; always performing their own devotions in secret, and seldom condescending to converse with the Negroes in a friendly and instructive manner. To me, therefore, it was not so much the subject of wonder, as matter of regret, to observe, that while the superstition of Mahomet has, in this manner, scattered a few faint beams of learning among these poor people, the precious light of Christianity is altogether excluded. I could not but lament, that although the Coast of Africa has now been known and frequented by the Europeans for more than two hundred years, yet the Negroes still remain entire strangers to the doctrines of our holy religion. We are anxious to draw from obscurity the opinions and records of antiquity, the beauties of Arabian and Asiatic literature, &c.; but while our libraries are thus stored with the learning of various countries, we distribute with a parsimonious hand, the blessings of religious truth, to the benighted nations of the earth. The natives of Asia derive but little advantage in this respect from an intercourse with us; and even the poor Africans, whom we affect to consider as barbarians, look upon us, I fear, as little better than a race of formidable but ignorant heathens. When I produced Richardson's Arabic grammar to some Slatees on the Gambia, they were astonished to think that any European should understand, and write, the sacred language of their religion. At first, they suspected that it might have been written by some of the slaves carried from the Coast; but, on a closer examination, they were satisfied that no Bushreen could write such beautiful Arabic; and one of them offered to give me an ass, and sixteen bars of goods, if I would part with the book. Perhaps, a short and easy introduction to Christianity, such as is found in some of the catechisms for children, elegantly printed in Arabic, and distributed on different parts of the Coast, might have a wonderful effect. The expence would be but trifling; curiosity would induce many to read it; and the evident superiority which it would possess over their present manuscripts, both in point of elegance and cheapness, might at last obtain it a place among the school books of Africa.

The reflections which I have thus ventured to submit to my readers on this important subject, naturally suggested themselves to my mind, on perceiving the encouragement which was thus given to learning, (such as it is,) in many parts of Africa. I have observed, that the pupils at Kamalia were most of them the children of Pagans; their parents, therefore, could have had no predilection for the doctrines of Mahomet. Their aim was their children's improvement; and if a more enlightened system had presented itself, it would probably have been preferred. The children, too, wanted not a spirit of emulation; which it is the aim of the tutor to encourage. When any one of them has read through the Koran, and performed a certain number of public prayers, a feast is prepared by the schoolmaster, and the scholar undergoes an examination, or (in European terms,) *takes out his degree*. I attended at three different inaugurations of this sort, and heard with pleasure, the distinct and intelligent answers which the scholars frequently gave to the Bushreens, who assembled on those occasions, and acted as examiners. When the Bushreens had satisfied themselves respecting the learning and abilities of the scholar, the last page of the Koran was put into his hand, and he was desired to read it aloud : after the boy had finished this lesson, he pressed the paper against his forehead, and pronounced the word *Amen;* upon which all the Bushreens rose, and shaking him cordially by the hand, bestowed upon him the title of Bushreen.

When a scholar has undergone this examination, his parents are informed that he has completed his education, and that it is incumbent on them to redeem their son, by giving to the schoolmaster a slave, or the price of a slave, in exchange; which is always done, if the parents can afford to do it ; if not, the boy remains the domestic slave of the schoolmaster until he can, by his own industry, collect goods sufficient to ransome himself.

About a week after the departure of Karfa, three Moors arrived at Kamalia with a considerable quantity of salt, and other merchandize, which they had obtained on credit, from a merchant of Fezzan, who had lately arrived at Kancaba. Their engagement was to pay him his price when the goods were sold, which they expected would be in the course of a month. Being rigid Bushreens, they were accommodated with two of Karfa's huts, and sold their goods to very great advantage.

On the 24th of January, Karfa returned to Kamalia with a number of people, and thirteen prime slaves which he had purchased. He likewise brought with him a young girl whom he had married at Kancaba, as his fourth wife, and had given her parents three prime slaves for her. She was kindly received at the door of the baloon by Karfa's other wives, who conducted their new acquaintance and co-partner into one of the best huts, which they had caused to be swept and white-washed, on purpose to receive her. *

My clothes were by this time become so very ragged, that I was almost ashamed to appear out of doors; but Karfa, on the day after his arrival, generously presented me with such a garment and trowsers, as are commonly worn in the country.

The slaves which Karfa had brought with him were all of them prisoners of war; they had been taken by the Bambarran army in the kingdoms of Wassela and Kaarta, and carried to Sego, where some of them had remained three years in irons. From Sego they were sent, in company with a number of other captives, up the Niger in two large canoes, and offered for sale at Yamina, Bammakoo, and Kancaba; at which places the greater number of the captives were bartered for gold-dust, and the remainder sent forward to Kankaree.

Eleven of them confessed to me that they had been slaves from their infancy; but the other two refused to give any account

* The Negroes white-wash their huts with a mixture of bone-ashes and water, to which is commonly added a little gum.

of their former condition. They were all very inquisitive; but they viewed me at first with looks of horror, and repeatedly asked if my countrymen were cannibals. They were very desirous to know what became of the slaves after they had crossed the salt water. I told them, that they were employed in cultivating the land; but they would not believe me; and one of them putting his hand upon the ground, said with great simplicity, " have you really got such ground as this, to set your feet upon?" A deeply rooted idea, that the whites purchase Negroes for the purpose of devouring them, or of selling them to others, that they may be devoured hereafter, naturally makes the slaves contemplate a journey towards the Coast with great terror; insomuch that the Slatees are forced to keep them constantly in irons, and watch them very closely, to prevent their escape. They are commonly secured, by putting the right leg of one, and the left of another, into the same pair of fetters. By supporting the fetters with a string, they can walk, though very slowly. Every four slaves are likewise fastened together by the necks, with a strong rope of twisted thongs; and in the night, an additional pair of fetters is put on their hands, and sometimes a light iron chain passed round their necks.

Such of them as evince marks of discontent, are secured in a different manner. A thick billet of wood is cut about three feet long, and a smooth notch being made upon one side of it, the ankle of the slave is bolted to the smooth part by means of a strong iron staple, one prong of which passes on each side of the ankle. All these fetters and bolts are made from native iron; in the present case they were put on by the blacksmith

as soon as the slaves arrived from Kancaba, and were not
taken off until the morning on which the coffle departed for
Gambia.

In other respects, the treatment of the slaves during their stay
at Kamalia, was far from being harsh or cruel. They were led
out in their fetters, every morning, to the shade of the tamarind
tree, where they were encouraged to play at games of hazard,
and sing diverting songs, to keep up their spirits; for though
some of them sustained the hardships of their situation with
amazing fortitude, the greater part were very much dejected,
and would sit all day in a sort of sullen melancholy, with their
eyes fixed upon the ground. In the evening, their irons were
examined, and their hand fetters put on; after which they were
conducted into two large huts, where they were guarded
during the night by Karfa's domestic slaves. But notwithstanding all this, about a week after their arrival, one of the
slaves had the address to procure a small knife, with which he
opened the rings of his fetters, cut the rope, and made his
escape: more of them would probably have got off, had they
assisted each other; but the slave no sooner found himself at
liberty, than he refused to stop, and assist in breaking the
chain which was fastened round the necks of his companions.

As all the Slatees and slaves belonging to the coffle were
now assembled, either at Kamalia, or at some of the neighbouring villages, it might have been expected that we should
have set out immediately for Gambia; but though the day of
our departure was frequently fixed, it was always found ex-
pedient to change it. Some of the people had not prepared

their dry provisions; others had gone to visit their relations, or collect some trifling debts; and, last of all, it was necessary to consult whether the day would be a lucky one. On account of one of these, or other such causes, our departure was put off, day after day, until the month of February was far advanced; after which all the Slatees agreed to remain in their present quarters, until the *fast moon was over*. And here I may remark, that loss of time, is an object of no great importance in the eyes of a Negro. If he has any thing of consequence to perform, it is a matter of indifference to him whether he does it to-day or to-morrow, or a month or two hence: so long as he can spend the present moment with any degree of comfort, he gives himself very little concern about the future.

The fast of Rhamadan was observed with great strictness, by all the Bushreens; but, instead of compelling me to follow their example, as the Moors did on a similar occasion, Karfa frankly told me that I was at liberty to pursue my own inclination. In order, however, to manifest a respect for their religious opinions, I voluntarily fasted three days, which was thought sufficient to screen me from the reproachful epithet of Kafir. During the fast, all the Slatees belonging to the coffle assembled every morning in Karfa's house, where the schoolmaster read to them some religious lessons, from a large folio volume, the author of which was an Arab, of the name of *Sheiffa*. In the evening, such of the women as had embraced Mahomedanism assembled, and said their prayers publicly at the Misura. They were all dressed in white, and went through the different prostrations, prescribed by their religion, with becoming solemnity. Indeed,

T t

during .the whole fast of Rhamadan, the Negroes behaved themselves with the greatest meekness and humility; forming a striking contrast to the savage intolerance and brutal bigotry, which at this period characterize the Moors.

When the fast month was almost at an end, the Bushreens assembled at the Misura, to watch for the appearance of the new moon; but the evening being rather cloudy, they were for some time disappointed, and a number of them had gone home with a resolution to fast another day, when on a sudden this delightful object showed her sharp horns from behind a cloud, and was welcomed with the clapping of hands, beating of drums, firing muskets, and other marks of rejoicing. As this moon is reckoned extremely lucky, Karfa gave orders that all the people belonging to the coffle should immediately pack up their dry provisions, and hold themselves in readiness; and on the 16th of April, the Slatees held a consultation, and fixed on the 19th of the same month, as the day on which the coffle should depart from Kamalia. This resolution freed me from much uneasiness; for our departure had already been so long deferred, that I was apprehensive it might still be put off until the commencement of the rainy season; and although Karfa behaved towards me with the greatest kindness, I found my situation very unpleasant. The Slatees were unfriendly to me; and the trading Moors, who were at this time at Kamalia, continued to plot mischief against me, from the first day of their arrival. Under these circumstances, I reflected, that my life in a great measure depended on the good opinion of an individual, who was daily hearing malicious stories concerning the Europeans; and I could hardly expect that he would always judge with impartiality between me and his countrymen. Time had, indeed, reconciled me, in some degree, to their mode of life; and a smoky hut, or a scanty supper, gave me no great uneasiness; but I became at last wearied out with a constant state of alarm and anxiety, and felt a painful longing for the manifold blessings of civilized society.

On the morning of the 17th, a circumstance occurred, which wrought a considerable change in my favour. The three trading Moors, who had lodged under Karfa's protection, ever since their arrival at Kamalia, and had gained the esteem of all the Bushreens, by an appearance of great sanctity, suddenly packed up their effects, and, without once thanking Karfa for his kindness towards them, marched over the hills to Bala. Every one was astonished at this unexpected removal; but the affair was cleared up in the evening, by the arrival of the Fezzan merchant from Kancaba (mentioned in p. 317); who assured Karfa, that these Moors had borrowed all their salt and goods from him, and had sent for him to come to Kamalia, and receive payment. When he was told that they had fled to the westward, he wiped a tear from each eye with the sleeve of his cloak, and exclaimed, " these *shirrukas* (robbers) are Mahomedans, but they are not " men; they have robbed me of two hundred minkallies." From this merchant, I received information of the capture of our Mediterranean convoy by the French, in October 1795.

April 19th. The long wished-for day of our departure was at length arrived; and the Slatees having taken the irons from their slaves, assembled with them at the door of Karfa's house,

where the bundles were all tied up, and every one had his load
assigned him. The coffle, on its departure from Kamalia, consisted of twenty-seven slaves for sale, the property of Karfa and
four other Slatees; but we were afterwards joined by five at
Maraboo, and three at Bala; making in all thirty-five slaves.
The free men were fourteen in number, but most of them had one
or two wives, and some domestic slaves; and the schoolmaster,
who was now upon his return for Woradoo, the place of his
nativity, took with him eight of his scholars; so that the
number of free people and domestic slaves amounted to thirty-
eight, and the whole amount of the coffle was seventy-three.
Among the free men were six Jillakeas (singing men), whose
musical talents were frequently exerted either to divert our
fatigue, or obtain us a welcome from strangers. When we
departed from Kamalia, we were followed for about half a mile,
by most of the inhabitants of the town, some of them crying,
and others shaking hands with their relations, who were now
about to leave them; and when we had gained a piece of rising
ground, from which we had a view of Kamalia, all the people belonging to the coffle were ordered to sit down in one place, with
their faces towards the west, and the townspeople were desired
to sit down in another place, with their faces towards Kamalia.
In this situation, the schoolmaster, with two of the principal
Slatees, having taken their places between the two parties, pronounced a long and solemn prayer; after which they walked
three times round the coffle, making an impression in the ground
with the ends of their spears, and muttering something by way
of charm. When this ceremony was ended, all the people be-

longing to the coffle sprang up, and without taking a formal
farewell of their friends, set forwards. As many of the slaves had
remained for years in irons, the sudden exertion of walking
quick, with heavy loads upon their heads, occasioned spasmodic
contractions of their legs; and we had not proceeded above a
mile, before it was found necessary to take two of them from
the rope, and allow them to walk more slowly until we reached
Maraboo, a walled village, where some people were waiting to
join the coffle. Here we stopt about two hours, to allow the
strangers time to pack up their provisions, and then continued
our route to Bala, which town we reached about four in the
afternoon. The inhabitants of Bala, at this season of the year,
subsist chiefly on fish, which they take in great plenty from
the streams in the neighbourhood. We remained here until
the afternoon of the next day, the 20th, when we proceeded
to Worumbang, the frontier village of Manding towards Jallonkadoo. As we proposed shortly to enter the Jallonka Wilderness,
the people of this village furnished us with great plenty of provisions; and on the morning of the 21st, we entered the woods
to the westward of Worumbang. After having travelled some
little way, a consultation was held, whether we should continue
our route through the Wilderness, or save one day's provisions
by going to Kinytakooro, a town in Jallonkadoo. After debating
the matter for some time, it was agreed that we should take the
road for Kinytakooro; but as that town was a long day's
journey distant, it was necessary to take some refreshment.
Accordingly every person opened his provision bag, and brought
a handfull or two of meal, to the place where Karfa and the

Slatees were sitting. When every one had brought his quota, and the whole was properly arranged in small gourd shells, the schoolmaster offered up a short prayer; the substance of which was, that God and the holy Prophet might preserve us from robbers and all bad people, that our provisions might never fail us, nor our limbs become fatigued. This ceremony being ended, every one partook of the meal, and drank a little water; after which we set forward (rather running than walking), until we came to the river Kokoro, a branch of the Senegal, where we halted about ten minutes. The banks of this river are very high; and from the grass and brushwood which had been left by the stream, it was evident that at this place, the water had risen more than twenty feet perpendicular, during the rainy season. At this time it was only a small stream, such as would turn a mill, swarming with fish; and on account of the number of crocodiles, and the danger of being carried past the ford by the force of the stream in the rainy season, it is called *Kokoro* (dangerous). From this place we continued to travel with the greatest expedition, and in the afternoon crossed two small branches of the Kokoro. About sunset we came in sight of Kinytakooro, a considerable town, nearly square, situated in the middle of a large and well cultivated plain: before we entered the town we halted, until the people who had fallen behind came up. During this day's travel, two slaves, a woman and a girl belonging to a Slatee of Bala, were so much fatigued that they could not keep up with the coffle; they were severely whipped, and dragged along until about three o'clock in the afternoon, when they were both affected with vomiting, by which it was discovered that they had *eaten clay*. This practice is by no means uncommon amongst the Negroes; but whether it arises from a vitiated appetite, or from a settled intention to destroy themselves, I cannot affirm. They were permitted to lie down in the woods, and three people remained with them until they had rested themselves; but they did not arrive at the town until past midnight; and were then so much exhausted, that the Slatee gave up all thoughts of taking them across the woods in their present condition, and determined to return with them to Bala, and wait for another opportunity.

As this was the first town beyond the limits of Manding, greater etiquette than usual was observed. Every person was ordered to keep in his proper station, and we marched towards the town, in a sort of procession, nearly as follows. In front, five or six singing men, all of them belonging to the coffle; these were followed by the other free people; then came the slaves fastened in the usual way by a rope round their necks, four of them to a rope, and a man with a spear between each four; after them came the domestic slaves, and in the rear the women of free condition, wives of the Slatees, &c. In this manner we proceeded, until we came within a hundred yards of the gate; when the singing men began a loud song, well calculated to flatter the vanity of the inhabitants, by extolling their known hospitality to strangers, and their particular friendship for the Mandingoes. When we entered the town we proceeded to the Bentang, where the people gathered round us to hear our *dentegi* (history); this was related publicly by two of the singing men: they enumerated every little circumstance which had happened to the coffle; beginning with the events of the present day, and relating every thing, in a backward series, until they reached Kamalia. When this history was ended, the master of the town gave them a small present; and all the people of the coffle, both free and enslaved, were invited, by some person or other, and accommodated with lodging and provisions for the night.

CHAPTER XXV.

The Coffle crosses the Jallonka Wilderness.—Miserable Fate of one of the female Slaves;—arrives at Sooseeta;—proceeds to Manna. —Some Account of the Jalonkas.—Crosses the main Stream of the Senegal.—Bridge of a singular Construction.—Arrives at Malacotta.—Remarkable Conduct of the King of the Jaloffs.

WE continued at Kenytakooro until noon of the 22d of April, when we removed to a village about seven miles to the westward; the inhabitants of which being apprehensive of hostilities from the Foulahs of Fooladoo, were at this time employed in constructing small temporary huts among the rocks, on the side of a high hill close to the village. The situation was almost impregnable, being every where surrounded with high precipices, except on the eastern side, where the natives had left a pathway sufficient to allow one person at a time to ascend. Upon the brow of the hill, immediately over this path, I observed several heaps of large loose stones, which the people told me were intended to be thrown down upon the Foulahs, if they should attempt the hill.

At daybreak, on the 23d, we departed from this village, and entered the Jallonka Wilderness. We passed, in the course of the morning, the ruins of two small towns, which had lately been burnt by the Foulahs. The fire must have been very intense; for I observed that the walls of many of the huts were

U u

slightly vitrified, and appeared at a distance as if covered with a red varnish. About ten o'clock we came to the river Wonda, which is somewhat larger than the river Kokoro; but the stream was at this time rather muddy, which Karfa assured me was occasioned by amazing shoals of fish. They were indeed seen in all directions, and in such abundance, that I fancied the water itself tasted and smelt fishy. As soon as we had crossed the river, Karfa gave orders that all the people of the coffle should in future keep close together, and travel in their proper station: the guides and young men were accordingly placed in the van, the women and slaves in the centre, and the free men in the rear. In this order, we travelled with uncommon expedition, through a woody, but beautiful country, interspersed with a pleasing variety of hill and dale, and abounding with partridges, guinea-fowls, and deer, until sunset; when we arrived at a most romantic stream called Co-meissang. My arms and neck having been exposed to the sun during the whole day, and irritated by the rubbing of my dress in walking, were now very much inflamed and covered with blisters; and I was happy to embrace the opportunity, while the coffle rested on the bank of this river, to bathe myself in the stream. This practice, together with the cool of the evening, much diminished the inflammation. About three miles to the westward of the Co-meissang we halted in a thick wood, and kindled our fires for the night. We were all, by this time, very much fatigued; having, as I judged, travelled this day thirty miles; but no person was heard to complain. Whilst supper was preparing, Karfa made one of the slaves break some branches from the trees for my bed.

When we had finished our supper of kouskous, moistened with some boiling water, and put the slaves in irons, we all lay down to sleep ; but we were frequently disturbed in the night by the howling of wild beasts; and we found the small brown ants very troublesome.

April 24th. Before daybreak the Bushreens said their morning prayers, and most of the free people drank a little *moening* (a sort of gruel), part of which was likewise given to such of the slaves as appeared least able to sustain the fatigues of the day. One of Karfa's female slaves was very sulky, and when some gruel was offered to her, she refused to drink it. As soon as day dawned we set out, and travelled the whole morning over a wild and rocky country, by which my feet were much bruised; and I was sadly apprehensive that I should not be able to keep up with the coffle during the day; but I was, in a great measure, relieved from this anxiety, when I observed that others were more exhausted than myself. In particular, the woman slave, who had refused victuals in the morning, began now to lag behind, and complain dreadfully of pains in her legs. Her load was taken from her, and given to another slave, and she was ordered to keep in the front of the coffle. About eleven o'clock, as we were resting by a small rivulet, some of the people discovered a hive of bees in a hollow tree, and they were proceeding to obtain the honey, when the largest swarm I ever beheld, flew out, and attacking the people of the coffle, made us fly in all directions. I took the alarm first, and I believe was the only person who escaped with impunity. When our enemies thought fit to desist from pursuing us, and every person was employed

U u 2

in picking out the stings he had received, it was discovered
that the poor woman abovementioned, whose name was
Nealee, was not come up ; and as many of the slaves in their
retreat had left their bundles behind them, it became necessary
for some persons to return, and bring them.   In order to do
this with safety, fire was set to the grass, a considerable way to
the eastward of the hive, and the wind driving the fire furiously
along, the party pushed through the smoke, and recovered the
bundles.   They likewise brought with them poor Nealee, whom
they found lying by the rivulet.   She was very much exhausted, and had crept to the stream, in hopes to defend herself
from the bees by throwing water over her body ; but this
proved ineffectual ; for she was stung in the most dreadful
manner.

When the Slatees had picked out the stings as far as they
could, she was washed with water, and then rubbed with bruised
leaves ; but the wretched woman obstinately refused to proceed
any farther ; declaring, that she would rather die than walk
another step. As entreaties and threats were used in vain, the
whip was at length applied ; and after bearing patiently a few
strokes, she started up, and walked with tolerable expedition for
four or five hours longer, when she made an attempt to run away
from the coffle, but was so very weak, that she fell down in the
grass. Though she was unable to rise, the whip was a second time
applied, but without effect ; upon which Karfa desired two of
the Slatees to place her upon the ass which carried our dry
provisions ; but she could not sit erect ; and the ass being very
refractory, it was found impossible to carry her forward in that

manner. The Slatees however were unwilling to abandon her, the day's journey being nearly ended : they therefore made a sort of litter of bamboo canes, upon which she was placed, and tied on it with slips of bark : this litter was carried upon the heads of two slaves, one walking before the other, and they were followed by two others, who relieved them occasionally. In this manner the woman was carried forward until it was dark, when we reached a stream of water, at the foot of a high hill called Gankaran-Kooro; and here we stopt for the night, and set about preparing our supper. As we had only eat one handful of meal since the preceding night, and travelled all day in a hot sun, many of the slaves, who had loads upon their heads, were very much fatigued ; and some of them *snapt their fingers*, which among the Negroes is a sure sign of desperation. The Slatees immediately put them all in irons; and such of them as had evinced signs of great despondency, were kept apart from the rest, and had their hands tied. In the morning they were found greatly recovered.

April 25th. At daybreak poor Nealee was awakened ; but her limbs were now become so stiff and painful, that she could neither walk nor stand; she was therefore lifted, like a corpse, upon the back of the ass; and the Slatees endeavoured to secure her in that situation, by fastening her hands together under the ass's neck, and her feet under the belly, with long slips of bark ; but the ass was so very unruly, that no sort of treatment could induce him to proceed with his load ; and as Nealee made no exertion to prevent herself from falling, she was quickly thrown off, and had one of her legs much bruised. Every attempt to

carry her forward being thus found ineffectual, the general cry
of the coffle was, *kang-tegi, kang-tegi*, " cut her throat, cut her
throat ;" an operation I did not wish to see performed, and
therefore marched onwards with the foremost of the coffle.   I
had not walked above a mile, when one of Karfa's domestic
slaves came up to me, with poor Nealee's garment upon the end
of his bow, and exclaimed *Nealee affilita* (Nealee is lost).   I
asked him whether the Slatees had given him the garment, as a
reward for cutting her throat ; he replied, that Karfa and the
schoolmaster would not consent to that measure, but had left
her on the road ; where undoubtedly she soon perished, and
was probably devoured by wild beasts.

The sad fate of this wretched woman, notwithstanding the
outcry beforementioned, made a strong impression on the minds
of the whole coffle, and the schoolmaster fasted the whole of
the ensuing day, in consequence of it.   We proceeded in deep
silence, and soon afterward crossed the river Furkoomah, which
was about as large as the river Wonda.   We now travelled
with great expedition, every one being apprehensive he might
otherwise meet with the fate of poor Nealee.   It was however
with great difficulty that I could keep up, although I threw
away my spear, and every thing that could in the least obstruct me.   About noon we saw a large herd of elephants, but
they suffered us to pass unmolested, and in the evening we
halted near a thicket of bamboo, but found no water ; so
that we were forced to proceed four miles farther, to a small
stream, where we stopt for the night.   We had marched this
day, as I judged, about twenty-six miles.

April 26th. This morning two of the schoolmaster's pupils complained much of pains in their legs, and one of the slaves walked lame, the soles of his feet being very much blistered and inflamed; we proceeded, notwithstanding, and about eleven o'clock began to ascend a rocky hill called Boki-Kooro, and it was past two in the afternoon before we reached the level ground on the other side. This was the most rocky road we had yet encountered, and it hurt our feet much. In a short time we arrived at a pretty large river called Boki, which we forded: it ran smooth and clear, over a bed of whinstone. About a mile to the westward of the river, we came to a road which leads to the north-east towards Gadou, and seeing the marks of many horses' feet upon the soft sand, the Slatees conjectured that a party of plunderers had lately rode that way, to fall upon some town of Gadou; and lest they should discover, upon their return, that we had passed, and attempt to pursue us by the marks of our feet, the coffle was ordered to disperse, and travel in a loose manner through the high grass and bushes. A little before it was dark, having crossed the ridge of hills to the westward of the river Boki, we came to a well called *cullong qui* (white sand well), and here we rested for the night.

April 27th. We departed from the well early in the morning, and walked on, with the greatest alacrity, in hopes of reaching a town before night. The road, during the forenoon, led through extensive thickets of dry bamboos. About two o'clock we came to a stream called Nunkolo, where we were each of us regaled with a handful of meal, which, according to a superstitious custom, was not to be eaten until it was first moistened with water from this stream. About four o'clock we

reached Sooseeta, a small Jallonka village, situated in the district of Kullo, which comprehends all that tract of country
lying along the banks of the Black river, or main branch of the
Senegal. These were the first human habitations we had seen,
since we left the village to the westward of Kenytakooro;
having travelled in the course of the last five days, upwards of
one hundred miles. Here, after a great deal of entreaty, we
were provided with huts to sleep in; but the master of the
village plainly told us that he could not give us any provisions,
as there had lately been a great scarcity in this part of the
country. He assured us, that before they had gathered in their
present crops, the whole inhabitants of Kullo had been for
twenty-nine days without tasting corn; during which time,
they supported themselves entirely upon the yellow powder
which is found in the pods of the *nitta*, so called by the
natives, a species of mimosa; and upon the seeds of the bamboo
cane, which, when properly pounded and dressed, taste very
much like rice. As our dry provisions were not yet exhausted,
a considerable quantity of kouskous was dressed for supper,
and many of the villagers were invited to take part of the
repast; but they made a very bad return for this kindness; for
in the night they seized upon one of the schoolmaster's boys,
who had fallen asleep under the Bentang tree, and carried him
away. The boy fortunately awoke before he was far from the
village, and setting up a loud scream, the man who carried him,
put his hand upon his mouth, and run with him into the
woods; but afterward understanding that he belonged to the
schoolmaster, whose place of residence is only three day's
journey distant, he thought, I suppose, that he could not

retain him as a slave, without the schoolmaster's knowledge; and therefore stripped off the boy's clothes, and permitted him to return.

April 28th. Early in the morning we departed from Sooseeta, and about ten o'clock, came to an unwalled town called Manna; the inhabitants of which were employed in collecting the fruit of the nitta trees, which are very numerous in this neighbourhood. The pods are long and narrow, and contain a few black seeds enveloped in the fine mealy powder before mentioned; the meal itself is of a bright yellow colour, resembling the flour of sulphur, and has a sweet mucilaginous taste: when eaten by itself it is clammy, but when mixed with milk or water, it constitutes a very pleasant and nourishing article of diet.

The language of the people of Manna, is the same that is spoken all over that extensive and hilly country called Jallonkadoo. Some of the words have a great affinity to the Mandingo, but the natives themselves consider it as a distinct language: their numerals are these,

One	——	*Kidding.*
Two	——	*Fidding.*
Three	——	*Sarra.*
Four	——	*Nani.*
Five	——	*Soolo.*
Six	——	*Seni.*
Seven	——	*Soolo ma fidding.*
Eight	——	*Soolo ma sarra.*
Nine	——	*Soolo ma nani.*
Ten	——	*Nuff.*

X x

The Jallonkas, like the Mandingoes, are governed by a number of petty chiefs, who are, in a great measure, independent of each other: they have no common sovereign, and the chiefs are seldom upon such terms of friendship as to assist each other, even in war time.   The chief of Manna, with a number of his people, accompanied us to the banks of the Bafing, or Black river (a principal branch of the Senegal) which we crossed upon a bridge of bamboos, of a very singular construction; some idea of which may be formed from the annexed engraving.   The river at this place is smooth and deep, and has very little current.   Two tall trees, when tied together by the tops, are sufficiently long to reach from one side to the other; the roots resting upon the rocks, and the tops floating in the water.   When a few trees have been placed in this direction, they are covered with dry bamboos, so as to form a floating bridge, with a sloping gangway at each end, where the trees rest upon the rocks. This bridge is carried away every year by the swelling of the river in the rainy season, and is constantly rebuilt by the inhabitants of Manna, who, on that account, expect a small tribute from every passenger.

In the afternoon we passed several villages, at none of which could we procure a lodging; and in the twilight we received information that two hundred Jallonkas had assembled near a town called Melo, with a view to plunder the coffle. This induced us to alter our course, and we travelled with great secresy until midnight, when we approached a town called Koba.   Before we entered the town, the names of all the people belonging to the coffle were called over, and a freeman and three slaves were

A VIEW OF A BRIDGE OVER THE BA·FING OR BLACK RIVER.

J. C. Barron, del. from a Sketch by Mr. Park.

Engraved by W. C. Wilson.

found to be missing. Every person immediately concluded that the slaves had murdered the freeman, and made their escape. It was therefore agreed that six people should go back as far as the last village, and endeavour to find his body, or collect some information concerning the slaves. In the meantime the coffle was ordered to lie concealed in a cotton field near a large nitta tree, and nobody to speak, except in a whisper. It was towards morning before the six men returned, having heard nothing of the man or the slaves. As none of us had tasted victuals for the last twenty-four hours, it was agreed that we should go into Koba, and endeavour to procure some provisions. We accordingly entered the town before it was quite day, and Karfa purchased from the chief man, for three strings of beads, a considerable quantity of ground nuts, which we roasted and eat for breakfast: we were afterwards provided with huts, and rested here for the day.

About eleven o'clock, to our great joy and surprise, the freeman and slaves, who had parted from the coffle the preceding night, entered the town. One of the slaves, it seems, had hurt his foot, and the night being very dark, they soon lost sight of the coffle. The freeman, as soon as he found himself alone with the slaves, was aware of his own danger, and insisted on putting them in irons. The slaves were at first rather unwilling to submit, but when he threatened to stab them one by one with his spear, they made no further resistance; and he remained with them among the bushes until morning, when he let them out of irons, and came to the town in hopes of hearing which route the coffle had taken. The information that we received concerning the Jallonkas, who intended to rob the coffle, was this day confirmed, and we were forced to remain here until the afternoon of the 30th; when Karfa hired a number of people to protect us, and we proceeded to a village called Tinkingtang. Departing from this village on the day following, we crossed a high ridge of mountains to the west of the Black river, and travelled over a rough stony country until sunset, when we arrived at Lingicotta, a small village in the district of Woradoo. Here we shook out the last handful of meal from our dry provision bags; this being the second day (since we crossed the Black river) that we had travelled from morning until night, without tasting one morsel of food.

May 2d. We departed from Lingicotta; but the slaves being very much fatigued, we halted for the night at a village about nine miles to the westward, and procured some provisions through the interest of the schoolmaster; who now sent forward a messenger to Malacotta, his native town, to inform his friends of his arrival in the country, and to desire them to provide the necessary quantity of victuals to entertain the coffle for two or three days.

May 3d. We set out for Malacotta, and about noon arrived at a village, near a considerable stream of water which flows to the westward; here we determined to stop for the return of the messenger which had been sent to Malacotta the day before; and as the natives assured me there were no crocodiles in this stream, I went and bathed myself. Very few people here can swim; for they came in numbers to dissuade me from venturing into a pool, where they said the water would come

over my head. About two o'clock the messenger returned
from Malacotta; and the schoolmaster's elder brother being
impatient to see him, came along with the messenger to meet
him at this village. The interview between the two brothers,
who had not seen each other for nine years, was very natural
and affecting. They fell upon each other's neck, and it was
sometime before either of them could speak. At length, when
the schoolmaster had a little recovered himself, he took his
brother by the hand, and turning round, " This is the man"
(said he, pointing to Karfa) " who has been my father in
" Manding; I would have pointed him out sooner to you, but
" my heart was too full."

We reached Malacotta in the evening, where we were well
received. This is an unwalled town; the huts for the most part
are made of split cane, twisted into a sort of wicker-work, and
plastered over with mud. Here we remained three days, and
were each day presented with a bullock from the schoolmaster;
we were likewise well entertained by the townspeople, who
appear to be very active and industrious. They make very
good soap, by boiling ground nuts in water, and then adding
a ley of wood ashes. They likewise manufacture excellent
iron, which they carry to Bondou to barter for salt. A party
of the townspeople had lately returned from a trading expedition of this kind, and brought information concerning a war
between Almami Abdulkader, King of Foota Torra, and Damel,
King of the Jaloffs. The events of this war soon became a
favourite subject with the singing men, and the common topic
of conversation in all the kingdoms bordering upon the Senegal

and Gambia; and as the account is somewhat singular, I shall here abridge it, for the reader's information. The King of Foota Torra, inflamed with a zeal for propagating his religion, had sent an embassy to Damel, similar to that which he had sent to Kasson, as related in page 79. The ambassador, on the present occasion, was accompanied by two of the principal Bushreens, who carried each a large knife, fixed on the top of a long pole. As soon as he had procured admission into the presence of Damel, and announced the pleasure of his sovereign, he ordered the Bushreens to present the emblems of his mission. The two knives were accordingly laid before Damel, and the ambassador explained himself as follows: " With this knife, (said he) Abdulkader will con- " descend to shave the head of Damel, if Damel will embrace " the Mahomedan faith; and with this other knife, Abdulkader " will cut the throat of Damel, if Damel refuses to embrace " it:—take your choice." Damel coolly told the ambassador that he had no choice to make: he neither chose to have his head shaved, nor his throat cut; and with this answer the ambassador was civilly dismissed. Abdulkader took his mea- sures accordingly, and with a powerful army invaded Damel's country. The inhabitants of the towns and villages filled up their wells, destroyed their provisions, carried off their effects, and abandoned their dwellings, as he approached. By this means he was led on from place to place, until he had advanced three day's journey into the country of the Jaloffs. He had, indeed, met with no opposition; but his army had suffered so much from the scarcity of water, that several of his men had died by the way. This induced him to direct his march towards a watering place in the woods, where his men, having quenched their thirst, and being overcome with fatigue, lay down carelessly to sleep among the bushes. In this situation they were attacked by Damel before daybreak, and compleatly routed. Many of them were trampled to death as they lay asleep, by the Jaloff horses; others were killed in attempting to make their escape; and a still greater number were taken prisoners. Among the latter, was Abdulkader himself. This ambitious, or rather frantic prince, who, but a month before, had sent the threatening message to Damel, was now himself led into his presence as a miserable captive. The behaviour of Damel, on this occasion, is never mentioned by the singing men, but in terms of the highest approbation; and it was, indeed, so extraordinary, in an African prince, that the reader may find it difficult to give credit to the recital. When his royal prisoner was brought before him in irons, and thrown upon the ground, the magnanimous Damel, instead of setting his foot upon his neck, and stabbing him with his spear, according to custom in such cases, addressed him as follows. " Abdulka-" der, answer me this question. If the chance of war had placed " me in your situation, and you in mine, how would you have " treated me?"." I would have thrust my spear into your heart;" returned Abdulkader with great firmness, " and I know that a " similar fate awaits me." " Not so, (said Damel) my spear is " indeed red with the blood of your subjects killed in battle, and " I could now give it a deeper stain, by dipping it in your own; " but this would not build up my towns, nor bring to life the

" thousands who fell in the woods. I will not therefore kill
" you in cold blood, but I will retain you as my slave, until I
" perceive that your presence in your own kingdom will be no
" longer dangerous to your neighbours; and then I will con-
" sider of the proper way of disposing of you." Abdulkader
was accordingly retained, and worked as a slave, for three
months; at the end of which period, Damel listened to the
solicitations of the inhabitants of Foota Torra, and restored to
them their king. Strange as this story may appear, I have no
doubt of the truth of it; it was told me at Malacotta by the
Negroes; it was afterwards related to me by the Europeans
on the Gambia; by some of the French at Goree; and confirmed by nine slaves, who were taken prisoners along with
Abdulkader, by the watering place in the woods, and carried
in the same ship with me to the West Indies.

CHAPTER XXVI.

The Caravan proceeds to Konkodoo, and crosses the Falemé River.—Its Arrival at Baniserile, Kirwani, and Tambacunda. —Incidents on the Road.—A matrimonial Case.—Specimen of the Shea Tree.—The Caravan proceeds through many Towns and Villages, and arrives at length on the Banks of the Gambia, —passes through Medina, the Capital of Woolli, and finally stops at Jindey.—The Author, accompanied by Karfa, proceeds to Pisania.—Various Occurrences previous to his Departure from Africa,—takes his Passage in an American Ship.—Short Account of his Voyage to Great Britain by the Way of the West Indies.

On the 7th of May, we departed from Malacotta, and having crossed the *Ba lee*, " Honey river," a branch of the Senegal, we arrived in the evening at a walled town called Bintingala ; where we rested two days. From thence, in one day more, we proceeded to Dindikoo, a small town situated at the bottom of a high ridge of hills, from which this district is named *Konkodoo*, " the hilly country." These hills are very productive of gold. I was shewn a small quantity of this metal, which had been lately collected : the grains were about the usual size, but much flatter than those of Manding, and were

Y y

found in white quartz, which had been broken to pieces by hammers. At this town I met with a Negro, whose hair and skin were of a dull white colour. He was of that sort which are called in the Spanish West Indies *Albinos*, or white Negroes. The skin is cadaverous and unsightly, and the natives considered this complexion (I believe truly) as the effect of disease.

May 11th. At daybreak we departed from Dindikoo, and after a toilsome day's travel, arrived in the evening at Satadoo, the capital of a district of the same name. This town was formerly of considerable extent; but many families had left it in consequence of the predatory incursions of the Foulahs of Foota Jalla, who made it a practice to come secretly through the woods, and carry off people from the corn-fields, and even from the wells near the town. In the afternoon of the 12th, we crossed the Falemé river, the same which I had formerly crossed at Bondou in my journey eastward. This river, at this season of the year, is easily forded at this place, the stream being only about two feet deep. The water is very pure, and flows rapidly over a bed of sand and gravel. We lodged for the night at a small village called Medina, the sole property of a Mandingo merchant, who, by a long intercourse with Europeans, has been induced to adopt some of their customs. His victuals were served up in pewter dishes, and even his houses were built after the fashion of the English houses on the Gambia.

May 13th. In the morning, as we were preparing to depart, a coffle of slaves belonging to some Serawoolli traders, crossed the river, and agreed to proceed with us to Baniserile, the capital of Dentila; a very long day's journey from this place. We accordingly set out together, and travelled with great expedition, through the woods, until noon; when one of the Serawoolli slaves dropt the load from his head, for which he was smartly whipped. The load was replaced; but he had not proceeded above a mile before he let it fall a second time, for which he received the same punishment. After this he travelled in great pain until about two o'clock, when we stopt to breathe a little, by a pool of water, the day being remarkably hot. The poor slave was now so completely exhausted that his master was obliged to release him from the rope, for he lay motionless on the ground. A Serawoolli therefore undertook to remain with him, and endeavour to bring him to the town during the cool of the night: in the meanwhile we continued our route, and after a very hard day's travel, arrived at Baniserile late in the evening.

One of our Slatees was a native of this place, from which he had been absent three years. This man invited me to go with him to his house; at the gate of which his friends met him, with many expressions of joy; shaking hands with him, embracing him, and singing and dancing before him. As soon as he had seated himself upon a mat, by the threshold of his door, a young woman (his intended bride) brought a little water in a calabash, and kneeling down before him, desired him to wash his hands: when he had done this, the girl with a tear of joy sparkling in her eyes, drank the water; this being considered as the greatest proof she could possibly give him of her fidelity and attachment. About eight o'clock the same evening, the Serawoolli, who had been left in the woods to take care of the fatigued slave, returned and told us that he was dead: the general opinion, however, was that he himself had killed him, or left him to perish on the road; for the Serawoollies are said to be infinitely more cruel in their treatment of slaves than the Mandingoes. We remained at Baniserile two days, in order to purchase native iron, Shea-butter, and some other articles for sale on the Gambia; and here the Slatee who had invited me to his house, and who possessed three slaves, part of the coffle, having obtained information that the price on the Coast was very low, determined to separate from us, and remain, with his slaves, where he was, until an opportunity should offer of disposing of them to advantage; giving us to understand that he should complete his nuptials, with the young woman before mentioned, in the meantime.

May 16th. We departed from Baniserile, and travelled through thick woods until noon, when we saw at a distance, the town of Julifunda, but did not approach it; as we proposed to rest for the night at a large town called Kirwani, which we reached about four o'clock in the afternoon. This town stands in a valley, and the country, for more than a mile round it, is cleared of wood, and well cultivated. The inhabitants appear to be very active and industrious, and seem to have carried the system of agriculture to some degree of perfection; for they collect the dung of their cattle into large heaps during the dry season, for the purpose of manuring their land with it at the proper time. I saw nothing like this in any other part of Africa. Near the town are several smelting furnaces, from which the natives obtain very good iron. They afterwards hammer the metal into small bars, about a foot in length and two inches in breadth, one of which bars is sufficient to make two Mandingo corn paddles. On the morning after our arrival, we were visited by a Slatee of this place, who informed Karfa that among some slaves he had lately purchased, was a native of Foota Jalla; and as that country was at no great distance, he could not safely employ him in the labours of the field, lest he should effect his escape. The Slatee was therefore desirous of exchanging this slave for one of Karfa's, and offered some cloth and Shea-butter, to induce Karfa to comply with the proposal, which was accepted. The Slatee thereupon sent a boy to order the slave in question to bring him a few ground nuts. The poor creature soon afterwards entered the court in which we were sitting, having no suspicion of what was negotiating, until the master caused the gate to be shut, and told him to sit down. The slave now saw his danger, and perceiving the gate to be shut upon him, threw down the nuts and jumped over the fence. He was immediately pursued and overtaken by the Slatees, who brought him back, and secured him in irons, after which one of Karfa's slaves was released and delivered in exchange. The unfortunate captive was at first very much dejected, but in the course of a few days his melancholy gradually subsided; and he became at length as cheerful as any of his companions.

Departing from Kirwani on the morning of the 20th, we entered the Tenda Wilderness of two days' journey. The woods were very thick, and the country shelved towards the

south-west. About ten o'clock we met a coffle of twenty-six
people, and seven loaded asses returning from the Gambia.
Most of the men were armed with muskets, and had broad
belts of scarlet cloth over their shoulders, and European hats
upon their heads. They informed us that there was very little
demand for slaves on the Coast, as no vessel had arrived for
some months past. On hearing this, the Serawoollies, who
had travelled with us from the Falemé river, separated themselves and their slaves from the coffle. They had not, they
said, the means of maintaining their slaves in Gambia, until a
vessel should arrive; and were unwilling to sell them to dis-
advantage: they therefore departed to the northward for
Kajaaga. We continued our route through the Wilderness,
and travelled all day through a rugged country, covered with
extensive thickets of bamboo. At sunset, to our great joy, we
arrived at a pool of water near a large Tabba tree, whence the
place is called Tabba-gee, and here we rested a few hours.
The water at this season of the year is by no means plentiful
in these woods; and as the days were insufferably hot, Karfa
proposed to travel in the night. Accordingly, about eleven
o'clock, the slaves were taken out of their irons, and the
people of the coffle received orders to keep close together; as
well to prevent the slaves from attempting to escape, as on
account of the wild beasts. We travelled with great alacrity
until daybreak, when it was discovered that a free woman had
parted from the coffle in the night: her name was called until
the woods resounded; but no answer being given, we conjectured
that she had either mistaken the road, or that a lion had seized

her unperceived. At length it was agreed that four people should go back a few miles to a small rivulet, where some of the coffle had stopt to drink, as we passed it in the night; and that the coffle should wait for their return. The sun was about an hour high before the people came back with the woman, whom they found lying fast asleep by the stream. We now resumed our journey, and about eleven o'clock reached a walled town called Tambacunda, where we were well received. Here we remained four days, on account of a *palaver* which was held on the following occasion: Modi Lemina, one of the Slatees belonging to the coffle, had formerly married a woman of this town, who had borne him two children; he afterwards went to Manding, and remained there eight years, without sending any account of himself, during all that time, to his deserted wife; who, seeing no prospect of his return, at the end of three years had married another man, to whom she had likewise borne two children. Lemina now claimed his wife; but the second husband refused to deliver her up; insisting that by the laws of Africa, when a man has been three years absent from his wife, without giving her notice of his being alive, the woman is at liberty to marry again. After all the circumstances had been fully investigated in an assembly of the chief men, it was determined that the wife should make her choice, and be at liberty either to return to the first husband, or continue with the second, as she alone should think proper. Favourable as this determination was to the lady, she found it a difficult matter to make up her mind, and requested time for consideration: but I think I could per-

ceive that *first love* would carry the day. Lemina was indeed
somewhat older than his rival, but he was also much richer.
What weight this circumstance had in the scale of his wife's
affections, I pretend not to say.

On the morning of the 26th, as we departed from Tambacunda,
Karfa observed to me, that there were no Shea trees farther to
the westward than this town. I had collected and brought
with me from Manding the leaves and flowers of this tree;
but they were so greatly bruised on the road that I thought
it best to gather another specimen at this place; and accordingly collected that from which the annexed engraving is
taken. The appearance of the fruit evidently places the Shea
tree in the natural order of *sapotæ*, and it has some resemblance to the *madhuca* tree, described by Lieutenant Charles
Hamilton, in the Asiatic Researches, Vol. I. p. 300. About one
o'clock, we reached Sibikillin, a walled village, but the inhabitants having the character of inhospitality towards strangers,
and of being much addicted to theft, we did not think proper
to enter the gate. We rested a short time under a tree,
and then continued our route until it was dark, when we
halted for the night by a small stream running towards the
Gambia. Next day the road led over a wild and rocky country, every where rising into hills, and abounding with monkeys
and wild beasts. In the rivulets among the hills, we found
great plenty of fish. This was a very hard day's journey, and
it was not until sunset, that we reached the village of Koomboo,
near to which are the ruins of a large town formerly destroyed
by war. The inhabitants of Koomboo, like those of Sibikillin,

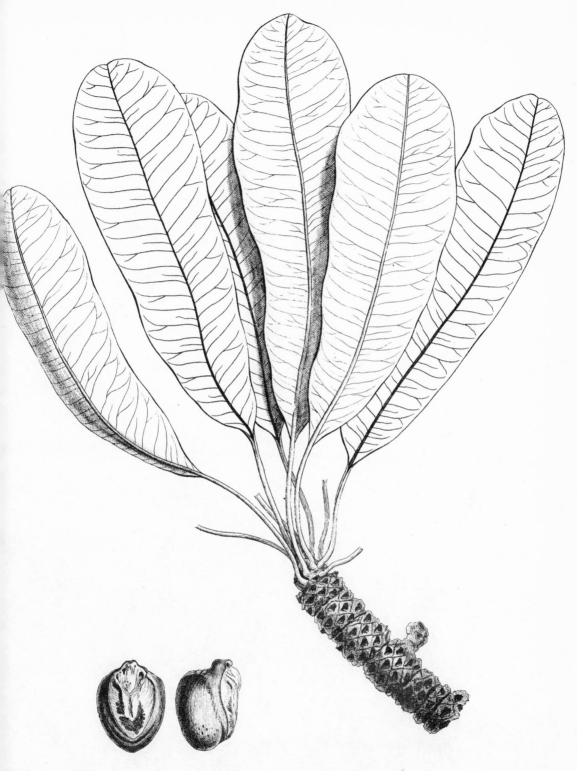

Shea or the Butter Tree

Mackenzie sculp

Published as the Act directs. January 1.1799. by George Nicol, Pall Mall

have so bad a reputation, that strangers seldom lodge in the village; we accordingly rested for the night in the fields, where we erected temporary huts for our protection, there being great appearance of rain.

May 28th. We departed from Koomboo, and slept at a Foulah town about seven miles to the westward; from which on the day following, having crossed a considerable branch of the Gambia, called Neola Koba, we reached a well inhabited part of the country. Here are several towns within sight of each other, collectively called Tenda, but each is distinguished also by its particular name. We lodged at one of them called Koba Tenda, where we remained the day following, in order to procure provisions for our support in crossing the Simbani woods. On the 30th we reached Jallacotta; a considerable town, but much infested by Foulah banditti, who come through the woods from Bondou, and steal every thing they can lay their hands on. A few days before our arrival, they had stolen twenty head of cattle, and on the day following made a second attempt; but were beaten off, and one of them taken prisoner. Here, one of the slaves belonging to the coffle, who had travelled with great difficulty for the last three days, was found unable to proceed any farther: his master (a singing man) proposed therefore to exchange him for a young slave girl, belonging to one of the townspeople. The poor girl was ignorant of her fate, until the bundles were all tied up in the morning, and the coffle ready to depart; when, coming with some other young women to see the coffle set out, her master took her by the hand, and delivered her to the singing man. Never was a face of serenity more sud-

Z z

denly changed into one of the deepest distress: the terror she
manifested on having the load put upon her head, and the
rope fastened round her neck, and the sorrow with which she
bade adieu to her companions, were truly affecting. About
nine o'clock, we crossed a large plain covered with *ciboa* trees
(a species of palm), and came to the river Nerico, a branch of the
Gambia. This was but a small river at this time, but in the rainy
season it is often dangerous to travellers. As soon as we had
crossed this river, the singing men began to vociferate a particular song, expressive of their joy at having got safe into the west
country, or, as they expressed it, *the land of the setting sun*. The
country was found to be very level, and the soil a mixture of
clay and sand. In the afternoon it rained hard, and we had
recourse to the common Negro umbrella, a large ciboa leaf,
which, being placed upon the head, completely defends the
whole body from the rain. We lodged for the night under
the shade of a large tabba tree, near the ruins of a village. On
the morning following, we crossed a stream called Noulico,
and about two o'clock, to my infinite joy, I saw myself once
more on the banks of the Gambia, which at this place being
deep and smooth, is navigable; but the people told me that a
little lower down, the stream is so shallow that the coffles frequently cross it on foot. On the south side of the river opposite to this place, is a large plain of clayey ground, called
Toombi Toorila. It is a sort of morass, in which people are
frequently lost, it being more than a day's journey across it.
In the afternoon we met a man and two women, with bundles
of cotton cloth upon their heads. They were going, they

said, for Dentila, to purchase iron, there being a great scarcity of that article on the Gambia. A little before it was dark, we arrived at a village in the kingdom of Woolli, called Seesukunda. Near this village there are great plenty of nitta trees, and the slaves in passing along had collected large bunches of the fruit; but such was the superstition of the inhabitants, that they would not permit any of the fruit to be brought into the village. They had been told, they said, that some catastrophe would happen to the place, when people lived upon nittas, and neglected to cultivate corn.

June 2d. We departed from Seesukunda, and passed a number of villages, at none of which was the coffle permitted to stop, although we were all very much fatigued: it was four o'clock in the afternoon before we reached Baraconda, where we rested one day. Departing from Baraconda on the morning of the 4th, we reached in a few hours Medina, the capital of the King of Woolli's dominions, from whom the reader may recollect I received an hospitable reception in the beginning of December, 1795, in my journey eastward.* I immediately inquired concerning the health of my good old benefactor, and learnt with great concern that he was dangerously ill. As Karfa would not allow the coffle to stop, I could not present my respects to the king in person; but I sent him word, by the officer to whom we paid customs, that his prayers for my safety had not been unavailing. We continued our route until sunset, when we lodged at a small village a little to the westward of Kootakunda, and on the day following arrived at Jindey;

Vide p. 34.

Z z 2

where, eighteen months before, I had parted from my friend Dr.
Laidley; an interval, during which I had not beheld the face
of a Christian, nor once heard the delightful sound of my
native language.

Being now arrived within a short distance of Pisania, from
whence my journey originally commenced, and learning that
my friend Karfa was not likely to meet with an immediate
opportunity of selling his slaves on the Gambia; it occurred to
me to suggest to him, that he would find it for his interest to
leave them at Jindey, until a market should offer. Karfa
agreed with me in this opinion; and hired, from the chief man
of the town, huts for their accommodation, and a piece of land
on which to employ them, in raising corn, and other provisions
for their maintenance. With regard to himself, he declared that
he would not quit me until my departure from Africa. We set
out accordingly, Karfa, myself, and one of the Foulahs belonging to the coffle, early on the morning of the 9th; but although
I was now approaching the end of my tedious and toilsome
journey; and expected, in another day, to meet with countrymen
and friends, I could not part, for the last time, with my unfortunate fellow-travellers, doomed, as I knew most of them to
be, to a life of captivity and slavery in a foreign land, without
great emotion. During a wearisome peregrination of more
than five hundred British miles, exposed to the burning rays
of a tropical sun, these poor slaves, amidst their own infinitely
greater sufferings, would commiserate mine; and frequently,
of their own accord, bring water to quench my thirst, and at
night collect branches and leaves to prepare me a bed in the

Wilderness. We parted with reciprocal expressions of regret and benediction. My good wishes and prayers were all I could bestow upon them; and it afforded me some consolation to be told, that they were sensible I had no more to give.

My anxiety to get forward admitting of no delay on the road, we reached Tendacunda in the evening, and were hospitably received at the house of an aged black female called Seniora Camilla, a person who had resided many years at the English factory, and spoke our language. I was known to her before I had left the Gambia, at the outset of my journey; but my dress and figure were now so different from the usual appearance of an European, that she was very excusable in mistaking me for a Moor. When I told her my name and country, she surveyed me with great astonishment, and seemed unwilling to give credit to the testimony of her senses. She assured me that none of the traders on the Gambia, ever expected to see me again; having been informed long ago, that the Moors of Ludamar had murdered me, as they had murdered Major Houghton. I inquired for my two attendants, Johnson and Demba, and learnt, with great sorrow, that neither of them was returned. Karfa, who had never before heard people converse in English, listened to us with great attention. Every thing he saw seemed wonderful. The furniture of the house, the chairs, &c. and particularly beds with curtains, were objects of his great admiration; and he asked me a thousand questions concerning the utility and necessity of different articles; to some of which I found it difficult to give satisfactory answers.

On the morning of the 10th, Mr. Robert Ainsley, having

learnt that I was at Tendacunda, came to meet me, and politely offered me the use of his horse. He informed me that Dr. Laidley had removed all his property to a place called Kaye, a little farther down the river, and that he was then gone to Doomasansa with his vessel, to purchase rice; but would return in a day or two. He therefore invited me to stay with him at Pisania, until the Doctor's return. I accepted the invitation, and being accompanied by my friend Karfa, reached Pisania about ten o'clock. Mr. Ainsley's schooner was lying at anchor before the place. This was the most surprising object which Karfa had yet seen. He could not easily comprehend the use of the masts, sails, and rigging; nor did he conceive that it was possible, by any sort of contrivance, to make so large a body move forwards by the common force of the wind. The manner of fastening together the different planks which composed the vessel, and filling up the seams so as to exclude the water, was perfectly new to him; and I found that the schooner with her cable and anchor, kept Karfa in deep meditation the greater part of the day.

About noon on the 12th, Dr. Laidley returned from Doomasansa, and received me with great joy and satisfaction, as one risen from the dead. Finding that the wearing apparel which I had left under his care was not sold or sent to England, I lost no time in resuming the English dress; and disrobing my chin of its venerable incumbrance. Karfa surveyed me in my British apparel with great delight; but regretted exceedingly that I had taken off my beard; the loss of which, he said, had converted me from a man into a boy. Doctor Laidley readily undertook to discharge all the pecuniary engagements which I had entered into since my departure from the Gambia, and took my draft upon the Association for the amount. My agreement with Karfa (as I have already related), was to pay him the value of one prime slave; for which I had given him my bill upon Dr. Laidley, before we departed from Kamalia: for, in case of my death on the road, I was unwilling that my benefactor should be a loser. But this good creature had continued to manifest towards me so much kindness, that I thought I made him but an inadequate recompence, when I told him that he was now to receive double the sum I had originally promised; and Dr. Laidley assured him that he was ready to deliver the goods to that amount, whenever he thought proper to send for them. Karfa was overpowered by this unexpected token of my gratitude, and still more so, when he heard that I intended to send a handsome present to the good old schoolmaster, Fankooma, at Malacotta. He promised to carry up the goods along with his own, and Dr. Laidley assured him, that he would exert himself in assisting him to dispose of his slaves to the best advantage, the moment a slave vessel should arrive. These, and other instances of attention and kindness shewn him by Dr. Laidley, were not lost upon Karfa. He would often say to me, " my journey has " indeed been prosperous!" But, observing the improved state of our manufactures, and our manifest superiority in the arts of civilized life, he would sometimes appear pensive, and exclaim with an involuntary sigh, *fato fing inta feng*, " black " men are nothing." At other times, he would ask me with great seriousness, what could possibly have induced me, who was no trader, to think of exploring so miserable a country as Africa? He meant by this to signify that, after what I must have witnessed in my own country, nothing in Africa could in his opinion deserve a moment's attention. I have preserved these little traits of character in this worthy Negro, not only from regard to the man, but also because they appear to me to demonstrate that he possessed a mind *above his condition*: and to such of my readers as love to contemplate human nature in all its varieties, and to trace its progress from rudeness to refinement, I hope the account I have given of this poor African will not be unacceptable.

No European vessel had arrived at Gambia for many months previous to my return from the interior; and as the rainy season was now setting in, I persuaded Karfa to return to his people at Jindey. He parted with me on the 14th with great tenderness; but as I had little hopes of being able to quit Africa for the remainder of the year, I told him, as the fact was, that I expected to see him again before my departure. In this, however, I was luckily disappointed; and my narrative now hastens to its conclusion; for on the 15th, the ship Charles-Town, an American vessel, commanded by Mr. Charles Harris, entered the river. She came for slaves, intending to touch at Goree to fill up; and to proceed from thence to South Carolina. As the European merchants on the Gambia, had at this time a great many slaves on hand, they agreed with the Captain to purchase the whole of his cargo, consisting chiefly of rum and tobacco, and deliver him slaves to the amount, in the course of two days.

This afforded me such an opportunity of returning (though by a circuitous route) to my native country, as I thought was not to be neglected. I therefore immediately engaged my passage in this vessel for America; and having taken leave of Dr. Laidley, to whose kindness I was so largely indebted, and my other friends on the river, I embarked at Kaye on the 17th day of June.

Our passage down the river was tedious and fatiguing; and the weather was so hot, moist, and unhealthy, that before our arrival at Goree, four of the seamen, the surgeon, and three of the slaves had died of fevers. At Goree we were detained for want of provisions, until the beginning of October.

The number of slaves received on board this vessel, both on the Gambia, and at Goree, was one hundred and thirty; of whom about twenty-five had been, I suppose, of free condition in Africa; as most of those, being Bushreens, could write a little Arabic. Nine of them had become captives in the religious war between Abdulkader and Damel, mentioned in the latter part of the preceding Chapter. Two of the others had seen me as I passed through Bondou, and many of them had heard of me in the interior countries. My conversation with them, in their native language, gave them great comfort; and as the surgeon was dead, I consented to act in a medical capacity in his room for the remainder of the voyage. They had in truth need of every consolation in my power to bestow; not that I observed any wanton acts of cruelty practised either by the master, or the seamen, towards them; but the mode of confining and securing Negroes in the American slave ships, (owing chiefly to the

weakness of their crews,) being abundantly more rigid and severe than in British vessels employed in the same traffic, made
these poor creatures to suffer greatly, and a general sickness prevailed amongst them. Besides the three who died on the
Gambia, and six or eight while we remained at Goree, eleven
perished at sea, and many of the survivors were reduced to a
very weak and emaciated condition.

In the midst of these distresses, the vessel, after having been
three weeks at sea, became so extremely leaky, as to require
constant exertion at the pumps. It was found necessary, therefore, to take some of the ablest of the Negro men out of irons,
and employ them in this labour; in which they were often
worked beyond their strength. This produced a complication of
miseries not easily to be described. We were, however, relieved
much sooner than I expected; for the leak continuing to gain
upon us, notwithstanding our utmost exertions to clear the vessel, the seamen insisted on bearing away for the West Indies, as
affording the only chance of saving our lives. Accordingly,
after some objections on the part of the master, we directed our
course for Antigua, and fortunately made that island in about
thirty-five days after our departure from Goree. Yet even at
this juncture we narrowly escaped destruction; for on approaching the north-west side of the island, we struck on the Diamond
Rock, and got into St. John's harbour with great difficulty.
The vessel was afterwards condemned as unfit for sea, and the
slaves, as I have heard, were ordered to be sold for the benefit
of the owners.

At this island I remained ten days; when the Chesterfield

Packet, homeward bound from the Leeward Islands, touching at St. John's for the Antigua mail, I took my passage in that vessel. We sailed on the 24th of November; and, after a short but tempestuous voyage, arrived at Falmouth on the 22d of December: from whence I immediately set out for London; having been absent from England two years and seven months.

THE END.

A VOCABULARY

OF THE

MANDINGO LANGUAGE.

ABOVE, *santo.*

Absent, *inteegee;* (*literally,* " not here.")

Abuse, *v. anenni.*

Add, *akeejee.*

Afraid, *silantee.*

Afternoon, *oora.*

Air, *fonio.*

Alike, *beakillin.*

Alive, *a beegee,* (is here.)

All, *bea.*

Always, *toomotoma.*

And, *ning.*

Angry, *jusu bota;* (*literally,* " the heart comes out.")

Angel, *melika.*

Arm, *boulla;* (the same for *hand.*)

Arrived, *footăta.*

Arrow, *binni.*

Ascend, *silli.*

Asleep, *sinouta.*

Assist, *maquoi.*

Axe, *terang.*

Back, *ko.*

Bad, *jou.*

Bag, *bota.*

Barter, *v. fallan.*

Bastard, *janka ding;* (*literally,* "nobody's child.")

Beads, *connoo.*

Beard, *bora.*

Beat, *v. agossi.*

Bees, *leekissi.*

Bed, *larong.*

Beer, *dolo;* (the same for strong liquor of any kind.)

Before, *neata;* (" within sight.")

Behind, *kofi.*

Belly, *konno.*

Big, *awarata.*

3 B

Bind or tie, *aseeti.*

Bird, *cono.*

Bite, *v. keeng.*

Black, *fing.*

Blood, *jollie.*

Blue, *fingma;* (blackish.)

Boil, *v. fagee.*

Bone, *cooloo.*

Book, *kittāba.*

Borrow, *la.*

Bottom, *joo.*

Bow, *kalla.*

Boy, *kea ding;* (*literally*, "male child".)

Brave, *fattee.*

Bread, *munko.*

Break, *v. affāra;* (the same word signifies "to kill" or "to destroy.")

Breasts, *sonjoo.*

Bring, *insambo.*

Brother, *ba-ding-kea;* (*literally* "mother's male child.")

Burn, *v. agēni.*

Buy (or sell), *saun.*

Call, *v. akilli.*

Carry, *asāmbo.*

Cat, *neancon.*

Catch, *v. amuta.*

Chest or coffer, *koonio.*

Child, *ding;* (if very young, *dingding*)

Cloth, *jauno.*

Cold, *ninno.*

Come, *na.*

Coming *abenāli.*

Completely, *betiki.*

Cook, *v. tabbee.*

Corn, *neo.*

Country, *doo.*

Cow, *nessee moosa.*

Crowd, *n. setima.*

Cry, *v. akumbo.*

Cunning, *n. a. kissee.*

Cut, *v. tegi.*

Danger, *torro.*

Dark, *dibbie.*

Daughter, *ding moosa;* (*literally* "female child.")

Day, *teelee.*

Dead, *asāta.*

Deep, *adoonta.*

Desist, *attoo.*

Dew, *combi.*

Die, *v. sa.*

Dirt, *no.*

Disease, *jankra.*

Dispute, *degama.*

Dog, *woola.*

Door, *da;* (this is a word of very extensive use, being applied to whatever opens and shuts.)

Down, *ad. dooma.*

Dream, *v. sibota.*

Dream, *n. s. sibo*

Drink, *v. ameen.*

Dry, (arid) *ajāta.*

Ear, *toola.*

Earth, (soil) *banko.*

Earth, (globe) *banko kang.*

East, *teelee bo;* ("sunrise.")

Eat, *adummo.*

Elephant, *samma.*

Empty, *fing tigee;* ("nothing here.")

Enough, *keyento.*

Entertain, (a guest) *fanda.*

Expert, *cumering;* ("active, clever, &c.")

Eye, *nea.*

Face, (the same as for the eye.)

Fall, *v. bui.*

Far off, *jangfata.*

Fast, *v. soong.*

Fat, *keng.*

Father, *fa.*

Fear, *v. seelan.*

Feather, *tee;* (it signifies also *hair* and *wool.*)

Female, *moosa.*

Fever, *candea.*

Few, *do.*

Fight *v. akilli.*

Fill, *afundi.*

Finger, *boulla konding.*

Fire, *deemba.*

Fish, *yeo.*

Flesh, *sooboo.*

Food, *kinnee.*

Fool, *fooring.*

Foot, *sing;* (signifies also " the leg.")

Forget, *neānata.*

Free, *horea.*

Fresh, *kinde* (signifies also, *healthy*).

Friend, *barrio.*

Fruit, *eree ding;* (" child of the tree.")

Full, *affāta.*

Give, *insong.*

Glad, *lāta.*

Go, *v. ta.*

God, *alla.*

Gold, *sanoo.*

Good, *bettie.*

Great, *baa.*

Grass, *bing.*

Gray, *aqueta.*

Guard, *v. tenkoong.*

Half, *tella.*

Handsome, *aniniāta.*

Hang up, *deng.*

Hate, *v. akoong.*

He, *etti.*

Head, *koon.*

Hear, *moi.*

Heart, *jusu.*

Heaven, *santo;* (the Mahomedan Negroes commonly say, *il jinna.*)

Heavy, *acooliata.*

Hell, *johaniba.*

Hen, *soosee moosa.*

Herb, *jambo.*

3 B 2

Here, *jang.*

Hide, *n. goolo.*

Hill, *konko.*

Hog, *lea.*

Hole, *dinka.*

Honey, *lee.*

Horn, *bini.*

Horse, *soo.*

Hot, *candiāta.*

House, *boong.*

Hungry, *konkola.*

I, *inta.*

Idle, *nare.*

Increase, *aboonia.*

Industrious, *sayāta.*

Interpret, *konno sor;* (literally, *to pierce the belly.*)

Iron, *nega.*

Island, *jouio.*

Jump, *v. soun.*

Kill, *affāra.*

King, *mansa.*

Knife, *mooro.*

Know, *alla.*

Lamp, *fitina.*

Laugh, *v. jilli.*

Lend, *infoo.*

Lie (down), *v. la jang.*

Lie (falsity) *fonio.*

Lift, *achicka.*

Lightning, *sanfata.*

Lion, *jatta;* (in the interior countries, *wara.*)

Little, *miessa.*

Long, *jang.*

Look, *v. affille.*

Lose, *afeele.*

Lost, *affeeleeta.*

Love, *v. konie.*

Make, *v. dada.*

Male, *kea.*

Man (homo) *mo.*

Man (vir) *fato.*

Many, *sitimata.*

Market, *loe.*

Master, *marree.*

Mat, *basso.*

Meet, *v. beng.*

Middle, *taima.*

Milk, *nunno.*

Milk, *v. beetee.*

Mine, *pr. talem.*

Money, *naphula;* (it signifies also *merchandize,* or any *effects of value.*)

Month, *korro;* (the same word signifies the *moon.*)

Morning, *somo.*

Mother, *ba.*

Mouth, *da.*

Narrative, *dentigi.*

Name, *atto.*

Near (nigh), *mun jang;* (not far.)

Neck, *kang.*

Never, *abada.*

Night, *sooton.*

No, *inta;* (literally, *is not.*)

Noon, *teelee kooniata;* (literally, the *sun over head.*)

North, *saheel.*

Nose, *noong.*

Now, *seng.*

Oil, *toulou.*

Obtain, *sutte.*

Old, *accottata.*

Only, *kinsing.*

Open, *v. yelli.*

Out of, *banta.*

Pain, *deeming.*

Paper, *coitoo.*

Pass, *v. tambi.*

Past, *atambita;* (gone by.)

Pay, *v. jo.*

Pen, *kalla.*

People, *molo.*

Pierce, *sor.*

Pity, *v. dimi.*

Pleasure, *di.*

Pleasant, *adiāta.*

Plenty, *asiāta.*

Poor, *doiāta.*

Present (gift), *boonia.*

Promise, *v. moindee.*

Proud, *telingabalia;* (literally, *strait bodied.*)

Pull, *asabba.*

Push, *āneury.*

Put down, *alondi.*

Quarrel, *quiāta.*

Quick, *catǎba.*

Quiet, *dea.*

Quiver, *n. s. toong.*

Rain, *sangee;* (literally, *water from above.*)

Rat, *nīnee.*

Read, *akarra.*

Red, *woolima.*

Release, *affering;* (untie.)

Rest, *lo.*

Restore, *serrat.*

Return, *v. n. ascita.*

Ripe, *mota.*

Rise, *v. wooli.*

River, *ba;* (the same as for *mother.*)

Road, *seelo.*

Rob, *boitāca.*

Rock, *kooro.*

Rope, *julie.*

Rotten, *accorata.*

Row, *v. ajah.*

Run, *boorie.*

Sad, *doi.*

Safe, *torro inteege;* (literally, *no danger.*)

Salt, *ko.*

Sand, *kini kini.*

Sandals, *samata.*

Say, *affo.*

Sea, *babagee.*

Seat, *serong.*

See, *eāgee.*

Send, *kee.*

Separate, *atulla.*

Shake, *jiggi jiggi.*

Shame, *māla.*

Shew, *aita.*

Ship, *caloon.*

Short, *sutta.*

Shut, *tou.*

Sick, *mun kinde.*

Side, *carra.*

Silent, *dering.*

Silver, *cody.*

Sing, *jilli ;* (the same *to dance*)

Sister, *ba ding moosa ;* (mother's female child.)

Sit, *see.*

Sky, *sang.*

Slave, *jong.*

Sleep, *v. sinoo.*

Smell, *v. soomboola.*

Smoke, *seisee.*

Snake, *sau.*

Something, *fenke.*

Son, *ding kea ;* (male child.)

Soon, *sang sang ;* (now now.)

Sour, *accoomiata.*

South, *boulla ba ;* (literally, *the right hand.*)

Speak, *akummo.*

Spear, *tamba.*

Spin, *v. a. worondi.*

Spoon, *dosa.*

Star, *lolo.*

Steal, *soonia.*

Stink, *v. n. kassa.*

Stone, *birro*

Stop, *munia.*

Stranger, *leuntōng.*

Strike, *abooti.*

Sun, *teelee.*

Swear, *kolli.*

Sweet, *teemiāta.*

Swell, *foonoo.*

Swim, *noo.*

Sword, *fong.*

Tail, *finnio.*

Thief, *soon.*

Thin, *feata ;* (slender.)

Think, *meira.*

Thirst, *mindo.*

Thread, *bori.*

Throw, *fy.*

Thunder, *sangfata.* (In contradistinction to lightning, it is *Kallam Alla* (Arab.) " the voice of God.")

Tie, *v. asseetee.*

To-day, *bee.*

To-morrow, *sinny.*

Tongue, *ning.*

Touch, *v. ma.*

Town, *kunda.*

Trade, *v. feeree.*

Tree, *eree.*

True, *tonia.*

Trust, *v. la.*

Turn, *aelima.*

Understand, *moi.*

Until, *hāning.*

Walk, *tāma.*

War, *killi.*

Wash, *v. coo.*

Water, *gee.*

Weary, *umbatata.*

Weep, *akussi.*

Weigh, *simang.*

Well, *n. a. awa.*

Well, *n. s. cullong.*

West, *teelee gee.*

Wet, *sinunta.*

What, *mun.*

Where, *minto.*

White, *qui.*

Who, *jema.*

Why, *munkang.*

Wind, *n. funnio.*

Wolf, *soolo.*

Woman, *moosa.*

Wilderness, *woolla.*

Yes, *awa.*

Yesterday, *koona.*

You, *eeta*, when simply pronounced; when joined to any other word, it is *ee.*

Young, *juna.*

The following QUESTIONS *and* ANSWERS *may be useful in the West Indies.*

Do you understand Mandingo ? - *ee Mandingo kummo moi ?*

I understand it, - - - *ya moi.*

I do not understand you, - - *ma moi.*

Come hither, - - - *nā nā re.*

Is your Father or Mother living ? *ee fā, ou ee bā abeegee ?*

———— alive, - - - *abeegee.*

———— dead, - - - *asāta.*

Have you any brothers or sisters ? *ee bā ding abeegee ?*

Where are they? - -	*biminto?*
Are they in Africa? - -	*abbe fato fing doo?*
Are they on board the ship? -	*abbe Tobaubo Caloon o konno?*
Point them out. - - -	*aitanna.*
What is the matter with you? -	*mun bela?*
Are you in health? - -	*ko ee kinde?*
I am sick. - - - -	*mun kinde.*
Shew me your tongue. - -	*ee ning aitanna.*
Give me your hand. - -	*ee boulla adima.*
Are you hungry? - -	*konkolabinna?*
I am hungry. - - -	*konkolabinna.*
Are you thirsty? - - -	*mindolabinna?*
I am thirsty. - - -	*the same word repeated.*
I am not hungry. - - -	*konko inteegee.*
I am not thirsty. - - -	*mindo inteegee.*
Does your head ach? - -	*ee koon bideemina?*
It does ach. - - -	*bideemina.*
It does not ach. - - -	*intadeeming.*
Does your stomach pain you? -	*ee konno bideemina?*
Do you sleep well? - -	*ko ee sinoo betiki?*
Are you feverish? - -	*acandeata?*
Do not be afraid. - - -	*kanna seelan.*
There is no danger. - -	*torro inteegee.*
Drink this medicine. - -	*ning borri ameen.*
It will do you good. - -	*aee kissi.*

APPENDIX.

GEOGRAPHICAL ILLUSTRATIONS

OF

MR. PARK'S JOURNEY.

BY

MAJOR RENNELL.

GEOGRAPHICAL ILLUSTRATIONS.

CHAPTER I.

Concerning the Ideas entertained by the Ancient Geographers, as well as the Moderns, down to the Times of Delisle and D'Anville, respecting the Course of the River Niger.

THE late journey of Mr. PARK, into the interior of WESTERN AFRICA, has brought to our knowledge more important facts respecting its Geography (both *moral* and *physical*), than have been collected by any former traveller. By pointing out to us the positions of the sources of the great rivers SENEGAL, GAMBIA, and NIGER,* we are instructed where to look for the elevated parts of the country; and even for the *most elevated* point in the western quarter of Africa, by the place from whence the Niger and Gambia turn in opposite directions to the east and west. We are taught, moreover, the common boundary of the desert and fruitful parts of the country, and of the MOORS and

---

* I here use the word NIGER, as being the best understood by Europeans; but the *proper* name of this river in the country seems to be *Guin* or *Jin*. (Hartmann's Edrisi, p. 32. 48. 51.) At the same time, it is more commonly designed by the term JOLIBA, meaning the *Great Water*, or great river. In like manner, the GANGES has two names, *Padda*, the proper name; *Gonga*, the great river.

The Moors and Arabs call it NEEL ABEED, the *River of Slaves*; but they have also a name to express the great water, that is, NEEL KIBBEER. *Neel* appears to be employed in Africa, as *Gonga* in India, to express any great river.

By *Niger*, the ancients meant merely to express the River of the Black People, or *Ethiopians*. The term was Roman: for the Greeks believed it to be the head, or a branch, of the *Egyptian Nile*.

NEGROES; which latter is the more interesting, as it may be termed a boundary in *moral* geography; from the opposite qualities of mind, as well as of body, of the Moors and Negroes: for that physical geography gives rise to habits, which often determine national character, must be allowed by every person, who is a diligent observer of mankind.

It must be acknowledged, that the absolute extent of Mr. Park's progress in Africa, compared with the amazing size of that continent, appears but small, although it be nearly 1100 British miles in a direct line, reckoned from its western extremity, Cape Verd. But considered in itself, it is no inconsiderable line of travel; being more extensive than the usual southern tour of Europe.

But moreover, it affords a triumph to the learned, in that it confirms some points of fact, both of geography and natural history, which have appeared in ancient authors, but to which our own want of knowledge has denied credit. I allude more particularly to the *course* of the *Niger*, and the history of the *Lotophagi*. That the Greeks and Romans, who had formed great establishments in Africa, and the latter in particular, who had penetrated to the Niger,* should have had better opportunities of knowing the interior part of the country, than we, who live at a distance from it, and possess only a few scattered factories near the sea coast, is not to be wondered at: but the proof of such facts should teach us to be less hasty in decrying the authority of ancient authors; since the fault may arise from a want of comprehension on our parts, or from an assumption of false principles on theirs.

Few geographical facts have been more questioned in modern times, than the course of the great inland river of Africa, generally understood by the name of NIGER; some describing it to run to the *west*, others to the *east*; but of these opinions, I believe the former has been espoused by the most numerous party, by far.* Although Mr. Park's authority, founded on ocular demonstration, sets this question *for ever* at rest, by determining the course of

* Pliny, lib. v. c. 4.

† M. J. Lalande, almost at the moment of Mr. Park's investigation, has determined its course to be to the west; notwithstanding the forcible reasoning of his countryman D'An ville. (Mémoire sur l'Intérieur de l'Afrique.) Mr. Bruce was of the same opinion. Vol. iii. p. 720. 724.

the river to be from *west* to *east*, as Major Houghton's information had previously induced a belief of, yet it may not be amiss to trace the history of the opinions, concerning the course of this celebrated river, from the earliest date of profane history.

HERODOTUS,* more than twenty-two centuries ago, describes, from the information of the Africans, a great river of Africa, far removed to the south of the Great Desert, and abounding with crocodiles. That it flowed from *west* to *east*, dividing *Africa*, in like manner as the Danube does *Europe*. That the people from the borders of the Mediterranean, who made the discovery, were carried to a great city on the banks of the river in question; and that the people of this quarter were *black*; that is, much blacker than their visitors. Our author, indeed, took this river to be the remote branch of the Egyptian Nile, and reasons on the circumstance, accordingly: but even this argument serves to express in a more forcible manner, the supposed direction of its course.

PLINY also believed that the *Nile* came from the west; but he is far from identifying it with the *Niger*, which he describes as a distinct river. But we have at least his negative opinion respecting its western course; for he speaks of the *Bambotus* river as running into the Western ocean; meaning to express by it either the Gambia or Senegal river, and not the Niger.†

PTOLEMY is positive in describing the Niger as a separate stream from the Senegal and Gambia, which two rivers are designed by him under the names of *Daradus* and *Stachir*; and they are by no means ill expressed; falling into the sea on different sides of the *Arsinarium* promontory, or Cape Verd.‡ The Niger of Ptolemy is made to extend from west to east, over half the breadth of Africa, between the Atlantic ocean, and the course of the Nile.

These may suffice for the ancient authorities, which in very early times fixed the course of the Niger in the systems of geography, to be *from west to east*. Who it was that first led the way, in the opposite opinion, I know not; but we find EDRISI, in the twelfth century, not only conducting the *Nile of the Negroes*, or Niger, *westward*, and into the *Atlantic*, but also *deriving*

---

* Euterpe, c. 32.   † Lib. v. c. 9.

‡ Probably a corruption of *Senhagi*; or *Assenhagi*, as the early Portuguese discoverers write it. These were a great tribe.

it from the *Egyptian* Nile; which is diametrically opposite to the opinion of Herodotus.

Such an opinion marks the very imperfect state of his knowledge of African geography; and should induce a degree of caution in receiving other opinions of the same author, where they rest absolutely on his own authority. It is very probable that the waters which collect on the *west* of *Nubia*, may *run to the west*, and be lost in lakes: and it is possible, though very improbable, that a branch of the Nile may take the same course: but fortified by the present state of our knowledge, we may certainly pronounce the general scope of the intelligence communicated by Edrisi, respecting the course of the Niger, to be erroneous.

I conceive, however, that his error may easily be accounted for, in this way. He was probably told, that the waters on the west of Nubia, &c. ran to the westward. He also knew that a great river (the Senegal) discharged itself into the Atlantic, nearly in the same parallel; and moreover, that a great river, whose *line of direction* lay between the *east* and *west*, and between Nubia and the just mentioned *embouchure*, watered a very extensive tract, in the midland part of Africa. Now, what so natural (admitting the fact of the western waters from Nubia, and which I trust, I shall go near to prove in the sequel) as to suppose, when he had found a *head*, and a *tail* of a great river, together with a long extent of course of a river between them, that they were parts of each other? It must also be taken into the account, that he supposed the continent of Africa to be about 1000 miles narrower than it really is, in the line between Nubia and the mouth of the Senegal.

ABULFEDA followed Edrisi in the same opinion, respecting the Niger; which he calls a *twin* river with that of Egypt. He also calls it the *Nile of Gana*. Abulfeda also knew, and has described, the general form of the continent of Africa: and, of course knew that it was surrounded by the sea.* But his descriptions are limited to the north and north-east parts. He wrote in the fourteenth century.

It was Edrisi, probably, who influenced and determined the opinions of the moderns, respecting this question. An author, long supposed to be of the

* This was previous to the Portuguese discoveries.

same region with that which he describes,* and who had entered more into the *detail* of the African geography, than any other, would, according to the usual mode of decision, on such pretensions, be preferred to those who went before him, and had treated the subject in a more general way. Mankind had no criterion by which to judge of the truth.

Since then the Arabian geographer, who had written the most extensively on the subject, had conducted the Niger into the Atlantic, we cannot wonder that the early Portuguese discoverers, who doubtless learnt from the Arabian authors the particulars of African geography, should adopt the same idea; and that they should regard the *Senegal* river as the *Niger*; as we find it, in the histories of their discoveries in the fifteenth century. The Portuguese, who at this period took the lead, in matters of navigation and discovery, might well be expected to set the fashion, in what related to African geography. So that in despite of Ptolemy, and of the ancients in general, the great inland river of Africa was described to run *to* the *west*; and to form the head of the Senegal river. Nay more, it was at last supposed to be the *parent stock* of all the great *western* rivers of Africa.

Sanuto, whose Geography of Africa, is dated 1588, describes one branch of the Niger to be the *Rio Grande*, the other the river of *Sestos*; regarding the Senegal as a different river.

M. DELISLE's map of Africa (1707) gives the Niger a direct course through Africa, from *Bornou*, in the east, and terminating in the river of Senegal on the west. But in his maps of 1722 and 1727, this was corrected: the source of the Senegal was placed at a shallow lake named *Maberia*, between the 14th and 15th degrees of longitude east of Cape Verd; and in latitude 12°; whilst the river of TOMBUCTOO, named *Guien*, was described to issue from another lake, in the same neighbourhood, and to flow *towards* Bornou, where it terminated in a third lake.

The cause of this change, may be easily traced, in the intelligence collected by the French traders and settlers in GALLAM:† the substance of which

* He was commonly called the *Nubian* Geographer.

† Gallam is one of the names of the country in which Fort St. Joseph is situated; and is often applied to the settlement itself.

is to be found in Labat's collection, published in 1728; although the detail differs in some points.   He says, Vol. ii. p. 161, *et seq.* that the MANDINGA merchants report that the Niger (by which he always means the Senegal river) springs from the lake Maberia, whose situation could not be ascertained.   That the Gambia river was a branch of the Niger ; separating from it at Baracota (a position also unknown) and that it passed through a marshy lake, in its way to *Baraconda*; where the English and Portuguese had settlements. That the Niger, at a point below Baracota, sent forth another branch, namely the *Falemé* river ; which encompassed the country of *Bambouk*, and afterwards joined the *Niger* in the country of *Gallam*.   And finally, that the same Niger, by its separation into two branches, formed a very considerable island above Kasson   It may be remarked, that a belief of these circumstances, manifests a gross state of ignorance respecting the interior of the country ; since such de-rivations from rivers, are found only in *alluvial* tracts : and it happens, that scarcely any levels vary more than those, through which the rivers in question pass ; as will appear in the sequel.

They likewise report (p. 163) that on the east of the lake Maberia lies the kingdom of *Guinbala*; within which, is the river of *Guien*, which passes near the city of Tombuctoo.   Again (Vol. iii. p. 361 to 364) it is said that Tombuctoo is not situated on the bank of the Niger, but at about 6 leagues inland from it : and that in passing to it, from Gallam (which is reported to be a journey of thirty-two days only), they go through Timbi, five journies short of Tombuctoo ; where they leave the bank of the river, to avoid too great a *detour.*

Labat does not state in positive terms that the Niger or river of Senegal af-fords a continuous navigation, from the falls of Govinea (above Gallam) to Tombuctoo : but that he believed it, is strongly implied, by what appears after-wards, in p. 367, 368 ; that is, a project of a trade to Tombuctoo ; " by keep-ing an establishment of vessels above the falls ; which vessels might ascend the Niger to a point opposite to Tombuctoo, thereby saving the great expence and fatigue of a land journey."

Here then, we trace the idea of the lake of Maberia, the supposed head of the Niger ; and the river of Tombuctoo, under the name of Guien ; and

moreover, (although these are not expressly said to communicate) a continued navigation from Gallam to Tombuctoo. But it must surely have struck
those on the spot, to inquire whether any boats ever descended from Tombuctoo to the falls of Govinea?

It is certain that Delisle, (as well as D'Anville, whose general ideas are
much the same, in this particular *) regards the river Guien, as having no
communication with the lake Maberia, but makes it flow from a different
lake, at no great distance to the northward: so that these geographers so
far understood the matter right; and denied the practicability of a continuous navigation to Tombuctoo: but then, they erred very greatly in
placing the head of the Senegal, either so remotely, or in the eastern
quarter; since it rises in the south-east.

We must regard the geography of M. D'Anville, as the most perfect of
all, previous to the inquiries made by the AFRICAN ASSOCIATION. The
researches made under the direction of this Association, have already
established on record, from the reports of Major Houghton, and of Mr.
Magra, although in a vague way, the general position of the sources of the
Joliba, or Niger, in or near the country of Manding; as well as its easterly or north-easterly course, towards Tombuctoo; the position of Bammakoo, situated near the highest navigable point of its course; of Sego, and
Jenné, along its banks; the separation of its waters, into two channels, in
the quarter of Tombuctoo; together with a vague idea of the position of
that city itself. It will be shewn, in the sequel, that Mr. Park's observations do not contradict, but establish these positions; drawing them out of
the obscurity in which, by the very nature of the information, they were
necessarily involved; and fixing, in some degree of just relative position
and proportion, those particulars which before remained at large, considered in a geographical sense.

Concerning the errors of former geographers, they are more easily de-

---

* D'Anville differs from Delisle in extending very greatly, the distance between Gallam and Tombuctoo; and by representing the Maberia lake, as one source alone, and
that the least distant, of those of the river Senegal.

tected than the *causes* of them. They must, however, be ascribed, partly to the ignorance of the African merchants; but, in all probability, in a much greater part, to the want of understanding each other's language; a defect that has led to many errors, that are oftentimes charged to the account of wilful falsehood, or, at least, to an indifference to the cause of truth.

I can easily conceive that the caravan merchants, in passing from Tombuctoo to Gallam (or the contrary), might have *deceived themselves* into a belief, that the principal rivers which they had either crossed or skirted in their way, might communicate with each other: for it appears clearly, by Mr. Park's observations, that the eastern branch of the Senegal, and the western branch of the Joliba, approach very near to each other, in the early part of their courses; so that, during the whole journey, the merchants might never be farther distant from *a river* to the southward of them, than a few journies.

As to the story, so long credited, of the Niger being the parent river, from whence all the western rivers were derived, we may remark, that ignorance, in every country through which large rivers take their course, is very ready to derive them *all* from *one source*; and that source very probably, a *lake*. Within our own times, the *Burrampooter* and *Ava* rivers were thus described in the maps. Pliny reports, that the Euphrates and Tigris are united in Armenia, by the medium of a lake:* and Edrisi, as we have seen, derived the Nile and Niger, from one and the same lake.†

It will appear that the lake Maberia, taken by D'Anville and Delisle for the head of the Senegal river, or that which runs to the *west*, is meant for no other than the lake of *Dibbie*, formed by the river Joliba, or that which runs to the *east*; and which Mr. Park's inquiries have brought to our knowledge. Again, we recognize the river Guien, or Guin, of Labat,

---

* Pliny, lib. vi. c. 27.

† Thomson believed it. After speaking of the Nile, he says,—

    His *brother Niger* too, and all the floods

    In which the full-form'd maids of Afric lave

    Their jetty limbs.——   *Summer*, 811.

of D'Anville, and of Delisle, in the northern branch of the same Joliba, issuing out of the lake Dibbie; and which, together with the southern branch from the same lake, forms an island, reported to be 90 or 100 miles in length, named Jinbala by Mr. Park. There is a town on the side of the northern branch, also named Jinbala; but whether the island may take its name from this town, or from the river, whose *proper name*, from about this point, seems to be *Guin*, or *Jin*, I know not. M. D'Anville has described, in this position, the country of Guinbala, subject to Tonka Quata : the same who is said by Labat to be sovereign of the country which contains the lake of Maberia, and the river of Guien. *

Here, then, we have an explication of the error of those, who, from the supposed information of the Mandinga merchants, supposed the lake Maberia (answering to the Dibbie of Park), to form the source of the Senegal river; and who took the river of Guin, or Jinbala, for a distinct river, instead of a branch, issuing from that lake. The Mandingas might very truly have informed the French settlers, that the lake Maberia, and the rivers Joliba and Guin would convey them to Tombuctoo; but did they say also, that the river of Senegal would convey them to the lake Maberia? The French merchants, perhaps, taking for granted that the navigation was continuous, might never inquire whether their informants were speaking of *one* or of *two* rivers : and the others might at the same time be speaking of *two* distinct rivers, and be ignorant of the prepossessions of their inquirers !

It may be added, that, whether from the difficulties that grew out of the subject, when the geographical documents came to be analyzed, or whether it was from actual information, both Delisle and D'Anville describe *two* lakes, near each other; one at the supposed head of the Senegal river, the other at that of the Tombuctoo river. I think it most probable, that it was occasioned by the want of their being made to comprehend, that the waters ran *eastward to*, and not *westward from* the lake Maberia; so that when they were told that the Tombuctoo river issued from a lake, they

* Labat, Vol. ii. p. 161. 163. and iii. p. 361.

concluded it must be a different one from that at the head of the Senegal. Certain it is, however, that these geographers believed, that the waters ran to the *west*, from this lake.

I have now brought to a conclusion, what was meant to be said on the subject of the descriptions, and mistakes, of former geographers; in the course of which it may be observed, that a period of twenty-two centuries has brought matters round again to the same point. And having thus cleared the ground, I next proceed to the more important part of the subject, the proper discoveries of Mr. Park.

CHAPTER II.

Concerning the Geographical Discoveries of Mr. Park.

SINCE the scope and design of Mr. Park's routes have been already set forth in the beginning of the present work, it would be useless to say more on that head; and as the particular map of his progress will explain the relative circumstances of the Geography, nothing more will be necessary, than to call the attention of the reader to such particulars as may not readily occur to him on inspection of the Map; or which, from their nature, cannot well be inserted in it.

The discoveries of this gentleman (as has been said before), give a new face to the *physical* geography of *Western* Africa. They prove, by the courses of the great rivers, and from other notices, that a belt of mountains, which extends from west to east, occupies the parallels between 10 and 11 degrees of north latitude, and at least between the 2d and 10th degrees of west longitude (from Greenwich). This belt, moreover, other authorities extend some degrees still farther to the west and south, in different branches, and apparently of less height. One of these, follows the upper part of the Gambia river; another the Rio Grande, to a low point of its course; and a third appears to shut up the western coast of Guinea.* Accordingly, this chain approaches much nearer to the equatorial parts of Africa, than was before supposed; and thus we are enabled to understand fully what Abulfeda † meant, when he said, that after the continent of Africa has extended southward ‡ from the Strait of Gibraltar, to the neigh-

* Meaning Serra Leona, &c. &c.

† Prolegomena.

‡ Abulfeda in effect, *literally* meant *southward*; for, like Ptolemy, and Strabo, he had no idea that the coast of Africa projected to the *westward*, beyond the Straits, but rather supposed it to trend to the *eastward* of south.

bourhood of the Equator, it turns to the east, *passing at the back of the mountains of Komri*, which give rise to the *Nile*.* The mountains in question, then, ought to be those intended by Abulfeda; who by the name *Komri*, evidently meant to express the *Mountains* of the *Moon*; from which Ptolemy derives the remote source of the Nile.† As Abulfeda supposed the source of the Nile to be very far to the south or south-west (in which I agree generally with him), this chain may be supposed to pass onward from the abovementioned quarter, to the *east*, and *south* of *east*, shutting up Abyssinia on the south. This, at least, seems the only way in which we can fairly understand Abulfeda; in confirmation of whose description, *a part* of the ridge has been actually found by Mr. Park.‡ According to Leo (p. 249), the country of *Melli* is bordered on the south by mountains; and these must be nearly in the same parallel with the mountains of *Kong*, seen by Mr. Park.

Mr. BEAUFOY was informed that the countries on the south and south-west of the Niger, lying opposite to, and to the westward of, Kassina, were also *mountainous* and *woody*. In particular in the line between Kassina and Assentai, the country is said to be formed of a succession of hills, with woods of vast extent, and some mountains of a *stupendous height*.§

As the source of the Nile is confessedly very far to the south of the

* When the above is considered, we can understand that Abulfeda supposed the bays of Benin and St. Thomas to be 11 or 12 degrees more to the *east*, than they really are; and he might well suppose that " the sea came in at the back of the mountains that gave rise to the Nile."

That the *Nile of Egypt*, and not the *Niger*, is meant, we learn in another place in the same author, where he speaks of the *Egyptian* Nile, and traces it to Egypt. Prolegomena, article Rivers.

† *Komri*, or rather *Kummeree*, is the Arabic term for *lunar*; and is the adjective of *Kummer*, the moon. [Mr. Hastings.]

‡ The mountains of Kong were seen by Mr. Park; but no other part of the chain.

§ African Association, 1790, and 1791, quarto ed. p. 117. 123; octavo, 176. 186. Also quarto, 174; octavo, 260.

As two editions of this work are in the hands of the public, I have referred to both throughout this work; distinguishing them respectively by Q. and O.

parallel of 10 degrees north, this chain of mountains, admitting it to continue its general easterly course, must bend to the southward, after it passes Kong and Melli, in order to pass *above* the sources of the Nile; the principal of which I conceive to be situated in the country of DARFOOR.

The highest part of the portion of this chain, pointed out by Mr. Park's discoveries, is situated between the 5th and 9th degrees of west longitude; for within this space are situated the sources of the Gambia, which run to the west-north-west; of the Senegal, running to the north-west; and of the Joliba (or Niger) to the east-north-east.* There is, however, a general slope of the country, extending to a great distance northward, formed by a gradation of summits of lesser mountains and hills, as is shewn by the early part of the courses of the rivers; in particular, that of the Niger, which appears to run near 100 miles on a northerly course, before it turns finally to the eastward.

A large portion of the tract bordering on the northern foot of the mountains, from whence the branches of the Senegal river issue, is covered with thick forests. Mr. Park's track on his return lay through these woods; one part of which is named the *Jallonka Wilderness*, in which no habitations were seen during five days of forced marching. The hardships endured, even by the *free* men of this caravan, almost exceed belief.†

The head of the principal branch of the Senegal river is about 80 geographical miles to the west of that of the Joliba; and the head of the Gambia, is again, about 100 west of the Senegal. The branches of the latter are very numerous, and intersect the country for about 200 miles from east to west, in the line of the caravan route: and it was this circumstance that detained Mr. Park, during a great part of the periodical rainy season, in

* The Rio Grande has its source very far to the south of this chain; first running to the north, till it touches the foot of this very ridge of mountains, by which it is turned to the west. [Vide Mr. Watt's Plan and Journal.]

† The caravan in question was composed chiefly of slaves going from Manding to the ports of the Gambia.

Manding; a state of things, perhaps little expected, in a country regarded *here*, as the most thirsty on the globe. *

We may conclude that similar circumstances take place, with respect to the Joliba; only that as its course is such as to intercept all the streams that descend from the Kong mountains on the south, whilst Mr. Park's travels along it, were confined to the northern bank, he had no opportunity of knowing it, any farther than by seeing various openings on that side; and by being told that he could not possibly *make his way* there. No doubt, it receives some large streams also, when its course diverges far enough from the mountains as to allow the waters room to collect.

At the lowest point to which Mr. Park traced it, and which (although about 420 British miles in direct distance from its source) could only be reckoned the early part of its course, it was a very considerable body of water; the largest, he says, that he had seen (in Africa,) and it abounded with crocodiles. The rainy season was but just begun; and the river might have been forded at Sego, where its bed expands to a vast breadth. Still, however, we must not estimate the bulk of the Niger, that *Niger* which was in the contemplation of Pliny and the Romans, by the measure of its bulk at Sego, and Silla.† If we suppose it to be the same river which passes by Kassina (and we know of no other), which place is 700 miles, or more, to the eastward of Silla, it would doubtless receive by the way great additional supplies of water, and be at least a much deeper river than where Mr. Park saw it. And here it may not be amiss to remark, for the use of those who

---

* There is in Africa, a rainy season; and also a periodical change of wind, as in the same latitudes in India: in effect, a MONSOON.

† It may be conceived that the Romans, who, according to Pliny, (lib. v. 4.), held the dominion of the countries as far as the Niger, penetrated to it by the route of Gadamis, Fezzan, Taboo, and Kassina, as the most direct, and convenient one, from the Mediterranean. There are very clear proofs of the conquest of the three former by Balbus. (Pliny, lib. v. 5.) It was known to Pliny that the Niger swelled periodically like the Nile, and at the same season; which we have also in proof from Major Houghton's *Report*; and from Mr. Park's *Observations*. Pliny says, moreover, that its productions were the same with those of the Nile. (Lib. v. c. 8.)

are not conversant with the subject, that rivers make the greatest display of their waters, in proportion to their bulk, at a moderate distance from their sources; and are often wider *above*, than *below*.*

There can be no doubt but that the *Joliba*, is a noble stream; and the prince of the *western* rivers of Africa, as the *Nile* of the *eastern:* but the African rivers, however, rank lower than those of Asia and America.

Mr. Park judged that the Senegal river below the falls of *F'low*, or *Félou* (as Labat writes it), was about the bulk of the *Tweed* at *Melross*, in summer. This was indeed, in the dry season; but as the river does not begin to swell periodically till many months after that, Mr. Park, did not of course see it, at its lowest pitch. And yet this was the assemblage of all the principal branches of the river, save the *Falemé*, which was itself about three feet deep at the same season. But the Senegal is even fordable in some places *below* the conflux of the Falemé, according to Labat:† for the Moors cross it in the dry season, and commit depredations on some of the lands to the south. However, almost the whole of the towns and villages are placed on the south side, with a view of being in security for the longest possible term.

The Senegal river then, is by no means a very capital stream, except in the

---

* In the Proceedings of the African Association, (Q p. 122; O. 183, *et seq.*) the river of Kassina is described to run *to the west,* and *to pass on to* Tombuctoo; where it is said to be named *Gnewa*; possibly intended for Joliba, for the *n* and *l* are more commonly interchanged than the *m* and *n.*‡ It will very probably turn out that there is an error in the above statement, and that it runs from W to E in the country of Kassina as well as at Tombuctoo. It would seem also to be a larger river in the *east*, than in the *west*; a presumption in favour of an easterly course. But perhaps, the best argument is, that it certainly runs *from* Tombuctoo to the *east*. It must then either be one and the same river, or there must be a receptacle common to both, lying between Tombuctoo and Kassina! and we have not heard of any such. Much more will be said concerning this subject, in the latter part of the Memoir.

† See Labat, Vol. ii. p. 172, where the impediments to the navigation are described. They do not appear to arise from differences in the general level, but to a ledge of rocks.

‡ Abderachman Aga calls it Gülbi; (or Julbee). Hartmann's Edrisi, quarto ed. p. 22. It is incumbent on me to acknowledge the obligations I owe to M. Hartmann, for his arrangement of th matter of Edrisi's Africa; and for his invaluable Elucidations, and Notes.

c

rainy season; when, like all the other tropical rivers, its bed is filled, and very commonly will not contain the additional waters. Mr. Park observed by the mark of the highest point of swelling of the river *Kokoro* (or eastern branch of the Senegal), that it had been twenty feet higher than when he crossed it, in the line of the southern route. The *main* branch of this river, the *Ba-fing*, or Black River, was not fordable, and was crossed over a temporary bridge of a very singular construction. Alligators, or crocodiles are found in all these branches, at the height at which Mr. Park passed them.

The Falemé river has also a remote source, and drains a great extent of country.

Concerning the Gambia Mr. Park had fewer notices. It is remarkable that the position pointed out to him for the source of this river, agrees very nearly with that found in Dr. Wadstrom's map; from notices collected from another quarter. This is very satisfactory. I learn also from Dr. Afzelius that the distance across, between the approximating parts of the courses of the Gambia and Rio Grande, is four journies.

Mr. Park crossed in his way, six different streams that fall into the Gambia from the north-east. Amongst these the principal one is the Nerico, which flows from the quarter of Bondou; and is reckoned the eastern boundary of a tract which the Africans of this region style the Country of the *West*, expressed by that of the *setting sun*. This tract is on a lower level than that to the east; is flat, and the soil composed of clay and sand. It appears that the whole tract through which Mr. Park *returned* is covered with wood, cleared only in certain inhabited spots (*Numidian fashion*): of which, the great tract, named the Jallonka Wilderness, is composed of primeval forests.*

The Bambara and Kaarta countries are also exceedingly woody, but less so than the other tract; and the woods are of an inferior growth.

According to the ideas collected from Mr. Park's observations, the

---

* Thomson seems to have understood this, when he says,

—— beneath *primeval* trees, that cast
Their ample shade o'er NIGER's yellow stream.

Summer, v. 705.

general levels of the countries, near the sources of the great rivers are thus distributed:

Between the countries of Bondou and Neola on the west, Bambara and Kaarta on the east, the country forms a very elevated level, falling *rapidly* to the eastward; but only *by degrees*, to the westward: and narrowing in breadth, from 330 miles in the south (in the line between Bambara and Neola) to the narrow space of 60 or 70 in the north, between Kaarta and Kajaaga; and probably diminishing to nothing, as it advances into the *Great Desert*; thus forming a great triangular space, whose vertex is on the north of the little kingdom of Kasson. This vast upland tract is divided into other degrees of level, of which the highest comprizes the eastern and largest part of the whole. The eastern boundary of this particular level, is, of course, that of the upper level, generally, in the part where it overlooks Kaarta and Bambara: and its termination, in the opposite quarter, is at a *great descent*, west of the principal branch of the Senegal river, in Woradoo; from which place, the edge of it may be conceived to run northward, to join *another descent* of the same kind, which forms the falls of *Govinea*, over which the great body of the Senegal river is precipitated, from this *upper* level, to the intermediate one.

The upper level contains the political divisions of Manding, Jallonkadu, Fooladu, Kasson, Gadou, and some other smaller states. And the second, or intermediate level, contains Bambouk, Konkadoo, Satadoo, Dentila, and some others; and is bounded on the south-west, by the great slope of country at Kirwanney, where the waters first begin to flow towards the west. On the north-west it is bounded by the great descent which forms the *second* or *lower* fall of the Senegal river, named F'low. This fall is about 30 miles below Govinea, 48 above Fort St. Joseph: and here the river being arrived at the lowest level of the country, continues navigable with little interruption to the sea.* The Falemé river of course, must run on a far lower level than the other heads of the Senegal river.

The Gambia has a small impediment to its navigation at Baraconda, in the country of Woolli; but although this is usually termed a *fall*, Mr.

* Labat, Vol. ii. p. 172. See his description of the navigation.

Park was informed that it did not impede the passage of canoes: so that it ought more properly to be termed a *rapide*, according to the *American* phrase; that is to say, a *slope*, down which the water runs, with more than ordinary rapidity, but which does not, however, totally impede the passage of canoes, or small boats.

The Joliba (Niger) descends from the high level of Manding, into Bambara, on the eastward, with a rapid and furious course, at Bammakoo, about 150 miles below its source; after which it glides smoothly along, and affords an uninterrupted navigation to Houssa, and probably by Kassina to Wangarah; by the two first of which places, a very large and navigable stream does certainly pass, under the same name as is applied by the Arabs and Moors to the Joliba, that is, Neel Abeed, or River of Slaves: a name that marks the idea of the people of the country through which it flows, in the minds of those people.

Mr. Watt was informed, when at *Teembo,* the capital of the FOULAH kingdom, in 1794, that in the way from thence to Tombuctoo, (concerning which his inquiries were pointed) a part of the road, lay along the side of a *Great Water,* to which they came in about thirty days from Teembo. There can be no question but that the *Great Water* was the *Joliba* river; whose very name, as we have said, in the Manding language literally imports the same meaning: or more properly, the *Great River.* Some have concluded that the Foulahs intended by it a great *inland sea*; but this is highly improbable, although there are, no doubt, such in other quarters of Africa, which serve as receptacles for those rivers which do not reach the sea. But, in the present case, the distance itself points to the Joliba; for, a month's journey from Teembo, would reach beyond Yamina, but fall short of Sego: and we are told from the same authority, that in order to go to Tombuctoo, they pass through the countries of Beliah, Bowriah, Manda, Sego, &c. Beliah, we know not the situation of, but may conceive it to lie on the north-east, or east-north-east of Teembo; because Mr. Park points out Bowriah, under the name of Boori, adjacent to Manding, which is obviously recognized in the Manda of Mr. Watt: and Sego, there can be no doubt about. What is farther said concerning the great breadth of the water, may either apply to the lake Dibbie, or may be African hyperbole. The sense appears clear enough.

I have extracted in a note, the intelligence concerning the Great Water: and also that, concerning the *Nyalas*. Mr. Park has also heard of the Nyalas, or *Gaungays*, but is clearly of opinion that the interpreter of Mr. Watt, either misunderstood the story, or was himself misinformed. *

* " I had a good deal of conversation with some men of a particular tribe of Mandingas called *Nyalas*. These are great travellers, and much respected by all the nations of Africa. It is from *this nation* that all the *Gaungays* or workers in leather, come; and they are likewise employed as the speakers on all embassies: as they are not only good orators, but are so far privileged, that no one, not even kings, can take offence at any thing they say. Any one who travels with them, is sure of being protected; and, to use their own terms, they can pass between contending armies, who will defer the battle till they have passed. I inquired about Tombuctoo." &c.—One of them said, that " about a month's journey beyond Teembo, we should come to a *large Water,* which our eyes would not be able to reach across; but which to the taste was sweet and good: that we should then coast along, touching at different towns for refreshment; but that there was one country inhabited by bad people, who would rob and murder us, if they could; where we should not stop, but keep far out, at a distance from the shore;" &c. They engaged to carry him thither for the price of *four slaves.* [Watt's Journal, MS. p. 181.]

CHAPTER III.

Construction of the Geography of Mr. Park's Expedition into Africa.

I NEXT proceed to the detail of Mr. Park's geographical materials. Should it be objected that I have been too diffuse and particular, in this part, I can only say, that since the information itself could not, from its nature be correct, it became the more necessary to investigate it closely, and also to place, not only the *result* but the *detail* of the investigation, together with the *original documents* themselves, in the form of notes, in the hands of the public, that the true grounds of the construction, might be known. For whether it may happen, that no further lights should ever be obtained, concerning the subject; or whether some other traveller, more *fortunate* (for he cannot possess more zeal, enterprize, temper, or firmness) should complete Mr. Park's work; in either case, the original documents, as well as the mode of working them up, should be recorded; in the *former*, that we may know how to *appreciate* them; in the *latter*, how best to *improve* them. The successor of Mr. Park, cannot have too extensive a knowledge of the detail of his predecessor's work; in order that he may know what parts require correction; and how to avoid delays, from a useless attention to objects, that are already attained.

Two new Maps have been constructed for the occasion. The one contains the PROGRESS OF DISCOVERY AND IMPROVEMENT in various parts of North Africa; the other, the GEOGRAPHY of Mr. PARK's EXPEDITION, as well as the result of his particular inquiries in the same quarter; on a more extended scale. The *present* remarks and discussions refer particularly to the latter.

In the construction of this map, it is first required to state those points, on which Mr. Park's *outset* depends; as also those which affect the position of Fort St. Joseph, near to which he passed; as they differ from the maps in present use. And, as some positions in the journey of Mess. Watt and Winterbottom, serve very much to aid the improvement of the geography, it will be proper to speak of them also.

Cape Verd, and Fort St. Louis, at the mouth of the Senegal river, are placed according to the observations and results of M. Fleurieu.*

Jillifrey, on the Gambia river is, from the mean of the longitudes set forth by D'Anville, D'Apres, and Woodville, and which do not differ amongst themselves, more than $4\frac{1}{2}$ minutes. †

The detail of the coasts, as well as the lower parts of the rivers between Cape Verd, and Cape Verga, are also from the charts of M. Woodville. That part between Cape Verd and latitude 18°, is adjusted to M. Fleurieu's result of longitude, whilst the particulars are from D'Anville and Woodville.

The course of the Rio Grande from the sea to the *break* near the river Dunso, is from Dr. Wadstrom's map. The Dunso river, crossed by Mr. Watt, appears evidently to be a continuation of the same river; several branches of which flow from the south-east. And the high tract of mountainous land beyond it, is no doubt a branch of the great ridge above commemorated, under the name of Komri, in the work of Abulfeda.

The route of Mr. Watt is described from a sketch communicated by the late Mr. BEAUFOY,‡ in which the scale appears, on a reference to the original journal, to be intended for *British* miles. I have regarded them

---

* That is, Cape Verd in latitude 14°.48′, longitude 17° 34′ west of Greenwich: St. Louis in latitude 16° 5′ (by D'Anville), longitude 16° 8′ by Fleurieu.

† D'Anville	16°	9′	30″	
D'Apres	16	5	0	Mean, 16° 7′
Woodville	16	8	3	

Latitude 13° 16′

‡ The public cannot but recollect the obligations due to this gentleman, on the score of his persevering industry, and laudable zeal, in the work of extending our knowledge of the interior parts of Africa. Accordingly his loss to society, in this department, is likely to be felt for some time, if not for ever: the researches in Africa being a path of his own choosing; a path which, more than any other person, he had contributed to open, and to render smooth; and in which he seemed destined to succeed!

accordingly; whence Laby and Teembo are placed much nearer to the coast, than Dr. Wadstrom's map represents: for it appears by the Journal, that Kissey, at the head of the river of the same name, is no more than eight journies from Teembo. Nor has the map more than 120 geographic miles between them, admitting the scale to be British miles, as I have concluded. *

The nearest point in Mr. Park's route falls at 112 G. miles to the northward of the extreme point of Mr. Watt's; and the river Gambia lay nearly midway between them. Thus, the map of Mr. Watt forms a most useful point of comparison; and adds confirmation to the report of the natives, respecting the course of the Gambia; for Mr. Park was told, that it was *crossed* in the way from the Falemé river, to Foota Jallo, of which Teembo is the capital.

Pisania, on the Gambia (called also Kuttijar Factory), the place of Mr. Park's outset† is stated by D'Anville to be 170 G. miles above Jillifrey, by the difference of longitude; but by M. Woodville's map, no more than 156; which answers better to the statement of the land journey; for Mr. Park was told that it was no more than $6\frac{1}{2}$ journies of a messenger. ‡

---

* Dr. Afzelius supposes that the town of Kissey may be, in direct distance, about 36 geographical miles to the north-east by east of Serra Leona. Hence, Teembo should be no more than 156 from Serra Leona. On the general map it is 170. I have adhered to the bearing lines on Mr. Watt's map; but think it probable that Teembo, and the whole route may be *more to the south.*

† This is the residence of Dr. LAIDLEY, a gentleman to whom Mr. PARK and the ASSOCIATION are under great obligations. He received Mr. Park into his house, and treated him more like a child of the family than a stranger. He cured Mr. Park of a serious illness, which confined him for many weeks: and when Mr. Park was disappointed of the goods necessary for his expences, which were to have been sent out with Consul Willis, the Doctor supplied him with every possible necessary, he had occasion for; taking his bills upon the Association for the amount.

‡ A journey of an ordinary traveller may be taken at about 17 geographical miles in direct distance; that of messengers in India, is equal to about 25, or 100 English miles by the road, in three days.

Pisania then, is placed in longitude 13° 28', according to this result; and in latitude 13° 35' north, according to Mr. Park's observation, by sextant.

The causes of the *apparent wanderings* of Mr. Park having been explained in the former part of this work, it will be no farther necessary to trace his course, than merely to explain the connection of the different parts of the *data* for the general construction.

Since the scale of the Map is fixed by the computed distances arising on the intervals of time employed in Mr. Park's route, it is possible that some readers may be startled at the idea of following such an apparently vague authority. Those, however, who have been much in the habit of observing their rate of travelling, will be easily convinced that distances *may be* approximated; and those in particular who have been much accustomed to travel in countries, where *time* regulates the *distance*; or who have been in habits of working up geographical materials of this kind, will be the most easily convinced. It will of course be understood, that calculations of this kind can only be received from persons of judgment and experience: and also, that when opportunities of checking them, occur, they are always resorted to; after which, of course, no alternative remains, but to adopt the corrected distance.

In the present case, the *rate of travelling of camels,* * does not apply; as Mr. Park's journey outwards was made on horseback, and his return chiefly on foot. Nor are camels, indeed, in use in that line of route. The checks to be employed, are the number of journies reported by the travelling merchants, from different points of Mr. Park's route to Sego and Tombuctoo; and also those from the quarters of Morocco, Tunis, and Fezzan, to Tombuctoo; using as a scale, the rate arising on the route between Fezzan and Egypt, Morocco and Jarra, as the *best known* lines of distance. These, altogether, furnish such kind of authority as will, I trust, lead to a satisfactory conclusion; as the general coincidence is certainly very striking.

My mode of procedure has been, to calculate, in the first instance,

* See Phil. Trans. for 1791.

d

Mr. Park's bearings and distances, and then to correct the bearings by his observed latitudes, as far as these extend : and beyond that, I have taken his bearing by compass, and allowed the *supposed quantity* of variation.

The result of these calculations, together with the addition of his line of distance from Sego to Tombuctoo, was then compared with the popular report of the distance between the several stations of Woolli, Fort St. Joseph, Bambouk, and Tombuctoo. It was found that these reports did not materially differ from the aggregate distance given by Mr. Park; although they fell short of it; a difference which might naturally have been expected, and which I have ventured to alter. The difference, however, does not exceed twenty-four geographic miles; a mere trifle in African geography. The position of Tombuctoo, so obtained, differs only half a degree in latitude, and still less in longitude, from that arising from the intersection of the lines of distance from Morocco on the N W, and Fezzan on the N E: of which a particular account will be given in the sequel.

A great part of Mr. Park's geographical memorandums are totally lost: but fortunately his bearings by compass during a great part of the way, are preserved. In other parts, he has preserved only the calculation of latitude and longitude, arising from them; which, however, of course furnish the means of obtaining the bearings, if necessary. As he omitted to take observations to determine the quantity of the variation of the compass, after he lost the means of correcting his course by observations of latitude, which was at Jarra, about midway in his route :* it becomes a question of some importance, what quantity to allow on those long lines of distance between Jarra and Silla; Silla and Manding.

It appears on inquiry, that the quantity of variation is no more known, any where *within* the continent of *Africa*, than within that of *New Holland*. And it happens moreover, that the *lines of equal quantities* of variation, do not run across Africa with that degree of regularity and parallelism, which takes place over great part of the Atlantic and Indian oceans (at least this is what appears clearly to my judgment) : so that it became necessary to inquire, what quantity prevails in the surrounding seas; and what the general

* The places of observation are marked on the Map by asterisks.

direction, as well as the *particular nature*, and *tendency*, of the curves, of the lines of equal quantities?

The variation lines on the globe have occupied a good deal of my attention at different periods of my life, and therefore the application of such new observations as the assiduity and kindness of my friends had procured for me on this occasion, was less difficult, than if the subject had been new to me. A dissertation on the subject, would be out of place here; and therefore I shall only give the result of my inquiries, in abstract; after premising, that the theoretical part belonging to the interior of Africa, is founded on a *supposed continuation* of those lines of equal quantities, whose *tendency* has been already ascertained, in the surrounding seas. I am perfectly aware, that some may regard the assumption as too great: but they will no doubt admit, at the same time, that it is difficult to conceive a more probable arrangement: and what is much more to the purpose, is, that if we are compelled to abandon the system, in the gross, the quantity of variation in the line of Mr. Park's travels, cannot be greatly different from what we have assumed. For, whether the line of 18° in the *south Atlantic*, be a continuation of that in the *north* Atlantic, or of that in the *Indian sea*, much the same result will follow: only that in the former case, the quantity will be somewhat greater.

It would appear, that between the East Indies and South America, Europe and South Africa, there are *four* distinct sets of what may be termed *concentric curves* of variation lines, on the globe, and whose highest points of convexity are opposed to each other, within the great body of Northern Africa. The accompanying sketch will best explain it.* It would appear moreover, that from the place of opposition of these curves, in Africa, where

---

* This sketch is not pretended to be minutely accurate; it being morally impossible to procure recent observations in every part, from the rapid change that takes place in the quantity of the variation, in one and the same spot. However, the observations that determine the course of the lines in the Atlantic (and which are marked on the sketch) are from observations so late as 1793. The same is to be said of those in the western quarter of the Mediterranean; and those beyond the Cape of Good Hope, to longitude 30° east, are of the year 1789.

It is obvious that a critical knowledge of the *quantity* of the variation in any particular

the quantity of variation is 18°, it *decreases* with great rapidity, and finally to nothing, in going *eastwards* to *India*, or *south-westward* to *south America :* and that from the same point, it *increases*, in going *N N W*, towards *Ireland*, or to the *opposite quarter*, towards the coast of *Caffraria*. But the change is not in any proportion so rapid in the *increase*, in going *north* or *south*, as in the *decrease*, in going *east* or *west*. Such are the outlines of this system; by which, if a person was to set out from Cape Verd, or Cape Blanco, to traverse Africa from W S W to E N E, to Upper or Lower Egypt, he would find at setting out, from $15\frac{1}{2}$ to $16\frac{1}{2}$ degrees of westerly variation, which would increase to 18° about the centre of the continent, and afterwards decrease to a less quantity than at his setting out. Mr. Park's travels being comprized between Cape Verd and the centre of Africa, will therefore be in the quarter that has from 16 to 18 degrees; and the part more particularly, where, from the want of observations of latitude, we must depend on his compass bearings, nearer 18° than 17°.* I shall now proceed to the detail of Mr. Park's materials.

Leaving Pisania, Mr. Park proceeded eastward to Medina,† the capital

place, and at a given time, is of less importance to the present question, than that of the *bearing* of the *lines* of equal quantities, at any *recent* period : and this object is, I think, tolerably well obtained, by the materials before me. Any change that may have taken place since 1793, is in favour of a greater quantity of variation, within the limits of Mr. Park's travels.

In the Atlantic, the increase appears to be about a degree in seven years. In the Indian ocean, less: and in the Red Sea, there seems to have been little alteration between 1762, and 1776.

The lines, as far as they are founded on *authority*, are *continuous* ; but *broken* in the parts *assumed*.

* It is in proof of the existence of this quantity of variation, that, on closing Mr. Park's route at Woolli, there appeared to be only a small deficiency of distance on the Map, when 17° variation were allowed. Had the quantity allowed been less, this ought not to have happened, as Jarra is placed according to its latitude.

† Major Houghton's point of outset in 1791 was Medina. His route falls into that of Mr. Park at several points, and finally branches off from it about 30 miles short of the Falemé river, which the Major crossed at Calcullo, near 20 miles higher up than Naye, where Mr. Park crossed it.

of Woolli; and thence to the E N E, through the countries of Bondou, Kajaaga, and Kasson; the two latter of which are separated by the river of Senegal.

In his way, he took observations of latitude at Kolor, Koorkoorany, and Joag, on this side the river: by which means we are enabled to correct the parallels. The *distance* at *present* is left as it stands in the Journal, with a view of correcting it afterwards. The result of these bearings and distances (the particulars of which appear below),* places Joag at 247 miles east of Pisania; and the latitude, by two different observations, was found to be 14° 25'. †

At Joag Mr. Park was informed that Dramanet, which is about $2\frac{1}{2}$

	Hours	G. Miles direct.	Bearings by compass.	Country	Lat. by obs.	REMARKS.
* Pisania to Jindey	- 6	- 16	- - SE by E	- - Yani	13° 35'	On these bearings 17° westerly variation were allowed. The diff. lat. was then 89; departure easterly 237. But the diff. lat. by obs. being only 50, the course should be E. 11¼ N. instead of E. 20½, as before; and the departure 247. But I have finally corrected the easting, by reducing it 24 miles, or to 223.
Kootacunda	5	13	E			
Tabajang -	2½	6	E ½ N			
Medina -	5¼	15	ditto			
Konjour -	3	8	E ½ S			
Mallaing -	2	6	E by S	Woolli		
Kolor -	5	12	ENE	- -	13° 49'	
Tambacunda	5¼	14	SE by E			
Kooniakarry	5	13	E by N			
Koojar -	3	9	E ½ N			
At a well -	13	34	E by N	Woods		
Tallica -	4	10	E			
Ganada -	4	10	E ½ N			
Koorkoorany	4½	12	ESE	- -	13° 53'	
Dooggi -	1	3	E by N			
Buggil -	4½	14	E ½ N	Bondou		
Soobroodka	7	18	E by N			
Naye - -	7	16	ENE			
Fattyacunda	3¼	7	ditto			
Kimmoo -	4½	12	ditto		14° 25	
Joag - -	6	16	E by N	Kajaaga		

† According to this result, Joag would be in longitude 9° 12', and Fort St. Joseph in 9° 21'; which is about 38 min. more easterly than M. D'Anville's Map of the Senegal allows: of which more in the sequel.

miles to the *eastward* of Fort St. Joseph, was 10 miles to the *westward* of him. That fort is said to be in 14° 34', or 9 min. north of Joag; so that it ought to lie to the north-west, rather than to the west: and accordingly, there is found, in the map in Labat,* a place named Gacouva, no doubt meant for Joag, on the SE of St. Joseph; and in point of distance answering to it. Other places in the same map of Labat, are also recognized in the route of Mr. Park; so that the connection between it and the French settlement on the Senegal, is very clearly made out; which is a circumstance of some importance in this geography.

It will appear that the *reckoning* kept by Mr. Park gave 89 min. difference of latitude between Pisania and Joag, whilst the observation gave 50 only. About 9 minutes may be placed to the account of *excess of distance*, and 30 will then remain, on the whole distance of 253 geographic miles. In other words, the *dead reckoning*, corrected by allowing 17 degrees of westerly variation, gave a course of E 20°½ N; which, however, by the observations of latitude, is shewn to be E 11°¼ N (or E by N) making a difference of 9¼ degrees. But this I regard as coming very near, considering the circumstances under which the reckoning was kept.

From Joag we accompany Mr. Park to Kooniakarry and Jarra. The reckoning between the two first gives about 23¼ min. difference of latitude, 55 of easting.† And hence the latitude of Kooniakarry will be 14° 48' by account; but the observation taken at Jumbo, in its neighbourhood, giving only 14° 34', the account is 14 to the north; equal to about a point and quarter in bearing. The same mode of correction has

*In Vol. iv. p. 92.

	Hours	G. miles direct.	Bearings by compass.	Lat. by observ.	Country.
† Joag to } Sammee }	7	18	E by N	14° 25' }	Kajaaga
Kayee -	3½	9	Ditto		
Teesee -	7½	18	NE by N	}	
Medina -	—	12	SE by E		Kasson
Jumbo -	—	12	Ditto	14° 34'	
Kooniakarry	—	3	E by S		

been applied here, as in the former part of the route; that is, the *whole distance* has been (for the present) allowed; with the difference of latitude by observation; and hence Kooniakarry will fall $59\frac{1}{2}$ geographic miles to the east of Joag.

The route from Kooniakarry to Jarra* may be divided into two parts; first, to Feesurah, a place of *observation*, south-eastward; and secondly, to Jarra, north-eastward.

The account to Feesurah agrees very nearly with the bearings and distance. The latitude by observation was $14°\ 5'$, and the easting from Kooniakarry, corrected, 47 miles. Then, to Jarra, the account also agrees very nearly; the latitude was $15°\ 5'$, that is, just one degree north of Feesurah; and the easting from thence 33 miles.

The aggregate of easting, between Joag and Jarra, is then $139\frac{1}{2}$ miles.†

It may be observed, that throughout this journey, generally, the reckon-

* The register of the bearings and distance between Kooniakarry and Jarra, being lost or mislaid, Mr. Park gave them from memory only; but the observations of latitude at two places within that space, were preserved, as well as the latitude by account at two other places.

	Hours	G. miles direct.	Bearings by compass.	Lat. by observ.	Country.
Kooniakarry to	—	—	—	14° 34′	
Soomo -	—	17	SE $\frac{1}{2}$ E		
Kanjee -	—	17	Do.	14° 10	Kasson
Leekarago -	—	8	Easterly		
Feesurah -	—	14	E by S	14° 5′	
Karancalla -	—	18	Easterly		
Kemmoo -	—	8	E by N		
Marina -	—	13	Northerly		Kaarta
Toordah -	—	8	Do.		
Funingkeddy	—	12	N by E $\frac{1}{2}$ E		
Simbing -	—	16	N by E		Ludamar
Jarra -	—	2	NNE	15° 5′	

† Equal to 144 min. of longitude; whence Joag being by account in long. 9° 12

Add 144 min. - - - 2 24

Long. of Jarra, by Mr. Park's original calculation - 6 48

ing has been to the northward of the observations; and that, by about *ten* degrees on the *whole* traverse, when 17 degrees of variation have been allowed. It will hardly be supposed that the difference arises from allowing too much variation by *ten* degrees; but it is singular, that the error should, in all cases but *one*, lie the same way. I do not by any means regard the error as considerable, circumstances considered:* nor is it of any consequence in the parts where the observations of latitude serve to correct it: as between Pisania and Jarra.

Mr. Park was plundered of his sextant at Jarra, which accident of course put an end to his observations of latitude; and thus, unfortunately, left the remaining *half* (very nearly) of his geography in a state of uncertainty, as to parallel. This point, therefore, must be regarded as the most advanced geographical station, that rests on any *certain basis* of parallel. However, the remaining part of the route will not appear to be much out, when it is seen how nearly the bearing of Sego, as determined by Mr. Park, agreed with the line of direction pointed out from Jarra.

It is, no doubt, a favourable circumstance, that the instrument was not lost at an earlier period, and before the commencement of the intricate route between the pass of the Senegal river and Jarra; to which may be added, the advantage of a *known parallel*, from whence to set off the very important bearing of Tombuctoo. In effect, the bearing was pointed out from Benowm, but this place being nearly east from Jarra, and the bearing in question E $\frac{1}{2}$ N, no error of any magnitude can be looked for.

Jarra (called also Yarra), has already appeared in the Maps drawn for the Association, and was originally taken from M. Delisle's Map; but was neglected, or overlooked, by M. D'Anville. In the former Map it was placed somewhat more to the west, and in a higher parallel by about $\frac{1}{4}$ of a degree.

Between Jarra and Wassiboo, Mr. Park's reckoning, as it appears wrought up in his table of day's works, gives 41 min. diff. of latitude N, and

† Mr. Carmichael came within 6 or 7 degrees in the bearing between Aleppo and Bussorah, on a distance of 720 British miles. But the advantages were prodigiously in his favour; the road being straight, the country open, and the camel walking an equable pace. (See Phil. Trans. for 1791.)

1° 31′ diff. longitude E ; which reduced to departure, in miles, is 89, and produces a course of E 26° S. But he allowed *no variation* after he left Jarra : and as I allow 17°, the course must be taken at E 9° S, distance 96½ geographic miles. From this arises a diff. lat. of 16′ only ; departure 95 : and, hence, Wassiboo should be in latitude 14° 49′, and 95 east of Jarra. *

Mr. Park was so lucky as to preserve his original bearings,† between

	Diff. Lat. S.	Diff. Lon. E.		N.	E.
*JARRA to			Doolinkeaboo - -	7	24
Queira - - -	11′	25′	Diggani § - -	19	8
Sherilla - -	14	40	Seracorro - -	5	9
Dama - - -	11	4	SEGO - -	6	3
Wawra - -	5	8	Lat. by account 13° 4′ ⎱	121 S	281 E
Dingyee - - -	—	7	Diff. lon. 4° 41′ E ⎰		
Wassiboo ‖ - -	—	7	Sansanding - -	10 N	15 E
Satile - - -	18	31	Sibiti - - -	—	7
Galloo - - -	1	21	Nyara - - -	3	16
Moorja - - -	4 N	14	Modiboo - -	3	19
Datiliboo - - -	9 S	38	Silla - - -	2	12
Fanimboo - - -	12	24	Lat. by account 13° 22′ ⎱	18 N	69 E
Jiosorra - - -	7	18	Diff. lon. 1° 9′ E - ⎰		

No variation was allowed in this calculation.

† Original bearings between Wassiboo ‖ and Diggani. §

Places.	Dist.	Bearings.
Wassiboo to		
Satile - - -	30	SE b E
Galloo - - -	20	ESE
Moorja - - -	15	E b N
Datiliboo - - -	25	SE b E
Fanimboo - -	35	ESE
Jiosorra - - -	20	ESE
Doolinkeaboo - -	15	SE b E
Lions - - -	18	SE b S
‡ Diggani - -	7	South

‡ On working these bearings over again, it appeared that Mr. Park had made a mistake ; and thence inferred a wrong position for Diggani, Sego, &c. in his table of latitudes and longitudes. I mention this, to shew that he has acted fairly, in exposing his whole process ; and even his errors.

e

Wassiboo, and Diggani (a place about 15′ short of Sego) ; and *these alone*, out of all that were taken during the route. These give a course of E $27°\frac{1}{2}$ S, 174 geographical miles ; so that when 17° of variation are allowed, the true course will be E $10\frac{1}{2}$ S ; the diff. lat. 31,7 ; departure 171,1 ; whence Diggani should be in lat. 14° 17′, and 266,1 east of Jarra.

Between Diggani and Sego (returning again to the table of latitude and longitude), Mr. Park's account gives E 43 S 15′ ; or corrected E 26 S, which gives diff. lat. 6,6 ; departure 13,5 : so that Sego, the capital town of Bambara, falls, by this account, in lat. 14° 10′ 30″ and 279,6 east of Jarra. *

In this position, it bears E $10\frac{1}{2}$ S from Jarra, distant 284 geographical miles. It is important to mention, that whilst at Jarra, the bearing of Sego was pointed out to Mr. Park by compass, E S E, or E $22°\frac{1}{2}$ S. His route made it E $27°\frac{1}{2}$ S, or 5° more to the south. This difference, so trifling in a distance of about 330 of our miles, on a straight line (in other words, the distance from London to Edinburgh), is not worth investigating. If we could suppose the report of the natives to be true, it would place Sego nearly 25 minutes more to the north. For my own part, I do not believe that any person, from mere judgment, unassisted by geographical records, and so far removed as to be out of the hearing of cannon, and of the view of con-flagrations (two circumstances that aid the most in fixing the line of direc-tion between distant places), could ever come nearer than *several* degrees of the bearing of two places that are 330 British miles asunder. †

Having at length reached the banks of the *long sought for* river NIGER (or JOLIBA), near which the city of Tombuctoo stands, Mr. Park pro-ceeded along it several days' journey, towards the city in question, on a course E $15\frac{1}{2}$ N by compass, but corrected E $32\frac{1}{2}$ N 70 G. miles ; which giving a diff. lat. of $37\frac{1}{2}$, departure 59, places Silla, the extreme point of his expedition, in latitude 14° 48′ ; and longitude by reckoning 0° 59′ west

* This being equal to 4° 47′ difference of longitude, Sego, by Mr. Park's reckoning, would lie in 2° 1′ west of Greenwich.

† The informant might possibly be influenced by the bearing of *that portion* of the road *nearest* to him, which is more *easterly* than the part towards Sego.

of Greenwich; but, as will be hereafter shewn, when corrected, 1° 24′ west. Here, then, terminates his journey eastward, at a point somewhat more than 16 degrees east of Cape Verd, and precisely in the same parallel. The line of distance arising from this difference of longitude is about 941 G. miles, or 1090 British, within the western extremity of Africa; a point which, although short by 200 miles of the desired station, Tombuctoo, the attainment of which would unquestionably have been attended with great *eclat*, was yet far beyond what any other European, whose travels have been communicated to the European world, had ever reached.*

* It may not be known to the generality of readers, that, in the former part of this century, Tombuctoo was as much the object of geographical research amongst the French, as it has been of late with the English. D'Anville was particularly anxious about it, as may be seen in the Mem. of the Academy of Inscrip. Vol. xxvi. p. 73.

CHAPTER IV.

The Construction of the Geography continued.

At Silla, Mr. Park was informed that Tombuctoo was yet fourteen journies of the caravan distant from him; and these he has calculated at 200
G. miles only, in a direct line from Silla; as it appears that a bend in
the course of the river, prevents a direct line of route towards it. As to the
bearing, he unfortunately could not, as at Jarra, obtain a consistent account
of it. The natives always pointed *along the general course of the river*;
although, as it may be supposed, it occasionally deviated to the right and
left. It has been seen, in the bearing of Sego, how nearly it was given by
judgment; but then the two cases differ very widely. The route is
entirely by *land*, from *Jarra* to *Sego*, by which the idea of the general line
of direction is better preserved, than when broken into so many small
parts, by a *river navigation*, the more ordinary mode of communication
(as it appears) between Silla and Tombuctoo. There were, no doubt,
people, could Mr. Park have been able to meet with them, who having
made the journey by land, could have furnished him with better information: but the reader, who already knows under what suspicious circumstances Mr. Park travelled in this quarter, will easily conceive that he
was precluded from any communication with *those*, who alone could have
given the information: that is, the *Moorish merchants*, and their dependants.

The bearing of Tombuctoo from Benowm, was pointed out to Mr.
Park, by a merchant of some consideration, who had resided at Walet,
and had visited both Tombuctoo and Houssa. But the *exceeding great
distance* of Tombuctoo and Benowm, (it being nearly twice the distance of
Sego from Jarra), will not admit such a degree of confidence in the report,
as to allow it to *supersede* all other authorities, however it may *aid* the task

of approximating the position. But, notwithstanding, it will appear, that on the whole, it coincides most wonderfully with the other *data*.

The bearing in question, pointed out at different times, was commonly E by S, by compass: and Mr. Park never found his informant vary more than half a point, which was to the southward; or E by S $\frac{1}{2}$ S. But the idea left on his mind, was E by S; which, allowing 17 degrees variation, is about east half north; or more correctly, E $5\frac{3}{4}$ N. And hence, admitting the distance of 200 G. miles between Silla and Tombuctoo, which supposes a space of about 500 such miles between Benowm and Tombuctoo, this latter would fall at about 50 minutes of latitude northward from Benowm (whose parallel is the same with that of Jarra, 15° 5'), and consequently in 15° 55'. The *obliquity* of the intermediate meridians, might increase the parallel some minutes, and we may call it roundly 16°.

Such then was the received opinion at Benowm, concerning the *parallel* of Tombuctoo: for, it will appear, that the distance on the *Rhumb*, which determines the difference of latitude, cannot be taken lower, than has been stated.

If the *general course* of the Joliba, after its escape from the mountains, may be admitted to have any weight in the determination of the question (since Mr. Park says, that they always pointed *along it*, to express the line of direction, in which Tombuctoo lay), this will point to a higher parallel, by about half a degree, than the bearing from Benowm; that is to $16\frac{1}{2}$ degrees. And, it may be remarked, that the difference between these results falls yet short of what would have arisen on an error of 5 degrees in the bearing; such as was experienced in that of Sego from Jarra.

Mr. Park was informed whilst at Benowm, that Walet, the capital of Beeroo, was ten journies distant, and this latter eleven journies short of Tombuctoo. According to Mr. Park's information, Walet stands at about 240 G. miles, to the eastward of Benowm; (which would require no less than 24 such miles per day, and appears out of rule, unless meant for journies of *couriers*, which is possible enough.) But what is most to our point, is, that by the information he received, concerning the position of Walet, it appears to lie from Benowm, in the same line of direction which points to Tombuctoo, when placed in 16½. Now, as Walet lies in the shortest route from Benowm to Tombuctoo, one might infer, of course, that it lies also the *nearest* to the line of direction towards Tombuctoo, of any of the places pointed out : and, I confess, I am strongly inclined to adopt the highest parallel, on this very account.

These alone, are the authorities for the position of Tombuctoo, derived from Mr. Park's observations and inquiries; and which differ, as we have seen, no more than half a degree in the parallel : that is, from 16°, to 16°½. The reader may recollect, that these are very far indeed to the southward of those assigned to it, by M. D'Anville and myself, in former publications; as we mistook its position so far, as to place it between 19°, and 20°.

Before I proceed to state the authorities for its position, derived from the northern stations, it will be proper to compare the calculation of distance made by Mr. Park, with the reports of merchants and travellers; in order finally to deduce the longitude of Tombuctoo from the west; and afford a fair ground of comparison, between the authorities from the opposite quarters.

It has appeared that Sego, *according to Mr. Park's calculation*, falls in latitude 14° 10', longitude 2° 1' west of Greenwich : and accordingly, the direct distance between it and Medina, the capital of Woolli, will be by this account 618 G. miles. Now, the merchants reckon 36 journies between them. The daily rate between Fezzan and Egypt having come out by construction 16,3* per day, on 53 days, and about 16¼ between Morocco and Jarra, on 50 days, I may venture to assume the highest of the two rates on 36 days; and this gives about 587, or only 31 short of Mr. Park's result.

Again, between Fort St. Joseph and Tombuctoo, M. D'Anville (Mem. Insc. Vol. xxvi. p. 73.) allows 240 French leagues. These are rated at 2,64 G. miles, or 23¾ to a degree, on his scale; consequently there results a distance of 634 G. miles. M. Lalande (Afrique, p. 23.) allows 250 leagues, which give about 660 miles. Ben Ali went from St. Joseph to Tombuctoo, by way of Tisheet and Aroan, in forty-eight days. The

* Strictly 16,292.

detour may be taken at eight days more than the direct road (for Mr. Park furnishes the positions of Tisheet and Aroan very satisfactorily), whence 40 remain, which at 16,3, produce 652 miles.

Lastly, although the following be a very vague kind of computation, it may not altogether be useless. Major Houghton's guide undertook to carry him to Tombuctoo, from Ferbanna in Bambouk, and to return again in ninety days. Ferbanna is much about the same distance, as St. Joseph, from Tombuctoo. Perhaps no more than ten days can well be allowed for rest and refreshment, and then forty days will be the length of the journey.

The mean of the three first reports, is about 649 : and on the Map, the space between St. Joseph and Tombuctoo, according to Mr. Park's result, is 667, or 18 more.

There is then, a difference of 31 only, on the accounts between Woolli and Sego : 18, between St. Joseph and Tombuctoo : both pointing to an excess, on the part of our traveller. I am however far from offering these results, on the ground of inducing a belief that such *small differences* can be *ascertained* by such *coarse* materials; but rather to shew that in the general scope of the authorities, there was more of coincidence, than of disagreement, if the circumstances are rightly appreciated.

As it appears, however, that Mr. Park and Major Houghton formed different estimates of the distance between Medina and the river Falemé ; and that the former exceeds by about 36 miles; and moreover, that on Mr. Park's return by the southern route, he found by the number and scale of his journies, that he had allowed too great an extent to the space between the rivers Falemé and Gambia ; I say, it clearly appears that an excess may be admitted in this part. It may be added, that, according to the report of the African travellers, at Pisania, concerning the arrangement of the journies, there is an excess on the west of Kasson ; whilst the space on the east of it, agrees pretty well. Or, strictly speaking, perhaps the space is a *little under*-rated on the east, and *much over*-rated on the west. If the mean of the differences between Pisania and Tombuctoo, Fort St. Joseph and Tombuctoo, 31, and 18, that is, 24 miles be taken off, the result will be satisfactory ; as it agrees pretty well with the excess found in the southern route, on Mr. Park's return.

This naturally leads me to the discussion of the position of Fort St. Joseph, as a point connecting the upper and lower part of the Senegal river: or in other words, the routes of the French, *below*, with those of the English, in the *interior* of the country.

The French report concerning this position also points to an excess of distance from the westward; even more than that arising from the difference between Mr. Park's reckoning and the reports of the merchants; for it amounts to about 37 miles.

Could it be ascertained that a measured survey of the Senegal river, to the height of Fort St. Joseph, had been taken, as Labat says (Vol. ii. p. 157.) was actually done, by the order of the Sieur Brüe, this would settle the matter at once. But *cursory* surveys have so often been called *actual* and *measured* ones, that one must be in possession of better authority, before the survey of the Senegal river can be relied on, as an absolute measure of distance. Nor is there, in the list of places in the *Con. de Temps*, any intimation of the longitude of St. Joseph by triangles, or measurement. Here follows a statement of the means used in fixing the position of this place.

M. D'Anville, in his map of the Senegal and Gambia rivers (1751) places St. Joseph 7° 44′ east of Ferro, which being in 17° 37′ west of Greenwich, Fort St. Joseph should be in 9° 53′. This is 32′ to the west of the position arising on Mr. Park's route; which gives 9° 21′. But M. D'Anville supposes a difference of longitude of 6° 9′ 15″ only, between Fort St. Louis, at the mouth of the Senegal river, and Fort St. Joseph: and as I have followed M. Fleurieu's ideas in placing St. Louis in 16° 8′ longitude, St. Joseph of course falls in 9° 59′, rejecting the seconds; making a difference of 37 G. miles, or 38 min. from Mr. Park; that is, 13 miles more than the mean of the differences between the authorities for the position of Tombuctoo. *

* It is proper to remark that M. D'Anville took the longitude of Cape Verd 18½ min. more to the east, in respect of Ferro, than M. Fleurieu: and Fort St. Louis, more to the west in respect to Cape Verd, by 10¼ min.

M. D'Anville moreover, allows no more than 3° 2′ 30″ diff. lon. between Pisania and Fort St. Joseph, which by the *corrected distance* of Mr. Park, is no less than 3° 42′.

It is obvious, that as neither St. Louis nor Jillifrey, are exactly determined, in respect of Cape Verd, or of each other, it would be idle to
attempt a critical adjustment of them; and therefore I have adopted the
position arising from Mr. Park's route, corrected by 24 miles, or 25 min. of
longitude, more to the west; so that Fort St. Joseph stands in the map in
lon. 9° 46′, lat. 14° 34′.

In consequence of this correction, all the eastern positions, Joag, Jarra,
Sego, &c. must of course *recede* 25 minutes to the westward of the arrangement heretofore made, on the construction of Mr. Park's geographical
materials. Hence I place

Joag, in 9° 37′ west, instead of 9° 12
Jarra, in 7 13 ———— 6 48
Sego, in 2 26 ———— 2 1
Silla, in 1 24 ———— 0 59
And Tombuctoo, in 1 33 east, ———— 1 58*

I now proceed to state the reports of the distance to Tombuctoo, from
the NW, N, and NE.

From Tatta † on the southern frontier of Morocco, 9½ journies to the
SSE of the capital, (equal to 157 G. miles) the distance is 50 journies of
he caravan, according to Mr. Matra.

From Mourzouk, the capital of Fezzan, (taken to be in latitude 27° 48′
and longitude 15° 3′ east, or directly south of Mesurata), 64 journies, according to the report of Ben Ali. And from Tunis, 77 journies, through
Kabes and Gadamis, according to Mr. Magrah.

On the route between Mourzouk and Cairo, as well as between Morocco
and Jarra, it has been already stated (p. xxxviii), that 16,3 and 16,25 were
the mean rates: and the former was accordingly adopted between Woolli
and Sego. At the same rate, the 50 days from Tatta, give 815 G. miles, and
the 59½ from Morocco, 970. The 64 from Mourzouk give 1043; and
the 77 from Tunis, 1255.

---

* The latitudes remain as they were.

† For further particulars respecting Tatta, see Afr. Assoc. Q.; p. 225: and O. 333.

Now the above assumed position of Tombuctoo, falls exactly at the given distance from Morocco through Tatta; and 18 short of that from Fezzan (Mourzouk); but 61 beyond that from Tunis. The coincidence therefore of the three lines of distance from the Gambia, from Morocco and Fezzan, may be regarded as complete, since, in using the same rate nearly across the whole continent of Africa, from Cape Verd to Egypt, a difference of 18 miles only, arises. And hence, the public mind may well be satisfied at present respecting this important position. Whichsoever of the two determinations may be right, is of little consequence: but I hold it to be more prudent to adhere to that line which is the result of computation in detail, and corrected as above, than to the long lines given in the aggregate, and in which there is more risk of error. And thus I close the subject of the position of Tombuctoo; placing it in latitude 16° 30′, longitude 1° 33′ east of Greenwich.

Something, however, is proper to be said, concerning the rate of travelling adopted on the present occasion, as it differs materially from that allowed on long lines of distance, in the Proceedings of the Association, in 1790. I there allowed $16\frac{1}{2}$ for a single day, but diminished the rate according to the *length* of the lines of distance. It would appear that the proportion of diminution allowed, although proper enough in countries, where obstacles interpose to change the line of direction, is not applicable to that part of Africa, where the great Deserts are crossed in so straight a line, as hardly to increase the *simple* winding, arising on each day's course, in any considerable degree; and that even the *simple* winding is less than elsewhere. And hence $16\frac{1}{4}$, or more, arises on the camel routes, on long lines of distance, across the Desert; and on the pilgrims' routes, where it appears the camels travel with light burthens. It was through misconception of this rate, that I placed Tombuctoo, so far to the north. I am ignorant of the cause of M. D'Anville's error.

The particulars of the geography between Silla and Tombuctoo, are copied exactly from Mr. Park's map; and require but little elucidation. Jinné, a large town, is two short journies below Silla: and Tombuctoo, twelve still lower down. It would appear that all the journies were conceived to be *short*, as Mr. Park allows only 200 G. miles for the aggregate of the 14.

Two days below Jinné, the Joliba expands itself into a considerable lake, already mentioned by the name of Dibbie; from whence the river again issues in a number of streams. These unite at a lower point, and then form *two* large branches, which separating widely from each other, form an island near 100 miles in length, whose name being Ginbala, or Jinbala, we recognize in it, the Guinbala country of M. D'Anville; as in the northern branch of the river that bounds it, the river of Guin, mistaken by him for the original head of the Tombuctoo river (or Niger); as he also mistook the lake of Dibbie for that of the Senegal river. Such were the errors in the African geography, to the date of the AFRICAN ASSOCIATION: one of which errors conducted the *Senegal* river through 500 miles of the space which is, in reality, occupied by the *Niger*.

The position of Houssa will be adjusted in the map of Africa.

The important station of Tombuctoo, being adjusted, together with the positions dependent on it, I proceed with Mr. Park, on his return by the south, to his original point of outset in the west : taking it up at Sego, by which he passed in his way.

Along this line, an account of the bearings by compass was kept, as well as circumstances would permit, until the instrument was rendered useless, by robbers, near Sibidooloo. This was, however, the most important part of the route, as it lay along the side of the Joliba, the knowledge of whose course is, by this means, prolonged to about 350 British miles. Mr. Park moreover committed to paper, a tracing of its general windings; and obtained notices respecting the place of its source, during his long residence at Kamaliah, in the country of Manding, (commonly called Mandinga.)

Kamaliah is about 40 G. miles SW of Sibidooloo;* and to this place Mr. Park contrived to extend his line of bearings from Sego. He also learnt, that Jarra lay ten journies to the north-westward of Kamaliah; which agrees satisfactorily to the result from Sego, as it leaves 154 G.

* It lies nearly midway between the Joliba and Senegal rivers.

miles, for the ten journies; and Kamaliah itself falls in lat. 12° 46'; 227½ from Sego, in a direction of W 21 S; corrected by the allowance of 17° variation.

The town of Bammako, where the Joliba first becomes navigable (or perhaps to which point it is navigable upwards, in a continuous course from Tombuctoo), lies about fifty miles short of Kamaliah.* It is reckoned by the natives, ten journies only from Sego. †

At Kamaliah the source of the Joliba (or Niger), was pointed out to Mr. Park, at a bearing of south, a very little west, seven journies distant; and for these, he allows 108 G. miles. The name of the place is Sankary, and seems meant by the Songo of D'Anville; which, however, he supposed to be at the source of the Gambia river, in the kingdom of Mandinga. Such were the crude ideas heretofore entertained of this geography.

Here it may be proper to mention, that Mr. Park, whilst at Kooniakarry, in Kasson, in his way out, meditated a route to the south-eastward, through Kasson, Fooladoo, and Manding; which route was to have brought him to the Joliba in twenty days. The place on the Joliba is not mentioned: possibly it might be Yamina. This route, however, he was not permitted to take. Had he pursued it, his personal sufferings might probably have been less; but our knowledge of the geography would probably have been less, also.

It has been mentioned, that the space between Jarra and Kamaliah, is checked by the report of the road distance between them. It is proper also to state, as a further proof of the consistency of the respective positions of Jarra and Kong, that the distance across, agrees generally with the report of the Shereef Imhammed, who says, that Yarba, (meant for Yarra, or Jarra,) is eighteen to twenty days journey to the NW of Gonjah, meaning Kong. (Proc. Af. Assoc. chap. xii.) Mr. Park was told that

* Bammako, by Mr. Park's original bearings, lies from Sego W 8° S, 178 G. miles: and Kamaliah W 7°½ N, 51½. These are corrected to W 25° S, and W 9°½ S.

† Perhaps the long journies of the slave caravans, such as Mr. Park experienced, to the westward of this place.

Kong, was ten journies to the southward, or SSW of Sego; and he saw a part of the great ridge of *blue mountains* of Kong, as he coasted the Niger westward. These notices agree well with the Shereef's report.

Between Kamaliah and Woolli, there is yet a greater degree of uncertainty respecting the *data* for the geographical construction; for in this long line of near 400 geographical miles, the line of direction is collected from the places of the sun and stars; the compass being useless, whilst the traveller was in motion. Besides, the rapidity of the march, and the height of the woods, were unfavourable to any attempts of that kind, had bodily fatigue and hunger, left him either the inclination or the ability: for, in effect, it was one long forced march through the Jallonka Wilderness, under the terrors of famine, or being left behind to perish, by wild beasts.

Under such circumstances, it was full as much as could reasonably be expected, to obtain some general idea of the line of direction, on which he travelled; together with the proportional lengths of the several intervals, by keeping an account of the time; leaving the *absolute scale* to be determined by the extent of the space. In this, he succeeded so well, that the middle part of the line, when produced to the capital of Woolli, appears to be no more than half a point out of the bearing; as is shewn by Labat's map of Bambouk (Vol. iv. p. 92), in which the course of the river of Falemé, which Mr. Park crossed in his way home, as well as out, is described; and affords much assistance in adjusting his position on that river, on his return.

It is first necessary to state, that M. D'Anville, in his map of Senegal, &c. (1751) has totally disregarded the scale of Labat's map, as well as most of the bearings in it; having preferred to it some other authority; perhaps some tracing of the two rivers. M. D'Anville allows no more than thirty-seven geographical miles between the two passes Naye and Kayee on the Falemé and Senegal rivers; when Mr. Park allows sixty-two. Now Labat's scale agrees with the latter: for he allows 28¾ French leagues for this interval, equal to 2,16 geographical miles per league, according to Mr. Park's calculation. The leagues were therefore probably of road measure: as a league in direct distance appears to be equal to 2,64. Hence M. D'Anville, seems to have misconceived the matter; and has applied the same erroneous scale to the course of the Falemé river, upwards; which he has shortened by about twenty-six geographical miles; carrying that part no higher than to latitude 13°, which by the original (or rather the proportioned) scale, should be extended to 12° 34'.

This Map of Labat, then, gives the position of Ferbanna on the Falemé river; * as also the southern boundaries of Bondou and Bambouk, with other particulars. Mr. Park, when at the pass of the Falemé river, between Satadoo and Medina,† obtained some general notices concerning his position, in respect of the above points. For he learnt that Ferbanna (Tenda) lay at some distance lower down the river: that Bondou (by the account of a fellow-traveller who was on his way thither) lay six journies to the northward; and he learnt also the general position of Bambouk. To this may be added, that he kept on his right hand (to the N), and even touched the foot of it at Dindi-koo, a ridge of mountains, answering to that which, in Labat's map, crosses the Falemé *above* Ferbanna; and which is also found precisely at the corresponding point, with Dindikoo. Moreover, it preserves in Labat, the same distance from the southern boundary of Bambouk, as that seen by Park. And finally, it appears, by the description of the southern route pointed out by the King of Bambouk (see Mem. 1793, p. 11.), that Mr. Park passed to the *southward* of Ferbanna, and yet *not far* from it. For the king's road from Ferbanna (Tenda) led eastward, through Concoudou (the Konkodoo of Park, a province) as also through Silloumana, Gangaran, Gadou, and Manding. Now there is every reasonable proof that (bating Ferbanna) this is the very route by which Mr. Park returned. His route went through Gangaran (Gankaran), on the one hand, Konkodoo on the other. Sillou-Mana is very probably intended for Kullo-Manna,‡ a famous pass over the *Black River,*

---

* Not the Ferbanna of Bambouk, at which Major Houghton resided ; but Ferbanna Tenda, through which the King of Bambouk described the southern route of the Slatees to lead, from Woolli to Manding. (See Mem. Af. Assoc. 1793 ; p. 11.)

† There are several places of this name. The one in question lies to the south of Bambouk.

‡ Kullo is a province of Jallankadoo, occupying both banks of the Ba-fing, or Black River ; and Manna the name of the town. [Park.]

or main stream of the Senegal, where a bridge of a very singular construction is thrown across occasionally, for the use of the caravans. It is unlikely that bridges should occur at *two* places in the southern route, and more particularly as the one at Manna is placed there, because the steep rocky banks, and narrow channel of the river, are peculiarly adapted to that kind of bridge.

It may therefore be concluded, that from Konkodoo, the king's road, instead of turning to the S W to Satadoo, leads straight on to the westward to Ferbanna, and thence into the Woolli road, either at Baneserile or Kirwanny; being a branch, only, of the great southern road, leading directly across the mountains; whilst the other makes a bend to the south, to avoid them; which bend, according to Mr. Park's description of his route, is so much like that in Labat's map above Ferbanna, that I cannot help suspecting the Dambanna of Labat to be meant for the Dindikoo of Mr. Park. I return to the construction of the route.

Ferbanna, in Labat, is placed 33 leagues on a bearing of S 11° E from Cacullo, another pass on the same river Falemé, in latitude 13° 54′, by Major Houghton's observation: and which is about 20 miles south of Naye, where Mr. Park crossed it in his way out. The 33 leagues according to the *proportional* scale furnished by Mr. Park's route (2,16 each) give $71\frac{1}{4}$ G. miles for the distance of Ferbanna from Cacullo: or latitude 12° 46′. From this point, Labat describes the course of the river 24 miles higher up, in a S E by E direction. About this place, we may suppose that Mr. Park crossed the Falemé on his return; since it agrees with the circumstances of the mountains, the bend of the road above described, and the distance of Bambouk and Bondou; to which may be added, the general accordance of the bearing from Manding. Medina, a village, stood on the west bank of the Falemé, at the pass; and Satadoo, the capital of the province, at two miles to the eastward of it. It is certain that neither Satadoo, nor Konkodoo, appear in Labat's map. In that, Macanna is the name of the country bordering on the south of Bambouk; but Mr. Park calls it Konkodoo, which means the *country of mountains*; and appears very characteristic. (These mountains extend through Bambouk and Kasson, and are productive in gold.) Again, Combregoudou in Labat, occupies the places of Satadoo and Dentila in Mr. Park's descriptions: and we must therefore conclude, that either these countries have more than one name, or have changed their names in the course of the century.

On the whole, it cannot well be doubted that the adjustment of the southern route, to the northern, in this place, is tolerably exact; and it is indeed a matter of the first importance to the geography. One circumstance is very much in its favour: at Kirwanny on this route Mr. Park was told, that the course of the Gambia river lay three journies southward, or one journey within the boundary of Foota-Jallo: and Dr. Afzelius was informed, that the same river runs at the distance of four journies from the mountains which skirt the Rio Grande on the north-east. These notices accord perfectly with the relative positions of Kirwanny, and the course of the Rio Grande, which are about 112 G. miles asunder, on the construction.

This adjustment, moreover, goes as well to the proportioning of the longitudinal distance, on the line between Kamaliah and Woolli, by means of the course of the river Falemé, extended from a known point in the northern route.

On Mr. Park's original map, I find 201 G. miles on that portion of the southern line, east of the Falemé river; 181 on the west: whilst the respective intervals on my construction, are 211, and 185. But Mr. Park observed, that there was a greater portion of distance to be travelled through, on his return, than he had expected. His reckoning was, according to the sea phrase, *ahead of the ship:* which was, no doubt, occasioned by his omitting to take the variation of the compass into the account, after he had lost his sextant at Jarra.

It appears on the examination of his journal, that between the river Falemé and Baraconda, in Woolli (a few miles short of Medina), they employed nine whole days, and part of a tenth; a great part of which journey lay through the wildernesses of Tenda and Simbani. Six of the days are remarked to be either *long* or *very long:* and one in particular was a *very hard day's work.* Allowing six miles for the fraction of the day, the nine whole ones require 19 G. miles of direct distance, each: and as the road diverged considerably from the *direct line* (to the southward, falling in with the Gambia pretty high up) they may be taken somewhat higher. The five forced marches through the Jallonka wilderness are also calculated at 19 each, direct: and which may produce 25 road miles: I should conceive those through the Tenda and Simbani wildernesses to be equal to 26, at a medium; and some of them more than 30.*

Thus I have brought the grand outline of Mr. Park's Geography to a conclusion; and cannot do otherwise than sympathize with him in his feelings, when he arrived at " *the hospitable door of* Dr. LAIDLEY," at Pisania, after an absence of eighteen months, unheard of, during the whole time; whether enjoying the triumphs of exploring new paths; whether pining in hopeless captivity, amongst the barbarous Moors of Jarra; or fostered by the kind hands of Mandinga Negroes.

It remains that something should be said regarding the connection of Mr. Park's Geography with that of Labat, between the rivers Senegal and Falemé; as well as concerning the positions of the *falls* of the Senegal river.

Labat's scale has already been adjusted to Mr. Park's, in p. xlv, where 2,16 G. miles were found equivalent to one of Labat's leagues, in direct distance.

Kayee, the pass on the Senegal river, where Mr. Park crossed it, is given at 16¾ leagues above Fort St. Joseph, in Labat's Map, (Vol. iv. p. 92.) and the falls of F'low (Felou in Labat), 5½ still higher up. Kayee may therefore be taken at 36 miles, and F'low 48, above St. Joseph; the bearing a *point or more* to the southward of east.

F'low is the *lower* fall, (below which the river continues navigable generally, to the sea,) and Govinea, the *upper* fall. The distance between them is very differently represented, by different persons; but I believe, is from 12 to 14 leagues, perhaps 30 G. miles, direct. It is true that Labat says,

* Mr. Park seems to reckon 18 G. miles, in a direct distance, a long journey: and 16 to 17 seems to have been his ordinary rate, when left to himself. This is also the ordinary rate of travelling, with those who perform journies on foot, or with loaded beasts.

in more than one place,* that they are 40 leagues asunder; but as his Map (in Vol. iv. p. 92.) has less than 12 leagues; and as M. P. D. also says (p 78.) 12 leagues: and as, moreover, the King of Kasson's residence is said to be *midway between* the two falls; and that residence appearing to be Kooniakarry, a place visited by Mr. Park; and which is no more than about 22′ from the lower fall, and at 13′ distant from the north bank of the river; it cannot well be otherwise than that the two falls are within 30 G. miles of each other. And hence it may be concluded, that *quatorze* and not *quarante*, was in the original manuscript.

The distance between Kooniakarry and the Senegal river, 13 miles, points to a WNW course, or thereabouts, of the river between the falls; not much different from its general course, lower down. But as the Ba-fing, or principal arm of this river, must run almost directly to the north, from the place where Mr. Park crossed it, in Jallonkadoo, it is highly probable, that the two great branches unite at no great distance above the upper fall; for the same ridge of mountains that occasions the fall, may, perhaps, occasion a junction of the different streams above it.

These falls are said by Labat to be from 30 to 40 *toises* perpendicular; or 180 to 240 French feet. We must recollect that P. Hinnepen states the fall of Niagara at 600 feet, which subsequent accounts have reduced to 150.† The reader will, however, find very curious descriptions of these falls, and of the river itself, in Labat, Vol. ii. p. 156, 160.

---

* Vol. ii. p. 156. Vol. iii. 290 and 358.

† See Ellicott's Letter in Europ. Mag. Vol. xxiv.

CHAPTER V.

Construction of the New Map of North Africa.*—New Arrangement of the Course of the Nile—Its distant Fountains yet unexplored by Europeans. —A central Position in Africa, determined.—Edrisi's Line of Distance, consistent.—Errors of Leo.

IN order that the reader may be enabled to judge of the improved state of the new map of NORTH AFRICA, I shall set before him a list of the

* Table of the principal latitudes and longitudes in the Map.

	In the map.		By M. Fleurieu.	Con. de Temps.	Bruce.
	Latitude.	Longitude.	Longitude.		
*Cadiz - - -	36° 21′ N	6° 19′ W	6° 19′		
C. Spartel - -	35 48	5 57	6 2	5 54	
C. Cantin - -	32 33	9 15	9 11		
C. de Geer - -	30 28	9 54	10 31	9 53	
C. Bajador - -	26 20	14 17	14 49	14 28	
*I. Ferro - - -	27 51	17 37	17 37		
C. Blanco -	20 47	16 58	16 58		
*C. Verd - -	14 48	17 34	17 35		
†C. Palmas - -	4 30	7 41			
†I. St. Thomas -	0 18 N	6 37 E			
Tunis - -	36 44	10 20			
Tripoly -	32 54	13 15	— —	13 20	
Mourzouk - -	27 48	15 3			
*Suez - -	30 2	32 28			
Cairo - -	30 3	31 20	— —	31 29	
Koseir - -	26 8	34 8	— —	— —	*31 4
Sennar - -	13 35	33 30 30″			
Source of the Nile in Abyssinia }	10 59	36 55	— —	— —	*36 55
†C. Guardafui -	11 43	51 12			
Syene - -	24 —	33 30	— —	— —	*33 30

* The longitudes thus marked, are from celestial observation, either at the place, or in the vicinage.

† From timekeepers: the two first by Capt. Price, the latter by Capt. Richardson.

authorities, together with an outline of the construction. To enter into a detail of both, would require a volume: I shall therefore barely *specify* the authorities for the sea coasts, and for such parts of the interior as have been aforetimes described by geographers; and confine the *detail* to modern discoveries, and to such parts, as those discoveries have helped to improve: and more especially to the points which determine the courses of the Niger and Nile.

The western and southern coasts, from the Strait of Gibraltar to the Equator, have been newly constructed for the present purpose. M. Fleurieu's authorities have been followed in respect of Cape Verd, Cape Blanco, and the Canary Islands. The coasts of Morocco and Fez, rest on the authority of Don Tofino's charts, in the Spanish atlas: and between Morocco and Cape Blanco, various authorities have been admitted, in the different parts: as it appeared to me, that M. Fleurieu had not rightly conceived the position of Cape Bajador.

The coasts on the south and east of Cape Verd, are drawn in conformity to the ideas of Captain Price. This gentleman, in the Royal Charlotte East India ship in 1793, had an opportunity of adjusting the longitudes of some important points; which longitudes Mr. Dalrymple applied to the correction of the existing charts of the coast, and with his accustomed liberality and zeal for the improvement of science, permitted me to avail myself of the use of these corrections, previous to his own publication of them, in a different form. It is to the same invaluable Journal of Capt. Price, that I am indebted for some of the most important notices respecting the variation of the compass, along the coast of Guinea, &c.; and without which notices, the approximation of the quantity of variation in the interior of Africa, could not have been accomplished. (See above, page xxvi.)

The result is, that the coast of Guinea has several degrees *more* of *extent* from east to west; and that the breadth of South Africa at the Equator, is *less*, than M. D'Anville had supposed.

No alteration has been made in the coasts within the Mediterranean, save in the form and position of the Gulf of Alexandretta, and the adjacent coasts.

The Red Sea, or Arabian Gulf, as well as the *whole* course of the Nile, have been re-constructed for the present purpose. For the former, a great collection of new materials has been furnished by Mr. Dalrymple. This includes a new chart of the whole Gulf by Captain White, made in 1795 : but I have not followed either *that* or any other *single* authority *throughout* : but have made such alterations as appeared to be warranted, on an examination and comparison of the different materials.

The upper part of the Gulf, between Suez and Yambo, is however, preserved entire, as Capt. White drew it.

The position of the Gulf, is thus adjusted :

Capt. White, by two observations of eclipses of Jupiter's first satellite, found the longitude of Suez to be 30° 28′ 30″ east of Greenwich : and a mean of 76 lunar observations differed less than a minute from the former.

The difference of longitude between Suez and Mocha, near the entrance of the Gulf, is, by the mean of five different accounts, 11° 4′, which added to 32° 28′ gives 43° 32′ for the longitude of Mocha : and which is nearly a mean between the different results, by timekeepers. But until a greater number of celestial observations are taken at the mouth of the Gulf, its position cannot be deemed exact.

Cape Guardafui, is placed by *timekeeper* observations, in 51° 12′ longitude : 11° 43′ of latitude.

The adjustment of the lower part of the course of the Nile, to the shores of the Red Sea, differs very much from M. D'Anville's map. He supposed that the Nile, in its course from the lower Cataract (near Syene) to Cairo, gradually approached towards the Arabian Gulf : but late observations shew that it runs nearly parallel to it, throughout that extent, which is about 7 degrees of latitude. Hence the distance across, between the port of Kosire and Ghinna, on the Nile, is much less than M. D'Anville supposed; he having allowed about 110 G. miles, although 90 is about the truth.*

It may be proper to state, that the line between Kosire and Ghinna is by no means the *shortest*, that can be drawn between the Nile and the Red

* Mr. Bruce reckoned 44½ hours of the caravan (with camels) between Kosire and Kuft (that is Coptos), near Ghinna : Mr. Irwin 46 from Kosire to Banute, situated at

Sea, because it runs *obliquely* between them. The distance appears to be no greater than 72 miles on an E N E course, from Ghinna to the nearest part of the coast.

Cairo, by the mean of several accounts, is about 59 G. miles to the west of Suez, equal to 1° 8′ of longitude.† So that Cairo should stand in

the Nile, at five hours above Ghinna. The camel's rate is 2½ British miles by the road: consequently less than two G. miles in direct distance.

M. Savary had much the same idea of the distance; for he reckons it 33 French leagues. (Vol. ii. letter z.) But his map has 70 G. miles only: Pocock's 90.

Mr. Irwin reckons the bearing WNW from Kosire to Ghinna; doubtless by compass. The variation might be 13 to 14 degrees; whence Ghinna would bear W 9° N from Kosire: Banute, which is stated to be about five hours to the south of Ghinna, will therefore by this account bear 1°½ N of W from Kosire. Mr. Irwin was certainly very near the mark; though a little too much northerly. It appears that Banute is in lat. 25° 47′ 30″ in D'Anville, and is 8 min. N of Negada; at which place, Mr. Bruce observed the latitude to be 25° 53′ 30″. Consequently D'Anville is 14 min. too far south in this part. Apply this to Banute, and we have 26° 1′ 30″. Kosire lies in 26° 8′, and Banute is then to the south of it, in reality, by several minutes. At Syene, Mr. Bruce's latitude is 11 min. north of D'Anville's. Not to go into extremes, I have taken Banute at 5 min. S of Kosire, Ghinna 3 min. N of it; or 26° 11′. D'Anville places Ghinna in 26° 1′. It was of importance that these parallels of the places should be adjusted.

† The principal authorities are the following:

M. Niebuhr reckoned between Suez and the Lake of the Pilgrims, situated at 6,9 G. miles E 38 N from Cairo, - - - - - 28ʰ 40ᵐ

M. Volney, - - - - -		29 —
Dr. Pocock, - - - - -		29 15
	mean	28 58
Add from the Lake to Cairo, as it is usually reckoned, -		3 —
	or say 32 hours	31 58

But as there are (besides the just mentioned 3 hours, in a direction of about 40° from the general line of direction) 3¼ hours more between Suez and Ajerud, at much the same angle, a considerable reduction of the direct distance must take place, probably about 1¾ hour: whence there remains 30¼. And as Dr. Shaw states the general report of the distance to be 30 hours, it may be conceived that this is the actual distance, by the *shortest* route, which leaves the Lake and Ajerud to the north. And for these, 59 G. miles direct may be allowed. M. D'Anville allowed 60.

31° 20′. The *Con. de Temps* has 31° 29′; but it is probable that Suez is the best determined of the two places.

Mr. Bruce had observations of longitude at Kosire and Syene (or Assuan). The first he gives at 34° 4′: and Capt. White at 34° 3′. But as Capt. White gives its latitude at 26° 18′, whilst Mr. Bruce found it only 26° 8′, we may suppose that the former did not approach the coast near enough to discriminate particulars. Mr. Bruce's parallel intersects the coast in Capt. White's chart, in lon. 34° 8′: and I have adopted that for the place of Kosire. Capt. White may perhaps have mistaken the *old* for *new* Kosire.

Syene is given at 33° 30′ by Mr. Bruce, making 2° 10′ east from Cairo; whereas M. D'Anville has no more than 41 minutes of easting. Hence arises a difference of 12 degrees in the bearing: M. D'Anville's being about N 9 W; Bruce's N 21 W: or nearly parallel to the shore of the Red Sea.

The longitude of Sennar is 33° 30′ 30″ according to Mr. Bruce. In this particular is found the widest difference between D'Anville and Bruce; the former placing it no less than 3° 50′ more to the west; that is, D'Anville has it, 1° 41′ *west* of Cairo, Bruce 2° 9′ *east* of it.

In effect, then, the general course of the Nile below Sennar lies to the *west* of north, instead of the contrary, as described in the imperfect materials offered to M. D'Anville. For we cannot doubt the *general* truth of Mr. Bruce's geographical positions, although we may not be inclined to allow them every point of accuracy. In the observation of longitude at Kosire, we have seen that he comes very near to Capt. White: and his longitude of Cairo, is more exact, or more in harmony with Capt. White's observations at Suez, than the longitude recorded in the *Con. de Temps*. We have moreover another observation of longitude taken by Mr. Bruce at the eastern source of the Nile, 36° 55′ 30″, (lat. 10° 59′), from whence one route leads eastward to the shore of the Red Sea at Masua, another westward to Sennar. Admitting his observations to be ever so coarsely made, these routes must have afforded so considerable a check, to the distance between Masua and Sennar, as to have precluded any very great error, in a difference of lon--

gitude of about six degrees only; so that there is little question but that M. D'Anville's statement is wrong.

From Sennar, Mr. Bruce has a new and interesting route, northward to Syene. Dongola lay wide to the west of this route; and he has not informed us on what authority it is placed in his map. Still, however, the change in the position of the Nile, must carry Dongola to the eastward with it, of course; and in Bruce's map it is found at 1° 18′ diff. long. to the east of D'Anville's ;* equal to 73 G. miles. The latitude of Dongola is also ½ a degree to the south of the parallel assigned by D'Anville, that is, 19½ instead of 20°. With respect to that of Sennar, D'Anville was right.

In describing the western head of the Nile (and which has no existence in Mr. Bruce's map), it may be thought that I have advanced into the regions of conjecture; but I trust that I have not gone beyond the limits implied by the authorities. To enter into a detail of these, together with the deductions and combinations arising from them, would occupy too much room here; especially as they are designed for another place. It may be sufficient to state, that the branch in question, called the *White* River, or *Abiad*,† is admitted by Mr. Bruce himself, to be a more *bulky* stream than the Abyssinian branch. That M. Maillet was told, that it holds a course which is distant from 12 to 20 journies from the eastern branch. That Ledyard was told at Cairo, by certain persons from *Darfoor*, that the Nile has its fountains in their country situated 55 journies to the westward of Sennar :‡ and whose *frontier* province, *Kordofan*, is placed by Bruce, adjoining to the west of the country of Sennar. And finally, that Ptolemy, Edrisi, and Abulfeda, all place the head of the Nile in a quarter far remote from Abyssinia. Ptolemy, in particular, has described the eastern source, in such a way, as that it cannot be taken for any other than the Abyssinian branch (*i. e.* Bruce's Nile); and yet he at the same

* That is, M. D. places it 36 min. *west* of Cairo: Mr. B. 42 min. *east* of it.

† This must not be confounded with the *Neel Abeed*, the name applied by the Arabs, to the Niger.

‡ See Mr. Ledyard's communications in African Association, for 1790,—91. He says 55 journies, *or* four or five hundred miles. There must, of course, be an error, either in the number of the journies, or of the miles.

time describes a larger, and more distant, source, to proceed from the SW ;
answering to the White River. His *Coloe* lake, is clearly the *Tzana* of Bruce:
and may possibly have been meant to express *Galla,* the name of the southern division of Abyssinia.*

Having completed this part of the subject, I proceed to the inland positions in the western and central parts of the continent.

M. D'Anville has been followed in the geography of Barbary and Morocco, with the exception of an adjustment of the interior of the latter, to the
coasts; which are drawn from the charts in the atlas of Don Tofino, in
which the capes of Cantin, Geer, &c. are placed more to the east, in respect
of the strait, than in D'Anville.

The lower parts of the Senegal, Gambia, and Rio Grande, are from M.
D'Anville's, and Dr. Wadstrom's maps.

Of Mr. Park's route and discoveries, it is needless to say more, than that
the particular map which contains them, has been copied into this; forming
a most important member of it.

The routes and positions formerly introduced from materials collected by
the African Association, in the northern part of the continent, are revised and
reconstructed; perhaps with more effect, as our knowledge and experience
of the subject increases.

Fezzan is placed, as before, due south from Mesurata : its capital Mourzouk, being $17\frac{1}{2}$ journies of the caravan, distant. Edrisi affords a slight check
to the *bearing*, as well as to the distance, by means of Wadan, which lies
nearly midway, and is five journies west of Sort, a known position on the
coast : and also eight journies of his scale from Zuela, a known position in
Fezzan.†

---

* Mr. Bruce has fallen into an error, which may mislead those who do not attend to his
map. He says, Vol. iii. p. 720, that " the ground declines southward, from the parallel
of five degrees north:" but in the map at the end of Vol. v. the waters, as we have just said,
begin to flow southward, from the latitude of 8° north. I believe, with him, that farther
to the west, the southern slope may not begin short of the 5th degree of latitude.

† The day's journey of Edrisi is taken at 18 Arabic miles, or about 19 G. in direct
distance. Strictly speaking, it should be 19,06, as $56\frac{2}{3}$ Arabic miles are equal to a degree.

h

A description of the caravan routes from Tripoly, to Mourzouk, Egypt, and the Niger, will be found in the Proceedings of the Association, published in 1790, and 1791 (chapters x. and xii.)

The point on which the *central* and *eastern* positions depend, is GHINNY; or GHANA, (as Edrisi and Abulfeda call it) a city, and capital of a kingdom situated nearly midway between the Indian Sea and the Atlantic, on the E and W; and between the Mediterranean and the Ethiopic Seas, on the N and S. Fortunately, this point, on which so many others depend, can be satisfactorily approximated: though by this, I do not mean to any degree of nicety, where an extent of 70 degrees, nearly, is in question.

According to Edrisi, Ghana lies 37 journies from *Germa*, through Agadez, or Agadost. Germa, an ancient and ruined city of Fezzan, lies to the ESE of Mourzouk, about four journies.* The position of Germa therefore will be about lat. 27° 25': lon. 16° 20' E. Agadez in 25 of Edrisi's journies from Germa,† and is said to bear S by W, or SSW from the capital of Fezzan.‡ Again, Agadez is given at 48 caravan journies from Gadamis, which latter is 24 such journies in a southerly direction from Tunis.§ The road to Agadez makes a considerable angle, by passing through Tegerhy, situated 80 miles only, to the SW or WSW of Mourzouk : ‖ and hence the direct distance of 48 journies must undergo some diminution. The result places Agadez S by W ¼ W from Mourzouk, 479 G. miles distant ; which only exceeds by six miles the distance arising on the 25 journies from Germa : and its position will be at a few minutes above the parallel of 20 degrees, and a little more than half a degree of longitude west of Tripoly. The position receives some further check, from the circumstance of Tegerhy being midway between Kabes and Agadez.**

Ghana is 12 days of Edrisi's scale to the southward of Agadez, or about 229 G. miles.†† It appears that Ghana lies somewhat to the east of the

* Mr. Beaufoy's MSS.   ‖ Af. Assos. 1790, Q. p. 88 ; O. p. 133.
† Edrisi, p. 39.   ** Af. Assoc. 1793, page 29, *et seq.*
‡ Mr. Beaufoy's MSS.   †† Edrisi, p. 39.
§ Af. Assoc. 1793, p. 29.

line which passes through Agadez from Germa ; whence some little deduction should be made from the aggregate distance of 37 days, or 705 miles ; and I have therefore taken 700 as the general line of distance from Germa to Ghana.

Mr. Matra was told, at Morocco, that Ghinny (Ghana of Edrisi) was 40 journies from Kabra, the port of Tombuctoo, along the bank of the Niger. These, taken at the caravan rate between Fezzan and Egypt; Morocco and Jarra ; &c. that is at 16,3 per day, produce 652 G. miles. The intersection of this line with that from Germa, places Ghana in lat. 16° 10′, lon. 13° 2′ E of Greenwich ; in which position it stands at 760 miles from the city of Benin, on the coast of Guinea.*

De Barros says, that when the Portugueze first explored the *Coast of Guinea* (about 1469) the king of Benin held his kingdom of the king of *Ogane*, as his superior lord ; and that ambassadors were sent accordingly, to obtain a confirmation of his authority. The distance of Ogane (doubtless meant for Ghana) from Benin, was stated to be 250 leagues of Portugal ; which being of 18 to a degree, are equal to about 833 G. miles. And if from these we deduct $\frac{1}{7}$ for the inflections of the road, there remain 740 for the direct line ; which, as the reader will perceive, is very near the former result. Thus the determination of this important point, appears satisfactory.†

Before I speak further concerning Ghana and Melli, with a view to identify them with the same countries mentioned by Leo, it will be proper to *close* the line of distance eastward to Nubia.

Between Ghana on the west, and Dongola on the east,‡ the interval on

* By some oversight, Ghana is placed in the map, too far to the east, by 8 minutes of longitude.

† I cannot learn with any degree of certainty, from whence the name GUINEA, applied to the SW coast of Africa, is derived. Some have supposed it to be from the capital or country of the superior monarch, in the interior of the continent ; but it is certain that the same name is applied by Sanuto (in 1588) to the coast between the river Gambia and Cape Mesurada. But Sanuto may have taken the idea from Leo, who was in an error with respect to the matter of Guinea, at large.

‡ Placed as above on the authority of Mr. Bruce.

the map is about 1118 G. miles, in an E by N direction, nearly. Edrisi gives a chain of distance between them: and although we cannot ascertain the *exact* bearing of the several parts, yet enough is known, to enable us to approximate the general *bent* of it; which is to the *south*; and the degree of curvature seems to be such, as to increase the distance 50 or 60 miles; say 55, and then the line of Edrisi may be taken at 1173 G. miles.* Now as he reckons 66 journies, each will be no more than $17\frac{3}{4}$: and his usual standard is 19, or $1\frac{1}{4}$ more. This difference may easily arise on some of the longer portions of the line; which, although given in the aggregate, may be broken into several parts, and each of them inflected from the other in some degree. Such, for instance, may be the case of the line of 30 days between Dongola and Kauga; although the bearing of it, on the whole, is SW by W, or WSW. Therefore the interval of space between Ghana and

* The chain of bearings and distances is thus ascertained: Edrisi allows 66 journies between Ghana and Dongola: of which 36 are between Ghana and Kauga; 30 between the latter and Dongola (Damokla of Edrisi). Of the thirty six, eighteen are clearly shewn to point *eastward*; partly by direct information, partly by the context. For Kauga is said to be 10 journies to the *east* of Semegonda: (Ed. p. 13.) and between the latter and Sekmara, 8 journies, is about E by S and W by N; as we learn from the triangle formed by the points of Sekmara, Semegonda, and Reghebil; the latter place being six days *southward* from the former, and nine from Semegonda. And lastly, the 18 journies between Ghana and Sekmara, are checked by the *bearing* and *distance* between Reghebil and *Ghanara*; and the *distance* between Ghanara and Ghana—(See the map). For Reghebil is said (Edrisi, p. 12.) to lie 11 journies to the *east* of Ghanara, whilst the latter is also 11 journies from Ghana. The context shews, that if *Sekmara* is 18 journies from Ghana, and Reghebil 6 days *south* from Sekmara, whilst Ghanara preserves the relative position above described, that Sekmara must lie to the *eastward* of *Ghana*.

Kauga ought unquestionably to lie to the southward of Dongola, by $2\frac{1}{2}$ or 3 degrees. For it is 20 journies to the southward of Kuku, which is itself about the parallel of Tamalma, which is 12 journies from Matthan, the capital of Bornou; *northward*. And this Matthan, as will be shewn presently, lies in the same parallel with *Dongola*. Thus, I may assume, without any great hazard, an easterly bearing between Ghana and Kauga; E 25 N between Kauga and Dongola.

For the authorities for the above particulars, see Edrisi, pages 10, 11, 12, 13. It would be almost endless to note each separate authority.

Dongola seems to be satisfactorily filled up. Or, if we take the whole number of computed journies between Pisania on the Gambia river, and Dongola on the Nile, at 158; of which 92 are between Pisania and Ghana, 66 between the latter and Dongola; there will be on the former, according to our construction, a ratio of about 16,6 G. miles per day, on the direct line; and 16,9 on the latter.

To the *northward* of this line, and in the quarter towards *Nubia*, are situated the countries or kingdoms of Bornou (or Kanem) Tagua, Kuku, Kuar, and Zagawa: and in the quarter towards *Ghana*, are Zanfara, and Zegzeg. Most of them are mentioned, as well by Leo, as by Edrisi.

There is a route to the capital of Bornou given in the Proceedings of the Association, 1790-91, by which it is placed at about SE $\frac{1}{2}$ S from Mourzouk, distant 660 G. miles; whence it falls on the map exactly in the same parallel with Dongola, and at 524 miles to the west of it: so that the country of Bornou occupies the middle space between Nubia and Ghana; Fezzan and Sennar.* There is little doubt that Bornou is the Kanem of Edrisi, said to border on Nubia. Angimi (or Gimi) in particular, one of its cities, is said to be near Nubia, on the east.† There is a city of the name of Kanem, in the way from Fezzan to the capital of Bornou, as we learn not only from Mr. Beaufoy's MSS. but from a note in Hartmann:‡ but this cannot be the capital of Kanem, intended by Edrisi; because neither the bearings nor the distances to it, from Dongola and Nubia agree; and also, because the bearing and distance from Dongola *do* agree exactly to the capital pointed out, by Mr. Beaufoy: and which Edrisi names Matthan, or Matsan. This capital he places at 31 days journey to the west of Nubia, whose position, however, is too uncertain to reckon upon: but Abulfeda says that Zagua, or Zagara, is 20 journies *west* from Dongola; § and Matthan, according to Edrisi, is eight journies from Zagua, (p. 15). It has already been noticed that the capital of Bornou falls in the same parallel

* The capital of Bornou falls in lat. 24° 32', lon. 22° 57'. The empire is said to be very extensive; and its sovereign more powerful than the Emperor of Morocco: Af. Assoc. 1790, Q. p. 152; O. p. 229.

† Edrisi, p. 14.   ‡ Hartmann's Edrisi, page 63, note (v.)   § Article Soudan.

with Dongola; and here we learn that Zagua, is also in the same parallel with it; consequently, the whole 28 journies from Dongola, may be taken on the same *westerly* bearing; and the result will be, a distance of 534 miles; differing only 10 from the interval on the map. Consequently, the Matthan of Edrisi may be taken for the capital of Bornou, pointed out by the above authority.

The countries of Zagua (or Zagara) and Tagua, fill up the space between the kingdom of Bornou and Nubia. The former appears to be a small province, perhaps a dependency of Bornou. The situation of its capital is inferred above, to be eight journies to the east of that of Bornou.

Tagua lies between Zagua and Dongola, and its capital at 13 journies from Matthan, (p. 15). Northward it extends to the tract of *Al Wahat*, the western province of Upper Egypt. Thus, its position cannot be mistaken.

The country of Kuku (this must not be mistaken for Kauga) lies to the NW of Tagua; NE of Bornou; and joins on the NE to Al Wahat. This is an extensive country, bordering on the Desert of Libya, and partakes of its nature. Its capital of the same name is situated at 20 journies to the *north* of Kauga. It is also 14 to the *eastward* of Tamalma, which is itself 12 to the *northward* of Matthan. Hence Kuku may be approximated, in position. (Edrisi, page 13, *et seq.*)

A river runs from N to S by Kuku, and is received into a lake at a great distance from Kuku; perhaps the lake of Kauga: and the river itself may form a part of that, said to run near Angimi,* of which more in the sequel.

Kuar, or Kawar, lies to the northward of Kuku and of Bornou; and extends eastward to Al Wahat. It is bounded on the north by that extensive Desert which separates Egypt from Fezzan; and which contains the *wandering* tribe of *Lebeta* or *Levata*; as also various *Oases*, or fertile islands; amongst the rest, those of Augela, Berdoa, Seewah, and that which con-

* Angimi is a city eight days journey from Matthan, six from Zagua; and towards Nubia and the Niger; consequently to the SE of Matthan; and *apparently*, not far to the northward of Kauga. Edrisi, p. 14.

tained the temple of *Jupiter Ammon*. This Desert I regard as the proper Desert of LIBYA: and it may be a question whether the tribe of *Lebeta*, although now found in the interior of the country, may not have originally inhabited the sea coast; and that the Greeks denominated Africa from *them*.* This was the part of Africa the nearest, and first colonized by the Greeks; and it is a known fact, that the *Adyrmachidæ*, and *Nasamones*, who, in the days of Herodotus, inhabited the *coasts*, were at a succeeding period, found in the *inland* parts about *Ammon* and *Augela*.

The capital of Kuar is by Edrisi placed adjacent to Fezzan; but there is either some mistake in this, or I do not comprehend the matter rightly. (Ed. p. 39, 40.) Tamalma, a city of Kuar, is only 12 days from Matthan (p. 14.), so that the Desert of Bilma, or Bulma, must lie between it and Fezzan. Mederam Isa, another of its cities, is said to be only two davs from Zuela, or Zawila, a city of Fezzan: and Izer, a third city, is placed in the same neighbourhood, and near a large lake. Either then, these cities belong to Fezzan, and are by mistake classed as belonging to Kuar; or they *really* belong, as well as Tamalma, (of which there is no doubt) to Kuar. I am inclined to the *latter* opinion, for the following reasons. In the catalogue of places, in Fezzan (in Af. Assoc.) there is no mention either of Izer, Isa, Bulmala, or of a lake near the former. But there is a remarkable salt lake near Dumboo, on the northern frontier of Bornou, which from its relative position to Tamalma, may well be the one intended by Edrisi: especially as Bulmala, (p. 40.) which may be meant for Bulma, occurs in the same neighbourhood. The salt lakes of Dumboo are said to be situated in the Desert of Bilma;† which Desert appears to be a prolongation of the Libyan Desert to the SW.

---

* Mr. Park mentions a wandering tribe named *Libey*, whom he had seen in his travels. He compares them, in respect of their habits and modes of life, to *gipsies*.

† From the borders of these lakes, Kissina and other countries are supplied with salt, by the people of Agadez, who annually employ 1000 camels in this commerce. Af. Assoc. 1790, Q. p. 157. 167; and O. p. 236. 251.

There is reason to suspect, that the great salt lake of Dumboo, is the *Chelonides Palus* of Ptolemy.

Zanfara is said by Labat, to be 50 journies from Tombuctoo.* Leo places it between Wangara and Zegzeg; which latter, by the same authority, being to the SE of Cano (or Ganat) Zanfara must necessarily border on the NE of Ghana; having Bornou on the east, Agadez and Kassina (which we formerly erroneously spelt *Cashnab*) on the west. Here it may be proper to observe, that in the present political division of Africa, Kassina comprizes generally the provinces between Fezzan and the Niger; and that Zanfara is its eastern boundary. Of course Ghana, which in the 15th century was paramount in the centre of Africa, is now become a province of Kassina.

To the *south* of the line between Ghana and Nubia, very few particulars are known to Europeans. The knowledge of Edrisi, was limited to this line itself: and the only country known to him on the south of the Niger, was *Melli*, which he calls *Lamlem*. Nor did the knowledge of Leo, extend beyond the countries contiguous to the south bank of the Niger; nor to any country west of Tombuctoo; although by mistake, he places Ghana and Melli, there. This may serve to shew, that the people on the north side of the Niger, have very little communication with those, who live beyond the great belt of mountains, which runs across Africa, at about the 10th degree.

Nor did the inquiries of Mr. Beaufoy produce any thing more than the *names* of certain of the adjacent countries; the only one of which that can be *placed*, is *Begarmee* (perhaps the Begama of Edrisi) said to be 20 journies to the S E of Bornou, and separated from it by several small deserts.† It seems to be the country intended by the Gorham of D'Anville.

Kororofa and Guber are said in Mr. Beaufoy's MSS. to lie to the west of Begarmee; the latter bordering on Wangara. Neither of these, can well be in a lower parallel than 11° or 12 degrees. But *Darfoor*, a country of considerable extent and population, and apparently the farthest removed of any that has a communication with Egypt, is pointed out to our notice by Mr. Ledyard, as has been already shewn.‡

---

* Labat, Vol. iii. p. 363.

† African Association, 1790; Q. p. 155; O. p. 234.

‡ African Association. See Ledyard's Communications, in Af. Assoc. 1790, 1791.

In the present limited state of our knowledge respecting the interior of Africa, it would be mis-spending time to attempt to follow Leo, in his detail of provinces and nations, in the parts remote from the immediate scene of our discoveries; or of the routes communicated to the Association. But it is of the utmost importance to the argument respecting the *course* of the *Niger*, that I should clear up some of his errors regarding the positions of *Ghana* (his *Ginea*) and *Melli*.

Leo says, p. 248, 249, that the merchants of *his* country (I conceive he means Barbary, call the country in question, Gheneoa; that its proper inhabitants call it Genni: but the Portugueze, and other Europeans, Ginea.* He says that it is situated to the *west* of Tombuctoo, that is between Tombuctoo and Gualata :† that it has an extent of several hundred miles *along the Niger*, even to the place where it discharges itself into the sea. Again, says he, the kingdom of Melli *borders on* Ginea, *southward*; and on the west, are vast forests, which extend to the sea. And finally, he places the kingdom of *Gago* to the *east* of Melli.

Now nothing is more certain, than that the space on the west of Tombuctoo and Gago, is occupied by nations, very different from those of Ginea (by which Ghana is to be understood) and Melli: as also that the space assigned by Leo, to Ginea, is a remarkably *dry, sandy*, country; being either adjacent to, or forming a part of the Sahara: whereas Ginea is described by him to be a tract, which, during the inundations of the Niger, in July, August, and September, is inclosed like an island.

It is however not improbable, that Leo, who it appears had visited Tombuctoo (but who certainly never saw the Niger, which is about 12 miles beyond it), might confound the city of Jenné, which is situated in a small island in the Niger, and to the west of Tombuctoo, with the kingdom of Ghana (his Ginea), on the east: but as to Melli, that is quite out of the question, in respect of any mistake of the like kind; and could only be placed on the west of Gago, in order that it might preserve its southerly position in respect of Ginea. Thus one mistake seems to have produced the other.

---

* Abulfeda, Edrisi, and Ibn Al Wardi call it Ghana, and Ganah.

† Gualata is described by Leo to be situated 500 miles from Tombuctoo towards Nun.

The position of Ghana (or Ginny according to Mr. Matra), at 40 journies to the eastward of Tombuctoo, has been already detailed, in page lix. And this is, no doubt, the Ginea intended by those, from whom Leo collected his information respecting the country itself, whose geography he has so much erred in.

The kingdom of Melli had been reported to Cadamosta, when he made inquiries concerning the interior of Africa, about the year 1455. He was told that Tombuctoo, (whose general position was not ill described to him, at about 60 journies inland from Arguin,*) was supplied with *mineral* salt from Tegazza, 40 journies to the westward. That the same salt mine supplied Melli, 30 journies beyond Tombuctoo, the salt passing through the latter place.† (We must here suppose that the *capital* of Melli, called by the same name as the country, is meant as the term of this journey). Hence we should naturally look for Melli on the *eastward* of Tombuctoo, as will presently appear, and not on the SW, as is expressed in Astley.‡ No doubt, SE was meant : for Edrisi has a city of the name of *Malel*, at 10 journies to the south of Berissa,§ and 12 from the city of Ghana : and this position actually falls at 30 journies to the E S E of Tombuctoo ; agreeing to the distance reported by Cadamosta.

But Edrisi does not call the country *Melli*, but *Lamlem*. However, it can be no other than the Melli of Leo, and Cadamosta : for Edrisi says (p. 8 and 11), that it is situated to the south of Ghana and Berissa, and has on the east the country of Wangara (Vancara), which agrees to the tract in which Malel is situated. Hartmann supposes, (p. 39,) with great appearance of truth, that Lamlem is a transposition of Melli : and I have met with similar instances in the translation of Arabic words and numbers. Thus Leo's ideas were evidently wrong, respecting the situations of Ghana and Melli; which lie to the *eastward* of Tombuctoo, although he places them to the *west*.

---

* He was told that Hoden or Whaden, was 70 leagues east of Arguin, and Tegazza six journies from Hoden. Tombuctoo was 40 days from thence. Astley, Vol. i. p. 20, and 577, 578.   † Astley, Vol. i. p. 578. Some Remarks on the Salt Mines are added, at the end of this Chapter.   ‡ Ib. Vol. ii. p. 74.

§ Berissa is 12 journies west of Ghana. Edrisi.

The place of Melli is occupied, in his description, by Guber (which Mr. Beaufoy learnt, was to the south of Wangara); whilst that of Ghana remains unoccupied; unless we suppose it to be included in the empire of Tombuctoo, which is implied (p. 254), when he speaks of Wangara (Guangara) as being troubled on the *west* by the King of Tombuctoo, and on the *east* by him of Bornou: and as he also speaks of Tombuctoo as the largest empire in Nigritia, (p. 4.)

In the position of Wangara,* he is right; for it lies between Zanfara, and Bornou: but he seems not to have known that it was intersected by the Niger, and formed of its alluvions, as Edrisi points out to us.† But Leo learnt one important particular as a merchant, that the *southern* quarter of it, produced *gold*, in abundance. As I shall have occasion to speak more fully of this country, when the *course* of the Niger comes under consideration, it will be unnecessary to say more of it, in this place.

Kassina is removed by Leo, from the banks of the Niger, its proper situation, far inland, to the east of Cano, or Ganat,‡ (p. 253.) This is another proof of his writing from hearsay. Kassina is not heard of, in Edrisi; it no doubt was included in Ghana, at that day.

Leo is silent respecting Tokrur or Tekrur. This appears to have been the metropolis of the great central empire of Africa, in the time of Edrisi and Abulfeda; and must have existed in later times; as the Tukorol, to whose prince the Portugueze sent an ambassador about the year 1493, may be taken for the same place. It may, however, have been swallowed up in the empire of Tombuctoo, which was founded after the time of Edrisi, and before the date of Leo's writing. But as the city of Tombuctoo gave name to the empire, so might Tokrur; and this latter may have fallen so much to decay, as to be little known in the present times: and this may account for Mr. Park's not being able to learn any tidings of it. And finally, as Leo had not heard of Houssa, we may conclude that it is a city of a yet later

---

* Guangara, (Leo.)   † Pages 11, and 12.

‡ It lies to the SSW of Agadez. Af. Ass. Q. p. 221; O. p. 326. M. D'Anville mistook the *Cano* of Leo (p. 253.) situated at 500 miles from the Niger, for *Ghana*. But the *Ganat* of our map, in the road from Fezzan to Agadez, must be meant.

date; and which may possibly have superseded Tokrur. Such a fluctuation of names, serves as much to confound geographers in the political division of Africa, as the various opinions of those who have written on the physical geography, do, respecting the relative position of places, and the courses of its rivers.

Remarks on the Positions of the Salt Mines in the Great Desert.

Edrisi understood that all the salt consumed in the kingdoms of Nigritia (particularly along the course of the Niger), was brought from *Ulil*, situated at 16 journies to the westward of Sala, and erroneously supposed by him to be an island, situated in the ocean, near the mouth of the Niger.* But by the *situation*, one would suppose that the salt mines of *Aroan*, 10 journies to the NNW of Tombuctoo, and in the road to Morocco, were meant; and from whence Tombuctoo is at present supplied. It is not easy to guess how an inland salt mine should have been mistaken for an island, in the ocean: but it is certain that both Edrisi and Abulfeda, supposed the Niger to discharge itself into the sea, near the meridian of Tombuctoo. Ibn Al Wardi† speaks of *Oulili*, as the principal city of *Soudan* (or Nigritia), situated on the *sea coast*, and having extensive salt works, from which salt was carried to the other states of Nigritia.

Mr. Park mentions the city of *Walet*, capital of Beeroo, which may perhaps be the *Oulili* intended by Ibn Al Wardi;‡ but it has no salt pits; for the inhabitants fetch salt from Shingarin, six journies to the northward of it:§ and Walet is more than 24 journies from Sala, instead of 16, as stated by Edrisi.

Cadamosta and Leo, in the third and fourth centuries after Edrisi,‖ say, that the people of Tombuctoo had their salt from *Tegazza*, 40 journies to

---

* Edrisi, p. 7.   † Hartmann's Edrisi, p. 29.   ‡ Oulili, Oualet?
§ Mr. Park's MSS.   ‖ Edrisi wrote in the 12th century; Cadamosta in the 15th, and Leo in the 16th.

the westward of that city; and that the salt was carried so far to the east as Melli, which is opposite to Kassina. By Tegazza, *Tisheet*,* the salt mine of Jarra seems to have been meant; but is far short of 40 journies from Tombuctoo. Now, if in the 12th century, salt was procurable so near to Tombuctoo as Aroan, or Shingarin (the salt pits of Walet), why should they have fetched it from a place 30 or 40 days distant, in the 15th and 16th? This requires explanation: for Edrisi states very particularly that salt was carried from *Ulil* in boats along the Niger, and distributed amongst the nations on its banks, from Sala to Kauga! †

Mr. Beaufoy, quoted as above, says, ‡ that there is a *salt lake*, or lakes, in Bornou; from whence Agadez, Kassina, and certain states on the south of the Niger, are supplied. This at least implies that there are no salt *mines* in the Desert, in the quarter *east* of Tombuctoo.

* Mr. Park's MSS.　　† Edrisi, p. 7.　　‡ African Association, 1790; Q. p. 157, 167; and O. p. 236, 251.

CHAPTER VI.

The Subject continued—Course of the River Niger, at large—has no Communication with the Nile—Ptolemy's Description of it consistent.

THE course of the *Niger* (or *Joliba*) as we have seen, is established, by ocular demonstration, as far as *Silla* ; and may, I conceive, be *admitted*, as far as *Houssa*, about 400 miles farther to the east, on the foundation of the information collected by Mr. Park ; since it agrees with the ideas communicated to Mr. Beaufoy, by an intelligent Moorish merchant, who had navigated the river: and as it agrees no less with the report of Mr. Magrah, obtained from Moorish merchants at Tunis ; and of Major Houghton from Bambouk. Thus, the first 700 G. miles of its course are *from* WEST *to* EAST ; or rather from WSW to ENE. There remains then, a space of *more* than double that distance, between Houssa and the nearest part of the Egyptian Nile, near Dongola: and yet more, to the known parts of the White river, or Abiad, the SW branch of the Nile.

I shall divide the matter respecting the course of this river, into three heads. 1. Respecting the continuity of its waters, from Houssa on the west, to Wangara on the east ; without regard to the direction of the stream. 2. Respecting the positive direction of the stream. And, 3, concerning its termination.

1. *Respecting the Continuity of its Waters.*

Edrisi gives the most positive information concerning the course of the Niger, or Nile of the Negroes, from east to west ; deriving it from the same lake through which the Egyptian Nile passes ; and describing it to terminate at 16 journies west of Sala (that is, a little to the west of the position occupied by Tombuctoo) ; and near the supposed island of Ulil before mentioned.* He thus cuts off about 1000 miles of the breadth of Africa. This

* Page 7 of Edrisi.

was an error common to all the ancient geographers, as well as to those of Arabia : for Ptolemy places the mouth of the Senegal river only two degrees more to the west, than Edrisi does that of the Niger.

Abulfeda believed, with Edrisi, that the Niger had a common source with the Nile, and ran westward.*

It is certain, that these *opinions* furnish no *proofs* of continuity of course : but it may be supposed that there was some foundation for them ; especially as Edrisi says, that salt was carried upon the Niger in boats from the island of Ulil, and distributed to the people on its banks, from Sala to Wangara, and Kauga.†

Mr. Matra was told‡ that from Kabra, the port of Tombuctoo, " people sometimes travelled *along the river* the space of 40 days, to Ginny (Ghana) a large city;" &c.

The Moorish merchant, with whom Mr. Beaufoy conversed, and whom he speaks of as a clear and intelligent man, says, " That the country of *Guinea* or Ginny, is on the *same river* with *Houssa*." (Mr. Beaufoy's MSS.)

Edrisi, besides mentioning the cities of Sala, Tokrur, Berissa, Ghana, and Ghanara, all of which he says are situated on the Niger, remarks that the *country of Wangara*, to which Ghanara belongs, is *surrounded* by that river,§ as it would appear by means of a subdivision of its waters; for Gatterer says, that Ghanara, one of its cities, stands on the *western* arm of the Guin,|| by which name he mentions the Niger ; of which more presently. Now, as Wangara extends, according to Edrisi, 300 *Arabic* miles along the river,** this extent, together with the distance of Wangara from Ghana, eight journies,†† or 152 miles, makes up 496 G. miles of the course of this river, eastward from Ghana ; which being itself 500 miles east of Houssa, there will be 969 miles in *direct* distance, traced eastward of Houssa : or on the whole, as Houssa is 700 miles below the source, about 1670 G.

---

* Article *Soudan.* † Edrisi, page 7. ‡ Mr. Beaufoy's MSS.
§ Edrisi, p. 7. 11. and 12. || Hartmann's Edrisi, p. 48. notes.
** Edrisi, p. 11. †† Ib. p. 11.

miles of water-course from the head of the Niger, above Manding, to the eastern extremity of Wangara!

In addition to these authorities, I may state from Leo, that the people of Tombuctoo convey their merchandize in boats (or rather canoes) to Ginea, *by the Niger:* and that at Kabra they embark for Melli, also. But it is proper to be noticed, that he says (p. 249), that this communication with Ginea takes place in the *rainy season only* (July, August, September), which would imply a deficiency of water for navigation, at other seasons.* Leo, however, certainly never saw the Niger, although he seems to report himself an eye-witness of many particulars relating to it. His intelligence is therefore often to be suspected; though it has probably happened, that being regarded as an original author, instead of a compiler, he has given weight to the systems of Edrisi and Abulfeda, respecting the course of the Niger.

Gatterer, as I have hinted before, calls the Niger, Guin, as well at Tokrur and Ghana, as at Wangara.† Now we learn from Mr. Park, that the northern branch of the Niger, above Tombuctoo, passes by the town of Jinbala, and collect also from Labat, that it is named the *river of Guin:* and here we have the same name extended even to Wangara; a presumptive proof of the prolongation of the same river!

Edrisi speaks of the same Niger, or Nile of the Negroes,‡ also, at Kauga, 10 journies to the east of Wangara; from which we collect that he must have supposed, that this *emanation* of the Egyptian Nile (as he supposed it to be) first ran to the north, and then turned to the west, through Nigritia. And if any consequence can be deduced from his account of the conveyance of salt, along the Niger to Kauga, where the catalogue of places supplied, ends, we should conclude that he supposed the navigable part of the river, *ended* at Kauga.

Although there can be no question that *a* river named *Nile* (or rather *Neel*), passes through the quarter of Kauga, Angimi, &c. since Edrisi,

---

* If this report of Leo has any *particular meaning*, and as the river in question carries a great body of water at all seasons, one must suppose that there are *falls* or *rapids*, in the river, when in its low state. Time may discover.

† Hartmann, p. 32, 48, 51.   ‡ Edrisi, p. 7, and 13.

Abulfeda, and Leo, speak of it, yet it would be advancing too far within the region of conjecture, in this place, to attempt to *decide* whether it has any communication with the western waters. I shall therefore reserve this discussion till the last; that it may not be allowed to have any weight in the decision of the great question concerning the continuity and direction of the Niger. Having therefore, as I conceive, established the fact of a *continuation* of the waters from Manding to Wangara, I shall next proceed to inquire into the authorities for the direction of the stream.

2. *The Direction of the Course of the Niger.*

Ocular demonstration has shewn, that its course is to the *eastward*, as far as Silla: and no reasonable doubt can be entertained that it continues the same course to Houssa, 400 miles farther to the eastward, even if the information communicated to Mr. Park, could be doubted. For the Moorish merchant before quoted, told Mr. Beaufoy, that he had himself *descended* the Joliba, from Kabra to Houssa, although he had forgot the exact number of days employed in the navigation; and whether it was 8 or 10 days, (Mr. Park was told 11). But one circumstance dwelt on his mind; which was, that " by the favour of a brisk wind, they returned to Kabra, *against the stream*, in as short an interval as they went down." (This is no new fact to those who are accustomed to inland navigations, even of the natural kind.)

The same Moor added, " that from Houssa, *going still with the stream*, boats went to Jinnee* and Ghinea; near the latter of which was the *sea*, into which the *Neel* (or Niger) discharged itself." That this Ghinea lies to the eastward of Houssa and Tombuctoo, has been already shewn; and that at the distance of 40 land journies.

Edrisi says that the navigation from Ghana to Tirka (which latter is in the way to Wangara, admitted by the same authority to lie to the east of Ghana†)

---

* It is certain that one city of Jinné or Jinnee stands *above* Tombuctoo and Houssa.
† Edrisi, p. 9, 11, and 12.

k

is *with the stream* of the Niger: * and if this be true, it ought unquestionably to have the same direction all the way from Houssa.

To these notices, of which the most full and positive, is that of an intelligent person who had visited the spot; are to be opposed the reports of Edrisi and Abulfeda, who wrote at a distance, and from the information of others. As to Leo, although his *declaration* is in favour of the two Arabian geographers, yet his authority loses all its weight, by his saying that the river runs to the *west*, *by Tombuctoo*; a fact which, I presume, no one will be hardy enough to contend for. And it will be found, that his *descriptions* do most completely do away his *declaration:* so that his testimony is turned against himself by the very context. For after saying that it runs *towards* the kingdoms of Ginea and Melli, he says also that they lie to the *west*, in respect of Tombuctoo. Now the contrary has already been made apparent, in page lxv, *et seq.*; so that in fact, Leo's descriptions go rather to prove, that the course of the Niger is to the *east*, than to the *west*. But after all, his descriptions are the result of hearsay, rather than of observation: and it is plain, that his idea of the course of the Niger, was regulated by the supposed situation of the countries it ran through. Nor had he in his mind the Coast of Guinea, according to our acceptation of the term, when he spoke of the country of Ginea: for in his description of Nigritia he says, that the *sea* on the *south*, was unknown† to him. Thus the testimonies appear to be clearly in favour of an *easterly* course of the Niger from Houssa to Wangara. I next proceed to the question respecting its termination.

3. *Concerning the Termination of the Niger.*

Mr. Beaufoy's Moor farther says, that " *below Ghinea*, is the *sea*, into which the river of Tombuctoo disembogues itself." This may therefore be considered as the *prevailing idea* at Houssa and Tombuctoo, at which places

---

* Sionita, p. 12, translates the passage thus: " *Via cursum Nili comitante.*" And Hartmann, p. 51, " *Nilum sequere.*"

D'Herbelot understood the same thing; article *Vankara.* † Leo, p. 2.

he had resided, altogether, about 12 years. By the word *sea*, it is well known, the Arabs mean to express a lake also; (and even sometimes a river.) Edrisi and others describe large lakes in Ghana and Wangara. * And when Leo says that the Niger falls into the *sea* which *borders* on *Ginea*, it is not improbable that the lakes of Ghana and Wangara are meant; and that he was under the same mistake *here*, in supposing Ginea to be in the neighbourhood of the sea, as in what relates to the position of Ginea itself. In other words, that hearing from the natives, that the Niger expanded itself into lakes *below Ghana* (or Ginea), he supposed the western ocean to be meant. For it appears (p. 2.) that *he had heard*, that the Niger had its source in the mountains on the *west*, and running thence to the *east*, expanded itself finally into a vast lake: but misled by the supposed situation of Ginea and Melli, he disregarded the information.

He also describes Ginea to be a country annually overflowed by the waters of the Niger, but omits to say the same of Wangara, to which the description more particularly applies. It may be, that as Wangara in more early times formed a part of the empire of Ghana (or Ginea), his ideas might have been collected from some history of those times. I therefore consider his description of Ginea (p. 248), to include both Ghana and Wangara.

Edrisi describes three large *fresh water* lakes in Wangara, and one in Ghana. † The description of Wangara appears to be that of an *alluvial* country, environed and intersected by the branches of the Niger, and annually overflowed in August. Perhaps August was the time of the highest flood: for Leo says that Ginea (apply this to Wangara, also) is overflowed in July, August, and September; which is indeed the season of swelling of the rivers of the tropical regions, generally. ‡

From this description may be inferred the very *low level* of the countries of Ghana and Wangara; which level or hollow forms a receptacle for the surplus waters of the Niger, collected during the rainy season: § and whose

* Edrisi, p. 10, 12, 13.   † See Edrisi, p. 10, 11, 12, 13.
‡ Ib. p. 11, *et seq.* Hartmann, p. 47, *et seq.*
§ And that probably, not only for the western waters, alone, but for the *eastern* also.

permanent lakes, apparently form receptacles for its waters, during the dry season also. The country of Wangara alone, is said by Edrisi and Ibn Al Wardi to have an extent of 300 miles .by 150 (*i. e.* Arabic miles, of 56⅔ to a degree); and Edrisi's statement of the distances through it, proves that its length lies in the same direction with the course of the Niger; that is, from *west* to *east.** Now I have no kind of difficulty in supposing that *any* river may be evaporated, provided it is spread out to a sufficient extent of surface: and it may be that the level, or hollow, of Wangara and part of Ghana, may present an extent of surface sufficient to produce this effect.† And hence these countries must be regarded as the *sink* of North Africa, at all seasons. No doubt the inhabitants are amply repaid by the fertility produced by the deposition of the waters: but besides this, in the southern quarter of Wangara, they collect an incredible quantity of gold sand, after the waters are gone off, which is carefully sought after, as soon as the rivers regain their beds.‡

It may be proper to oberve, that, according to the estimation which we ought to make, of the quantity of water collected into the Niger, it ought not to bear a proportion to that, collected into the great tropical rivers of Asia; since it receives no branches, but on *one* side. Of course, it does not drain so great a surface of country, as those which receive them on both sides. Moreover it drains only the tract situated to *leeward* of the great chain of mountains, which opposes the main body of the clouds; so that more water is discharged by the south, by the rivers of the Coast of Guinea, than by the *inland* rivers; or by those of Senegal and Gambia.

---

* Refer to Edrisi, p. 12, and 13; and to page lx above.

† There are many instances of this kind. In particular the *Hindmend*, or *Heermund*, a very considerable river of *Sigistan*, terminates in the lake of Zurrah (*Aria Palus*). The lake is about 100 miles long, and 20 broad, at the widest part; and is said to be *fresh*. The country it flows through, has all the characteristics of the alluvial tracts, at the mouths of great rivers; as Egypt, Bengal, &c. and is environed by mountains. This was the celebrated tract which is said to have formed the *appanage* of *Rustum*; and whose inhabitants, from the relief they afforded to CYRUS, were named *Euergetæ* by Alexander.

‡ Edrisi, p. 12. D'Herbelot, article Vankara.

Ben Ali reported to Mr. Beaufoy, that " it was believed, that the Tombuctoo river *terminated* in a *lake* in the Desert."

On the whole, it can scarcely be doubted that the Joliba or Niger terminates in lakes, in the eastern quarter of Africa; and those lakes seem to be situated in Wangara and Ghana. That it does not form the *upper part* of the Egyptian Nile, may be collected from *two* circumstances: first, the great *difference* of *level* that must necessarily exist, between the Niger and the Nile, admitting that the Niger reached the country of Abyssinia. For by that time, it would have run at least 2300 G. miles, in a direct line; and near 2000, after it had *descended* to the *level* of Sahara, or Great Desert. And the Nile, at the point where the White River (which, alone can be taken for the Niger, if the idea of a junction be admitted) falls in, has more than a thousand such miles to run, before it reaches the sea; and has moreover two or more *cataracts* to descend, in its way. Besides, Abyssinia is positively a *very elevated tract*. Mr. Bruce, (Vol. iii. p. 642.) inferred from his barometer, that the level of the source of the Nile, in Gojam, was more than *two* miles above the level of the sea: and this is repeated in pages 652, and 712; where he says " fully" two miles.

Again, in p. 719, he says, that the *flat* country of Sennar is *more than a mile* lower than the high country of Abyssinia, from whence (says he) the Nile runs with " *little descent*" into Egypt. Hence, the country of Sennar, and the mouth of the White River, of course, may be reckoned *about a mile*, above the level of the sea. It may however be asked, how this agrees with the idea of an easy descent?*

The second circumstance is, that the Niger throughout the tract of Nigritia, in common with all the rivers of that region, swells with the periodical rains, and is at its *highest pitch*, when the Nile is under the like circumstances in Egypt. Now, considering how long a time it would require, for the waters of Nigritia to reach Egypt, the effect ought surely to be, that

---

* Mr. Bruce mentions eight cataracts of the Nile; of which, *two* only are *below* Sennar. (Vol. iii. p. 644, *et seq.*) M. D'Anville marks *three* within the same space. The principal cataracts are those formed by the abrupt descent from the *upper* level of Gojam, to the *intermediate* one of Sennar; one of them being 280 feet. (See page 647.)

instead of what happens, at present, the Nile ought to be kept up to nearly its highest pitch, *a very long time* after the Niger.

Nor can I believe with P. Sicard and M. D'Anville, that the waters of Kauga and Bornou communicate with the river of Egypt. P. Sicard, it appears, had learnt from a *native* of Bornou, that the river which passed the capital of *his* country, communicated with the *Nile*, during the time of the inundation, by the medium of the *Bahr Azrac*, or Blue River.* M. D'Anville supposed this *Nile* to be meant for the river of Egypt; and the communication to be effected by the medium of the lake of Kauga; and that it flowed into the White River opposite Sennar. But the space of several hundred miles, which intervenes between this lake and the White River, is very unfavourable to such an opinion; even if the *levels* could be supposed to allow it. I rather conceive, that Sicard, not aware of the extensive application of the term *Neel*, or *Nile* (which in Africa seems to mean any great river), concluded that the river of Egypt alone, could be intended; whereas, I have no doubt but that the river which passes near Kauga and Angimi, was meant: (no matter whether it joins the Niger, or otherwise;) for Edrisi says, that Angimi, in Kanem, situated near the borders of Nubia, is only three journies from the *Nile* (implied to be *that* of the *Negroes*, that is, the *Niger*).† But Angimi must be more than 20 journies to the westward of Dongola, situated on the Egyptian Nile; for Zagua is 20 journies from Dongola to the *west*,‡ and Angimi 6 from Zagua,§ in a direction, which at least, *increases* the distance. Besides, a river of the name of *Nile*, or *Neel*, passes by Kauga,‖ which is 30 days to the south-westward of Dongola: and apparently about six from Angimi. Doubtless, this is the Nile intended by the informant of P. Sicard; and can have no relation to the Egyptian Nile, otherwise than in *name*.

---

* Mém. Acad. Inscrip. Vol. xxvi. p. 67. *Azrac,* or *blue,* is a term applied to certain rivers, by the Arabs, as *Mélas,* or *black,* by the Greeks. It is applied in Abyssinia to the eastern branch of the Nile, seemingly in contradistinction to the *Bahr Abiad,* or *White* River; whose waters are *muddy,* whilst those of the other are remarkably *clear.*

† Edrisi, p. 14.   ‡ Abulfeda, article Soudan.   § Edrisi, p. 14.
‖ Edrisi. p. 7.

But in the notices respecting the *western* course of a river, or rivers, from the confines of Nubia, Bornou, &c. I think I perceive abundant reason for belief, that such a course of waters does really exist; although perhaps, not exactly in the mode described.* There are notices of a considerable river in Bornou (or Kanem) called the Wad-al-Gazel, or River of the Antelopes, said to join the Nile during the time of the inundations: † of another at Kuku, more to the north, said to take its course *southward,* to the Nile.‡ Also, of *a* Nile near Angimi and Kauga, before spoken of. And finally, Edrisi § says, that a branch of the Egyptian Nile, issuing from the great lake at Tumi, in the south, forms the head of the Niger, or Nile of the Negroes.‖

Here it is well worth remarking, that Ptolemy describes a branch springing from the SE about the parallel of 10°, and amongst the *Nubi,* which branch flows into the *Gir,* a river distinct from the Niger, and appearing to answer to the river of Bornou, &c. This accords exactly with Edrisi's idea; only that it does *not* flow from the *same lake* as the Nile, separated from it only by a mountain. But M. D'Anville, in my idea, interprets very fairly the scope of the intelligence furnished by Edrisi; by supposing that the *sources* of the two rivers (or the *courses* of them) were *separated* only by a ridge of mountains.**

Leo says, that the head of the Niger is within 120 miles of the country of Bornou, and in the Desert of Seu: †† but these notices must be regarded as extremely vague.

Certain it is, that if the *eastern waters* of *Nigritia* do not run into the

* 1 am aware that Mr. Beaufoy was told that the river of Bornou runs to the NW, into the Desert of Bilma. [Af. Assoc. Q. p. 142: O. 215.]

† D'Anville, Mém. Inscrip. Vol. xxvi. p. 67.

‡ Edrisi, p. 13.   § Ib. p. 16.

‖ It appears that a report of the same kind was communicated to Mr. Beaufoy; namely, that a branch of the *Egyptian* Nile *runs into* the Desert of Bilma. (Af. Assoc. Q. p. 138: O. p. 209.) There does not, however, appear to be any foundation for believing that the Nile sends forth any branch above Egypt. All the notices of this kind may with more probability, be referred to a communication with the waters of *Kauga.*

** Mém. Inscrip. Vol. xxvi. p. 66.   †† Page 2. 255.

Nile (of which, in our idea, there does not appear a shadow of probability) they must either be evaporated in lakes, or lost in sands. The lake of Kauga offers itself in a position very convenient for the purpose, and a river taken by Edrisi for the Niger, is actually said to pass near it. It has also been shewn, that in the idea of Edrisi, the Kauga lake communicated with the *western* waters: but whether this is true, or otherwise, it is not possible to decide.

I do not pretend to follow Ptolemy in his decription of the rivers in the interior of Africa, with that precision which M. D'Anville has attempted: but *this* circumstance is clear enough, that he describes them to *terminate*, as well as to *begin*, *within* the continent. The same is to be said of Agathemerus.

It is apparent, that Ptolemy has carried the head of the Niger seven degrees too far to the *north*, and about four, or more, too far to the *west*: as also that his *inland* positions in Africa, as well along the Niger, as at a distance from it, are yet *more* to the west of the truth. But notwithstanding this geographical error, he proves that he knew many facts relating to the descriptive part of the subject. For instance, he places the source of the Niger, at the mountains of *Mandrus*, and amongst the nation of the *Mandori*. It has been seen, that the Joliba rises in the country adjacent to Manding. He marks also a large adjunct to the Niger, from amongst the *Maurali*, in the south, answering to the river from Malel (or Melli) in Edrisi. To these may be added another particular of agreement. The *Caphas* mountains of Ptolemy seem meant for those of *Kaffaba*, a country 9 or 10 journies to the eastward of Kong; 18 short of Assentai (or Ashantee) near the Coast of Guinea.* But I have a doubt where to place Ptolemy's metropolis of Nigritia, in modern geography. His ideas, however, corroborate in the strongest manner, the present system of geography.

Amongst the eastern waters, the *Gir* of Ptolemy, seems to be recognized in the river of Bornou, and its adjuncts: the Niger, in that of Tombuctoo and Wangara. The *Panagra* of the same geographer answers to Wangara; and his *Libya Palus*, which forms the *termination* of the Niger,

* Af. Assoc. 1790, ch. xii.

eastward, seems to be meant, either for the largest of the lakes, or for the lakes of that country (of which there are several), *collectively.* It is no impeachment of this opinion, that the *Libya Palus* is placed so far to the west as the meridian of Carthage, whilst the lakes of Wangara appear to be in that of Cyrene: for Ptolemy carries the river Gir, and the capital of the country which represents Bornou, into the centre of Africa; by which he has *shortened* the course of the Niger, in the same proportion as he had *extended* that of the Gir, or Wad-al-Gazel. Modern geographers, to the time of D'Anville, were guilty of the same kind of error: Ghana is about 6° too far west, in Delisle's map.

It may be best to omit any farther remarks on Ptolemy, at present, and to wait the result of future discoveries. In the mean time, those who are curious to read M. D'Anville's Memoir on the subject of " the Rivers in the interior of Africa," will find it in the Mém. Acad. Inscrip. Vol. xxvi.

CHAPTER VII.

Observations on the physical *and* political *Geography of North Africa—Naturally divisible into three Parts—Productive in Gold—Boundary of the Moors and Negroes—the* Foulahs, *the* Leucæthiopes *of the Ancients.*

To our view, North Africa appears to be composed of three distinct parts or members. The FIRST and smallest is a fertile region along the Mediterranean, lying opposite to Spain, France, and Italy (commonly distinguished by the name of Barbary); and which, could we suppose the western bason of the Mediterranean to have once been *dry land*, (bating a lake or recipient for the surrounding rivers), might be regarded as a part of Europe; as possessing much more of the European, than the African character.

The SECOND part is what may be deemed the *body* of North Africa, comprized between the Red Sea, and Cape Verd, on the east and west; and having the Great Desert (or *Sahara*) and its members, on the north; the Ethiopic ocean, and South Africa, on the opposite side. The prominent feature of this immense region, is a vast *belt of elevated land*, of great breadth, often swelling into lofty mountains, and running generally from west to east, about the tenth degree of latitude. Its western extremity seems to be C. Verd; the mountains of Abyssinia, the eastern. To the north, its ramifications are neither numerous, nor extensive, if we except the elevated tract which turns the Nile to the northward, beyond Abyssinia. Towards the south, no particulars are known, save that a multitude of rivers, some of them very large, descend from that side, and join the Atlantic and Ethiopic seas, from the Rio Grande on the west, to Cape Lopez on the east; proving incontestably that by far the greatest proportion of rain water falls on that side, during the periodical season of the S W winds; which corresponds in all its circumstances with the same monsoon in India.*

To the north of this belt, with the exception of the Egyptian Nile, the waters conform generally to the direction of the high land; passing at no great distance (comparatively) from its base, to the right and left: as if the surface of the Sahara had a general dip to the southward.† These rivers, moreover, receive all their supplies from the south; no streams of any bulk being collected in the Desert.

In order to produce this effect, there must necessarily be a vast hollow in the interior of Africa, between the high land of Nubia on the east, and Manding on the west; and of which the mountains and Desert form the other two sides. Nor is this state of things unexampled in the other continents. In Asia, the *hollow*, to whose waters the Caspian and Aral serve as recipients, is no less extensive than the one just mentioned; reckoning from the sources of the Wolga to those of the Oxus; (which latter has ever communicated with the Caspian, either throughout the year, or during a part of it:) the difference is, that in Asia, a greater portion of the hollow is filled up with water, than in Africa.

The THIRD part is of course, the Great Desert (or Sahara), and its members; consisting of the lesser deserts of Bornou, Bilma, Barca, Sort, &c. This may be considered as an OCEAN OF SAND,‡ presenting a surface equal in extent to about *one half of Europe*, and having its gulfs, and bays; as also its islands, fertile in groves and pastures, and in many instances containing a great population, subject to order and regular government. The

---

* A ridge stretches to the south, through the middle of South Africa, and forms an impenetrable barrier between the two coasts. M. CORREA DE SERRA informs me, that the Portugueze in Congo and Angola, have never been able to penetrate to the coast of the Indian ocean.

Mr. Bruce learnt (Vol. iii. p. 668.) that a high chain of mountains from 6° runs southward through the middle of Africa. He supposes the gold of Sofala to be drawn from these mountains. (p 669.)

† Circumstances have shewn, that it declines to the eastward also.

‡ " A wild expanse of lifeless sand and sky !" *Thomson.*

great body, or *western* division of this OCEAN, comprized between Fezzan and the Atlantic, is no less than 50 caravan journies across, from north to south; or from 750 to 800 G. miles; and double that extent, in length: without doubt the largest desert in the world. This division contains but a scanty portion of islands (or oases) and those also of small extent: but the eastern division has many; and some of them very large. Fezzan, Gadamis, Taboo, Ghanat, Agadez, Augela, Berdoa, are amongst the principal ones: besides which, there are a vast number of small ones. In effect, this is the part of Africa alluded to by Strabo,* when he says from *Cneius Piso,* that Africa may be compared to a leopard's skin. I conceive the reason why the oases are more common here, than in the west, is, that the *stratum* of sand is *shallower,* from *its* surface, to that of the earth which it covers. In other words, that the water contained in that earth, is nearer to the surface; as in most of the oases it springs up spontaneously.† Can any part of the cause be assigned to the prevalent easterly winds, which, by driving the finer particles of sand to leeward, may have heaped it up to a higher level in the Sahara, than elsewhere? ‡

The springs, no doubt, have *produced* the oases themselves, by enabling useful vegetables to flourish, and consequently population to be established.

---

* Page 130.

† Water is found at the depth of a few feet, in Fezzan (Afr. Assoc. Q̱ p. 96 : O. p. 146). The same is said by Pliny, concerning this quarter of Africa ; lib. v. c. 5. But farther to the N W, on the edge of the Desert, and in the country of Wadreag in particular (Shaw, p. 135.), wells are dug to an amazing depth, and water mixed with fine sand, springs up suddenly, and sometimes fatally to the workmen. The Doctor tells us, that the people call this abyss of sand and water, " the sea below ground." Exactly the same state of things exists in the country round London, where the sand has in several cases nearly filled up the wells. (See Phil. Trans. for 1797.) The famous well lately dug by EARL SPENCER (at Wimbledon), of more than 560 feet in depth, has several hundred feet of sand in it.

‡ Ships that have sailed at a great distance from the African coast, opposite to C. Blanco and C. Bojador, have had their rigging filled with fine sand, when the wind blew strong off shore. The accumulation of the *Bissago* shoals may have been partly owing to this cause also. They occupy the position where a great eddy of the general southerly current takes place, between C. Verd and Sherbro'.

That the Desert has a *dip* towards the east, as well as the south, seems to be proved by the course of the Niger, also. Moreover, the highest points of North Africa, that is to say, the mountains of Mandinga and Atlas, are situated very far to the west.

The Desert, for the most part, abounds with salt. But we hear of salt *mines* only, in the part contiguous to Nigritia, from whence salt is drawn for the use of those countries, as well as of the Moorish states adjoining; there being no salt in the Negro countries south of the Niger.* There are salt *lakes* also, in the eastern part of the Desert.

The great ridge of mountains, and its branches, are very productive in *gold*; but more particularly in the quarters opposite to Manding and Bambouk on the west, and Wangara, on the east. It may perhaps admit of a doubt, whether the gold is brought down at the present time, by the numerous fountains that form the heads of the Niger and Senegal rivers; or whether it has been deposited in the lower parts of their beds, at an earlier period of the world; and that the search, instead of being facilitated by the periodical floods, is, on the contrary, only to be pursued with effect, when the waters are low.

Tombuctoo is reckoned the mart of the Mandinga gold, from whence it is distributed over the northern quarters of Africa, by the merchants of Tunis, Tripoly, Fezzan, and Morocco; all of whom resort to Tombuctoo. Most of it, no doubt, afterwards finds its way into Europe. It may be remarked, also, that the *Gold Coast* of Guinea (so called, doubtless, from its being the place of traffic for gold dust), is situated nearly opposite to Manding: but whether the gold brought thither, has been washed out of the mountains, by the *northern* or *southern* streams, I know not: it may be by both; for a part of the gold of Wangara is brought for sale to the southern coast.†

---

* This quality of the African Desert was familiarly known to Herodotus (Melpom. c. 181, *et seq.*) He knew also that there was salt in abundance in the *northern* parts. But as it would appear that the inhabitants in that quarter can furnish themselves with salt of a better quality from the sea, the mines are not wrought.

† Some writers have said, that there are gold *mines* in the neighbourhood of Mina, on

Degombah, another country, said to be very productive in gold,* must, by its situation, lie directly opposite to the Gold Coast : for it lies immediately to the east of Kong (the Gonjah of Mr. Beaufoy, and the Conche of D'Anville).† The people of Fezzan trade to Kong.

The triangular hilly tract above commemorated, (p. xix.) which projects northward from the highest part of the belt, and contains Manding, Bambouk, &c. is also abundant in gold ; particularly in the quarter towards Bambouk, where it is found in mines; and that chiefly in the middle level.‡ (See also, p. xix.)

Wangara appears to have been, in its time, nearly as rich as Manding in this metal. The Arabs name it *Belad al Tebr*, or the *country of gold.*§ Edrisi, Ibn al Wardi, and Leo, bear testimony to its riches. They say that the gold is found in the sands, after the periodical inundation of the Niger

the Gold Coast; others, that the gold is rolled down by the rivers to that neighbourhood. Both may be true.

It is difficult to conceive any other adequate cause, than the exchange of the gold of the inland countries, for the introduction of so vast a quantity of *kowry* shells, which are carried from Europe to the Coast of Guinea, and pass for small money in the countries along the Niger, from Bambara to Kassina, both inclusive.

I am informed from authority, that about 100 tons of kowries are annually shipped from England alone, to Guinea. These are originally imported from the Maldive islands into Bengal; and from Bengal into England. In Bengal, 2400, more or less, are equal to a shilling: and yet notwithstanding the incredible smallness of the denomination, some article in the market may be purchased for a single kowry. But in the inland parts of Africa, they are about ten times as dear ; varying from 220 to 280. Mr. Beaufoy was told that in Kassina, they were at the rate of about 250: and Mr. Park reports, that they are about the same price at Sego : but *cheaper* at Tombuctoo, which is about the *centre* of the kowry country ; *dearer* towards Manding, which is the western extremity of it. Hence they are probably carried in the first instance to Tombuctoo, the gold market : and thence distributed to the east and west. Their circulation seems to be confined between Bornou and Manding. In Bournou they have a coinage of base metal.

* African Assoc. Q. p. 176 : O. p. 264.

† Mr. Park says that Kong signifies *mountain,* in the Mandinga language ; which language is in use from the frontier of Bambara, to the western sea.

‡ Labat, Vol. iv. ch. 2.

§ Bakui, and Herbelot; article Vankara.

(which is general over the country) is abated.* Leo, alone,† says, that the gold is found in the *southern* quarter of the kingdom ; which appears very probable, as the mountains lie on that side : so that it may be concluded, that the gold sand has not been brought there by the Niger, but by smaller rivers that descend immediately from those mountains. That a part of Wangara is bounded by mountains, we learn from Edrisi : for the lake on which Reghebil stands, has mountains hanging over its southern shore.‡

It is supposed that most of the countries bordering on these mountains, share in the riches contained within them, by means of the rivulets.§ But considering how amazingly productive in gold, the streams of this region are, it is wonderful that Pliny should not mention the Niger amongst the rivers that roll down golden sands : for although he speaks of the Tagus and others, in different quarters, no African river is mentioned.‖ And yet Herodotus knew that the Carthaginians bartered their goods for gold, with the Africans on the sea coast, beyond the Pillars of Hercules : which was contrived without the parties seeing each other.¶

The common boundary of the MOORS and NEGROES, in Africa, forms a striking feature, as well in the moral, as the political and physical, geography of this continent. The Moors, descendants of Arabs, intermixed with the various colonists of Africa, from the earliest to the latest times, overspread the habitable parts of the Desert, and the oases within it : and have pushed their conquests and establishments southward; pressing on the Negro aborigines, who have in several instances retired to the southward of the great rivers ; but in others, preserve their footing on the side towards the

---

* See Edrisi in particular, pages 11 and 12.

† Page 254.   ‡ Edrisi, page 12.

§ Mr. Bruce, Vol. iii. p. 647, says the same of the mountains of Dyre and Tegla, which are a continuation of the great belt, towards Abyssinia.

‖ Pliny, lib. xxxiii. c. 4.   ¶ Melpomene, c. 196.

Dr. Shaw (p. 302) speaks of the same mode of traffic, at present, between the Moors and Negroes : whence the place of traffic ought to be very far removed from the Mediterranean. There is a similar story related by Cadamosta of the exchange of salt for gold, in Melli ; and by Dr. Wadstrom on the windward coast of Guinea.

Desert; according to the strength, or openness of the situation. It is probable, however, that the Negroes, who are an agricultural people, never possessed any *considerable* portion of the Desert, which is so much better suited to the pastoral life of the Moors. It appears as if matters had not undergone much change in this respect, since the days of Herodotus; who fixes the boundary of the LIBYANS and ETHIOPIANS, in other words, of the MOORS and NEGROES, near the borders of the Niger; and he apparently pointed to the quarter in which Kassina or Ghana are now situated.*

The Negroes in the western quarter of the continent, are of two distinct races, of which the least numerous are named FOULAHS, or FOOLAHS. These, although they partake much of the Negro form and complexion, have neither their *jetty* colour, *thick lips*, or *crisped* hair. They have also a language distinct from the Mandinga, which is the prevailing one, in this quarter.

The original country of the Foulahs is said to be a tract of no great extent along the eastern branch of the Senegal river; situated between Manding and Kasson; Bambouk and Kaarta: and which bears the name of FOOLA-DOO, or the country of the Foulahs. But whether this be really the case, or whether they might not have come from the country within Serra Leona (called also the *Foulah* country), may be a question; of which, more in the sequel. The Foulahs occupy, at least as sovereigns, several provinces or kingdoms, interspersed throughout the tract, comprehended between the mountainous border of the country of Serra Leona, on the west, and that of Tombuctoo, on the east; as also, a large tract on the lower part of the Senegal river: and these provinces are insulated from each other in a very remarkable manner. Their religion is Mahomedanism, but with a great mixture of Paganism; and with less intolerance than is practiced by the Moors.

The principal of the Foulah States, is that within Serra Leona; and of which Teemboo is the capital. The next, in order, appears to be that bordering on the south of the Senegal river, and on the Jaloffs: and which is properly named Siratik. Others of less note, are Bondou, with Foota-Torra,

---

* See Euterpe, c. 32.; and Melpomene, c. 197.

adjacent to it, lying between the rivers Gambia and Falemé; Foola-doo, and Brooko, along the upper part of the Senegal river; Wassela, beyond the upper part of the Niger; and Massina, lower down on the same river, and joining to Tombuctoo on the west.

The Moors have in very few instances, established themselves on the south of the great rivers. They have advanced *farthest* to the *south* in the western quarter of Africa; so that the common boundary of the two races, passes, in respect of the parallels on the globe, with a considerable degree of obliquity, to the north, in its way from the river Senegal towards Nubia, and the Nile.*

Mr. Park arranges the Moorish States which form the *frontier* towards Nigritia, together with the Negro states opposed to them, on the south, in the line of his progress, in the following order:

The small Moorish state of Gedumah, situated on the north bank of the Senegal river, and the last that touches on it,† is opposed to the small Negro kingdom of Kajaaga, on the south. This latter occupies the extremity of the navigable course of the Senegal, terminated in this place, by the cataract of F'low.

From this point, the Negro and Foulah states occupy *both* banks of the Senegal river, to its source: and beyond that, *both* banks of the Niger (or Joliba) likewise, to the lake Dibbie, situated beyond the term of Mr. Park's expedition. This space is divided, unequally, between Kasson, a hilly strong country, but of small extent; and which has the Moors of Jaffnoo on the north: Kaarta, a considerable state, which has Ludamar for its opposite (a country held by Ali, a Moorish prince, who is loaded with infamy, on the score of maltreatment of the only two Europeans, who appear to have entered his country, in latter times): Bambara, of still more consideration, which has on the north, the Moorish kingdom of Beeroo, and Massina, a Foulah state.

Here Mr. Park's personal knowledge ends; but he learnt that Tombuctoo and Houssa, which succeed in order, to Massina, and occupy both sides of

---

* The common boundary of the Moors and Negroes, in the map of Mr. Park's route, is described by a blue line.

† The Moors appear to be masters of the northern bank of the Senegal through the greatest part of its navigable course: the Foulahs of the southern bank.

the Niger, are Moorish states, though with the greatest proportion of Negro subjects: so that the river may be considered as the boundary of the two races in this quarter.*

Of the countries between Houssa and Kassina we are ignorant. The Desert seems to approach very near the river (Niger) in that quarter, whence a Moorish population may be inferred. South of the river, we hear of Kaffaba, Gago, and other Negro countries; but without any distinct notices of position; and beyond these, Melli.

Kassina and Bornou, two great empires on the north of the river, appear to divide the largest portion of the remaining space, to the borders of Nubia; and extend a great way to the north; this region being composed of Desert and habitable country, intermixed; but perhaps, containing the largest proportion of the latter. In both these empires, the sovereigns are Mahomedans, but the bulk of their subjects are said to adhere to their ancient worship; that is to say, the lower orders are, almost universally, Negroes.†

From what has appeared, perhaps the boundary of Nigritia, as it respects the Negro population, may be expressed generally, and with a few exceptions, as follows: beginning from the west, the extent upwards of the navigable course of the Senegal river, generally—thence, a line drawn to Silla; from Silla to Tombuctoo, Houssa, and Berissa, along the river Niger; and thence through Asouda, Kanem, and Kuku, to Dongola, on the Nile.

Leo,‡ enumerates 12 states, or kingdoms of Nigritia: but amongst these, he includes Gualata, a tract only 300 miles S of the river Nun: as also, Cano (Ganat), adjacent to Fezzan; and Nubia. Kassina, Bornou, and Tombuctoo, are included, of course. §

---

* The Emperor of Morocco is said to have held, at one period, the sovereignty of some of the countries on the northern banks of the Senegal and Niger rivers. Labat, Vol. iii. p. 339, speaks of incursions made by his troops. † Af. Assoc. Q. p. 126 : O. p. 191.

‡ Page 4. § The Arabs and Moors, call NIGRITIA by the general name of SOUDAN. By *Belad Soudan*, or the country of Soudan, Abulfeda includes all the known part of Africa, south of the Great Desert, and Egypt. With him, Soudan is the southern quarter of the globe. D'Herbelot also allows it a wide range. *Affnoo* is another term for Nigritia, in use amongst the natives themselves. (See also Proceedings Af. Assoc. Q. p. 164 : O. p. 246.)

The kingdom of the Foulahs before mentioned, situated between the upper part of the Gambia river, and the coast of Serra Leona, and along the Rio Grande, has also a Mahomedan sovereign, but the bulk of the people appear to be of the ancient religion. It has been already said, that although they are a black people, they are less black than the Negroes, generally, and have neither crisped hair, nor thick lips: as also that they have a language distinct from the Mandinga. From these circumstances, added to that of situation, they appear clearly to be the *Leucæthiopes* of Ptolemy and Pliny. The former places them in the situation occupied by the Foulahs; that is, in the parallel of 9 degrees north; having to the north, the mountains of *Ryssadius*, which separate the courses of the *Stachir* and *Nia* rivers (Gambia and Rio Grande), and which therefore answer to the continuation of the great belt of high land, in our geography; in which there is, moreover, another point of agreement, the *Caphas* of Ptolemy, being the *Caffaba* of the map.*

Ptolemy, by the name, evidently meant to describe a people *less* black than the generality of the *Ethiopians*; and hence it may be gathered, that this nation had been traded with, and that some notices respecting it, had been communicated to him. It may also be remarked, that the navigation of HANNO, terminated on this coast; probably at Sherbro' river, or sound. And as this was also the term of the knowledge of Ptolemy, it may be justly suspected that this part of the coast was described from Carthaginian materials.†

Those who have perused the Journal of Messrs. Watt and Winterbottom, through the Foulah country, in 1794, and recollect how flattering a picture they give of the urbanity and hospitality of the Foulahs, will be gratified on finding that this nation was known and distinguished from the rest of the Ethiopians, at a remote period of antiquity.‡

* The *Soluentii* of Ptolemy may also be meant for the *Solimani* of Mr. Park.

† And it may also have been the scene of the traffic mentioned in page lxxxvii; as Dr. Wadstrom speaks of such a custom in this quarter, at the present day.

‡ Pliny (lib. v. c. 8.) also speaks of the *Leucæthiopes*, but seems to place them on *this side* of Nigritia. May it not be, that certain tribes of Foulahs were then established, as at present, along the Senegal river!

The contrast between the Moorish and Negro characters, is as great, as that between the nature of their respective countries; or between their form and complexion. The Moors appear to possess the vices of the Arabs, without their virtues; and to avail themselves of an intolerant religion, to oppress strangers: whilst the Negroes, and especially the Mandingas, unable to comprehend a doctrine, that substitutes opinion or belief, for the social duties, are content to remain in their humble state of ignorance. The hospitality shewn by these good people to Mr. Park, a destitute and forlorn stranger, raises them very high in the scale of humanity: and I know of no fitter title to confer on them, than that of the HINDOOS of AFRICA: at the same time, by no means intending to degrade the MAHOMEDANS of INDIA, by a comparison with the AFRICAN MOORS.

THE END.

Physician Travelers

AN ARNO PRESS/NEW YORK TIMES COLLECTION

Abel, Clarke.
Narrative of a Journey in the Interior of China. 1818.

Bancroft, Edward.
An Essay on the Natural History of Guiana. 1769.

Bell, John.
Observations on Italy. 1825.

Brown, Edward.
Account of Some Travels. 1673-1677.

Granville, Augustus Bozzi.
St. Petersburgh: Travels to and From That Capital. 1828.
(2 volumes)

Hamilton, Alexander.
Itinerarium. 1907.

Hodgkin, Thomas.
Narrative of a Journey to Morocco. 1866.

Holland, Henry.
Travels in the Ionian Isles, Albania, Thessaly, Macedonia, etc. 1815.

Holmes, Oliver Wendell.
Our Hundred Days in Europe. 1887.

Jeffries, John.
A Narrative of Two Aerial Voyages. 1786.

Kane, Elisha Kent.
Arctic Explorations in 1853, 1854, 1855. 1856. (2 volumes)

Linnaeus, Carl.
A Tour in Lapland. 1811.

Lister, Martin.
A Journey to Paris in 1698. 1698.

Park, Mungo.
Travels in the Interior Districts of Africa. 1799.

White, John.
Journal of a Voyage to New South Wales. 1790.

Wilde, William.
Lough Corrib: Its Shores and Islands. 1867.

Wittman, William.
Travels in Turkey, Asia Minor, Syria and Egypt. 1803.

Wurdeman, John G. F.
Notes on Cuba. 1844.